Celts in I

Papers from the Sixth Australian Conference of Celtic Studies, University of Sydney, July 2007

SYDNEY SERIES IN CELTIC STUDIES

1. Early Irish Contract Law
Neil McLeod

2. The Celts in Europe
Aedeen Cremin

3. Origins and Revivals: Proceedings of the
First Australian Conference of Celtic Studies
Geraint Evans, Bernard Martin and Jonathan M Wooding (eds)

4. Literature and Politics in the Celtic World:
Papers from the Third Australian Conference of Celtic Studies
Pamela O'Neill and Jonathan M Wooding (eds)

5. Celtic-Australian Identities: Irish- and Welsh-Australian Studies
from the 'Australian Identities' Conference, University College Dublin,
July 1996
Jonathan M Wooding and David Day (eds)

6. Nation and Federation in the Celtic World: papers from the
Fourth Australian Conference of Celtic Studies
Pamela O'Neill (ed)

7. Between Intrusions: Britain and Ireland
between the Romans and the Normans
Pamela O'Neill (ed)

8. Exile and Homecoming: papers from the
Fifth Australian Conference of Celtic Studies
Pamela O'Neill (ed)

Series Editor:
Pamela O'Neill

Celts in Legend and Reality

Papers from the Sixth Australian Conference of Celtic Studies
University of Sydney, July 2007

Edited by
Pamela O'Neill

Sydney Series in Celtic Studies 9
University of Sydney
2010

Published in Australia by
THE CELTIC STUDIES FOUNDATION
UNIVERSITY OF SYDNEY

in the
SYDNEY SERIES IN CELTIC STUDIES

ISBN: 978-1-74210-189-7

Papers delivered at the conference and submitted
for consideration for inclusion in this publication
were peer reviewed before being included.

Cover illustration: Fourteenth-century effigy in the Abbey Museum, Iona, Scotland (drawing J Drummond, *Sculptured Monuments in Iona & the West Highlands*, 1881). See pages 13–59.
Cover design by Pamela O'Neill.

Contents

Celts in Literature

Celts in the Diaspora

Preface

Pamela O'Neill ⊕

This collection consists of many of the papers that were presented at the Sixth Australian Conference of Celtic Studies, convened by Sybil Jack at the University of Sydney in July 2007. The theme of the conference, reflected in the title of this collection, was 'The Celts in legend and reality: ancient and modern'. As series editor of the Sydney Series in Celtic Studies, I have a strong commitment to the publication of papers from this conference series, and so, when Associate Professor Jack asked whether I would be willing to edit the papers for publication in the Series, I was happy to oblige. The process has been attended by more than a few difficulties, including communication breakdowns of the technical and human kinds and employment difficulties and a period of ill-health on my own part. I am therefore delighted that the collection presented here has taken such fine shape.

Overall, the collection represents the diversity of scholarship and identities in Australia — and beyond — with a Celtic flavour. This is very much reflective of the support base for Celtic Studies at the University of Sydney. Until the arrival of Anders Ahlqvist (about a year after this conference) as the inaugural Sir Warwick Fairfax Professor of Celtic Studies, Celtic was taught in an admirable but somewhat ad-hoc way by staff in various other academic departments, who taught according to their own scholarly interests, some of which were central to the discipline of Celtic Studies, others somewhat more peripheral. Similarly, the strong community campaign to establish the Chair saw support from many quarters, some closer than others to the centre of the discipline. The result is a valuable and varied group of supporters and scholars, who combine in their support for the existence of a Centre for Celtic Studies at

⊕ Centre for Celtic Studies, The University of Sydney.

the University of Sydney, and provide a broad, rich cultural and scholarly background against which the Centre's teaching and research work is carried out.

Celtic Studies is defined by peoples identified as having a common linguistic heritage, and expands to considerations of the cultural and historical development of those peoples. Australian manifestations of this have a natural tendency to encompass divergent modern strands of Celticism. The papers in this volume pre-date the arrival of Professor Ahlqvist, and whilst they represent the wide range of interest and energy devoted to Irish, Scottish, Welsh and Cornish topics in support of Celtic at Sydney, they perhaps also demonstrate how beneficial the arrival of Professor Ahlqvist will prove to be. His ability to reinforce the linguistic core of Celtic Studies at Sydney has been an essential development for the longevity of the discipline here. Without this core, one loses sight of the unifying principle by which it can be argued that these diverse strands share a common culture.

Papers in this collection explore aspects of peoples, things and ideas which have been considered 'Celtic' in a diversity of contexts. *Celts in the Material Record* sees plenary speaker David Caldwell and his colleagues seek a new paradigm for the classification of West Highland medieval stone sculpture, while other papers ponder the physical appearance of a *nemeton*, consider the Celtic presence on the continent, and debunk the myth of 'Celtic' mummies in the Gobi desert. In *Celts in History*, specific moments in time and space amongst 'Celts' are described and analysed, from professional-historian and personal perspectives. In *Celts in Law*, native Welsh law is considered, both as the legal system of Welsh rule and in the colonised context, and plenary speaker Ewen Cameron considers land law in the nineteenth and twentieth centuries. *Celts in Literature* includes discussions of early Celtic literature, as well as papers which take on the phenomenon of present-day literature with Celtic themes. Finally, *Celts in the Diaspora* includes studies of various manifestations of 'Celtic' identities in the Antipodes, including papers by plenary speakers Brad Patterson and Philip Payton.

The editing and production of this book have been done entirely by unpaid workers. I wish to thank the contributors for their papers, for their patience and understanding in the face of delays and infrequent communication, and for the professional way in which they have responded to requests for amendments and clarifications. Thanks are also due to the anonymous referees, who gave generously of their time and expertise to read and comment on contributions. I am grateful to Anders Ahlqvist and Tony Earls for support and assistance of various very welcome and unselfish kinds. Finally, the lion's share of the copy-editing and layout was carried out to an immensely high standard by Bran MacEachaidh, and I extend to him my heartfelt thanks for this very important contribution.

Celts in the Material Record

The image of a Celtic society: medieval West Highland sculpture

David H Caldwell, Fiona M McGibbon, Suzanne Miller and Nigel A Ruckley ⊕

Introduction

One of Scotland's most remarkable medieval legacies is the sculpture, predominantly grave-slabs and commemorative crosses, now generally labelled as West Highland. It is distributed throughout churches and burial grounds in the Hebrides, mainland Argyll and the western coastal fringe of Inverness-shire, including Arisaig, Morar and Knoydart (*illustration 1*). There are over 870 pieces at 86 locations, including 108 associated with the abbey and other churches on Iona, and 35 at the priory on Oronsay. There are heavy concentrations on Islay, and particularly in Knapdale and Mid Argyll, including 83 at the parish church of Kilmartin, 38 at Keills, 30 at Kilmory and 30 at Craignish. It is undoubtedly the case that this is just a proportion of those that were produced. Limited excavation at the chapel and burial-ground at Finlaggan on the island of Islay has demonstrated how there is potential to increase the corpus, in this case from 10 to at least 15.[1] Elsewhere in Scotland there are no medieval commemorative crosses, and while comprehensive data on grave monuments is not readily available, we doubt if there are as many as 870 pieces or any locations with as many as 20 slabs. Indeed, as far as we are aware, a concentration of medieval funerary and commemorative sculpture comparable to that in the West Highlands and Islands cannot be found anywhere else in Europe.

This paper stems from a multi-disciplinary research project

⊕ National Museums of Scotland.

1 This excavation was undertaken by D H Caldwell.

being undertaken by the authors. It seeks to characterise and explain this sculptural phenomenon through combining data derived from archaeological and historical studies with petrological examination of the sculpture, backed up with magnetic susceptibility measurements. This analytical work has had to rely on non-destructive techniques, and must be carried out in the field rather than in laboratory conditions. It has proved relatively simple and quick to take magnetic susceptibility readings for a great number of monuments, and so far this data has proved useful in refining rock-type characteristics that have been assigned by petrological analysis. It appears that it can also indicate broad groupings of rock types. A word of caution is, however, appropriate since much more detailed analysis is necessary, ideally including chemical analyses and detailed thin section petrology.[2]

Historical background

The Western Isles were subjected to Scandinavian invasion, settlement and influence from about 800. However, the disastrous naval expedition to Scotland by King Hakon IV of Norway in 1263 brought the Norwegians to realise that they could no longer exercise any overlordship in the Isle of Man and the Hebrides. By the Treaty of Perth in 1266, they ceded them to Alexander III, King of the Scots. These islands had formed the Kingdom of the Isles, ruled by two rival dynasties. One, based in the Isle of Man, was descended from a Scandinavian nobleman, Godred Crovan, who had fought with King Harald Hardrada of Norway against the English at Stamford Bridge in 1066. The last king of this line, Magnus, who died in 1265, may have continued to exercise some control over Lewis and Skye.

2 For previous reports on this project see D H Caldwell, K Eremin, S Miller, N A Ruckley, 'West Highland Sculpture, Scotland – Defining a Gaelic Lordship' 84–93 in G Helmig, B Scholkmann, M Untermann (eds), *Centre, Region, Periphery. Medieval Europe Basel 2002*, vol 1 (Hertingen, 2002); and S Miller, F McGibbon, D H Caldwell, N A Ruckley, 'Geological tools to interpret Scottish medieval carved sculpture; combined petrological and magnetic susceptibility analysis' 283–306 in M Magetti and B Messaga (eds), *Geomaterial in Cultural Heritage; Special Publication of the Geological Society of London 257* (London, 2006).

The rival dynasty was founded by a local prince or leader, Somerled, for whom, despite his Norse name, an Irish ancestry is claimed. He had annexed all, or most, of the kingdom prior to his death in 1164, and his descendants continued to hold the Islay and Mull groups of islands, and probably the Uists. They also held significant west coast territories from the Kings of Scots, including Kintyre and Lorne. Rival MacSorley kindreds (that is descendants of Somerled) — the MacDougalls, MacRuaris and MacDonalds — vied amongst themselves for recognition as Kings of the Isles.[3]

The Treaty of Perth incorporated these islands into the kingdom of Scotland and reduced those who claimed local kingship to the status of barons of the realm. Norwegian influence did not disappear overnight. The Bishops of the Isles continued to owe allegiance to the Archbishops of Nidaros (Trondheim) until the late fourteenth century and there are many aspects of medieval West Highland culture that can be seen to be rooted in a Scandinavian past. It is important, however, to understand that there is no serious doubt amongst scholars that, by 1266, Gaelic language and culture were again in the ascendancy in the whole area of the Kingdom of the Isles.

In the fourteenth century, the MacDonalds emerged as the most powerful lords in the West Highlands and Islands, eventually dominating territories even more extensive than their ancestor Somerled, including the vast earldom of Ross with its caput at Dingwall in the north-east, at the head of the Cromarty Firth. In effect, they revived the Kingdom of the Isles as a Celtic lordship, jealously guarding its cultural traditions from contamination from Lowland Scotland. These MacDonald Lords of the Isles also exercised considerable patronage in Gaelic Scotland beyond their own lands, and the MacDonalds of Dunyvaig in Islay came to hold extensive lands in the north of Ireland.

The fourteenth century also saw the rise to prominence of another important kindred, Clan Campbell, in mainland Argyll.

3 For a useful overview of this historical background see R A McDonald, *The Kingdom of the Isles. Scotland's Western Seaboard, c1100–c1336* (East Linton, 1997).

With the forfeiture of John II Lord of the Isles in 1493, the Campbells, led by the earls of Argyll, entered a period of hundreds of years when their ascendancy in the region was not effectively challenged.[4] Much of the corpus of West Highland sculpture is in areas where, and dates to a period when, the Campbells or their allies held sway. The bitter animosity between MacDonalds and Campbells, which is such a feature of Highland history, only dates from the seventeenth century.

The identification of West Highland sculpture

There is a long tradition of scholarly interest in the medieval sculpture of our region, starting with Edward Lhuyd, Keeper of the Ashmolean Museum in Oxford, at the very end of the seventeenth century.[5] Its identification and naming as West Highland sculpture largely derives from a survey by Kenneth Steer and John Bannerman in 1977, published by the *Royal Commission on the Ancient and Historical Monuments of Scotland* in a volume designed to complement the listing of the monuments of Argyll contained in the Commission's seven-volume inventory of that county. Apart from providing detailed information and excellent illustrations of much of the sculpture, the Steer and Bannerman volume made two main contributions to our understanding of the subject. Steer used his archaeological training to devise a classification of the monuments into five schools, while the historian Bannerman read the 109 surviving inscriptions and provided the detailed historical background to the names recorded in them. In attempting to move our understanding of the sculpture beyond the base established by these two scholars, our paper may appear to be critical, but let us record here our appreciation and admiration of what they achieved, and the hope that our work may be seen, in a small way, as building

4 For the Campbells, see S Boardman, *The Campbells 1250–1513* (Edinburgh, 2006); A Campbell, *A History of Clan Campbell*, volume 1, *From Origins to Flodden* (Edinburgh, 2000) and volume 2, *From Flodden to the Restoration* (Edinburgh, 2002).

5 See J L Campbell and D Thomson, *Edward Lluyd in the Scottish Highlands 1699–1700* (Oxford, 1963).

on their efforts.

Briefly, the story conjured up by Steer and Bannerman has the tradition of West Highland sculpture developing in the first half of the fourteenth century on the island of Iona. Iona remained an important centre of production into the sixteenth century and examples of Iona work can be found widely spread throughout the region. Steer and Bannerman believed that the carvers who originated this sculptural tradition may have been of Irish origin. They recognised that all of the rock used by the carvers must have been imported to Iona. The predominant rock in West Highland sculpture is Dalradian schist, types of which outcrop in Islay, in Knapdale up both sides of Loch Sween, and around Loch Awe (*illustration 2*). Having taken advice from a geologist, Geoffrey Collins, a quarry at Doide on the coast of Loch Sween was identified as a possible source for much of the rock used by the carvers. Collins was aware that several other rock types were used and he commented on this in an appendix.

Sometime after the establishment of the Iona school, others were established in Kintyre, around Loch Awe and Loch Sween, and in the sixteenth century on the island of Oronsay. The distribution of monuments of these schools is much more limited than Iona school ones, though examples of Loch Awe and Oronsay work can be found on Iona. Carvings that cannot readily be assigned to these schools were identified as the work of 'independent' carvers. The end of the tradition is said to coincide with the Reformation in the mid-sixteenth century.

Discussion of the artistic merit of West Highland sculpture has been rather limited. Suffice it to say here that most of the carvers were competent at laying out foliage designs and executing images in low relief of swords, galleys, tools, etc. The overall design schemes are normally well laid out. The craftsmen are at their weakest in producing effigies: they are awkwardly arranged and have unconvincing facial detail.

Towards a new understanding of West Highland sculpture

It is clear that there are serious flaws in the Steer and Bannerman scheme. Firstly, there is the problem of their hypothetical schools, and, secondly, the matter of the origins and dating of this sculptural tradition needs to be addressed. Up to now, no adequate attempt has been made to explain why the medieval West Highlands should have produced such a remarkable corpus of sculpture.

Steer and Bannerman were seduced into locating the origins and main output of West Highland sculpture on Iona because of the large corpus of stones there and the supposition that the stone carvers would have been closely connected with this important religious centre with its several churches. Iona, however, is 35 miles away, as the crow flies, from the nearest potential source of appropriate schist, and the sailing distance to the quarry at Doide is over 55 miles. Apparently, Steer and Bannerman felt no uneasiness about the necessity for carvers working on Iona to import slabs of rock from many miles away, carve them, and then re-export many of the finished products all over the West Highlands.

There are a few monuments on Iona which are carved from rock that occurs more locally and which was being used in the medieval period by masons on Iona for carving the dressings of doors, windows, etc in the island's churches and other buildings. The stone in question is a buff-coloured sandstone that outcrops at Carsaig, 20 miles away by sea, on the south shore of the Ross of Mull. There is a group of grave-slabs on Iona carved from this freestone. Five of these are associated with St Oran's Chapel (*Reilig Odhráin*), the burial place of the Lords of the Isles, and include slabs which may be typologically of early date. One, with a representation of a claymore, a type of sword that only came into use in the sixteenth century, is clearly of late date.[6] There is also a very fine effigy of an abbot or bishop in the presbytery of the abbey church which has been identified as Abbot Dominic (1467–c1498).[7] These pieces would

6 Royal Commission on the Ancient and Historical Monuments of Scotland, *Argyll Volume 4 Iona* (Edinburgh, 1982) 226 (no 171). In the introduction to this volume (p 25) it is estimated that there are nearly 60 slabs on Iona of Carsaig sandstone. The majority of these (about 50) have worn badly, and preserve no trace of decoration. They have not been adequately listed or described.

7 *Argyll 4*, 231 (no 202).

appear to have a good claim to be local work, of craftsmen based either on Iona or at the quarry at Carsaig. There is every likelihood that they would have been masons engaged on the island's building projects.

Otherwise, the medieval slabs and crosses on Iona are mostly carved from schists, but also slate. The use of schist, a hard rock, difficult to carve, for sculpture is very unusual in medieval Europe. Clearly, the lack of good local freestone has something to do with this preference for schist which, on the basis of slabs like illustration 23, goes back well into the thirteenth century. Magnetic susceptibility readings for the schists suggest the majority, with values of 0.75–1.25 x 10^{-3} SI, are similar to the chlorite calcite schist that outcrops at the quarry at Doide, but others with values of 0.45–0.7 x 10^{-3} SI are best compared with the hornblende schists around Loch Awe. Steer and Bannerman did identify some of these monuments as being of different schools than Iona, but nevertheless, on their model, we have Iona carvers importing rock from several different sources. A more likely scenario would seem to us to be that the monuments, with the exception of those of Carsaig sandstone, were imported from different regions of Argyll, just as most of the persons interred on the island came from further afield. The reputation of Iona as a holy place was such that many who could afford it would have preferred to have been buried there rather than in their local burial ground.

Turning to Iona school monuments elsewhere, most appear to be of chlorite calcite schist, but some, for instance at Kilmartin and Kilmory Knap, give magnetic susceptibility readings characteristic of Loch Awe hornblende schists.[8] At Lochaline in Morvern there are five Iona works of phyllite and slate from the West Highland slate belt, and at Ardchattan Priory in Lorn a slab of slate and another of Carsaig sandstone that may date to the sixteenth century. The latter has not been assigned to a school but should reasonably be

---

8 Royal Commission on the Ancient and Historical Monuments of Scotland, *Argyll Volume 7 Mid Argyll & Cowal Medieval & Later Monuments* (Edinburgh, 1992) 137 (no 81), 164–165 (nos 8, 9).

claimed as Iona work.[9] Other unassigned slabs that display Iona school characteristics include one of slate at Bracadale in Skye, and also on that island, at Borline and Dunvegan, slabs of biotite schist which could probably be sourced locally.

Some doubt has to be expressed at this stage about the integrity of Steer and Bannerman's Iona school as a unique stylistic grouping. This is not the place to give a detailed critical analysis, but suffice it to note two concerns that need resolution. Firstly, it is possible to see how their typologically early class I slabs, defined as having long shafted crosses (*illustration 3*), could have developed into class III slabs with cross-heads alone, and the cross-shafts be replaced by a sword or other decorative devices (*illustration 4*), but class II slabs, which have long narrow panels of decoration, mostly plant scroll, surrounded by a wide border and enriched and bevelled edges, seem to be different in character (*illustration 5*). They are invariably better finished off, as if they were the lids of sarcophagi. It is difficult to imagine the same carvers or workshops producing class I and class II monuments at the same time.[10] Secondly, military effigies seem almost invariably to have been classed as Iona products, though in practice there is little to compare stylistically, one with another, other than arms and armour (*illustration 6*). This does not necessarily seem a sound basis for grouping them all together.

The island of Oronsay, with its Augustinian priory founded by John I Lord of the Isles between about 1325 and 1353, was possibly second only to Iona as a religious centre in the later middle ages. Slabs of chlorite calcite schist were imported about 1500 to re-model the arcades of the cloister walk. The Iona and Oronsay school monuments are mostly of the same rock type, giving magnetic susceptibility readings of $0.75–0.88 \times 10^{-3}$ SI, thus within the same range as the rock at Doide. Three slabs and a cross-shaft,

---

9 Royal Commission on the Ancient and Historical Monuments of Scotland, *Argyll Volume 3 Mull, Tiree, Coll & Northern Argyll* (Edinburgh, 1980) 130–131 (nos 4, 5, 10, 11); *Argyll Volume 2 Lorn* (Edinburgh, 1974) 111 (no 9), 113 (no 14).

10 These classes of Iona monuments are defined in Steer and Bannerman, *Medieval Sculpture*, 17–20.

all identified by Steer and Bannerman as Iona work, are of a pelitic mica schist of unknown, but probably Argyll, origin. They give magnetic susceptibility readings of 0.47–0.52 x 10^{-3} SI.

Steer and Bannerman identified 17 slabs at Oronsay as belonging to an Oronsay school that flourished in the years from 1500 to 1560, and recognised slabs at six other burial grounds, as far away as the islands of Skye and Barra, as emanating from this island (*illustration 6*).[11] As with Iona, there is no local source of appropriate schist, but since it appears that it was imported in the early sixteenth century for rebuilding the cloisters, it does not appear unreasonable to believe that it was also shipped to the island for carving grave-slabs. Indeed, there is a cross-head at the priory which appears to have been discarded because it broke prior to being completed.[12] There are problems, however, with the exact definition, in stylistic terms, of the output of the Oronsay School. Representations of galleys with spread sails, circular designs incorporating crossed tri-lobe leaves, and plant scrolls with stems threaded over and under the leaves, are cited as typical motifs, but none of these are exclusive to Oronsay school work, and it is also evident that some pieces have been assigned to this school on the basis that they have an apparent Oronsay connection, rather than that they have an obvious design relationship. These include a slab at Iona with an inscription to the effect that it was bought for John MacIan of Ardnamurchan by his sister, Mariota, married to Malcolm MacDuffie, Lord of Dunevin in Colonsay, and therefore the local secular power for Oronsay.[13]

It is possible that all the so-called Oronsay school slabs on Oronsay are the work of one man, or at least one workshop, rather than anything so grand as a school. The man in question can be identified as Mael-Sechlainn Ó Cuinn, whose name occurs in inscriptions in the cloister arcade and on the Iona school cross at Oronsay. The name Mael-Sechlainn Ó Cuinn also appears on an Iona school military effigy on Iona, although Steer and Bannerman

11 Steer and Bannerman, *Medieval Sculpture*, 65–72.

12 Steer and Bannerman, *Medieval Sculpture*, 66, pl 28C.

13 Steer and Bannerman, *Medieval Sculpture*, 112–114, pl 25D.

speculate that this may belong to another member of the same family, perhaps in a previous generation.[14]

The Kintyre school slabs and crosses are of chlorite calcite schist and localised in Kintyre and the adjacent area of mainland Argyll, apart from one outlier at Nerabus on Islay. Steer and Bannerman suggested that this school might have been based at the Cistercian abbey of Saddell on the east coast of Kintyre, founded by Somerled or his son Reginald in the twelfth century. The problem with this is that it is some 80 miles away by sea — the only practical way to transport large, heavy pieces of stone — from Doide, and there is little evidence of any usable sources of chlorite calcite schist much closer. There are only two slabs and a cross at Saddell that are identified by the Royal Commission as of the Kintyre school, fewer than at other Kintyre churches. None have floriated crosses, with or without shafts, but many have swords and double plant scrolls containing clusters of tri-lobe leaves as dominant motifs (*illustration 8*). It is not hard to see a stylistic unity across these works, and Steer and Bannerman would appear to have good reason in suggesting that they span a relatively short space of time, at the outside from about 1425 to 1500.[15]

Most of the Kintyre slabs and crosses give magnetic susceptibility readings of 0.8–1.05 x 10^{-3} SI, within the range recorded for rock at the quarry at Doide. The two slabs at Saddell give 0.71 and 0.73 x 10^{-3} SI, and even lower readings have been recorded for single slabs at Kilchenzie and Keills. Further petrological examination of the Kintyre school monuments may demonstrate that they come from several different quarry sources.

The Loch Sween school slabs and crosses are also of chlorite calcite schist and mostly at Keills and Kilmory Knap on either side of Loch Sween. The magnetic susceptibility readings for the majority fall within the range 0.78–0.99 x 10^{-3} SI with one at each location

14 Steer and Bannerman, *Medieval Sculpture*, 105.

15 Steer and Bannerman, *Medieval Sculpture*, 44–50; Royal Commission on the Ancient and Historical Monuments of Scotland, *Argyll Volume 1 Kintyre* (Edinburgh, 1971) 142, 144.

less than 0.6×10^{-3} SI. Steer and Bannerman suggest that the school was based at Keills, on the not unreasonable grounds that there is a piece of carved stone there that appears to be a mason's trial piece. It is not so clear that there is a significant level of stylistic unity or progression spanning all the works of this school, which may extend over a longer period of time than the Kintyre school. Many of the carvings are, however, of a high quality.

The last school recognised by Steer and Bannerman turned out work which is generally of poorer quality than the others. It is one they located to the general area of Loch Awe. They considered, but rejected, the idea that the school should be associated with the cathedral of Argyll on the island of Lismore, for two reasons. Firstly, the distribution of Loch Awe monuments does not extend to the neighbouring area of Morvern but is largely confined to Mid Argyll, Lorn and Cowal. Secondly, they thought that the lack of inscriptions militated against attachment to a religious community.[16] Typical of the school are slabs with small military effigies standing in niches, or swords flanked by foliage scrolls (*illustration 10*). There does appear to be a considerable stylistic unity across this corpus of monuments.

The rock mostly used by the Loch Awe carvers appears to be a hornblende schist that outcrops in the region of the loch. Magnetic susceptibility readings on Loch Awe type monuments, however, suggest that a range of schists from different sources was used. Examples at Saddell Abbey, Kilmory Knap, Kilmartin and Craignish have been noted that give readings above the $0.45–0.7 \times 10^{-3}$ SI range expected for hornblende schist. There are also Loch Awe slabs at Craignish and Kilbride which are carved from locally available slate, and another such slab at Iona.[17] A slab which includes a small military effigy in a niche has recently been discovered at Saddell Abbey. It would thus appear to be related to the Loch Awe school, but it is made of sandstone, possibly from across the water in the

16 Steer and Bannerman, *Medieval Sculpture*, 50–57.

17 *Argyll 7,* 122–123 (nos 7, 9, 10); Steer and Bannerman, *Medieval Sculpture*, 50; *Argyll 4*, 228 (no 181).

island of Arran.[18]

Moving on from the works of these five schools to sculpture that is assigned to independent or local craftsmen, it is clear that a variety of rock types was utilised, including chlorite schist used for monuments distributed widely in burial grounds and churches throughout the region. A slab at Cill Chriosd in Skye is of slate, as is also a cross from Taynuilt (*illustration 11*), now in the collections of the National Museums of Scotland. At Bracadale on Skye there is a military effigy carved from biotite schist. At Rodel in Harris the tomb and effigy prepared in 1539 for William MacLeod are carved from the same biotite mica amphibolite schist as is used in the structure of the church itself. It was also used for the font from Borline in Skye (*illustration 12*), now in the collections of the National Museums of Scotland, commissioned by John MacLeod of Minginish in 1530.[19]

There is still a great deal of work to be done on determining the rock types selected for this sculpture, and sourcing them to particular quarries. Nevertheless, our initial assessment is that the geological evidence does not encourage belief in the Steer and Bannerman hypothesis. Three factors should be given greater weight than accorded them by Steer and Bannerman. Firstly, the rock for any monument was most likely to be quarried as near as possible to its location. Secondly, there were often good reasons for burial well away from home. These obviously included the perceived benefits to be gained from interment in ground sanctified by the presence of saints of old, or at religious houses like Iona and Oronsay where religious were on hand to pray for the dead. In such cases, what more natural than that a grave-slab should be commissioned locally for transportation to the final resting place with, or after, the body? Thirdly, the reputation of a particular carver might mean that he travelled considerable distances to undertake commissions. Steer and Bannerman recognised this in identifying 'independent

18 Council for Scottish Archaeology, *Discovery and Excavation in Scotland 2001* (Edinburgh, 2002) 24.

19 Steer and Bannerman, *Medieval Sculpture*, 99–100, pl 30, B-D.

carvers', but possibly all of them were more independent than they imagined.

It is important to point out that there is no corroborative evidence for Steer and Bannerman's scheme in the form of documentary references or archaeological evidence for workshops. They may unwittingly have limited their scope to create a scheme that best fitted their observations by making two assumptions, neither of which can be substantiated. The first of these is that it is reasonable to expect that the carvers should have worked in schools. Such schools, however, have been neither recorded nor predicted for other areas in the medieval period. In the absence of evidence for them, it would seem more appropriate to predict individual workshops and craftsmen, providing training from time to time for apprentices, many of whom would eventually have moved on to establish their own businesses. Under any circumstances, carvers must surely have taken an interest in the selection of the slabs they were to turn into grave-slabs, effigies and crosses. Those carvers who were settled, rather than itinerant, were surely more likely to have their workshops near suitable sources of stone rather than many miles away. A similar conclusion has been made for the carvers of medieval grave-slabs and covers in England.[20]

A second assumption that should be refuted is that there should have been a strong, or meaningful, link between the carvers and major churches, particularly at Iona, Oronsay and Saddell. The role of the clergy was to pray for the dead. The commemoration of the dead was primarily a matter for their kin and friends. As we will explore in more detail below, there is a surprising lack of overt Christian references on many West Highland monuments.

In creating a new model for the development of West Highland sculpture, more attention has to be given to its origins and dating. Steer and Bannerman favoured Irish roots, noting that the only known names of carvers have Irish-type surnames, Ó Cuinn and

20 L A S Butler, 'Some Early Northern Grave Covers – A Reassessment', *Archaeologia Aelania* 36 (4th series) (1958) 207–220; L A S Butler, 'Minor Medieval Monumental Sculpture in the East Midlands', *Archaeological Journal* 121 (1964) 111–153.

Ó Brolchán. A Mael-Sechlainn Ó Cuinn signed a warrior effigy (fourteenth–fifteenth century?) at Iona, and he, or another of the same name, signed the great Iona school cross at Oronsay and the rebuilt cloister arcades, both about 1500.[21] A fine Loch Sween school slab at Keills also has an inscription recording that it was made by an Ó Cuinn (*illustration 9*).[22] John Ó Brolchán is recorded on the cross at Ardchattan Priory as its maker in 1500, and he is likely to be related to the Donald Ó Brolchán who signed a capital of a pier in the abbey church of Iona in the fifteenth century.[23] There should be no surprise that masons and sculptors of Irish origin worked in the West Highlands in the medieval period, given the strong links between the Lords of the Isles, Clan Donald and Ireland. None of these works, however, take us back to the early stages of this sculptural tradition, and no group of Irish sculpture has as yet been identified as a likely model for West Highland work.

To a large extent the development of this sculptural tradition is best seen as a local phenomenon, but one for which roots should be sought in different locations. The well-developed forms, slabs and crosses, for which a date in the late fourteenth century or later can be given with some confidence, cannot readily be closely matched with work outside the West Highlands. That is not to say there is no awareness of developments elsewhere — just that a good case cannot be made for a major, direct infusion of designs, or indeed the importation of craftsmen, from any other area.[24] The development of West Highland sculpture design is based on local precedents and inventions. The same is not necessarily true of those works that can be identified as typologically early, some, perhaps, in reality dating to the thirteenth century and the first half of the succeeding

---

21 Steer and Bannerman, *Medieval Sculpture*, 105, 119–120.

22 *Argyll 7*, 91 (no 21).

23 Steer and Bannerman, *Medieval Sculpture*, 106–107, 134–135.

24 Steer and Bannerman, *Medieval Sculpture*, 21–22, suggest that their Class VII Iona slabs, characterised by two or three rows of small effigies set in niches, are copied from imported brasses. No convincing parallels have been adduced.

century. In assessing their inspiration or origins we recognise four different 'prime types'.

First of all we should consider the commemorative stone crosses, a fashion, by the fourteenth century, unique to the West Highlands. The idea of such crosses would seem to hark back to the high crosses of the eighth century at Iona, Kildalton on Islay, and elsewhere.[25] Whereas the latter have large ringed heads, many of the medieval crosses have small disc-heads which can be interpreted as being derived from — being a simplification of — the ring-headed form.[26] The disc-headed crosses at Kilchoman on Islay (*illustration 13*) and in the town-centre of Campbeltown can reasonably be dated to the mid to late fourteenth century on the basis of the inscriptions on them[27] and, relying on stylistic comparison, others may be placed that early. There is a vast gap in time between the eighth and the fourteenth centuries, and the range of decorative motives on the medieval crosses is distinctly different from the high crosses. Nevertheless, as our knowledge of all of this sculpture increases, it may even be possible to advance a case for a continuous tradition of producing stone crosses. It is notoriously difficult to provide reliable dates for many early sculptures, lacking distinctive decorative motifs, and it is possible that some of these are later than has been imagined.

There are the remains of a very fine cross at Kilmartin that may also help to bridge the chronological and typological gap between the

---

25 For a recent authoritative survey of these and other early sculptures see I Fisher, *Early Medieval Sculpture in the West Highlands and Islands* (Royal Commission on the Ancient and Historical Monuments of Scotland, Edinburgh, 2001).

26 Disc-headed crosses appear to have developed in Ireland from ring-headed ones in the eleventh or twelfth century. This is probably best seen as a parallel development rather than one closely linked with Scottish events. See F Henry, *Irish Art in the Romanesque Period 1020–1170 AD* (London, 1970) 123–147.

27 J Bannerman, *The Beatons – A medical kindred in the classical Gaelic tradition* (Edinburgh, 1998) 59; Steer and Bannerman, *Medieval Sculpture*, 159–160.

early and later crosses (*illustration 14*). It has been identified by the Royal Commission as the work of a sixteenth-century independent carver, but this high quality piece of sculpture is surely of twelfth- or thirteenth-century date. The image of the crucified Christ has a poise and sophistication that is different from other representations in local sculpture, and the cross has retained the tradition of having its arms linked by a ring.[28]

The second prime type to be considered is the slabs identified by Steer and Bannerman as Iona school class II (*illustration 5*). They bear no comparison to any elsewhere in the British Isles. They are often relatively thick, their edges normally bevelled and carved with roll and other mouldings including 'dog-tooth'. The surface of the slab is normally carved with a long thin panel of foliate decoration. There is rarely any ostensibly Christian symbolism, and where a sword is represented, it is invariably of an early type that could be of thirteenth-century date. On the other hand, Steer and Bannerman considered that the presence on some slabs of dog-tooth was an indication of a late date since there was a revival of such thirteenth-century detailing in Scotland in the late fifteenth and sixteenth centuries. They do not seem to have considered that this might be another indicator of an early date for these monuments. None of them have inscriptions.

The distribution of these stones is largely confined to Iona and the Argyll mainland. Of the 29 known, 15 are on Iona, one is on the Garvellach islands, two are at the cathedral of Argyll on the island of Lismore, one at Keills, five at Kilmory in Knapdale, two at Kilfinan in Cowal, three at Kilmartin and one at Kilbride in Lorn. There are two slabs on Iona, and another two at Finlaggan on Islay, that may be the typological precursors of these class II stones. All four have intertwined plant-scrolls forming a series of large circles occupying the full surface of the slabs. The plant-scrolls on one of the Finlaggan slabs (*illustration 15*), which include a pine-cone motif, are particularly reminiscent of those that decorate the throne of a late twelfth-century Scandinavian ivory king from the hoard

28 *Argyll 7*, 138–139 (no 89).

of chessmen and other pieces buried at Uig on the Isle of Lewis (*illustration 16*).[29] This comparison is particularly telling, since the closest parallel we have yet discovered to these class II slabs and their precursors is in the cathedral at Trondheim in Norway. It has a pattern of intertwined plant scrolls, including pine cones, forming a series of large circles, confined between broad chamfered edges (*illustration 17*). Like some other twelfth-century slabs at Trondheim, it is carved from locally available *grønskifer*, a hard type of soapstone.[30]

At this point some comment on the use of schist, especially chlorite schist, by the West Highland carvers may be appropriate. When newly made, their slabs and crosses would have been polished, dark green in colour. Although schist is very different in geological terms from the soapstone used at Trondheim, the visual effect was similar. Schist is not an easy stone to work, but if its colour was valued, this may help explain why it was so readily adopted by West Highland carvers. Little more can be offered at this stage on potential links with Norway, but the possibility that a significant strand in West Highland sculpture derives from a close link with Trondheim, especially in the twelfth century, is worthy of further research.

More obvious models for other early West Highland slabs can be found closer to Argyll than Trondheim. Our third prime type consists of Steer and Bannerman's Iona class I slabs. They have a central long-shafted cross, normally with a foliate head, flanked by other motifs, including swords and foliage scroll (*illustration 3*).

---

29 Most of the pieces from the hoard are now in the British Museum, some in the collections of the National Museums Scotland. The hoard is the subject of D H Caldwell, M Hall, C Wilkinson, 'The Lewis Hoard of Gaming Pieces; A Re-examination of their Context, Meanings, Discovery and Manufacture', *Medieval Archaeology* 53 (2009) 155–203. See also Caldwell, Hall and Wilkinson, *The Lewis Chessmen Unmasked* (National Museums Scotland: Edinburgh, 2010) and N Stratford, *The Lewis Chessmen and the enigma of the hoard* (London, 1997).

30 Ø Ekroll, *Her Hvilir … Nidarosdomens Gravsteinsutstilling* (Trondheim, 2001) 26 (no 4).

These slabs are obviously a local variant of a widespread medieval type of Christian grave-marker with dominant cross design. It may be suggested, however, that the main source of inspiration, and perhaps craftsmen, came initially across the Firth of Clyde from Ayrshire. From Ardrossan on the Ayrshire coast there is a sandstone sarcophagus (now in the museum in Saltcoats), the lid of which is carved with a central long-shafted cross with Calvary steps and a circular foliated head. On one side of the shaft is a band of foliage and on the other a sword, hanging from a loop of foliage. All the foliage is of 'stiff leaf' type and may be dated to the early or mid-thirteenth century (*illustration 18a*). The sword is of a characteristic Scottish type with lobated pommel and drooping quillons for which a thirteenth-century date is also likely (*illustration 18b*).

None of the class I slabs have stiff leaf foliage like the Ardrossan sarcophagus, demi-palmettes being preferred, but the 'trefoil' leaves on a slab at Kildalton old parish church on Islay (*illustration 18c*) are probably a later rendering of stiff leaf forms. Its sword (*illustration 18d*) is very similar to the Ardrossan one, but like the majority of such West Highland slabs, the cross shaft ends not in Calvary steps but in a semi-circular foliated base. A slab at Kilmartin, carved from a local chlorite schist, is one of the very few in the West Highlands with a long-shafted cross with Calvary steps, the norm on medieval slabs in the rest of Scotland, and appears on stylistic grounds to be of early date, probably thirteenth-century (*illustration 19*). It has foliage scroll to one side of the cross-shaft and a sword to the other, a typical arrangement for Iona class I slabs. Significantly, there is a grave slab at old St John's church in Ayr (*illustration 20*) which matches this pattern of motifs. Here the cross has a trefoil-shaped base which superficially seems closer than Calvary steps to the standard West Highland semi-circular bases. Although a political and cultural divide was to open up across the Firth of Clyde in the medieval period, links were strong in the thirteenth and early fourteenth centuries, and the comparisons made here suggest that Ayrshire could well have been the source of inspiration for Iona class I slabs.

Of the 16 surviving class I slabs, five are on Iona, three at Kilmory in Knapdale, one at Lochaline in Morvern and the rest on Islay: two of them at Finlaggan, one at Kilarrow and four at Kildalton. None of them have inscriptions or are otherwise identified. They are all dated to the fourteenth and fifteenth centuries by Steer and Bannerman, although the Royal Commission inventory volumes tend to narrow this down to the fourteenth century. It would not seem improbable that some should date to the late thirteenth century.

Our fourth prime type includes slabs with effigies, mostly military or ecclesiastical, and mostly full-size. What may be regarded as the earlier military effigies depict warriors holding upright spears, presumably shortened to fit neatly on the slabs (*illustration 6*). They are clad in aketons: quilted, long-sleeved, protective coats. On their heads they wear basinets — simple iron helmets — with mail coifs or aventails protecting the neck and shoulders. They have small shields and swords at their sides. One effigy at Iona wears a protective coat, possibly of leather or hide, which looks like the garment worn by the warders amongst the Lewis Chessmen.[31] A possible source of inspiration for the West Highland military effigies can be found close at hand, in the ruined church of St Mary, Rothesay, on the Isle of Bute (*illustration 21*). The effigy has been identified as that of John Menteith, who was dead by 1344. He was a grandson of Walter Stewart, first earl of Menteith. The slab is very worn but shows a warrior with basinet and protective coat or aketon, shield and sword, and a hunting horn.[32]

Clerics are shown in their vestments, chasubles — sometimes with a dalmatic underneath — stoles and albs (*illustration 22*). Bishops or abbots have crosiers while lesser clergy often have their hands clasped in prayer. A slab in Glasgow Cathedral with an image of a priest is of significance in tracing the inspiration for at least some of the ecclesiastical effigies. It is carved in flat relief with the hands clasped in prayer, like many examples in West Highland

31 *Argyll 4*, 234 (no 208); Stratford, *The Lewis Chessmen*, pls 27, 28.

32 Steer and Bannerman, *Medieval Sculpture*, 42, 161–162. Steer and Bannerman, perversely, considered this effigy to be derived from West Highland sculpture.

sculpture. Of particular relevance is the design round the edge of the slab of interlace and plant-scrolls, which would not look out of place on the surface of a West Highland slab or cross. The Glasgow monument, however, has been dated to about 1200.[33] Possibly of thirteenth-century date is an effigy in flat relief of a priest holding a chalice, at Shiskine on the isle of Arran. Although there is at least one slab at Iona with an image of a mitred abbot or bishop for which a thirteenth-century date might be postulated (*illustration 23*),[34] local effigies of priests that might reasonably be dated prior to the late fourteenth century have still to be identified.

The distribution of class I and class II slabs overlaps at only two places, Iona and Kilmory Knap. The presence of so many slabs of both classes at Iona can readily be explained by that island's reputation as a particularly holy place to be buried. Many of the monuments would undoubtedly have been commissioned in the territories from which bodies were shipped for interment. Kilmory is in a part of Argyll where the medieval pattern of land-holding is very complex. Otherwise, class I slabs are confined to Islay and Morvern, both MacDonald centres of power. Class II slabs, on the other hand, are to be found in territories dominated in the thirteenth century by the MacDougalls, Stewarts and Menteiths.

The Finlaggan proto-class II slabs require some comment. In the thirteenth century Finlaggan was a major castle. By the late fourteenth century it had been transformed into the centre of the Lordship of the Isles, a place where inauguration ceremonies were held for new lords and the Council of the Isles, comparable to a parliament, met in its own, purpose-built, council chamber. Indeed, its history as a ritual and administrative centre probably stretches back much further than the fourteenth century. The burial ground adjacent to the chapel was believed in the eighteenth century to be where the women and children of the Lords of the Isles were buried. Limited excavations do demonstrate the presence of burials, many of them male, extending back to early Christian times. It would be

33 Steer and Bannerman, *Medieval Sculpture*, 42.

34 *Argyll 4*, 229–230 (no 199).

possible to envisage office bearers of the MacDonalds, wives and others, being interred under slabs at Finlaggan brought in from their homelands on the Argyll mainland.[35]

The class I slabs can be seen as the underlying tradition for much of what followed in West Highland monumental sculpture. The influence of the class II slabs is less marked. We suggest that we are not just dealing here with fashion or simple matters of supply and demand. The distribution of the sculpture may reflect political realities. In the fourteenth and fifteenth centuries, the Hebrides and extensive tracts of the western mainland became part of the powerful Lordship of the MacDonald Lords of the Isles. Lorn, Cowal and other parts of mainland Argyll that remained free of MacDonald overlordship are dominated by grave-slabs of Steer and Bannerman's Loch Awe school. Loch Awe school monuments are a distinctive grouping within medieval West Highland sculpture, clearly part of the wider corpus, borrowing ideas from sculpture in the area of the Lordship of the Isles and no doubt contributing some too.

The function and distribution of West Highland sculpture

None of the above attempt at reinterpreting West Highland sculpture explains its overall distribution, and to that question we now turn our attention. We believe that to answer it, we have to look more minutely at the function of the monuments.

The distribution of West Highland sculpture appears to be one of the best examples from Britain of how a distinctive cultural phenomenon defines a regional identity. Much of the sculpture must have been transported by boat, and it would have been relatively simple for Clyde-coast dwellers in Ayrshire and Renfrewshire to import West Highland grave-slabs. They did not. The suspicion must be entertained that, despite trade in other commodities, they were not allowed to, or perhaps more likely, were not prepared to

35 For Finlaggan see D H Caldwell, *Islay, Jura and Colonsay. A Historical Guide* (Edinburgh, 2001) 163–175. The eighteenth-century account is in T Pennant, *A Tour in Scotland and Voyage to the Hebrides 1772* (Edinburgh, 1998) 214.

lie dead underneath such coverings. To take this speculation a step further, the lack of West Highland sculpture in the earldom of Ross and the north-east of Ulster, both firmly in MacDonald hands for much of the fifteenth century, may tell us something about the nature of their Lordship and the structure of population in these two regions — points to which we will return.

Even allowing for all the losses over the years, it would seem to have been the case that relatively few persons had a West Highland grave monument. The obvious conclusion is that those who did were the most important and wealthiest in medieval society. It is remarkable, however, that none of the surviving grave monuments with an inscription can be associated with the leaders of Clan Donald, and few with other leading families. Typically, they mark the burial place of mid-ranking families like the MacDuffies of Colonsay and the MacKinnons. The highest ranking MacDonald whose monument can be identified is Angus, apparently an obscure son of Angus Òg, the son of the last Lord of the Isles. His slab, probably dating to about 1500, is in the cloisters at Iona Abbey.[36] An exceptional group of three tombs with military effigies in St Clement's Church at Rodel on Harris commemorates three sixteenth-century chiefs of the powerful MacLeods of Dunvegan,[37] but have we lost all such monuments of the Lords of the Isles and others like the MacLeans of Duart and MacDonalds of Clanranald?

One answer may be that such families did not use local sculptors for their own monuments, though there is little evidence to back up this supposition. The head of the Campbells, the first Lord Campbell who died in 1453, had a Lowland sculptor carve effigies for himself and his wife. They are at Kilmun in Cowal.[38] There is a brass at Iona with a military effigy of the fourteenth century set in Tournai marble. It was believed in the seventeenth century to commemorate one of the MacLeans of Duart.[39]

---

36 Steer and Bannerman, *Medieval Sculpture*, 110–111, pl 5C.

37 Steer and Bannerman, *Medieval Sculpture*, 78–81, 97–99, pls 31–34.

38 *Argyll 7*, 179–181.

39 *Argyll 4*, 240–241.

The inscriptions on the burial monuments invariably give little information beyond the names of those interred after an opening *Hic iacet* (Here lies). Occasionally a date of death is recorded, the name of the person who commissioned the work, or the craftsman who did the carving. The names may only have a patronymic, making their identification difficult, a process not helped by the uncertainties caused by their translation into Latin. For clergy their rank and often the place where they served are given. The inscriptions are either in Lombardic capitals or black letter, the former generally being earlier than the latter.

Presumably few in medieval times could have read the inscriptions anyway. The position of the graves, and the symbolism and images on the monuments, were what must have allowed their identification. Overall, one of the most intriguing characteristics of many West Highland grave monuments is their lack of overt references to Christianity. The majority of medieval grave-slabs elsewhere in the British Isles have a cross as the main element in the design. Not so in the West Highlands, where crosses with long shafts are confined to the 16 class I slabs and a few other early slabs. Less than half of the corpus as a whole has a recognisable foliated or plaited cross design, normally positioned at the head of the stone. The majority of the inscriptions do not have any invocation seeking the prayers of the living or blessings from heaven, and there are relatively few other symbols of Christianity, except, of course, on the monuments commemorating clerics. Some of the effigies have little guardian angels at their shoulders, and a slab at Iona with a sword, instead of a cross design at the top, has a scene of a priest, with attendant, saying Mass.[40]

The swords that are such a prominent feature on many of the slabs were possibly intended to double as crosses, but their dominance in a range of patterns and designs of little religious significance suggests to us that West Highland grave-slabs were carved primarily to celebrate a warrior society. The lack of Christian symbolism on many of the slabs is compensated for by

40 *Argyll 4*, 222–223 (no 137).

the commemorative crosses. Many have crucifixion scenes. What is perhaps more surprising is the addition of secular objects and scenes, like the image of a warrior, a hunting scene and a galley on the late fourteenth-century cross of Ranald of Islay that formerly stood on the island of Texa (*illustraton 24*). The cross of Alexander MacMillan at Kilmory in Knapdale has a sword on one side of its shaft and a hunting scene on the other, complete with a huntsman with axe and hunting-horn.[41]

Several of the crosses have inscriptions identifying those they were intended to commemorate, but as with the grave-slabs, overt calls for the prayers of the living, or blessings from heaven, are mostly absent. A cross that stood at Kilchoman on Islay has an inscription saying it was for the soul of Duncan MacNerlin, and Mary and Michael. These last should probably be understood to be the Virgin Mary and the Archangel Michael. Another cross still at Kilchoman (*illustration 13*) was set up by Thomas the son of Patrick — apparently a fourteenth-century member of the medical family that later adopted the surname Beaton — for the souls of his wife, parents and all the faithful departed.[42]

There was clearly a distinction between grave-slabs and crosses. While the former commemorated and celebrated the dead, the latter, which may have been set up in the lifetime of at least some of those named on them, by their very form, were intended to invite prayers. Crosses were also commissioned by the highest ranks in West Highland society. The Ranald remembered by the cross on Texa was a son of John I Lord of the Isles and eponym of Clan Ranald. Another cross, on Eilean Mòr at the mouth of Loch Sween, was carved for Mariota de Ros, the wife of Donald Lord of the Isles.[43] Crosses were evidently fairly common in the West Highlands in the medieval period, with many of the burial grounds with medieval slabs known to have been home to at least one. Their presence goes some way to explain the lack of exhortations for prayers on the

41 Steer and Bannerman, *Medieval Sculpture*, pl 24.

42 Steer and Bannerman, *Medieval Sculpture*, 123–124 (nos 43, 44).

43 Steer and Bannerman, *Medieval Sculpture*, 125–127, 148–150.

gravestones themselves. This separation in function between slabs and crosses is unique to medieval West Highland society.

Clerics were important patrons of West Highland carvers. The evidence comes from 19 of the inscriptions, and effigies and symbolism on uninscribed monuments. The medieval clergy of the West Highlands were no different from their brothers and sisters elsewhere in their desire for their godly status to be recognised on Judgement Day by imagery and accoutrements, as well, we trust, as by the record of their achievements in life.

Effigies or representations of males in civilian clothing are rare, an exception being an effigy at Kilmory in Knapdale.[44] Craftsmen had a higher status in West Highland society than in the Lowlands. It is not surprising that several grave-slabs have symbols that suggest that they belonged to men of this type. For instance, a slab at Finlaggan has a representation of an anvil (*illustration 15*) that may be advertising the fact that it was carved in remembrance of a smith, perhaps one of the MacEacherns, hereditary smiths to the Lords of the Isles. In this case the anvil has been added to an older slab. A harp, and a harp key (?), on a slab at Keills (*illustration 9*), probably indicates that it commemorates the hereditary harpists of the Lords of the Isles, the MacIlshenochs, who had lands nearby in South Kintyre. At Kilmory Knap a slab with a large pair of cropping shears was commissioned for Henry Tulloch, perhaps a clothier who settled here in the fourteenth century. A slab at Kilchiaran on Islay with two figures identified as John and Donald also has a barrel (?), perhaps indicating that they were merchants. The lack of surnames or patronymics is presumably indicative of their lowly status, though perhaps not lack of wealth.[45]

Women appear to be poorly represented in West Highland sculpture. Indeed, there are only nine slabs with inscriptions in remembrance of women. These include an effigy of a prioress at Iona, Anna MacLean, who died in 1543. This effigy is confined to

44 *Argyll 7*, 169 (no 36).

45 *Argyll 5*, 195–196 (no 2), 280 (no 7); *Argyll 7*, 90–91 (no 21), 167 (no 28).

half the length of its slab, as is the representation of Mariota MacIan on her stone at Oronsay priory.[46] Images of women are all relatively small, like that on a slab at Kilarrow on Islay (*illustration 25*). A slab commemorating one Katherine daughter of Niall, perhaps a fifteenth-century MacEachan, at Kilchenzie in Kintyre, has a sword, while Mariota MacIan's, just mentioned, has a galley.[47]

The majority of images of men in West Highland sculpture are of warriors. The warriors continue to be dressed in aketons right through to the end of the tradition in the mid-sixteenth century. Documentary evidence backs up the use of these garments in this part of the world throughout the medieval period. We would suggest that they are not a sign of conservatism or poverty — a lack of resources to acquire plate armour. Rather they are being worn with pride by a caste of men whose power and raison d'etre was largely based on the employment of galleys as troop transporters. Their aketons may have been effective protection in battle against many a stab and blow, but as important must have been their qualities in keeping out wind and water when in an open boat. They were perhaps recognised by contemporaries primarily as an outfit for going raids by sea rather than just battle-dress.[48]

Only a few, probably early, warrior effigies are armed with spears (*illustration 6*), but small images of spearmen, also armed with basinets, aketons and swords, are a common device on slabs of the Loch Awe school (*illustration 10*).[49] It is an intriguing possibility that these images provide a benchmark of the status and quality of the deceased, relative to an Act of Parliament of 1318 concerning arming in time of war. This act may be supposed to result from

46 Steer and Bannerman, *Medieval Sculpture*, pls 26D, 27A-B.

47 *Argyll 4*, 227 (no 177); *Argyll 1*, 122 (no 4).

48 See D H Caldwell, 'Having the right kit: West Highlanders fighting in Ireland' 144–168 in S Duffy (ed), *The World of the Galloglass. Kings, warlords and warriors in Ireland and Scotland, 1200–1600* (Dublin, 2007) at pp 151–159.

49 There is not enough detail to indicate if they are wearing gauntlets, like at least some of the large warrior effigies.

King Robert I's experience of warfare, and be designed to produce the warriors with such kit that had led to his remarkable military successes. All men with £10 worth of goods were to have an aketon, basinet, gloves of plate, a spear and a sword, or else a habergeon (mail coat), a hat of iron and gloves of plate. All with goods to the value of a cow were to have a spear or a bow and arrows.[50] The core of King Robert's army at the battle of Loudoun Hill in 1307, where he won his first significant victory, consisted of Islesmen and Irish contingents.[51] If the images on the Loch Awe school slabs are commemorating such a warrior elite, some at least of the slabs may be rather earlier than has been supposed.

The most prevalent type of design or pattern in West Highland sculpture is foliage, normally stylised leaves arranged in scrolls or trellises. There is no apparent significance in this. It seems evident, however, that most other elements are meant to be read as statements about those commemorated, basically their status and desires. Heraldry, that essential medieval device for distinguishing individuals by design rather than words, is all but missing in West Highland art. As noted above, shields with heraldic devices are carried by some of the earlier military effigies, but otherwise, the cross at Lerags in Lorn, dated 1516, is exceptional in having Campbell arms.[52]

The prevalence of swords, not just as incidental elements in the overall design of slabs, but as the main, centrally placed motif, seems apt for a society which was strongly militarised and where the practice of warfare was held in high esteem. The swords invariably appear to be convincing representations of real types that we have reason to believe were made or used in the region.

---

50 T Thomson and C Innes (eds), *The Acts of the Parliaments of Scotland* (Edinburgh, 1814–1875) i, 473. Later arming acts are not relevant, being framed in different terms.

51 H Rothwell (ed), *The Chronicle of Walter of Guisborough* (London, 1957) 370, 377–78; W F Skene (ed), *John of Fordun's Chronicle of the Scottish Nation*, vol 2 (Edinburgh, 1872) ii, 335. See also D H Caldwell, 'The Scottish Foot in the Time of Wallace and Bruce' (forthcoming).

52 Steer and Bannerman, *Medieval Sculpture*, pl 35D.

There are representations on some sixteenth-century monuments of the characteristic two-handed sword of the Highlands, known as a claymore, with drooping quillons terminating in quatrefoils. Some swords, from their proportions, look as if they are 'halflang' swords, that is weapons with a grip sufficiently long to be grasped with both hands when occasion demanded. They were popular in the fifteenth century.

The vast majority of representations are of single-handed swords, and they and the supposed halflangs are invariably represented with drooping quillons and lobated (fingered) pommels. Drooping quillons are a design feature prevalent on swords used in Scotland and Ireland from the twelfth to the fifteenth century. On the basis of representations in West Highland sculpture, use into the sixteenth century might be argued. Over 20 such swords with drooping quillons are known to survive, including three with a Scottish provenance (two in the National Museums of Scotland, one from Ayr with Glasgow Museums and Galleries). At least 14 have an Irish provenance, where they are thought to have been taken and used by Scottish mercenaries. Only one of the swords in the National Museums of Scotland, one in Glasgow with an Irish provenance, and one in an American collection have a complete blade, guard and pommel, and are in good condition.[53]

The lobated pommels present an interesting problem. Amongst the 40 or so medieval single-handed and halflang swords from Scotland and Ireland there is only one with such a pommel, recovered from the River Blackwater in County Armagh. Two others, one from Cawood in Yorkshire and the other from Korsoygaden in Norway could, in these writers' opinion, be of West Highland origin.[54] It

53 The swords with a Scottish provenance are published in J G Mann, 'A Late Medieval Sword from Ireland', *Antiquaries Journal* 24 (1944) 94–99 and J G Scott, 'Three Medieval Swords from Scotland' 10–20 in D H Caldwell (ed), *Scottish Weapons & Fortifications 1100–1800* (Edinburgh, 1981). The Irish swords have recently been reviewed by A Halpin, 'Irish Medieval Swords, c1170–1600', *Proceedings of the Royal Irish Academy* 86 C (1986) 183–230.

54 D H Caldwell, 'Claymores – the Two-handed Swords of the Scottish

is possible that lobated pommels just do not have a good survival rate, though the extant ones do not look particularly fragile, or, is it the case that carvers were deliberately producing ideal images of swords? If lobated pommels are essentially a design feature of the twelfth century, is their continued representation in sculpture to the middle of the sixteenth century a conscious reproduction of an antique form?

A point of note with the effigies of warriors is that many are shown fastening on their sword belts, one hand grasping the scabbard and the other tugging on the end of the belt that has been passed through its buckle (*illustration 26*). We know of no other cases of this in sculpture elsewhere, except for an effigy at Dungiven Priory in the North of Ireland that is clearly either derivative of West Highland work, or carved by a Scottish worker.[55] Effigies of warriors elsewhere in Britain and Europe, if not showing the hands together in prayer, tend to show the sword in the act of being drawn. This is an understandable pose for a warrior, sometimes carved with some dynamism. None of the West Highland warrior effigies are shown at prayer, and only one, at Iona, is posed in the act of drawing his sword. It is one of the best in terms of quality of work, and is signed by its carver, Mael-Sechlainn Ó Cuinn.[56]

It is tempting to suggest that buckling on the sword belt related to the rite of knighthood. This act was much more significant as part of the ritual than dubbing with a sword, and may indicate the adoption by West Highland society of at least some of the cult and trappings of European chivalry.[57] There is little evidence for West Highland leaders seeking or valuing knighthood, but the significance of the symbolism on the grave slabs may be that the warriors are buckling on their own swords, whereas in the ceremony of knighting this was done by the person who was conferring the knighthood. Are

---

Highlanders', *London Park Lane Arms Fair* (2005) 47–53, at p 51.

55 Steer and Bannerman, *Medieval Sculpture*, pl 17E.

56 *Iona 4*, 235 (no 211).

57 We are grateful to Dr Philip Bennett of Edinburgh University for suggesting this to us.

we seeing here some ritual of 'self-knighting', a sign that these men belonged to an exclusive local club of warriors? If so, the club in question can be identified as the force of standing warriors, known as caterans (from Gaelic *ceatharn*) in Lowland sources. A late sixteenth-century report lists this force, with apparent exactness and accuracy, in the Hebrides as amounting to 6,171 men, and it seems likely that this system originated in the twelfth century. It may have been extended in medieval times to neighbouring areas of the mainland, and underlies the militarisation of West Highland society that largely distinguished it from the rest of the country and made it such a potent force in the politics of Scotland and Ireland.[58]

Our suspicion that there is some hidden symbolism involved in the representation of swords is considerably increased by our knowledge that medieval warriors from the West Highlands are described in many early sources as fighting with axes and bows, neither of which is represented to any extent in West Highland sculpture. The image of a warrior with an axe on the fourteenth-century cross of Ranald of Islay, from Texa, is exceptional (*illustration 24 a*), as is the huntsman with a bow on the sixteenth-century tomb of Alexander MacLeod at Rodel.[59]

Many West Highland monuments also have representations of galleys (*illustration 24 b*). They were the direct descendants of Viking longships and, indeed, many West Highland families, not least the MacDonald Lords of the Isles, had Scandinavian blood flowing in their veins. Galleys were clinker-built with high prow and stern and a central mast for a large rectangular sail. They were manned by crews, up to 72 or more strong, that could row these vessels at great speed for long distances. The galleys in local sculpture provide yet more evidence of the dangers in taking such representations too

---

58 The document in question can be found in W F Skene, *Celtic Scotland: A History of Ancient Alban*, vol 3 (Edinburgh, 1890) 428–440. The twelfth-century origin is speculation which will be dealt with more fully in a forthcoming paper by D H Caldwell.

59 Steer and Bannerman, *Medieval Sculpture*, pls 24C, 32B. For the arms and armour and tactics used in battle by West Highlanders see D H Caldwell, 'Having the Right Kit'.

literally. They have led scholars to assume that they were squatter than their Viking predecessors. A scaled-up replica, christened the *Ailech* in 1991, soon demonstrated various design faults, not least the difficulty of rowing her with any more than a few men. We think that the explanation for this is that the galleys in West Highland art are normally confined by the sides of a relatively narrow slab and their proportions have deliberately been distorted to give them more bulk. A grave-slab at Iona with a galley side-on to the slab shows what we may regard as more realistic proportions.[60]

A slab like that of Donald MacGillespie at Finlaggan (*illustration 26*), complete with identifying inscription, warrior effigy and representation of a galley, demonstrates the owner's position and status in a changing world.[61] Donald was crown tenant of Finlaggan in the mid-sixteenth century after the collapse of the Lordship of the Isles. The slab was presumably meant to show that he was a powerful gentleman of Clan Donald, one who captained a galley.

Another way of showing status was by the delineation of hunting scenes. Hunting with dogs was a pastime of the great in Highland society and some grave monuments show dogs attacking deer, like the 1539 slab of Murchadh MacDuffie at Oronsay (*illustration 27*). The 1528 tomb of Alexander MacLeod of Dunvegan at Rodel shows huntsmen, one with a bow, and dogs on leashes, setting off after some deer.[62]

Less obvious, but nevertheless intended to demonstrate status, are caskets, representations of which are surprisingly common (*illustration 9*). They are present on two of the slabs with inscriptions that commemorate women, one at Killean in Kintyre and the other at Kilmodan in Cowal,[63] prompting the thought that they also may be an indication of gender. Even if they were just containers for money, jewellery or other trinkets, for either sex, they would surely indicate wealth. We suggest that they may have been containers for

60 Caldwell, 'Having the Right Kit', 144–151; *Argyll 4*, 220 (no 127).

61 *Argyll 5*, 280 (no 11).

62 *Argyll 5*, 248 (no 17); Steer and Bannerman, *Medieval Sculpture*, pl 32B.

63 *Argyll 1*, 137 (no 11); *Argyll 7*, 154–155 (no 10).

documents. To have documents, particularly ones recording the holding of land, would have been a key sign of status.

Finally, we wish to comment here on a group of representations, of shears, combs and mirrors (*illustration 9*), which are identifiable on several slabs, sometimes all three together, often just shears alone, and normally a comb and mirror together. The shears in question probably represent the medieval equivalent of scissors for trimming the beard and hair. The implication of all three types of objects is a concern for personal appearance and hygiene, presumably attributes of men who did not labour the ground but kept themselves fit for warfare.

Our overall impression, then, is that West Highland sculpture is largely about commemorating a military caste in a culture that sought to be different from the rest of Scotland. This was an heroic society, more interested in proclaiming the prowess of its fighters than their hope of heaven. This investment in stone monuments was not inconsiderable, but the warrior elite mostly had no land or great houses to maintain; little to pass to succeeding generations but their reputation.

The distribution of West Highland sculpture does not fit exactly with the power and patronage of the Lords of the Isles. More research may show that it reflects the areas which provided the warriors who were hired as mercenaries to fight in Ireland. Payments and booty gained in that country may have been one of the main sources of wealth that paid for the monuments.

Envoy

This paper recounts progress to date on a major inter-disciplinary project. Many of the ideas expressed are tentative and much more detailed analysis requires to be done. We have suggested that the existing model that sees much of the sculpture emanating from five schools is not a good fit with the evidence, and there are difficulties in viewing Iona as a major centre from which slabs and crosses were exported. We believe that the carving of West Highland sculpture extends back into the thirteenth century, if not earlier, and that several monuments may be earlier than hitherto supposed.

While this sculpture is fundamentally a local development and has a distribution confined to the West Highlands, it is possible to recognise its roots in locally produced sculpture in the early medieval period, and in an awareness of twelfth- and thirteenth-century grave-slabs in Lowland Scotland and Norway. West Highland sculpture is chiefly the expression of a society that nurtured a professional caste of warriors and emphasised their status by commemorating the dead.

It is intended that future work will focus on identifying the work of individual craftsmen or workshops, partly by archaeological or art historical analysis of the design and execution of the monuments, and also by more detailed research on the rock types used and their sources. We hope that this will lead to a better understanding of where, when and how the sculpture was produced and, most importantly, why.

Illustrations

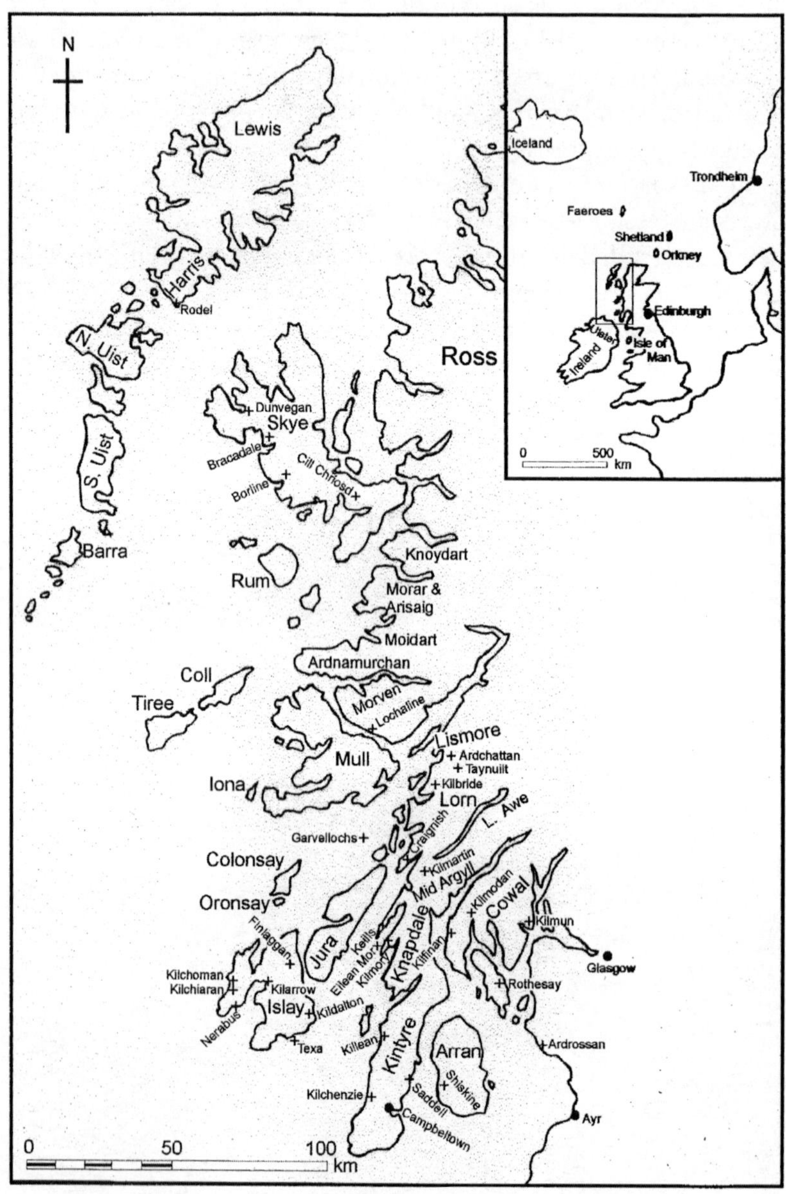

Illustration 1: *Map of the West Highlands and Islands of Scotland.*

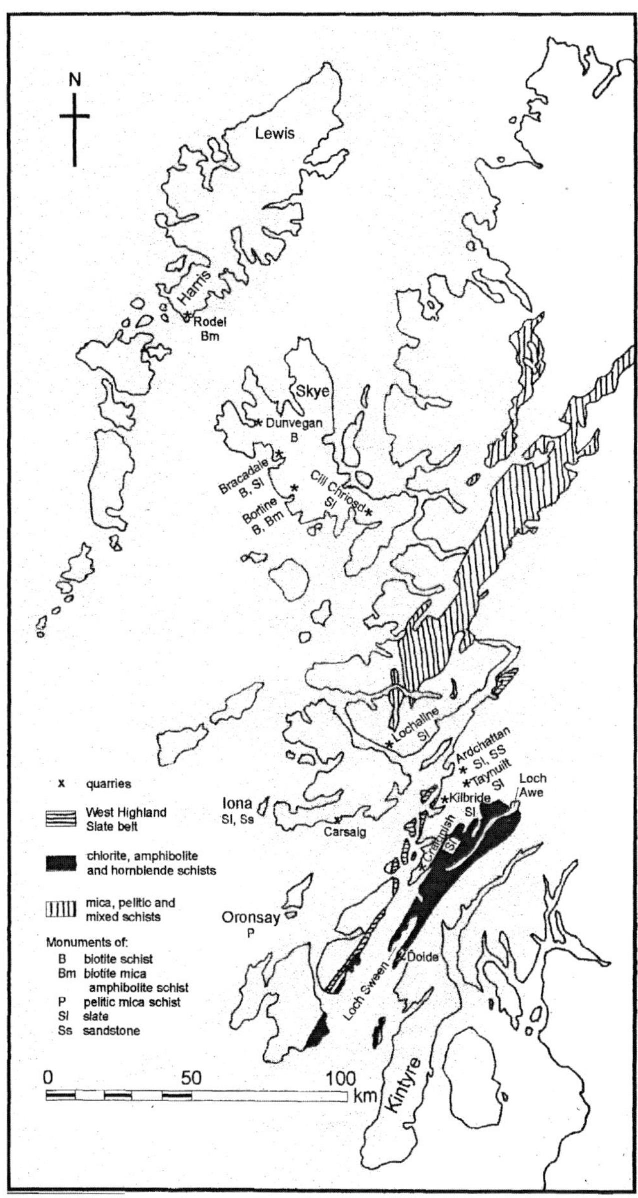

Illustration 2: *Map showing quarries, possible sources of rock used for West Highland sculpture, and distribution of some monuments made from rocks other than chlorite and hornblende schists.*

Illustration 3: *An Iona School class I slab in the chapel on Eilean Mòr, Finlaggan, Islay. Its small size (length 0.98m) may indicate that it covered a child's burial.* ***Argyll 5****, 279 (no 1).* Photo: *R C Graham,* ***The Carved Stones of Islay*** *(Glasgow, 1895), pl III, 8.*

Illustration 4: *An Iona School class III slab with floriated cross at the top and foliage scroll work, issuing from a lion and wyvern, covering the rest of the slab; length 1.9m. Other class III slabs have swords placed centrally. This one is now in the cloisters at Iona Abbey.* ***Argyll 4****, 225 (no 163).* Drawing: *J Drummond,* ***Sculptured Monuments in Iona & the West Highlands*** *(Edinburgh, 1881), pl XIII, 1.*

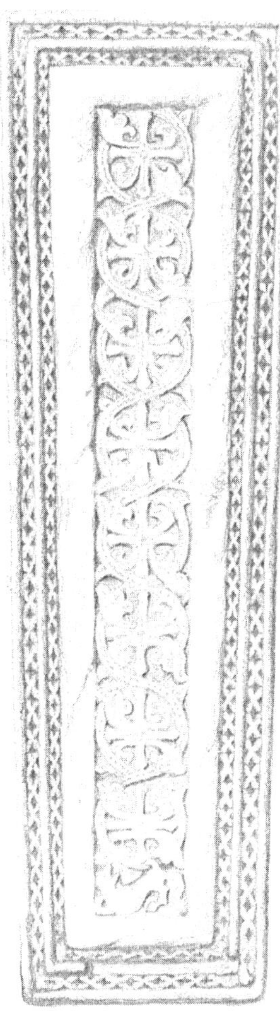

Illustration 5: *An Iona School class II slab now in the cloisters at Iona Abbey. It has a panel decorated with a plant scroll including crosses and terminating at the bottom in an animal; length 1.83m. The edge mouldings include two bands of dog-tooth ornament.* ***Argyll 4****, 227 (no 175).* Drawing: *Drummond,* ***Sculptured Monuments****, pl XXI, 2.*

Illustration 6: *An Iona School military effigy now in the Abbey Museum, Iona; length 2.1m. Inscriptions on it indicate it commemorates five successive generations of MacKinnons, the earliest being Gilbride, thought to have been active in the second half of the thirteenth century. The monument probably dates to the following century.* ***Argyll 4****, 233–34 (no 207).* Drawing: *Drummond,* ***Sculptured Monuments****, pl XL.*

Illustration 7: *An Oronsay School slab in the old burial ground of Kilarrow, Islay; length 1.74m. The sword is a sixteenth-century two-hander (claymore). The foliated cross at the top with a series of spokes interspersed with crossed tri-lobe leaves is of a design that occurs on more than one monument assigned to this school.* **Argyll 5**, *186 (no 12).* Photo: *Graham,* ***Carved Stones****, pl IX, 30.*

Illustration 8: *A Kintyre School slab in the chapel at Kilmory in Knapdale; length 1.96m. The positioning of the sword off-centre is typical of works of this school. There is a fine representation of a galley at the top, and the decoration also includes a comb, a pair of shears and a casket.* **Argyll 7**, *166 (no 18).* Drawing: *Drummond,* ***Sculptured Monuments****, pl LXVII, 2.*

Illustration 9: *A Loch Sween School slab in the old parish church at Keills in Knapdale; length 1.94m. The decorative motifs to the right of the sword include a harp with a harp key, a casket, a comb, pair of shears and a mirror. An inscription indicates it is the work of… Ó Cuinn. The presence of a harp and harp key suggests that it commemorates members of a family of harpists, perhaps the MacIlshenochs, hereditary harpists to the Lords of the Isles.* ***Argyll*** *7, 90–91 (no 21).* Drawing: *Drummond,* ***Sculptured Monuments****, pl LVIII, 1.*

Illustration 10: *A Loch Awe School slab in the Lapidarium at Kilmartin Parish Church; length 1.76m. The small figure of a warrior with a spear standing in a niche is typical of this school.* ***Argyll*** *7, 132 (no 14).* Drawing: *Drummond,* ***Sculptured Monuments****, pl LI, 2.*

Illustration 11: *The head of a cross carved from slate, formerly at Taynuilt, now displayed in the Museum of Scotland, Edinburgh; height 0.8m.* ***Argyll 2****, 167–168 (no 275).* Drawing: ***Proceedings of the Society of Antiquaries of Scotland*** *61 (1926–27) 146.*

Illustration 12: *A font carved from biotite mica amphibolite schist, from the old church at Borline, Skye; 0.33m x 0.47m. It is now displayed in the Museum of Scotland, Edinburgh. It is carved with the Crucifixion, St Michael slaying the dragon, the Virgin and Child and a bishop (St Maelrubha?). An inscription indicates it was made in 1530 for John MacLeod of Minginish. Steer and Bannerman,* ***Medieval Sculpture****, 99–100 (no 5).* Photo: *National Museums Scotland.*

Illustration 13: *An Iona School commemorative cross in the burial ground of the old Parish Church of Kilchoman, Islay; height 2.57m. An inscription indicates that the two figures below the Crucifixion represent a medical doctor, Thomas, who had the cross erected, and his father Patrick. Both were undoubtedly members of the Macbeths or Beatons of nearby Ballinaby. It is possible that Patrick was the doctor of that name who served King Robert Bruce.* ***Argyll 5****, 200 (no 13).* Photo: *Graham,* ***Carved Stones****, pl XIII.*

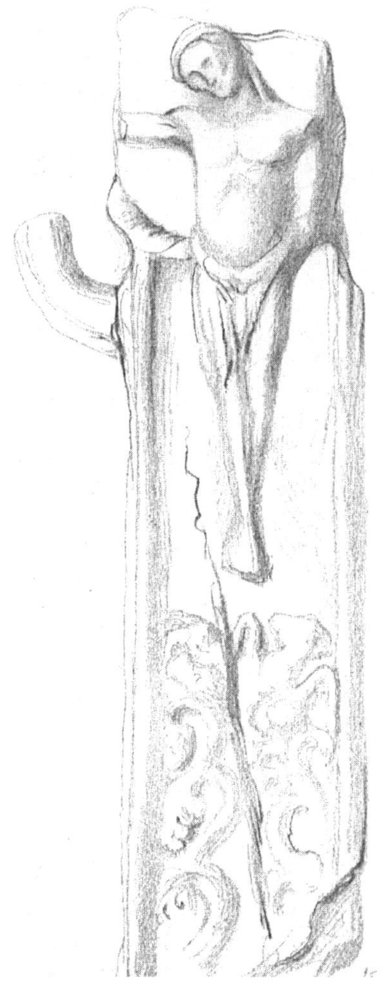

Illustration 14: *The shaft of a medieval ring-headed cross at Kilmartin. The cross has now been reconstructed and is inside the Parish church.* ***Argyll 7****, 138–139 (no 89).* Drawing: *Drummond,* ***Sculptured Monuments****, pl LIV, 2.*

Illustration 15: *A slab in the ruined chapel on Eilean Mòr, Finlaggan, Islay, a precursor, in stylistic terms, of the Iona School class II slabs; length 0.99m.* ***Argyll 5****, 280 (no 6).* Drawing: *D H Caldwell.*

Illustration 16: *The throne of an ivory king (no 79) chessman from the hoard recovered at Uig on Lewis, now in the British Museum, London.* Photo: *National Museums Scotland.*

Illustration 17: *Detail of the decoration on a twelfth-century slab in the cathedral, Trondheim, Norway.* Drawing: *D H Caldwell, after Ekroll,* ***Her Hvilir****, 26.*

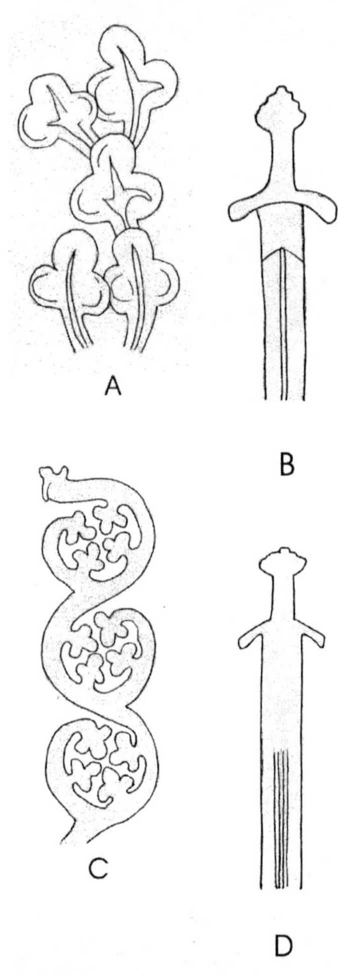

Illustration 18: *Details, (a) and (b) from the sandstone lid of a thirteenth-century sarcophagus discovered in the old parish church, Ardrossan — now in the North Ayrshire Museum in Saltcoats; and (c) and (d) from an Iona School class I slab in the burial ground of the old parish church of Kildalton, Islay.* ***Argyll 5****, 212 (no 6).* Drawings: *D H Caldwell.*

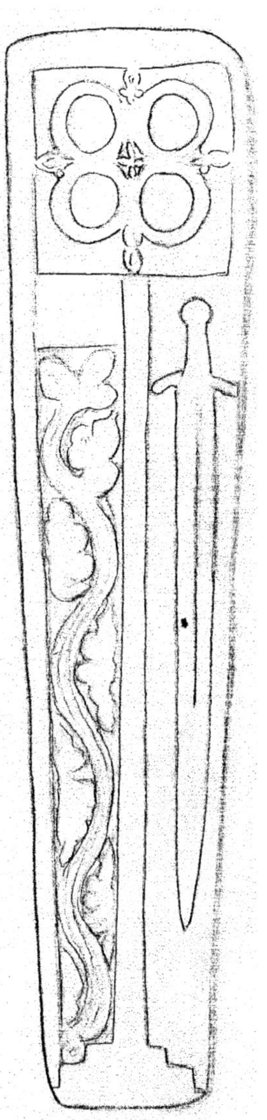

Illustration 19: *A slab in the Lapidarium at the Parish Church, Kilmartin, a precursor, in stylistic terms, of the Iona School class I slabs; length 1.89m.* ***Argyll 7****, 131 (no 5).* Drawing: *D H Caldwell.*

Illustration 20: *A sandstone slab in the tower of the old church of St John, Ayr, with a design scheme similar to Iona School class I slabs.* Drawing: *D H Caldwell.*

Illustration 21: *A military effigy, possibly of John Menteith, early to mid fourteenth-century, in the ruined church of St Mary, Rothesay, Bute.* Drawing: ***Proceedings of the Society of Antiquaries of Scotland*** *29 (1894–95) 363.*

Illustration 22: *The lower part of a slab, probably of early sixteenth-century date, from the chapel on the island of Texa, Islay, now in the Museum of Scotland, Edinburgh; length 0.91m. It depicts a priest in Eucharistic vestments, holding a chalice. On the basis of the inscription this was John MacAlister, Parson of Gigha.* ***Argyll 5****, 261 (no 2).* Photo: *National Museums Scotland.*

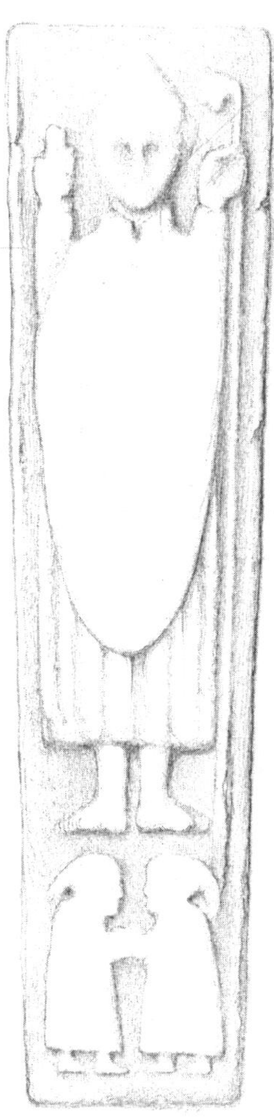

Illustration 23: *A thirteenth-century slab with the effigy of a mitred abbot or bishop, holding a crosier in his left hand, his right raised in blessing; beneath his feet are two monks; length 1.89m. It is in the nave of the Abbey Church, Iona.* ***Argyll 4****, 229–230 (no 199).* Drawing: *Drummond,* ***Sculptured Monuments****, pl XXXIII, 2.*

Illustration 24 a: *The shaft of a cross erected in memory of Ranald of Islay, the eponym of Clan Ranald, formerly in the burial ground of the chapel on Texa, Islay, but now in the Museum of Scotland, Edinburgh; height 1.02m. front: Ranald is shown as a warrior grasping a battle-axe.* ***Argyll 5****, 260–261 (no 1).* Photo: *Graham,* ***Carved Stones****, pl XXX, 105.*

Illustration 24 b: *The shaft of a cross erected in memory of Ranald of Islay, the eponym of Clan Ranald, formerly in the burial ground of the chapel on Texa, Islay, but now in the Museum of Scotland, Edinburgh; height 1.02m. back: a stag attacked by hounds and a galley.* ***Argyll 5****, 260–261 (no 1).* Photo: *Graham,* ***Carved Stones****, pl XXX, 105.*

Illustration 25: *A slab in the burial ground of the old parish church of Kilarrow, Bridgend, Islay, portraying a woman with a book and rosary; length 1.76m.* ***Argyll 5****, 188 (no 22).* Photo: *Graham,* ***Carved Stones****, pl VIII, no 26.*

Illustration 26: *A slab in the ruined chapel on Eilean Mòr, Finlaggan, Islay, with the effigy of Donald MacGillespie, dressed for war, a representation of a galley beneath his feet; length 1.87m. MacGillespie is listed as crown tenant of Finlaggan in a 1541 rental.* ***Argyll 5****, 280 (no 11).* Photo: *Graham,* ***Carved Stones****, pl II, 3.*

Illustration 27: *An Oronsay School slab in the 'Prior's House', Oronsay Priory, with an inscription recording that it was made for Mariota MacLean in commemoration of her husband Murchadh MacDuffie of Colonsay, who died in 1539. Apart from a fine representation of a hunting scene there is a claymore and a galley.* ***Argyll 5****, 248 (no 17).* Photo: *National Museums Scotland.*

Just what did a *nemeton* look like anyway?

Kristen Erskine ⊕

The problem with archaeology, according to Barry Raftery at least — though I am in agreement with him in this case — is that it deals with the end product of rituals. The alleged unwillingness of the upholders of Celtic religion to commit to writing anything relating to their rites and beliefs means that apart from the Coligny Calendar, the Bottoritta Tablet and the multitude of Romanised Celtic inscriptions on altars, weaponry and votive offerings, there is an absence of the actual litanies, incantations or prayers used by them. This lack is partly compensated for by archaeology, but what archaeology cannot provide us with is an account of the nature of the ceremonies conducted at assembly sites and cult centres.[1]

When the last rituals were carried out 1500 years ago and were not the sort to leave extensive inscriptions on stone monuments or obvious parcels of vellum and parchment with precise notes inscribed on them, archaeologists can find themselves floundering. Some ritual sites are a bonanza for the archaeologist, like the rivers, wells and lakes with depositions of stone, bronze, gold, silver and bone etc, chambered tombs and burial grounds as well as Roman-inspired temples. Assembly sites, on the other hand — those places where the Celtic tribes gathered at 'fixed times of the year' to bring grievances, hear judgements, celebrate festivals and the myriad other activities that would have taken place when a large group of people gathered together after months apart — have been generally neglected by archaeology (what's to see? an empty clearing in a forest?) and those that have been investigated in northern Britain have yielded virtually nothing from the period in question — the late bronze age to the early medieval (though pre-Christian). This is

⊕ Lismore NSW.

1 J Davies, *The Celts* (London, 2000) 77.

when the assistance of other disciplines, such as place-names, history and folklore, comes in handy. Amongst the assembly sites identified in the place-name record is one noted by classical commentators as occurring across the pan-Celtic world, the *nemeton*.

Watson translated *nemeton* as a neuter of *nemetos* ('sacred, noble'), found in the Gaulish personal name *Nemetos* and in compounds with other terms.[2] In Old Irish, *nemed* means sacred, noble or sacred place. Barrow followed Watson's interpretation and discussed the idea that nemeta possessed a holy or sacred significance and purpose in pagan Celtic society.[3] Rivet and Smith concurred that the name applied to 'natural sacred groves'.[4] They further noted that the word is based on an assumed **nemos* meaning heaven, from Sanskrit *nam* meaning to worship. This is supported by Ó hÓgáin, who suggested *nemeton* was based on the element *nem*, meaning sky, and argued that it was the word commonly used by the western Celts for a sacred centre.[5] The Celts' application of the word *nemeton* to a natural clearing is echoed in other Indo-European based languages: from Greek comes *nemos* for woods and from Latin, *nemus* for a forest sanctuary. *Nemed*, in the sense of 'holy place, sanctuary, church' is encountered fairly frequently in Irish literature. Even Saint Patrick had a *sen nemed* ('ancient sanctuary') and the Law of Adomnán stated that anyone who violated a *blai-nemed* ('sanctuary') could be punished with a fine.[6] Finally, the term *fid nemed*, translated as 'wood sanctuary', seems to be a common feature in the Irish landscape and references to them

2 W J Watson, *The Celtic Place-names of Scotland* (Edinburgh, 1926; repr 2004) 245.

3 G W S Barrow, 'The uses of place-names and Scottish history – pointers and pitfalls', 54–74 in S Taylor (ed), *The Uses of Place-Names* (Edinburgh, 1998) at pp 56-59.

4 A L F Rivet and C Smith, *The Place Names of Roman Britain* (London, 1979).

5 D Ó hÓgáin, *The Sacred Isle: Belief and Religion in pre-Christian Ireland* (Woodbridge, 1999) 70–1.

6 Watson, *Celtic Place-names*, 245. *Cáin Adomnáin*, ed P P Ó Néill and D N Dumville (Cambridge, 2003) §36.

occur fairly regularly in the literature.

So, in order to find the *nemeta*, history and onomastics are vital. From the classical records we find several instances of *nemeta*, these places of assembly that were considered sacred by the Celtic tribes that created them. The place-name appears throughout what we might describe as the pan-Celtic world, from Turkey's *Drunemeton* to Ireland's *fiodhneimidh* 'that the seers used to perform their rituals in'.[7] In Scotland, according to Watson, the *nemeton* has left its mark very distinctly on the place-names, and Watson and Barrow both feel that the history of the name appears to be the same as in Gaul and in Ireland — an institution, originally pagan, taken over by the Christian church.

Modern researchers are not agreed on when the word and its associated sites might have begun to be used, but the late bronze age is a likely guess: this was when the languages known as Celtic were being disseminated across Europe. From Turkey to Ireland, where there were Celtic-speaking peoples there appear to have been *nemeta*. In most cases the *nemeton* probably consisted of nothing more than a clearing in the woods, and this seems to have remained the case in northern Britain.[8]

Strabo was fairly dispassionate about the *Drunemeton* in the land of the Galatians, which he claimed was established by three Celtic tribes about 280 BCE.[9] Caesar wrote of another in Gaul, stating that 'at a fixed time of the year the (druids) meet in assembly in a holy place in the lands of the Carnutes, which is regarded as the centre of the whole of Gaul. All who have disputes come here from all sides and accept their decisions and judgements'.[10]

It sounds fairly standard, doesn't it? It could almost be the Old Bailey, except with druids instead of QCs.

Lucan, on the other hand, was rather more, shall we say, dramatic? He referred to the druids of Gaul, 'who dwell in deep

7 Ó hÓgáin, 71.

8 Davies, 89.

9 Strabo, *Geographica*, XII 5.1.

10 Caesar, *Gallic Wars*, 6.13.

groves and sequestered uninhabited woods', and added that 'they worship the gods in woods without making use of temples'.[11] In describing a grove in Marseilles, ordered destroyed by Caesar, he wrote that it was 'untouched by men's hands from ancient times, whose interlacing boughs enclosed a space of darkness and cold shade, and banished the sunlight from above [...] gods were worshipped there with savage rites, the altars were heaped with hideous offerings, and every tree was sprinkled with human gore'.[12]

In Britain, similarly obscene rites were apparently being carried out by Boudicca to ensure triumph over the Romans. According to Dio Cassius, she offered human sacrifices to the goddess of victory, Andraste, in a forest grove.[13] Further north, Tacitus tells us, there were groves on the island of Anglesey in Wales that were devoted to barbarous superstitions and were destroyed by Suetonius Paulinus around 61 BCE.[14]

Lucan's and Dio Cassius' descriptions pretty much sum up contemporary notions of a *nemeton* or sacred grove of the Celts. We may add, perhaps, the romantic ideal of white-robed druids with gold hooks trimming the oaks of mistletoe in the moonlight, that was only described by Pliny the Elder.[15] So, leaving aside the blood and guts and indeed the romance, what might these sacred sites of assembly have looked like?

In examining the possible physical appearance of a site whose only current indicator of existence is onomastics and occasionally historical records, I am going to stick primarily with the *nemeta* I know best: those of Pictland, the early medieval kingdom of north-eastern Scotland. The assertion that the tribes who eventually formed the nation of Pictland in the early medieval period used their *nemeta* as the Gauls apparently did is a little more contentious,

11 M Dillon and N Chadwick, *The Celtic Realms* (London, 1972; repr 2003) 177.

12 *Ibid.*

13 Dio Cassius, *Roman History*, LXII.7.

14 Tacitus, *Annals*, XIV.30.

15 Pliny the Elder, *Natural History*, XVI.95.

but most scholars accept that the place-name in eastern Scotland predates the wave of Gaelic that swept across the region with Christianity and the ascension of the Dál Riatan aristocracy.

Today, in nearly all of the places in north-eastern Scotland which bear a *nemeton*-derived placename, there is a little church with reasonably likely early medieval foundations, usually near a water source, built on a reasonably level area. There is a burial ground within the churchyard. Sometimes, if you're really lucky, there are Pictish symbol-stones or pillar stones in the vicinity as well.[16] In several places the *nemeton* prefix or suffix is affixed to a number of surrounding areas as well: hills, ridges, swamps, valleys. This has led to the question of so-called 'super' *nemeta* and whether their function was different to those places where the name is only attached to a single site. But we'll leave those for another day, another paper and perhaps even another researcher, like Simon Taylor of the University of Glasgow, who is already hard at work on just this subject, among others.

Oaks were particularly sacred to the druids. The name 'druid' itself has been supposed to have been derived from the word *dru*, which translates as 'oak'. In Welsh, 'oak' is *derw* and 'druid' is *derwydd*. So there has been an assumption by some that groves of oaks were the required vegetation. Without pollen core samples from the *nemeton* sites we can't really say for sure what kinds of trees made up the groves. However, we do know that in the fourth century, Columba, prior to his exile from Northern Ireland, built an oratory in Derry. He was unhappy about having an oak grove felled in order to clear the land for his chapel. To get around this, he repositioned the building to lie north-south rather than the traditional east-west alignment. Later in life, he admitted that though he feared Death and Hell, the sound of an axe in the grove of Derry frightened him still more.[17] This must be qualified though:

---

16 K Erskine, *From Groves to Churches: Sacred Sites in Pictland* (M Phil Thesis, University of Sydney, 2002).

17 M O'Donnell, *Betha Colaim Chille. Life of Columcille*, ed and trans A O'Kelleher and G Schoepperle (Urbana, 1918) 85.

rather than being a closet druid, from closer reading it is apparent that he recognised and respected the importance of continuity to the people he was ministering to.[18]

Columba didn't have to chop any trees down once he realigned the design of the chapel, so I'll go out on a limb and speculate that there was in fact a clearing large enough for him to build such a structure in. The passage of time and a lack of excavatory work means that we need to speculate heavily, but if people were receptive to a new religion being offered to them, the places where they were accustomed to assemble would have made the most sense as the places for the new religion to be disseminated from. The resistance to immediate and total religious change is brought forcefully home by an eighth-century list of superstitions and pagan rites in which there is a heading 'concerning shrines in groves which they call nimidae'.[19]

In north-eastern Scotland there is a total absence of pre-Christian shrines in groves. The first evidence we have of structures within the *nemeta* in Pictland are early medieval chapel or oratory foundations. On the continent and in southern Britain, where the Roman and Greek influences were greatest, we have evidence for pre-Christian construction, for ritual depositions and for the presence of many people[20] — which means people needed space to camp, for fires, for socialising and no doubt as somewhere for the druids to retire to.

Within the grove, while there might have been ritual sacrifices, there were certainly no burials. Burials took place elsewhere; the bodies of the dead were not part of the ritual space. In a few of the *nemeton* sites, excavations and field surveys have occasionally led to the identification of pre-Christian burials, but these are few and far between.

The classical commentators remarked on the use of *nemeta* as

18 M Beith, *Healing Threads – Traditional Medicines of the Highlands and Islands* (Edinburgh, 1995) 124.

19 Watson, *Celtic Place-names*, 244.

20 Davies, 89–90.

places of judgement and that is echoed in a piece of folklore passed on to me by Professor Ronnie Black of the Department of Celtic in Edinburgh. He recorded a story about Navity Moor in Sutherland, where an irascible old man who had been carrying on a feud with his neighbour for umpteen dozen years lay on his deathbed and asked his son to bury him just outside the church walls when he died. He urged his son to have the same done to his body when he passed on, so that 'we'll a' jump up at the first toot' (of the trumpet at the last judgement) and beat the aforementioned neighbour into Paradise. It seems that Navity Moor had long been regarded by the locals as the place where the final judgement would take place. Judgement by God was also passed on a farmer who was late for church at Nonakiln ('Church of the Nemeton' according to Watson, 'Church of St Ninian' to those who insist on seeing Nynia everywhere in Scotland[21]) in Ross and Cromarty: he had stopped on his way to kill a neighbour's bull that was annoying him before making his way to Sunday service. As he walked in, the roof fell in but no one was killed.[22] The sanctuary afforded by a *nemeton* is also remembered in the formal creation of Newmore Wood in Ross and Cromarty as a *comhraich*, or official church sanctuary, equal to that of Maelrubha's Applecross on the west coast of Scotland.[23] Sanctuary is also what is brought to mind with the legend of the witch in the Findhorn River valley who, on finding herself deceased, made at once for the church of Saint Fergus (another *nemeton* site) but the devil caught her at the gate and carried her off.[24]

In Pictland there is only one instance of a *fiodhneimidh*: Finavon in Fifeshire, within whose confines stood until recently what was attested as the largest tree in Scotland, a chestnut. The alleged oldest tree in Scotland, a yew tree, is also associated with a *nemeton*. It still stands, though much battered and burnt, in the churchyard at Fortingall on one bank of the River Lyon. Opposite is one of the

21 Watson, *Celtic Place-names*, pp 249 and 297.

22 Erskine, *From Groves to Churches*, 44.

23 Watson, *Celtic Place-names*, 70; Erskine, *From Groves to Churches*, 45.

24 Erskine, *From Groves to Churches*, 45.

riverbank *nemeta*, Duneaves ('the house of the *nemeton*'). Between the church and the *nemeton* lie three recumbent stone circles and the riverbank which touches Duneaves is gently undulating, with ideal spots for beaching a craft and coming ashore. Of the Pictish *nemeta*, several are on riverbanks, within close distance of some landmark — there are Wester and Easter Strathnoon on the opposite side of the Findhorn River from the aforementioned Saint Fergus' — which was built in a particularly rocky site but has within its churchyard a distinct lack of stones, because, according to legend, druids sifted the soil for some unknown purpose and removed all the stones larger than a hen's egg. There are also poor Nevie, known earlier as Neuchin Christe, whose chapel foundations are all but washed away, and the low-lying riverbank terrace at Newtyle Hill just south of Dunkeld, entered from the hill itself between two standing stones. By far the most isolated *nemeton* would have to be Eilean Neave, lying far in the north in Tongue parish. Lying 50 metres off the coast, it is nevertheless almost unreachable due to the treacherous waters and the scarcity of suitable landing sites. On the mainland, Cnoc Phobuill stands flat and at exactly the same elevation as the most likely assembly place on the island itself, which despite having no fresh water is reputedly the site of a chapel named for Columba. Dalnavie, Navidale — both valleys of the nemeton — and Inch Navie are other sites which incorporate the *nemeton* name with other landscape features.

The *nemeta* shared no single common landscape feature which might have been taken to have been essential to the choice of site. Many occurred on flat areas adjacent to rivers, but the diversity of site choice is apparent, with hills, bogs, riverbanks, cliff tops and unremarkable patches of agricultural land bearing *nemeton*-derived place-names. Of course we are hampered by the land use of more than 2000 years altering the landscape beyond recognition, but, given that the classical commentators were united in placing *nemeta* within groves, there could be a reasonable expectation of at least some similarity of placement. One possible way forward is to examine the surrounding place-names for elements referring to woodlands, although in a place like Pictland we are likely to find mostly frustration, given the extent of the Great Caledonian Forest and the propensity for Pictish words for woods, trees and shrubberies to survive in the place-name record.

Despite its limitations, archaeological evidence is of central importance. Without this, our deconstruction of the function and use of the *nemeton* sites is virtually at a standstill. In continental Europe, artefacts and sites relating to religion are far more abundant than those relating to any other aspect of people's lives. This evidence is invaluable when assessing the reliability of the accounts of the classical authors.

So what did a *nemeton* look like anyway? It would be useful to present a single, generic pattern for a *nemeton*, but the landscape evidence confounds me. Uniformity is a nice idea but should not be expected, and indeed, in Pictland at least, is not supported by the evidence. From the classical commentators we can infer that there was a substantial clearing most likely within a grove of trees, possibly with perishable artefacts, like wooden carvings, bone or the like. Equally, a *nemeton* in Pictland seems to have been a clearing on a riverbank that was reasonably flat, where people from nearby would have been able to gain access by travelling up or down river. *Nemeta* didn't need to be signposted, as they were known by the peoples who used them for hundreds of years. When Christianity became the religion of choice in Pictland, *nemeta* made ideal sites for situating a church, where the judgement of the new god could become known.

Celts, Romans and Germans in the Rhineland

Michael Nelson ⊕

What is now south-western Germany, northern Switzerland and Austria was in the fifth century BCE a Celtic-speaking area, according to the evidence of archaeology and place-names. The linguistic border with Germanic tribes in the north seems to have shifted south in the next centuries.[1] Caesar's campaigns in Gaul (58–51 BCE) brought him into contact with Germanic tribes on both sides of the Rhine, some of whom were allied with or cooperated with his Gallic enemies. He mounted two campaigns across the Rhine but he either did not want to, or could not, take his conquests further. For the next five centuries, the Rhine formed the border between Romanized Gaul and 'Free Germany' (*Germania Libera*) with its assortment of Germanic tribes. Caesar started the practice of recruiting Germanic troops as auxiliaries, and from the first century to the fifth century the Romans allowed or even forced Germanic-speaking groups to settle on their territory, including the left bank of the Rhine. From the third century on, the Gallo-Romans were subjected increasingly to raids from Germanic territory. The Romans responded sometimes by brutal punitive expeditions and sometimes by bribing the so-called barbarians with money and land. In the fifth century Roman rule in the west was replaced by a series of Germanic kingdoms. At first these were nominally under the sovereignty of the emperor in Constantinople. The ultimate

⊕ The University of Sydney.

1 W König, *dtv-Atlas zur deutschen Sprache* (München, 1985) 46–47. Examples of German river names from Celtic include the Lahn (**lugna*, curving river), Enns and Inn (**an*, bog; Irish *en*, water) and the Danube (**dan*, river). Celtic *magos* (plain, field) appears in Remagen and other names, *briga* and *dunum* (fort, mountain) in the Roman names for Bregenz/Brigantia and Kempten/Cambodunum.

result was that by the eighth century the border in western and southern continental Europe between the Germanic, Romance and Celtic languages became approximately what it is today, with later shrinkage of Celtic in western France and of Germanic in Belgium and Alsace-Lorraine.

The displacement of one language by another can come about more or less peacefully by migration and settlement, violently by expulsion of population, or voluntarily by adoption of a language which is more prestigious and useful than the existing one. Each of these processes can be illustrated by the expansion of the modern colonial languages English, French and Spanish, and by the fate of German. English became the language of the USA, Australia and New Zealand, where settlers outnumbered the original inhabitants. In Latin America the Spanish settlers may not always have outnumbered the locals but their language became universal because of its prestige as the language of the conquerors and the usefulness of a generally accepted language over a multitude of local ones. The expansion of German into eastern Europe was the result of the local rulers encouraging settlement by skilled farmers and artisans; most of the German communities were forcibly expelled after the defeat of the Third Reich, with the result that the border between Slavic and Germanic has retreated to the Oder-Neisse line and the Bavarian Forest.

The almost complete eclipse of Celtic by Latin and its derivatives is surprising when one considers the wealth and geographical extent of the Celtic area conquered by the Romans: first Gallia Cisalpina, then Gallia Transalpina in southern France and finally Caesar's conquests. The Romans imposed Latin as the language of administration and the military (with Romans in charge), but the tribal leaders who cooperated with the Romans (sometimes as hostages) were presumably already admirers and recipients of Roman civilisation. After the initial devastation and looting by Caesar and his followers, the benefits of the extension of Roman rule became apparent: infrastructure like roads and water supply, a regular monetary system, a literary instead of an oral culture, new trade routes, the development of towns out of existing Celtic settlements and the profits to be made near the camps of the legions. The Gauls adopted Mediterranean fashions and cuisine; for instance, dog meat went out of style, at least as a grave offering. While the Romans vigorously opposed the druids, they were tolerant of most other aspects of Celtic religions, so that this source of conflict between natives and colonists — so often seen in modern colonial history — seems to have been avoided. It can be assumed that Celtic dialects survived in country areas, although the Roman practice of settling veterans from elsewhere in the empire must have had an effect here too (tombstones of settlers and soldiers often reveal surprisingly distant origins).

The Rhine and Danube rivers were, for most of the empire, frontier areas with a strong military presence. Under Augustus (27 BCE–14 CE) a series of campaigns began to bring Germany into the Roman empire. The Elbe and Weser areas were reached by Roman forces. Indeed Germany was declared conquered and the beginnings of a colonial administration set up; but in 9 CE Varus' three legions were annihilated in the Teutoburg forest. Subsequent operations were only partially successful. The heavy losses they suffered did not seem to justify conquering a comparatively poor and backward country. Tiberius (14–37 CE), who had led some of the German campaigns, decided to adopt a purely defensive policy. This remained the basic policy on the Rhine frontier until Roman forces were withdrawn from the west in the fifth century Nevertheless, numerous emperors tried to make their name by brutal punitive expeditions into Germanic territory, giving themselves triumphs, adding the prestigious name of Germanicus to their titles, and striking coins showing *Germania victa* or *Germania capta*.[2] Looking back on the Flavian emperor Domitian's campaigns, Tacitus said

---

2 The following later emperors issued coins claiming victory over the Germans: Caracalla (211–217), Maximinus Thrax (235–238), Gallienus (253–268), Postumus (260–269), Claudius II (268–270), Probus (276–282), Constantinus I (306–30), Crispus (317–326), Constantinus II (317–340). Coins illustrated in *Die Alamannen*, herausgegeben vom Archäologischen Landesmuseum Baden-Württemberg (Stuttgart, 1997) 120.

sarcastically in his *Germania* (c 98 CE) that there were more victory celebrations than victories.[3] Throughout the period of the empire, the Romans wooed the more friendly Germanic tribes with gifts and honours, allowed settlers to cross the borders and recruited troops; indeed ultimately many senior officers and generals were of 'barbarian' origin.[4] In long periods of peace, there was border trade between Germany and Gaul. From the Germanic side came slaves, timber, amber, iron tools, wool, hides and foodstuffs including honey and cheese. Archaeological evidence shows that the German ruling class bought Roman textiles, glass, tableware and other luxury items — or stole them when invading Roman territory.[5]

Under Domitian (81–96) the Romans reorganised the area between Gallia Belgica, Galla Lugdenensis, Raetia and the Rhine as the provinces of Germania Inferior and Germania Superior. The name Germania possibly was given to support Domitian's claim to have conquered the Germans, since the population of these provinces, and especially of the cities established in them, was a mixture of Celts, Germans, Italians, and immigrants from elsewhere, including part of the Jewish diaspora.

Under Roman rule a chain of cities grew up in the Rhineland, deriving both from earlier Celtic settlements and from the military establishments on the left bank. The most important Roman cities in the two Germania provinces were (using the modern names) Cologne and Mainz, and later Trier; these were also early Christian bishoprics and never lost their ecclesiastical importance, since

---

3 "...proximis temporibus triumphati magis quam victi sunt" (in recent times, triumphed-over rather than defeated), *Germania*, 37.

4 M Martin, 'Zwischen den Fronten. Alamannen im römischen Heer' in *Die Alamannen*, herausgegeben vom Archäologischen Landesmuseum Baden-Württemberg (Stuttgart, 1997) 119–124. Alamannic officers took part in the campaign of Constantius II against Maxentius (350–353 CE).

5 S Martin-Kilcher, 'Handel und Importe. Das Imperium Romanum als Wirtschaftsraum' in *Imperium Romanum. Roms Provinzen an Neckar, Rhein und Donau*. Herausgegeben vom Archäologischen Landesmuseum Baden-Württemberg (Stuttgart, 2005) 426–434.

their archbishops were later Electors of the Holy Roman Empire. Cologne was in the area of a resettled German tribe, while Trier was in the area of the Trevi, a Celtic group. Saint Jerome (c347–420) is alleged to have become acquainted with the Celtic language in Trier.[6] A tendency for the major cities of the Rhineland to be on the left bank, usually with smaller outposts on the right bank, persists from Roman times: this applies to Basel (Switzerland) with its Baden exclave on the left bank, to French Strasbourg facing the small German town of Kehl, Mainz and Kastel, Cologne and Deutz, and exceptionally Neuss and Düsseldorf where the settlement on the right bank is the major city. The Netherlands cities of Nimwegen, Arnhem and Utrecht on the lower Rhine were also Roman towns. The Roman enthusiasm for baths is reflected in the spa cities of western Germany: Wiesbaden, Baden-Baden, and Aachen (*Aquae Granni*, named after a Celtic god).

What is now the Swiss left bank of the Rhine was a Celtic-speaking region during the Roman empire. Inscriptions record Celtic personal names, some using the characteristic letters 'X' and 'Đ'.[7] There was a large Roman town on the Rhine at modern Augst-Kaiseraugst. Because it was later abandoned in favour of nearby Basel, it has provided an excellent archaeological park and museum. In December 1961 a bulldozer bumped into a Roman wall in which an 84-piece silver table service and coins had been hidden before the destruction of the fortress in 351 or 252: at 57.5 kg one of the largest deposits of this nature ever found. By the time the archaeologists arrived two months later the locals had done some excavating of their own, most but not all of which was eventually recovered.[8]

On the other side of the Rhine, on the eastern and northern edges of the new territories acquired from 73–74, the Romans set

6 A Demandt, *Die Kelten* (München, 2005) 93.

7 W Drack und R Fellmann, *Die Römer in der Schweiz* (Stuttgart, 1988) 145–149.

8 B Rütti, 'Der Silberschatz von Kaiseraugst' in *Imperium Romanum. Römer, Christen, Alamannen – Die Spätantike am Oberrhein* [Catalogue of the exhibition in the Badisches Landesmuseum Karlsruhe] (Stuttgart, 2005) 226–233.

up the fortified frontier known as the Limes. The Limes, partly constructed of masonry and partly of a timber palisade, functioned both as a customs and immigration barrier and as an early warning of invasion. It was comparatively lightly manned (probably by auxiliaries) and the real defence lay in the powerful legions located in the hinterland. The best land in the new territories, known as the *agri decumates*,[9] was deforested and intensively settled, mainly by Gallo-Roman migrants and veterans. Thus an area which had once been Celtic again become predominantly Celtic. The native Germanic tribe, the Suebi, and other German migrants were also Romanised in the course of the two centuries of this colony's existence.[10]

The loss of the *agri decumates* to the Alamanni anticipates the later linguistic Germanisation of the Rhineland and upper Danube. The Alamanni were at first raiding parties of 'all the men', mainly from the Elbe region. Their most dangerous attack in 260 coincided with an internal crisis of the Roman empire. In the east, the Sassanid Persians defeated a Roman army and captured the emperor Valerian. In the west, the succession of Valerian's son Gallienus was disputed by Postumus who set up a separate Gallic empire which lasted until 273. Although the incursions of the Alamanni across the Alps into Italy were eventually stopped, the *agri decumates* had to be abandoned. Careful German archaeological research has suggested that the surviving Gallo-Roman population fled or were evacuated when the Romans decided to move the border south.[11] The Alamanni did not immediately resettle the area in large numbers, and it is estimated it was not until the seventh

---

9 However "agri decumates" is interpreted, the name suggests the special conditions of frontier territories. Discussion in *Reallexikon der Germanischen Altertumskunde* (Berlin und New York, 1984) 5.Band, 271–286.

10 E Schallmayer, *Der Limes. Geschichte einer Grenze* (München, 2006) 55.

11 G Fingerlin, 'Siedlungen und Siedlungstypen. Südwestdeutschland in frühalamannischer Zeit' in *Die Alamannen*, herausgegeben vom Archäologischen Landesmuseum Baden-Württemberg (Stuttgart, 1997) 125–126.

century that the population reached the Gallo-Roman figure. Study of the *fibulae* (clothes fasteners) found in Alamannic graves shows that many new settlers came from the Elbe and from Bohemia. The Alamanni did not generally repair the Roman buildings they had looted and burned during their invasion; even when they took over a Roman farm they preferred to live in timber buildings next to the ruins.[12]

The Germanisation of this area illustrates the processes by which languages can be displaced: by invasion, leading to death, flight or enslavement of the existing population; by migration and colonisation, creating a majority for the new language; and by the greater prestige and administrative usefulness of the new language.

The crisis of the third century was stabilised, with great effort, under a series of competent emperors such as Diocletian (284–305), Constantine (306–337) and Julian (360–363). Fortifications on the Rhine, Iller and Danube were strengthened. Defences and refuges for the population were built in towns and cities, including Rome's Aurelian wall. The end of the western Roman empire started with the arrival of the Huns and the consequent movements of Goths and other Germanic groups to the west. This was complicated by internal disputes among the Romans themselves using troops withdrawn from the frontiers. In the Rhineland, various Germanic groups were able to cross the frozen Rhine in late December 406 without finding significant opposition. By 500 Germanic leaders ruled in Italy, Gaul and Spain. But in most of the former Roman territories the Germanic ruling class was not sufficiently numerous to impose their language on the indigenous population.[13] This

---

12 H U Huber, 'Staatskrise im 3. Jahrhundert. Die Aufgabe der rechtsrheinischen Gebiete' in *Imperium Romanum. Roms Provinzen an Neckar, Rhein und Donau.* Herausgegeben vom Archäologischen Landesmuseum Baden-Württemberg (Stuttgart, 2005) 447–8. The process by which almost all of the Roman province became 'Alemannia' took about 40 years (approximately 260 to 300 CE) according to Huber.

13 K Rosen, *Die Völkerwanderung* (München, 2006) 100–101. Calculations based on cemeteries and palaeobotany substantially reduce the figures given in the classical sources for the 'barbarian' forces. At the battle of

only seems to have happened in the areas adjacent to the existing German-speaking area. Here there was direct migration of settlers who became the majority (thus the Alamannic-speaking territory eventually extended into Switzerland, western Austria and Alsace). The local Celtic-speaking people here presumably merged with the migrants in the process modern historians describe as ethnogenesis.

Of the various Germanic migratory groups, the great survivors were the Franks. Like the Alamanni, they started as an opportunistic tribal confederation and fought for and against the Romans, then defeated and absorbed Visigoths, Burgundians, Alamanni, Lombards, Frisians and Saxons. The key to their success as the only barbarian kingdom[14] to survive into the middle ages — indeed until 1792 — was cooperation with the Gallo-Romans and eventually the cultural Romanisation and westernisation of Germany itself within Latin Christianity.

Strasbourg (357) the Roman army of 13,000 had 247 killed, so it is likely that the other side had about the same number (perhaps 15,000), rather than the alleged 35,000 in the source. It is thought that 15,000 was about the maximum size of any army on the move given the problems of logistics. Geiserich's 419 Africa corps, reported as 80,000, was probably no more than 16,000.

14 The last to fall being the Anglo-Saxon kingdom in 1066.

The ancient Celts: classical perceptions and modern definitions

David Sheehan [⊕]

In a recent book on the ancient Celts, John Collis argued that current depictions of the ancient Celts as a pan-European ethnic group, such as one might find in the works of TGE Powell, Barry Cunliffe and Vincent and Ruth Megaw, are based upon outmoded nineteenth-century notions of interpreting archaeological, linguistic and historical evidence in ethnic terms.[1] Collis has examined the different and sometimes ambiguous ways in which classical writers classified and located Celts geographically, primarily from the perspective of an archaeologist interested in debunking the ethnic interpretation of La Tène culture as Celtic.[2] In particular, he has argued that there is a general trend in the classical sources towards greater geographic and ethnographic precision over time in how Celts were classified,[3] and that this trend demonstrates that we should place the origin of the Celts in central France, rather than in regions associated with the formation of Hallstatt and La Tène culture, such as central Europe, north-eastern France or south-western Germany.[4] He does not, however, offer any explanations as to why there are a range of different representations in the classical sources during the period for which we have the more detailed written records, that is, from the first century BCE to the fourth century CE.

⊕ The University of Melbourne.

1 J Collis, *The Celts: Origins, Myths and Inventions* (Gloucestershire, 2003) 11–12, 224.

2 *Ibid*, 117–118, 193.

3 *Ibid*, 103–4.

4 *Ibid*, 127–8.

Collis' empirical approach assumes that the *Celtae* were a distinct ethnic group who can be more clearly delineated from other peoples such as the *Galatae*, *Belgae*, or *Britanni*, whom Cunliffe and the Megaws would certainly regard as Celts. As a historian, I am interested in attempting to explain the apparent ambiguities and inconsistencies in the evidence and in how these sources may reveal ethnic diversity. Although some of the more problematic ambiguities may very well result from different writers patching together disparate information from different time periods, in much the same way as Collis has criticised modern writers for doing,[5] some of the inconsistencies may in fact not be inconsistencies at all. Classical writers may have appeared to conflate different peoples under the names *Galatae*, *Keltoi*, *Belgae* and *Germani* because their classificatory systems were unable to conceptually reconcile the actual ethnic complexity. As evidence for this, the sources reveal that some of these peoples were in fact intermingled with each other, were different in small degrees or felt strong kinship with each other. This paper briefly examines some evidence from Caesar, Diodorus Siculus and Strabo in support of this alternative reading. I will supplement these accounts with a couple of brief examples from later writers in order to show that the diversity of how Celts were represented continued over time.

The earliest written accounts of a people collectively called *Keltoi* in Greek (Celts in English) were usually brief and described Celts in very general geographic terms as 'barbarians' who inhabited western and north-western Europe. From the third century BCE to the second century CE, Celts were referred to in more complex ways by both Greek and Roman writers. The Greek term *Galatae* (Galatians or Gauls) first appears in the third century BCE, and by the second century BCE, although some writers such as Polybius were using the terms *Keltoi* and *Galatae* interchangeably, others such as Apollodorus of Athens made distinctions between these

5 J Collis, 'States without Centres? The Middle La Tène Period in Temperate Europe' 75–80 in B Arnold and D Blair Gibson (eds), *Celtic Chiefdom, Celtic State: The Evolution of Complex Social Systems in Prehistoric Europe* (Cambridge, 1995) at p 76–77.

terms.[6]

The most detailed account of the ethnicity of 'Celts' or 'Gauls' and 'Germans' is that of Julius Gaius Caesar, who conducted a military campaign in Gaul for seven years from 58 to 51 BCE. Caesar's account of the ethnicity of these peoples, in particular those of Gaul, however, is problematic for a number of reasons. His own cultural biases and personal political motivations cast some doubt upon the accuracy of his descriptions of certain peoples as Gauls and Germans. A discussion of these factors is, however, beyond the scope of this paper. I intend, instead, to focus upon a third factor: the tension and occasional contradiction between the classificatory systems Caesar used to describe northern Europeans and his narrative account of his time among them. While his description attempts to fit these peoples into neat ethnic categories, Caesar's narrative account frequently reveals a more complex ethnic situation. This is best demonstrated by examining the different ways in which he used the terms *Galli* (Gauls) and *Germani* (Germans).

Caesar used the term *Galli* in two different ways: as a specific group of peoples forming a separate nation inhabiting a specifically defined territory within Gaul, and as a general term for all peoples in or from Gaul. The first of these appears in the introduction to his book *The Gallic War* wherein he states '*Gallia* [Gaul] is a whole divided into three parts, one of which is inhabited by the *Belgae*, another by the *Aquitani*, and a third by a people called in their own tongue *Celtae* (Celts), in the Latin *Galli* (Gauls). All these are different one from another in language, institutions, and laws'.[7] Here, Caesar used the terms Celts and Gauls synonymously as applied to

6 Polybius, *The Histories*, ed and trans W R Paton (London, 1922–7) 2.17.3–9; 2.18.6–9; Apollodorus, *On the catalogue of Ships* in Stephanus of Byzantium, in *Fragmenta Historicorum Graecorum*, ed and trans C Müller and T Müller (Paris, 1885) V.1, 437, Fr. 60, Fr. 62. Translated into English by Collis, *The Celts*, 100; Strabo, *Geographica*, ed and trans H L Jones, *The Geography of Strabo* (Cambridge, Massachusetts; London, 1917–1944) 1.2.24.

7 J Caesar, *De Bello Gallico*, ed and trans H J Edwards, *The Gallic War* (Cambridge, 1917, this edition 2004) 1.1.

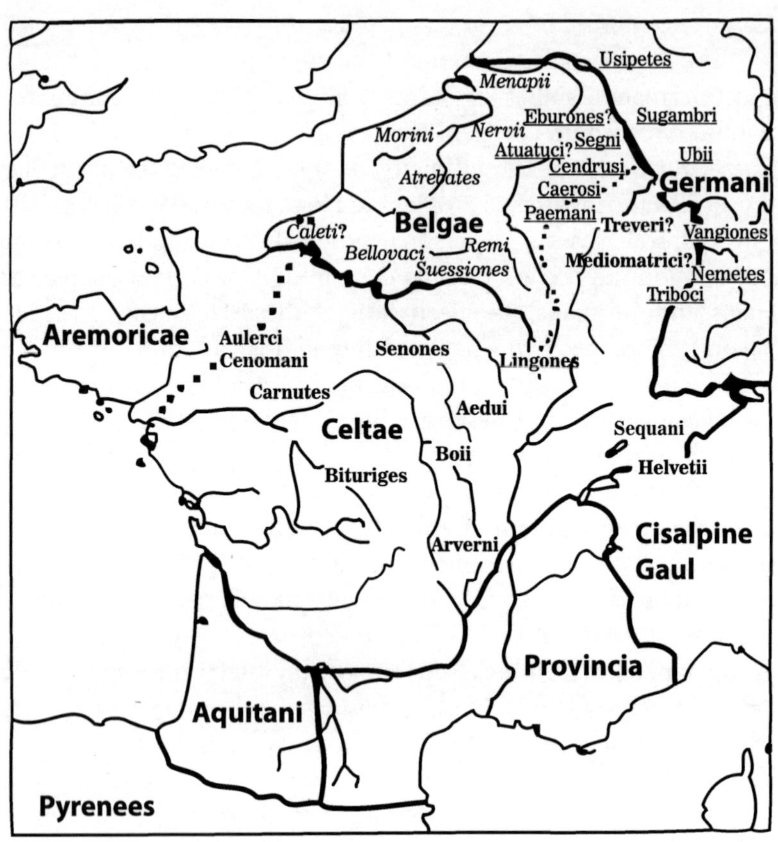

Figure 1: *Caesar's division of ethnic groups in Gaul: thick lines mark borders, dotted lines possible borders, square dots indicate Aremorica, Regular text=Celtae, Italic=Belgae, Underlined=Germani, ?=uncertain*

the peoples or 'tribes' living in a particular part of Gaul. It is in fact the one and only usage of the term *Celtae* in Caesar's writing, and thenceforth these people were referred to only as *Galli*. The clearest distinction he made between them and other Gauls was in terms of their territory. Thus, the territory of these *Celtae* was defined as being separated from that of the *Belgae* in the north by the Seine and Marne rivers, bounded in the west by the ocean, and separated from the *Aquitani* by the Garonne river in the south-west[8] (*figure 1*). The southern and south-eastern boundary is vague and not explicitly stated, but Caesar seems to have taken it for granted that his audience would know this to be Provincia (the Roman part of Gaul which stretched from Aquitania to the Alps), for he merely stated that the territory of the *Celtae* started at the Rhone.[9] 'Celtic' territory in the east was described as passing through the lands of the *Sequani* and *Helvetii*, where it touched the Rhine, after which its general trend was northward.[10] A possible subdivision of this category might include the peoples Caesar called the *Aremoricae* or 'maritime states', whom he located within the territory of the *Celtae* on the ocean coast[11] (*figure 1*).

Caesar referred to specific tribal groups within this territory, such as the *Aedui*, *Sequani*, *Senones*, *Arverni*, and *Helvetii*, for example.[12] This group of *Galli*, inhabiting a specific part of Gaul, was also referred to as a 'nation' by Caesar. In book three for example, Caesar recounted how he had sent one of his generals, Publius Crassus, to Aquitania to prevent auxiliary troops from the tribes there moving into Gaul, 'and the junction of the two great nations'.[13] This would tend to support his earlier definition of the *Celtae* as a distinct people in central Gaul. Caesar, however, was not entirely consistent in how he applied this usage at more specific

8 *Ibid*, 1.1. In fact he refers to it as 'Gallic territory'.

9 *Ibid*, 1.1; 3.20; 7.7. Provincia included the city of Narbo (Narbonne), after which Provincia would later be named during the reign of Augustus. Strabo, *Geography*, 4.1.1.

10 Caesar, *Gallic War*, 1.1. The territory of the Helvetii was bounded by the Alps, Provincia and Lake Geneva, the Rhine, and the Jura range. *Ibid*, 1.2.

11 *Ibid*, Veneti, Venelli, Osismi, Curiosolitae, Esubii, Aulerci, and Redones, 2.34; also includes the Ambibarii, Lemovices, and Caletes, 7.75; and possibly the Lexovii and Eburovices, 3.17; and the Diablintes, Namnetes and Ambiliati, 3.9.

12 *Ibid*, Aedui, Arverni, 1.31; 7.75; Senones, 5.54; Helvetii, 1.2; Sequani, rise and fall of, 1.31–32.

13 *Ibid*, 3.11.

levels. For example, one of the maritime states, the *Caleti* or *Caletes*, were described at different times as either *Belgae* or *Aremoricae*, which somewhat blurs the distinction he made between *Belgae* and *Celtae*.[14]

The differences between languages, laws and institutions mentioned in connection with the *Celtae* and other Gauls are also problematic. I use here only the issue of language as an example. Caesar's remark that their language differed from that of other Gauls is not possible to substantiate, and may have been merely an allusion to subtle dialect differences. Other references to languages spoken in Gaul are generally vague, or imply differences rather than explicitly state them. Caesar mentioned that one of his translators, Gaius Valerius Procillus, and Ariovistus, the leader of the Germanic tribe of the *Suebi*, both had knowledge of 'the Gallic language'.[15] In particular this must be a reference to the language spoken in central and eastern Gaul by the *Helvetii*, *Sequani* and *Aedui*, with whom Ariovistus was waging war. Procillus was sent by Caesar to speak with Ariovistus on their behalf as a Gallic interpreter, as Ariovistus is described as having learnt to speak this language freely after having spent a long time in Gaul. Two inferences arise. The first is that Ariovistus also spoke a native Germanic language. The second is that the Romans in that instance could only communicate with the Germans in Gallic, something to which I shall return later in this paper. Procillus was also said by Caesar to be a leading man from the Roman province of Gaul, which might also imply that the Gallic language spoken in central Gaul was either the same as that spoken in southern Gaul or equally well known.[16] There is also a reference to a man from *Hispania* (Spain), Quintus Junius, as having been sent by Caesar on many missions to Ambiorix, joint ruler of the *Eburones* among the *Belgae*. Junius, while not explicitly described as an interpreter, is described as having reported Ambiorix's remarks to Caesar, which might imply either that there was a common

14 Caleti as Belgae, *Ibid*, 2.4; as Aremoricae, 7.75.

15 *Ibid*, 1.47.

16 *Ibid*, 1.17.

'Gallic' language from Spain to northern Gaul, or that differences in dialect were so slight that communication was possible.[17] Whether or not Quintus Junius was a Celtiberian is not established, and he may, furthermore, have used a translator of his own (his knowledge of Gallic is not stated).[18]

The second and most prevalent use of the term *Galli* in Caesar's writing is a general one referring to all the people of Gaul, be they *Aquitani*, *Celtae* or *Belgae*. This usage was in most cases applied to anyone in or from the territory of Gaul. In book seven, for example, Caesar described how the *Galli* summoned a council of chiefs from all over Gaul to fight together against the Romans and how they made mention of a common Gallic ancestral heritage and reputation for prowess in war.[19] He also provided a list of tribes which included *Belgae* (*Bellovaci*, *Suessiones* and *Nervii*), *Celtae* (*Arverni*, *Aediu*, *Sequani*), and *Aremoricae* (*Veneti*, *Osismi*, *Venelli*) who participated.[20] This general usage was also applied by Caesar to *Galli* outside of Gaul. The *Volcae Tectosages* were described by him as Gauls dwelling in the Hercynian Forest (the Black Forest) in south-western Germany and living much the same as the Germans did, eating the same kinds of food and enduring the same hardships.[21] The *Boii* are described as having once been 'dwellers beyond the Rhine' but had crossed into *Noricum* and attacked *Noreia*[22] before

17 *Ibid*, 5.27–8.

18 The third possibility, that Ambiorix spoke Latin, although not impossible, is unlikely, given that Caesar speaks to leading men of influential Gallic tribes such as Dumnorix of the Aedui through Gallic interpreters, whereas Ambiorix hailed from an insignificant state in the far north of Gaul.

19 Caesar, *Gallic War*, 7.1. Caesar also referred to the unanimity of all Gaul in their common purpose of maintaining their liberty from Rome and recovering their ancient renown in war, 7.76.

20 *Ibid*, 7.75. This list is a shortened sample of the fuller lists Caesar gave.

21 *Ibid*, 6.24.

22 *Ibid*, 1.5. Although the kingdom of Noricum was a Gallic colony, roughly equating to modern Styria and Carinthia in Austria, Caesar never mentions the ethnicity of its inhabitants.

being settled in Gaul by Caesar near the territory of the *Aedui*.[23] The *Boii* were later also referred to as Gauls in this more general sense.[24]

This more general usage of *Galli* was especially applied to Gaul as a whole when Caesar wanted to make a distinction between Gauls and the Germans across the Rhine, for he described the Rhine as the natural border between the Gallic and Germanic peoples.[25] Caesar's description of the ethnicity of the peoples who inhabited northern Gaul between the Marne and Rhine rivers, however, is very ambiguous. Although he considered the *Belgae* to be Gauls, he also claimed that the *Remi*, a Belgic tribe, had informed him that most of the *Belgae* were of Germanic origin, and had crossed over the Rhine into Gaul many years ago and ejected the Gauls then living there.[26] Most of the *Belgae* took part in the confederation of Gallic tribes mentioned above, and in all likelihood spoke a Gallic language by Caesar's day. It would seem, however, that language was not a crucial determinant in how the ethnicity of some of these peoples was defined, as later examples from Strabo and Tacitus will show.

The definition of Germans in Caesar's *Gallic War* is even more ambiguous and contradictory than that of Gauls. Caesar applies three different usages of the term *Germani*. The first is the reference to the *Belgae* as Gauls of Germanic origin, as related above. It is unclear just what he meant by this designation. He may have meant Gallic-speaking Gauls who originally lived on the left bank (eastern side) of the Rhine in Germany, which would contradict Caesar's definition of the Rhine as the natural border between Gaul

---

23 *Ibid*, 1.28.

24 *Ibid*, 7.75.

25 *Ibid*, 1.1; Helvetii next to the Germans across the Rhine,1.2; the Ubii (Germani) on the German side of the Rhine near the Treveri (Gauls on the Middle Rhine Moselle) 6.9; 6.29; Tencteri and Usipetes (Germani) attempting to cross into Menapii (Belgae) lands near the northern mouth of the Rhine, 4.4.

26 *Ibid*, 2.3–4.

and Germany. There is also the possibility that these *Belgae* were originally a Germanic-speaking people who had gradually come to speak Gallic over many years through their closer association with Gauls, as Ariovistus had learnt to, but on a more permanent basis. The earliest of these immigrant *Belgae* were said to have been the only nation when all Gaul was attacked by the *Cimbri* and *Teutones* who prevented them from entering their borders.[27] In complete contradiction of this, Caesar also wrote that the *Atuatuci* were *Belgae* who were descendants of the *Cimbri* and the *Teutones*.[28]

Both the *Cimbri* and the *Teutones* were regarded by Caesar as Germans in the second sense, as a separate or distinct people who invaded Gaul.[29] A more explicit example of this type of German would be the Germanic coalition led by Ariovistus, chieftain of the *Suebi*, which crossed the Rhine, and included other Germans, such as the *Triboci*, *Harudes*, *Marcomani*, *Vangiones*, *Nemetes* and *Sedusii*.[30] These were Germans as invaders, but not initially so, as they were said to have been invited over by the *Arverni* and *Sequani* as mercenaries to fight the *Aedui*.[31] This suggests that language was not a barrier between Gauls and Germans, and that prior to the coming of Caesar some degree of bilingualism existed between the two peoples.

Caesar also described some Germans who were settlers in Belgic territory, such as the *Paemani*, *Caerosi*, *Condrusi*, *Segni* and *Eburones*.[32] These Germans appear to have had closer ties with

---

27 *Ibid*, 2.4.

28 *Ibid*, 2.29.

29 *Ibid*, 1.33, 40.

30 *Ibid*, 1.51; 1.43–44. The Tencteri and Usipetes also made incursions into the Menapii lands in the north, 4.4. Most of these were defeated and forced back over the Rhine by Caesar, although the Triboci at least were mentioned as still inhabiting their lands in book four, 4.10.

31 *Ibid*, 1.31.

32 *Ibid*, 2.4; Segni and Condrusi as Germani living between the territories of the Eburones and the Treveri, 6.32; Eburones were described as an undistinguished and insignificant state, 5.28; and they also fought

the Gauls than with other Germans over the Rhine. Whether they regarded themselves as Gauls, *Belgae* or Germans is a mystery. The *Eburones* seem to have regarded themselves as Gauls, if we are to believe the speech that Caesar puts into the mouth of Ambiorix, their leader.[33] Other Gauls, such as the *Treveri*, who were not referred to as *Belgae*, also had closer ties with the Germans on both sides of the Rhine. The *Eburones* and *Condrusi* were both described as clients or dependants of the *Treveri*.[34] The *Treveri* and the *Eburones* were also described as enlisting the help of Germans from across the Rhine to help fight the Romans.[35] The *Treveri* were described by Hirtius in book eight of the *Gallic War* as differing little from the Germans in their habits,[36] while he described some German peoples, such as the *Ubii*, as more civilised because they lived close to Gaul and therefore had become accustomed to Gallic fashions.[37] Given the level of cultural interaction and alliances, it seems highly plausible that there was some degree of bilingualism among the *Belgae*, other Gauls near the Rhine and the Germans on both sides of the river, especially when we bear in mind that such could exist between aggressive Germans such as Ariovistus and the peoples of central and eastern Gaul.

So although Caesar made a simple distinction between three peoples in Gaul, and between Gauls and Germans on the one hand, he also described a more complex ethnic mix both within and between these peoples. Both Belgic Gaul and south-western Germany offer the clearest examples of this, with 'Gallic Germans' in northern Gaul and 'German Gauls' in the Hercynian Forest.

---

against the Germans, 6.35, 42.

33 *Ibid*, 5.27.

34 Of the Treveri, Caesar wrote that "Their state is by far the most powerful in cavalry *of all the Gauls*, and possesses great forces of infantry; and, as above set forth, it touches the Rhine." *Ibid*, 5.3. The Eburones and Condrusi were clients or dependants of the Treveri. *Ibid*, 4.6.

35 *Ibid*, 6.5, 9.

36 *Ibid*, 8.25.

37 *Ibid*, 4.3.

While the presence of the Romans seems to have stimulated new alliances between peoples on both sides of the Rhine, it is likely that peoples had been crossing the Rhine in both directions for centuries. A closer examination of different usages of *Galli* and *Germani* in Caesar's *Gallic War* reveals an internal tension between his attempts to fit these peoples into neat categories, and yet describe the events in which they participated; events which reveal a multiplicity of changing loyalties and shifting allegiances between peoples whose high mobility and interaction contradicts any kind of neat generalised ethnic classification of peoples in Gaul.

We see in Diodorus a different conceptualisation of who 'Celts' were and where they lived. Firstly, Diodorus provides a mythic origin for the Gauls in a union between the Greek Heracles and the daughter of a powerful chieftain, which produced a son called Galates. Galates outdid everyone in bravery and feats of war, and expanded the territory of the tribe, going on to 'call his subjects *Galatae* [or Galatians/Gauls] after himself, and these in turn gave their name to all of *Galatia* [or Gaul]'.[38] Diodorus referred more generally to the land of Gaul as *Galatia*, and called its inhabitants *Galatae*, however he also used the term *Celtica*.[39] He also made a distinction between the peoples he called *Keltoi* and the rest of the *Galatae*. He wrote:

> The peoples who dwell in the interior above Massalia, and those on the slopes of the Alps, and those on this side of the Pyrenees mountains are called *Keltoi*, whereas the peoples who are established above this land of Celtica in the parts which stretch to the north, both along the ocean and along the *Hercynian* Mountain, and all the peoples who come after these, as far as Scythia, are known as *Galatae*; the Romans, however, include all these nations together under a

38 Diodorus Siculus, *Bibliotheca Historica*, ed and trans C H Oldfather, *The Library of History of Diodorus of Sicily* (London, 1933–67) 5.24.

39 *Ibid*, 5.24–25.1.

single name, calling them one and all Gauls.[40]

Diodorus never mentioned *Aquitani, Belgae* or *Germani*, or any of the specific tribal names of these peoples. The only specific people he mentioned in relation to the *Galatae* were the *Cimbri.* He regarded them as descendants of the Cimmerians and associated them with the Gauls who captured Rome, sacked Delphi and settled in Galatia (the central part of modern Turkey), where they later became known as Greco-Gauls.[41] So even though other writers before Diodorus, such as Caesar, referred to the *Cimbri* as *Germani*, Diodorus continued to regard them as *Galatae.* If he knew about Germans (and he must have because he knew Caesar's writing) he most probably made no distinction because he believed *Galatae* and Germans were kin and little different from each other, and therefore no distinction was needed.[42] Further proof of this may be evidenced by the fact that Diodorus described rivers such as the Danube and the Rhine as flowing through Galatia (Gaul), and mentioned how Caesar had built, in one day, a bridge across the Rhine to subdue the Galatae who lived beyond it.[43]

What Caesar called *Gallia* (Gaul), Strabo called ύπέρ τών Αλπεων Κελτική (Transalpine Celtica).[44] Strabo mentioned how previous writers (whom he did not name), had divided this land of Celtica into three parts: one inhabited by a people called the *Belgae*,

40 *Ibid*, 5.32.1–2.

41 *Ibid*, 5.32.4–6.

42 Caesar on the Cimbri as Germans, *Gallic War*, 1.33, 40; Diodorus on Caesar and his deeds, *Library*, 5.21.2–3.

43 Diodorus, *Library*, 5.25.3–5. Caesar twice built bridges to cross the Rhine in order to subdue Germanic tribes. The first bridge took him ten days to complete, after which he destroyed all the villages, buildings and crops of Sugambri. *Gallic War*, 4.17–19. On the second occasion it was to do battle with the Suebi, although they retreated and no battle ensued. It took him a few days to complete a bridge not far from where he had built the first one. *Ibid*, 6.9.

44 Strabo, *Geography*, 4.1.1.

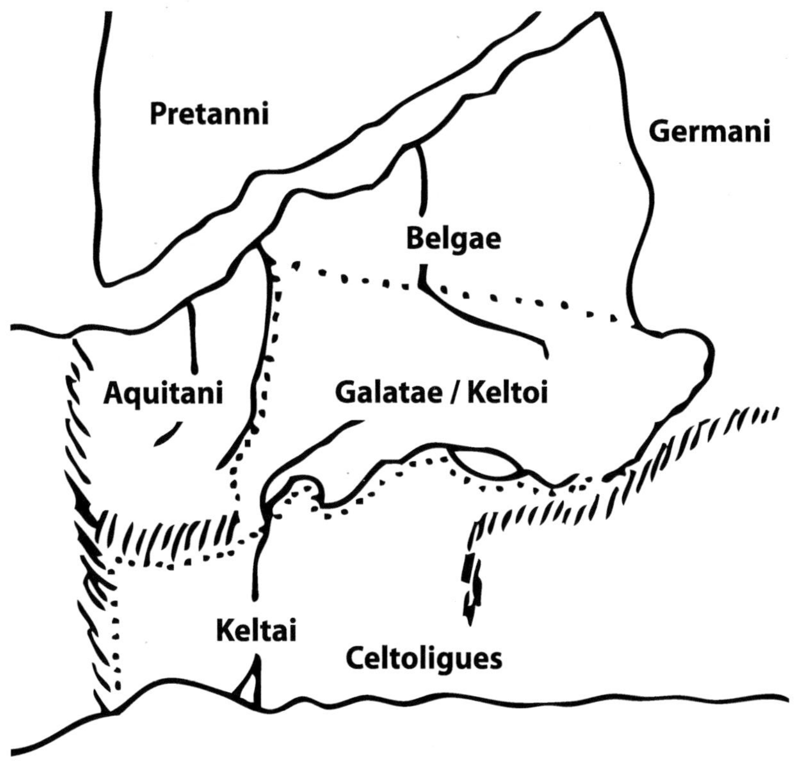

Figure 2: *Strabo's conception of Celtica*

another by the *Celtae* and a third by the *Aquitani*.[45] Writing in the past tense, Strabo attributed his own knowledge of the tripartite division of Gaul to a plurality of sources and added afterwards, 'thus the Deified Caesar, also, has put it in his Commentaries'.[46]

Strabo claimed that the *Aquitani* were wholly different from the Celtae with respect to their language and physique (which were closer to those of the Iberians).[47] The *Celtae* and *Belgae* were

45 *Ibid.*

46 *Ibid.*

47 *Ibid*, 4.1.1; 4.2.1.

both Γαλατικούς ('Galatic') in appearance, although they spoke slightly different languages. The governments and modes of life also differed slightly among the *Galatae* on the whole.[48] Strabo's description of the tribes inhabiting the eastern stretch of Celtica running up the Rhine and into Belgica also closely resembles that of Caesar, although it also includes a few striking differences in how he classifies their ethnicity. He only named two peoples specifically as *Belgae*, the *Veneti* and the *Osismii*, both of whom were classified by Caesar as Aremoricans or coastal Gauls dwelling in the region Caesar attributed to the *Celtae*.[49] In contrast to Caesar, he classified the *Nervii* as *Germani* (and possibly the *Treveri* as well, although the phrasing is inconclusive).[50]

Like Diodorus, Strabo also made a distinction between those he called *Keltoi* and the rest of the *Galatae*, and attempted to explain how the two terms became intertwined. He wrote that the true *Keltoi* were:

> the people who inhabit the dominion of Narbonitis [Narbonensis], whom the men of former times called '*Keltai*'; and it was from the *Keltai*, I think, that the *Galatae* as a whole were by the Greeks called '*Keltoi*' on account of the fame of the *Keltai*, or it may also be that the Massiliotes, as well as other Greek neighbours, contributed to this result, on account of their proximity.[51]

---

48 *Ibid*, 4.1.1.

49 *Ibid*, 4.4.1. Caesar, *Gallic War*, 7.75.

50 Strabo, *Geography*, 4.3.4. 'After the Mediomatrici and the Tribocchi, along the Rhenus, dwell the Treveri, near whom the bridge has been built by the Roman officers who are now conducting the Germanic war. The Ubii used to live opposite this region, across the Rhenus, though by their own consent they were transferred by Agrippa to the country this side the Rhenus. Next after the Treveri are the Nervii, *who are also a Germanic tribe* [my emphasis].'

51 Strabo, *Geography*, 4.1.14. Κελται or Keltai (nominative feminine) for the Latin *Celtae*. Κελτοι or Keltoi (nominative masculine) for Latin

Figure 3: *Strabo's description of central and eastern Europe*

Collis argues that Strabo seems to indicate here that only a small portion, perhaps a single tribe or a group of affiliated tribes of *Galatae*, were actually *Keltoi*, and that Strabo thought that the Greeks had transferred it as a collective name for neighbouring peoples.[52] Strabo, however, was often very inconsistent with his terminology, and his distinction between *Keltoi* and *Galatae* actually ranged far wider (*see figure 3*). For example, he described the territory on the eastern side of the Rhine north of the Danube as being beyond the land of *Celtica*, but inhabited by *Galatae* and *Germanoi (Germani)*.

Celti.

52 Collis, *The Celts*, 99.

This Germanic and Galatic territory stretched as far as the Dnieper (southern Russia), whereas the Illyrians, Thracians, and all the tribes of the *Keltoi* (and all the others who were intermingled with these) lived to the south of the Danube as far as Greece.[53] These *Keltoi* included the *Taurisci*, *Boii* and *Scordisci*, who lived south of the Danube in territory ranging from Austria to Serbia. These *Keltoi* were more generally described as being intermingled with Thracians and Illyrians.[54] Somewhat confusingly, however, he also described them as *Galatae*.[55]

Like Caesar, Strabo regarded the *Cimbri* as Germans.[56] In contrast, however, Strabo recognised some degree of kinship between 'Celts' and 'Germans' on both sides of the Rhine. Strabo described the *Germanoi* as being much the same as those of 'Celtic stock' in build and nature, only taller, wilder and with fairer hair, but otherwise similar in their forms of government, habits, and modes of life.[57] Strabo made further distinctions between different kinds of 'Celts' in relation to 'Germans'. For example, he suggested that the Romans thought of the *Germani* as 'genuine *Galatae*', adding that they had named them *Germani* because (according to Strabo) it meant 'genuine' in the Latin language.[58]

In other instances, Strabo associated the *Keltoi* with the

---

53 Strabo, *Geography*, 7.1.1.

54 *Ibid*, 7.5.1–7.5.2. The Scordisci were often used as allies for the Dacians in their wars against the Boii and Taurisci, 7.5.2. Some of the Dacians were also known as the Getae, 7.3.12.

55 Taurisci and Boii as Keltoi, *Ibid*, 7.3.11, 7.5.2; the Scordisci as Galatae. More precisely, the phrase "... the Scordisci who are called Galatae" might be taken to mean that he was merely mentioning that others had called them so, whereas he regarded them more properly as Keltoi. For example, Strabo called all three Keltoi, 7.3.2.

56 *Ibid*, 7.2.4.

57 *Ibid*, 4.4.2. He says that they were not only similar in respect to their nature and their governments, but they were also kinsmen to each other; He also said they varied slightly in that they were taller, wilder and had 'yellower hair' but were similar in build, habits and modes of life, 7.1.2.

58 *Ibid*, 7.1.2. Γερμανοι for *Germanoi* (*Germani*).

formation of new ethnic groups, such as the Celtoligurians who were a mix of Celts and Ligurians.[59] He also described a tribe in the eastern Alps called the *Iapodes* as 'at the same time both Celtic and Illyrian', adding that 'their armour is Celtic, and they are tattooed like the rest of the Illyrians and Thracians'.[60] One last point on Strabo is that he reported an interesting aspect of the early Greek historians: they often grouped several peoples together out of ignorance of the facts. He cited the example that when the ancient Greek historians could not decide whether a people were Celts or Scythians, they called them Celto-Scythians.[61]

Later accounts

Several later writers provide both general and specific information on Celts which differs from these earlier accounts or which explains the origins of Celts in mythic and legendary terms. Appian regarded the terms *Keltoi* and *Galatae* as different words for the same people, adding that in his time the *Keltoi* were called Γαλαται (*Galatae* or Galatians) or Γαλλοι (*Galloi* in Greek, *Galli* in Latin).[62] Curiously though, he also mentioned how the Greeks claimed that the *Keltoi* descended from Celtus, the son of Galatea and the Cyclops, Polyphemus, and added that the *Galatae* descended from Galas (another of their sons).[63] Like Caesar, Appian mentioned the *Nervii* as *Belgae*, but referred to them as the descendants of the *Cimbri* and *Teutones*, whereas Caesar referred to the *Atuatuci* thus.[64] Where some of his information is different from Caesar's and similar to Diodorus', the reverse is true in other parts. For example, Appian regarded the *Cimbri* as *Keltoi* or *Galatae*; however, he acknowledged

59 *Ibid*, 4.6.3.

60 *Ibid*, 7.5.2–4.

61 *Ibid*, 1.2.27.

62 Appian, *Historia Romana*, ed and trans H White, *Appian's Roman History* (London, 1955–1964) 6.1.1.

63 *Ibid*, 10.1.2.

64 *Ibid*, 4.1.4; Caesar, *Gallic War*, 2.29.

the Germans as a distinct people from the *Keltoi*.[65]

Ammianus Marcellinus referred to Celts as *Galli* (Gauls) more generally, but recounted several earlier accounts of the origins of the Celts in Gaul, one of which claimed that they were descended from an indigenous people called *Celtae*, after a much loved king, and *Galatae* (the Greek name for Gauls) after his mother. Other accounts in Tacitus and Ammianus can be read to support the notion of greater ethnic diversity in Gaul. Tacitus wrote that two Belgic tribes, the *Nervii* and the *Treveri* (both of which had participated in the rebellion of 57 BCE mentioned by Caesar) 'went out of their way to claim German descent. Such a glorious origin, they feel, should clear them of any resemblance to the nerveless Gauls'.[66] According to Ammianus, the druids claimed that part of the population were indigenous, but were joined by some settlers from remote islands and some from beyond the Rhine.[67] Although Tacitus' account differs from that of Caesar in the fine detail of describing two Belgic tribes as claiming descent from the Germans, both his and Ammianus' accounts would also seem to support a closer relationship between Celts and Germans than is traditionally recognised.

Conclusion

As Sims-Willliams has observed, one of the problems we face in interpreting classical representations of Celts is that what we are really looking at is a mental map of the distribution of classical terms,

65 Appian described Ariovistus as the king of the Γερμανοι (Germani in Latin) beyond the Rhine, and recalled how Caesar defeated his forces. In this passage one can see the classic civilisation versus barbarism paradigm which is evident in earlier writings and indeed, most Greek and Roman historiography of 'barbarian' peoples. For example, Appian describes the Germani as a people unequalled in size, savagery, bravery and ability to withstand harsh conditions, and claimed they were guided, not by intellect, but by passion, like wild beasts. Appian, *Roman History*, 4.1.3.

66 Tacitus, *Germania*, ed and trans M Hutton, revised by E H Warmington, (Cambridge, Massachusetts; London, 1914, revised 1970) 28.

67 Ammianus Marcellinus, *The Later Roman Empire (A.D. 354–378)* ed and trans W Hamilton (Middlesex, 1986) 15.9.1–8.

not a map of how the ethnic groups perceived their relationships with each other and with other northern peoples.[68] Some of the differences may be attributed to the fact that some classical writers were less interested in who the Celts actually were than in providing their audiences with familiar points of reference or entertaining them with exotic and outlandish information. Two examples shown above are Diodorus' reference to Heracles and Appian's reference to Galatea and the Cyclops, Polyphemus. Another explanation for the differences can be found in classical authors, such as Strabo, attempting to combine information from different time periods into a work of synthesis in much the same way as writers do today. The terminological confusion can then be seen as resulting from having to synthesise different classificatory systems from different times into a singular narrative form.

We cannot discount the possibility that the differences in the classification of *Celtae*, *Belgae* and the different kinds of *Germani* between Caesar, Strabo, Appian and Tacitus may merely reflect their occasionally awkward attempts to fit these peoples into neat categories in accordance with a Greco-Roman world-view which emphasised symmetry and order. But by the first century BCE Greek and Roman writers must have been reasonably well acquainted with northern peoples, for there is too much detail in their distinctions for them to be explained away as merely something invented as part of an indulgence in exotic fantasy or driven by personal political motivation. What these sources have in common is indeed their depiction of a plurality of ethnic identities within the larger conceptual constructs of *Keltoi* and *Galatae*. Despite the different terminologies used, the evidence from Caesar, Diodorus, Strabo, Tacitus and Ammianus can also be read as demonstrating a high degree of cultural interaction between, for example, Celts and Germans, which suggests to me that these ancient and modern categories are overly simplistic and largely artificial. The ease with which they seem to have communicated with each other, formed

68 P Sims-Williams, 'Celtomania and Celtoscepticism', *Cambrian Medieval Celtic Studies 36* (1998) 1–35, at p 25.

alliances together and lived among each other on the one hand, and fought with each other on the other hand, suggests a far more fluid relationship between the different peoples on both sides of the Rhine which may have been an ongoing process for centuries before the coming of the Romans. The evidence suggests not a sharp ethnic divide but a gradual shading of shared and changing ethnic identity between these peoples.

I suggest that when we conflate the sources as part of a grand narrative of the Celts, like Cunliffe, or attempt to impose specific modern distinctions between *Celtae* and *Galatae* and *Germani* on a geographic basis, as Collis has done, we are doing the same thing as those classical writers, and in the process, losing sight of the uniqueness of the ethnic situation among European peoples during the iron age. Alternatively, we can appreciate that the ambiguities and differences are really only relative to our preconceived notions of how ethnic groups are defined. That some members of the *Belgae*, such as the *Nervii* and *Treveri*, apparently spoke Celtic languages but proclaimed Germanic origins should alert us against being too quick to impose modern categories onto ancient peoples. That several writers noted similarities and kinship between *Galatae*, *Britanni* and *Germani*, or *Keltoi* intermingled with Iberians, Ligurians, Thracians and Illyrians, can also be read as showing that ethnicity was far more fluid during the iron age than a pan-Celtic interpretation allows for, or than can be understood from a purely empirical analysis of who were or were not Celts.

In conclusion I would add that we should not be too hasty in imposing modern definitions of ethnicity onto the ancient world. Classical descriptions of the ancient Celts, and other northern European peoples more generally, combined myth, legend and history in interesting ways. Whilst this paper has focused primarily upon the peoples of Gaul and Germany, I recognise that a deeper comparative analysis of the classical sources is needed for a better understanding of the ethnic complexity and diversity of past European peoples.

'Celts in the Gobi desert': a linguistico-archaeological mess

Aedeen Cremin ⊕

This paper was sparked by an article by Gabriel Coonan in the reputable British newspaper, *The Independent*, of 28 August 2006. Headlined The Mystery of China's Celtic Mummies, it was only the most recent of sensationalist articles published over the past 20 years, all of them based on the same information emanating from a few scholars. These articles and corollary websites are often brought to my attention by well-intentioned Celtophiles, to the extent that I feel the time has come to point out some flaws in the scholarship, even though I am by no means a specialist in the regions discussed.

As an archaeologist, I study material culture (how people interact with the physical world) and have become aware that it is varied and difficult to predict. The works I shall discuss seem to me to occlude this diversity of human behaviour — they are Eurocentric, essentialist and reductionist. The scholars concerned are undoubtedly sincere; they are making a genuine effort to state their case honestly; they write engagingly and even persuasively. But there are faults of logic, serious omissions of evidence, biased presentation and tendentious mapping, which regrettably feed exaggerated claims, not least among white supremacists.[1] More

---

⊕ The Australian National University.

My thanks to Creeda Fitzgibbon, who sent me the Coonan article; to Peter Jia and to Eileen and Terry Lustig, who encouraged me not only to publish but also to visit Hami, where Director Ya Her kindly opened up the museum for us. We are most grateful to him. I also have a long-standing debt of gratitude to the late Professor Ruaidhri de Valera, who taught me to scrutinise a map.

1 Accessed by web-searches for the terms 'Tarim Mummies' and 'Tocharian' [January 2008].

seriously, they may feed back into general scholarship. I shall attempt not so much to establish the truth — for it resides far away and in another time — but only to disestablish the more misleading statements. I shall do this first on general grounds, and then by discussing specific claims.

As this paper is concerned with popular perception, I deal only with two books written for the general public, published within the last ten years. They are *The Mummies of Urumchi* (New York, 1999) by Elizabeth Wayland Barber, a linguist, and *The Tarim Mummies: Ancient China and the Mystery of the Earliest Peoples from the West* (London, 2000), co-authored by James Mallory, an archaeologist, and Victor Mair, who is a scholar of Chinese literature.[2] These works are backed up by many scholarly articles and conference papers, the most accessible synthesis being the conference proceedings edited by Mair and published in two volumes as *The Bronze Age and Early Iron Age Peoples of Eastern Central Asia* (Washington DC, 1998).

The impetus for this wave of research came in 1987, when Mair visited the Provincial Museum at Urumchi, capital of Xinjiang, China's westernmost province. He saw there displays of human bodies in a remarkable state of preservation: they had been desiccated by the natural conditions prevailing in the Taklamakan desert, the former basin of the Tarim River. The bodies' garments were also well preserved. As there are in the Old World relatively few archaeological finds of textiles — compared to, say, stone, ceramic or metal artefacts — the Tarim textiles are of extraordinary importance, yielding woollen and silk textiles equal in quantity and quality probably only to the linen of Ancient Egypt and to the silk of early China.

---

2 Other important works by these authors are E W Barber, *Prehistoric Textiles: The Development of Cloth in the Neolithic and Bronze Ages with Special Reference to the Aegean* (Princeton, 1991) and *Women's Work. The First 20,000 years: Women, Cloth and Society in Early Times* (New York, 1994); J P Mallory, *In Search of the Indo-Europeans: Language, Archaeology and Myth* (London, 1989) and J P Mallory and D Q Adams, *The Oxford Introduction to Proto-Indo-European and the Proto-Indo-European World* (Oxford, 2006).

The desiccated bodies and clothing were already well-known and had been published in the earlier part of the twentieth century by European explorers, particularly Sir Aurel Stein (1862–1943), who had removed quantities of equally well-preserved documents from various monastery and city sites.[3] Mair would have been aware of all this, but what struck him was that the bodies were markedly 'Europoid'. One of them reminded him so much of his own brother that he has nicknamed him 'Ur-David'; he is also known as 'Cherchen man', or more prosaically as Zaghanluq 85M2 — i.e. body from grave 2 of the Zaghanluq cemetery, excavated 1985.[4] A point of interest is that both this man and the best-preserved of his three female companions had their faces painted with spiral designs in ochre. Later excavations in this cemetery revealed a woman who was actually tattooed, i.e. with pigment injected under the skin, on her forehead and all over her hands (89M2).[5] She too was Europoid.

It was well-known that many of the documents taken by the explorers were in Indo-European languages; and indeed some are the only record of the languages linguists define as Tocharian A and B (with a possible C).[6] It was also well-known that there had once

---

3 Barber, *Mummies*, 90–108; Mallory and Mair, *Tarim*, 62–63, 84–85, 184–188. See also M Juntunen and B N Schlyter 'Nordic Research on Central Asia: Past, Present and Future', 3–22 in M Juntunen and B N Schlyter (eds), *Return to the Silk Routes: Current Scandinavian research on Central Asia* (London, 1999).

4 Place-names are a problem, as there are variant spellings and degrees of precision; for convenience, I shall use whichever form is employed by the author under discussion. The official names are given in [Xinjiang Institute of Archaeology], *The Ancient Corpses of Xinjiang: The Peoples of Ancient Xinjiang and their Culture* (Ürümchi, 2001), bilingual Chinese-English text, translated by V Mair.

5 Mallory and Mair, *Tarim*, 192–194, figure 107 and plate VII; *Ancient Corpses*, 90, where the facial decoration is described as 'painted' in the caption, but 'tattooed' in the text at p 86. It looks more painted (in blue and red) than tattooed.

6 J Enwall, 'Towards a sociolinguistic history of Sinkiang', 119–134 in Juntunen and Schlyter (eds), *Return*. Tocharian studies are currently in a state of flux; see G Pinault, 'Tocharian and Indo-Iranian: relations

lived in the Gansu region of western China people who did not look Chinese. Known to the Chinese as Yuezhi, they had been displaced further west by the Xiongnu (Huns) and are today accepted as possibly the people known to the Greeks as the Tocharoi — who, by the second century BCE, according to Strabo, had overrun the Greek colony of Bactria (approximately modern Afghanistan and southern Tadjikistan).[7] Mair concluded that the mummies he was looking at came from this population.

Mair's discovery was very quickly diffused around the world and much enhanced by Barber's observation that cloth from another set of mummies (from Qizhilchoqa, Hami) was comparable to some found at the Austrian sites of Hallstatt and Hallein (the Dürrnberg). Her book makes an explicit connection between the three sites, which will be examined in more detail below.

But before we get caught up in the general excitement we should have a quick look at the region and its history.

The geographical definition of Central Asia is that its rivers all flow inland; they are fed by meltwater from the bordering mountains. Humans have lived in this area since at least the latter part of the ice age.[8] The end of the ice age (about 10,000 years ago) was followed

---

between two linguistic areas', 243–283 in N Sims-Williams (ed), *Indo-Iranian Languages and Peoples* (Proceedings of the British Academy 116, Oxford, 2002). I was pleased to learn that Harold Bailey, for whom this is a posthumous festschrift, did his first degree at the University of Western Australia.

7 Strabo XI.8.2, discussed by K Enoki, G A Kolshenko and Z Haidary, 'The Yüeh-Chih and their migrations', 171–189 in J Harmatta (ed), *History of civilizations of Central Asia. Volume II. The Development of Sedentary and Nomadic Civilizations* (Paris, 1994) at p 180. See also papers by E G Pulleyblank, especially his 'Why Tocharians', *Journal of Indo-European Studies* 23.3–4 (1995), reprinted as pp 416–430 in his *Central Asia and Non-Chinese Peoples of Ancient China* (Aldershot, 2002). See also F Thierry, 'Yuezhis et Kouchans: Pièges et dangers des sources chinoises', 421–539 in O Bopearachchi and M-F Boussac (eds), *Afghanistan: Ancien carrefour entre l'est et l'ouest* (Turnhout, 2005).

8 L I Miroshnikov, 'A Note on the Meaning of the Term "Central Asia" as Used in this Book', 477–480; A P Derevyanko and E Z Lü, 'Upper

by some fluctuations in climate which had considerable ecological effects, including desertification. Scholars consider that there was a dry, cold period around 6000 years ago which caused grassland to replace woodland throughout the Eurasian steppes, thus facilitating the spread of horse-breeding.[9] The existence of powerful states on the southern and eastern borders of the steppes created an economic incentive for horse-based nomadic pastoralism, exponentially increased by the development of the light-wheeled chariot, which transformed warfare in the eastern Mediterranean, western Asia and China.[10] The trade routes we today call the Silk Roads developed as the Chinese kingdoms found that silk was a commodity they could trade for horses from Ferghana (approximately southwest Kyrgyztan).

The Tarim basin, edged by fertile oases, provided watering-stops as well as food for travellers. As a result it became truly cosmopolitan: through the oases came traders, soldiers, missionaries and the administrators of whichever regional empire was nominally in power. From the first millennia BCE the sequence of empires was Xiongnu (Hun), Chinese Han, Kushan (Bactrian), Tibetans, Chinese Tang, Mongol and finally Türk (Uighur).[11] Thousands of

---

Paleolithic Cultures' 89–108 and map 3 at pp 46–47; Z An, 'Neolithic Communities in Eastern Parts of Central Asia, 153–168 and map 6 at pp 154–155. All in A H Dani and V M Masson (eds), *History of Civilizations of Central Asia. Volume I. The Dawn of Civilization: Earliest Times to 700 BC* (Paris, 1992).

9 G Matyushin, 'Problems of inhabiting central Eurasia', chapter 24 in M Levine, C Renfrew and K Boyle (eds), *Prehistoric Steppe Adaptation and the Horse* (Cambridge, 2003).

10 D Anthony, *The Horse, the Wheel, and Language: How Bronze-Age Riders from the Eurasian Steppes Changed the World* (Princeton, 2007). The subtitle accurately describes the author's views, which will doubtless be popular with the white supremacists. It is a massive work, with 38 pages of bibliography, and contains much information on Soviet archaeological excavations, too poorly indexed to be really useful.

11 The differing histories of the oases are conveniently assembled in L Hambis (ed), *L'Asie Centrale: Histoire et Civilisation* (Paris, 1977); see also Harmatta (ed), *History* volume II.

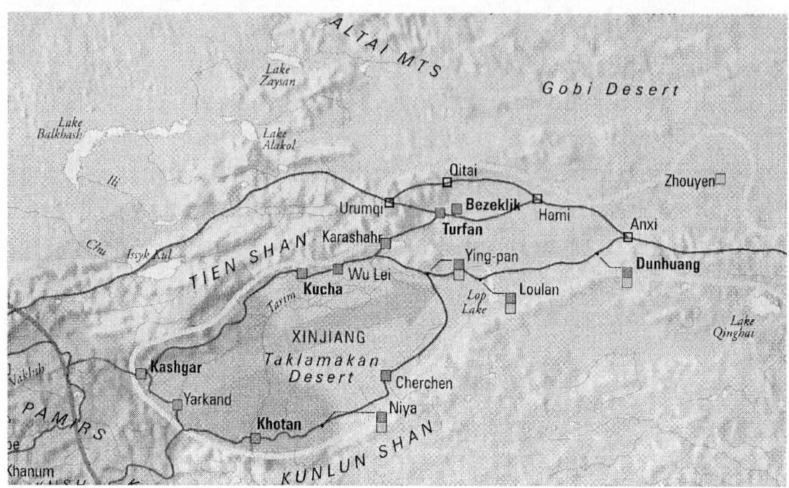

Figure 1: *Simplified map of the Silk Roads. The principal roads, coming from Samarkand and Bactria in the west, divide at Kashgar to skirt the Taklamakan Desert. The road from Tashkent goes north around the Tien Shan, while the road from the south comes through the Hindu Kush, skirting the Pamirs. China can only be accessed through the Gansu Corridor, east of Dunhuang. From Urumqi to Hami is about 450 km and from Hami to Cherchen about 700 km. The dark wavy line at the bottom left of this map is the edge of the Sassanian Empire (Iranian, 224–651 CE); the light line around the Taklamakan is the edge of the Han Empire (Chinese, c73–127 CE). The dark squares are sites with Buddhist art, lighter squares are sites with Chinese silk, and white squares are other important trade cities.* **Reproduced** *(cropped) from P G Bahn (ed),* Atlas of World Archaeology *(London, 2003) at p 135.*

---

administrative documents have been found in various languages, mostly Indo-European (Iranian, Gandhari and Loulan Prakrit, Sogdian, Khotan Saka, Tocharian), but also Tibetan and Chinese. The area is now within the Xinjiang Autonomous Region of China, formerly named Chinese Turkestan. Until recently the population was not Han Chinese.[12]

The dry, salt and cold conditions of the Taklamakan desiccated and preserved not only documents but also human bodies, of whom

12 Nowadays Han Chinese make up about 42% of the population, up from only 0.6% (300,000) in 1953; see Enwall, 'Sinkiang' at pp 131–134.

the earliest known is 1800 BCE (at Qäwrighul, Loulan). There seem to have been no specific attempts at embalming, though the bodies were sometime laid out on platforms so that air could circulate and facilitate the natural drying-out process. Funerary rites vary from oasis to oasis, but generally the bodies were clothed and accompanied by some grave-goods. Most of the corpses have large noses, deep eye-sockets and straight brownish or fair hair: they are 'Europoid' in appearance.

In 1998, Han Kangxin published a palaeoanthropological study of 300 skulls, and found that the Europoids could be classified into three sub-groups: 'proto-Europoid', 'Mediterranean' and 'Pamir-Fergana'. His diagram, reproduced at *Figure 2*, shows both the skull types and the radiocarbon dates 'before present' (BP), i.e. before 1950 CE.[13]

An independent study by Hemphill and Mallory of 1353 skulls from the Tarim Basin and adjacent regions from Russia to Pakistan has confirmed these findings and come to the conclusion that there was 'a population of unknown origin within the Tarim Basin during the early Bronze Age. After 1200 BC, this population experienced significant gene flow from highland populations of the Pamir and Ferghana Valley'. They also note that 'the occupants of Alwighul and Krorän [...] share closest affinities with Eastern Mediterranean populations'.[14] I interpret both studies as indicating that there was an indigenous population, augmented at different times by arrivals from the south or south-west.

---

13 K Han, 'The Physical Anthropology of the Ancient Populations of the Tarim Basin and Surrounding Areas', 558–572 in Mair (ed), *Bronze Age*, volume II. While the labelling seems to prejudge the conclusion, the data seem sound; the question is further examined in C P Thornton and T G Schurr, 'Genes, language, culture', *Oxford Journal of Archaeology* 23.1 (2004) 83–106 at pp 89–91.

14 B E Hemphill and J P Mallory, 'Horse-mounted invaders from the Russo-Kazakh steppes or agricultural colonists from western Central Asia? A craniometric investigation of the Bronze Age settlements of Xinjiang', *American Journal of Physical Anthropology* 124.3 (2004) 199–222, quotes at pp 199 and 217. As the title shows, this paper intercuts scientific data with historical conjecture in an unusual way.

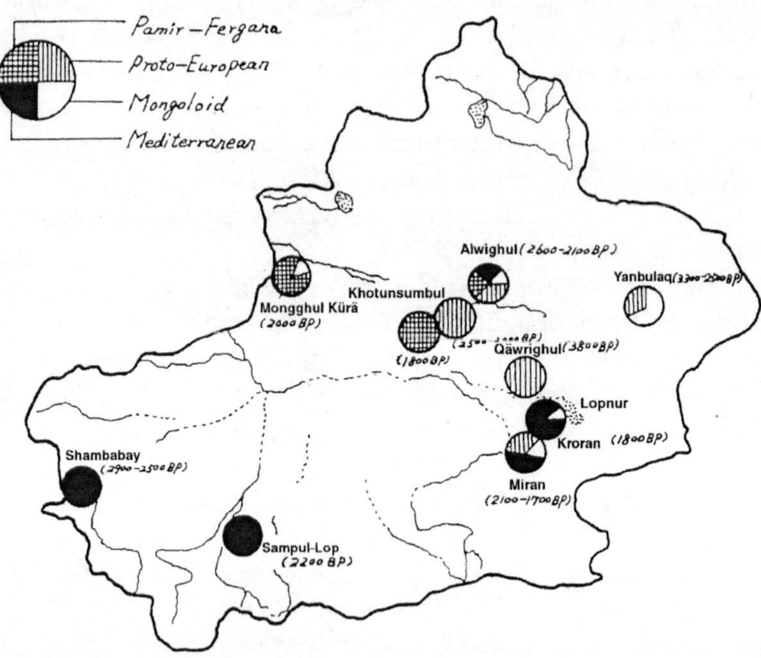

Figure 2: *Partial data about physical types in the Tarim, based on skulls, some from early excavations. It will be seen that the older skulls are proto-Europoid, in the north-east, c1800 to 500 BCE, the next-oldest being a clear Mediterranean group in the south, first millennium BCE, while the Pamir-Fergana group is in the northwest, c600 BCE to 300 CE. The 'Mongoloid' skulls are relatively few and mostly in the north or east, 1300 BCE to 300 CE.* **Reproduced** *from Han,* Physical Anthropology, *figure 1 at p 559; also shown in Mallory and Mair,* Tarim, *figure 138 at p 240.*

The mummies are mostly clothed in wool, often in twill, which is a common way to weave wool, as opposed to the plain 'tabby' used for cotton or linen. Wool dyes well and the clothes can be brightly coloured. Decorative patterns vary according to locality: at Qizilchoqa (Hami), northeast of the Taklamakan, there were both embroidered cloth and the famous 'tartans'; at Zaghunluq (Cherchen), in the south, there were fine stripes and decorative borders; at Subeshi (Astana) in the north, there was a horizontally striped skirt in green, red and brown. In the historic period, from the fifth century BCE, there was in the south a preference for floral patterns at Niya, and for animal patterns at Sampul (Lop), all in bright colours.[15]

Turning now to the sensationalist claims of 'Celts in China', there are three basic assumptions which are fallacious: fallacies so blatant that it would seem unnecessary to have to rebut them, but unfortunately it seems we must.

Fallacy 1: it is assumed that somebody who looks European speaks an Indo-European language. This is not the case. In the past there were in Europe several non-Indo-European languages, of which Etruscan and Iberian are particularly well-documented. Basques, Finns and Hungarians still speak non-Indo-European languages. The fallacy here is to think that language is somehow genetically transmitted. No. Language is culturally transmitted. There are today in Europe thousands of children of African origin who do not speak their parents' native language. Many Australians of Chinese descent do not speak Chinese and do not display any particular aptitude for it.

Fallacy 2: it is assumed that material culture (in this case clothing) is coterminous with social culture and/or language: 'if you wear plaid, you must be Celtic'. This is simply not true. There are many instances of people of differing languages, religions or ethnicities sharing a common material culture: e.g. the former Yugoslavia, northern Ireland, contemporary Australia. In addition, people have differing material cultures depending on their place of residence: the material culture of a Torres Straits Islands family will differ between the Islands and Sydney.

Fallacy 3: it is assumed that the written-down language is also the spoken vernacular. This is a fallacy to which Celticists should be particularly sensitive, given our ignorance of the languages spoken in Britain prior to the Roman conquest: for instance, we cannot say

15 Hami, Cherchen, Subeshi and Niya, *Ancient Corpses* at pp 67, 85, 98, 131–137; Sampul: D Keller and R Schorta (eds), *Fabulous Creatures from the Desert Sands: Central Asian Woolen Textiles from the Second Century BC to Second Century AD* (Riggisberger Berichte 10, Riggisberg, 2001).

where, or by whom, the ancestor of modern Welsh was spoken.[16] The many Indo-European documents from the Silk Road sites were written during periods of political or religious domination by Indo-European speakers from other regions (India, Iran, Bactria, etc.). They tell us very little about indigenous languages.

Looking at specific claims, I can do no better than to quote Coonan. His article was based on an interview with Mair.

> Solid as a warrior of the Caledonii tribe, the man's hair is reddish brown flecked with grey, framing high cheekbones, a long nose, full lips and a ginger beard. When he lived three thousand years ago, he stood six feet tall, and was buried wearing a red twill tunic and tartan leggings. He looks like a Bronze Age European. In fact, he's every inch a Celt. Even his DNA says so. But this is no early Celt from central Scotland. This is the mummified corpse of Cherchen Man, unearthed from the scorched sands of the Taklamakan Desert in the far-flung region of Xinjiang in western China. (*Independent* 28 August 2006)

Shall we gloss? Not to cavil, but just to show that the author's description cannot be taken as fully accurate —
'*Solid as a warrior of the Caledonii tribe*': the reference is to Tacitus' *Agricola* (11) 'the reddish hair and large limbs of the Caledonians proclaim a German origin'.
'*when he lived three thousand years ago*': the date is more likely 2600 years ago.[17]
'*he stood six feet tall*': well no, more like 5'8", but he was first

16 Extensively discussed in chapter 3 (76–121) of K H Jackson, *Language and History in Early Britain: A Chronological Survey of the Brittonic Languages, First to Twelfth Centuries AD* (Edinburgh, 1953); for Welsh see especially p 116.

17 Mallory and Mair, *Tarim* at pp 302 and 336.

advertised at 6'6".[18]

'*wearing a red twill tunic*': actually an open coat.

'*tartan leggings*': no. His stockings were hanks of coloured wool which had been felted together to make red, blue and yellow stripes.[19] Coonan is here confusing the Cherchen mummies with those of Hami, 700 km to the north-east, where there is indeed some 'tartan'-patterned cloth.

'*He looks like a Bronze Age European*': we do not know what such a person might look like, since the normal bronze age rite in Europe was cremation.

All of this boils down to saying that Coonan writes a good story but gets his facts a bit mixed up. The most serious mis-statement is about the DNA: 'Even his DNA says so'. It has been claimed that 'Scottish DNA is present in Tarim Basin mummies', a claim attributed to Victor Mair on websites. It appears to be based on analyses from two individuals — provenance and date unspecified.[20] The published DNA study shows a haplotype (H) which is the most frequent in modern European populations. But this same haplotype is also common in the Near East, Central Asia and South Asia. As there is not yet the same amount of DNA data from Asia as there is from Europe, we do not know what percentage of the population might have this haplotype and so the result is basically meaningless, particularly since we do not know what cemetery these samples came from. This did not deter the British television Channel Four 'Bodies of Evidence' program from claiming that the Xinjiang mummies 'were genetically related to present-day Swedes, Finns, Tuscans, Corsicans and Sardinians'.[21]

More recent DNA studies are giving more precise results and

---

18 Lower size in Mallory and Mair, *Tarim* at p 191. Earlier estimate in Barber, *Mummies*, at plate 2.

19 *Ancient Corpses* at p 82.

20 P Francalacci, 'DNA Analysis on Ancient Desiccated Corpses from Xinjiang (China): Further Results', 537–547 in Mair (ed), *Bronze Age*, volume II.

21 Accessed by website search for the term 'mummies' [June 2007].

show local consistency over time. The mitochondrial (maternal) DNA of 11 bronze age and 20 iron age bodies were tested by a Chinese scholar who found that 'the earlier mummies grouped closely with modern Sardinian and Basque examples' while 'the later Iron Age samples were extremely close to the modern Uighur and Kazak mtDNA samples'.[22]

We can now turn to our two books. Space does not permit detailed scrutiny but my purpose may be served by analysing some key statements.

Barber's book on the Urumchi mummies is chatty and informative. She explains that an efficient way to weave wool is in a twill pattern, in which the horizontal threads are passed over two verticals, rather than over one. Visually this gives a diagonal effect; more importantly the fabric is more tightly packed and thus warmer. Barber compares the tartan-like weave from Hami to some of the several hundred fragments recovered from the Austrian salt mines of Hallstatt and Hallein (Dürrnberg): 'though being four thousand miles apart, they parallel each other too closely for sheer chance'.[23] From this she concludes that there is an underlying weaving style confined to Proto-Indo-European (PIE) speakers, whom she supposes to have lived north of the Caucasus Mountains. This is Fallacy 2, as noted above.

Barber's map, reproduced at *Figure 3*, shows the 'apparent direction of the plaid plus twill technology in the 3rd and 2nd millennia BC'. It is important to look carefully at this map: the sweeping arrows so confidently drawn actually conceal the unknown, visible as blank spaces. In a well-studied area such as Britain or Italy a blank space is probably a genuine blank — there is nothing there — but in Central Asia blank spaces are areas that have hardly been explored. This author is yielding to the temptation of joining up the dots.

22 Y Cui 'Ancient DNA Analysis of Human Population in Xinjiang, China' (unpublished PhD, Jilin University, 2002), summarised in Thornton and Schurr, 'Genes', at pp 93–94.

23 Barber, *Mummies* at p 144.

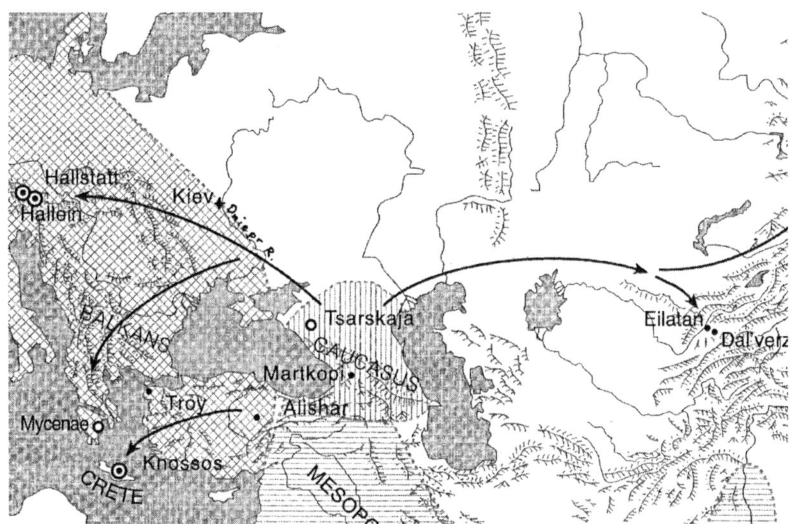

Figure 3: *Reproduced (cropped) from Barber,* Mummies, *figure 7.6. Circles show weave: black=twill; white=plaid; double=plaid+twill. Hatching shows loom-type: horizontal=horizontal loom; vertical=conjectured place of origin of vertical loom; cross-hatching=warp-weighted loom. Third-millennium loom-weights have since been recorded from the lower Don just north of the Caucasus, which should thus also be cross-hatched (Anthony,* Horse *at 295-297).*

As to the dots on the map, Barber is definitely disingenuous: Hami, Hallstatt and Hallein are all first-millennium BCE and should not be shown. Tsarskaya (Novosvobodnaya) is a plant-based textile, not wool, and should not be here either.[24] The 'plaid' in Crete is not an actual textile but a set of depictions on other artefacts which Barber interprets as realistic representations.[25] So that dot has to be removed as well. All that is now left on the map are sites with twill only — and we have to eliminate the two in Ferghana

---

24 N Shishlina, V P Golikov and O V Orfinskaya, 'Bronze Age Textiles of the Caspian Sea Maritime Steppes', 109–117 in J Davis-Kimball, E M Murphy, L Koryakova and L T Yablonsky (eds), *Kurgans, Ritual Sites and Settlements: Eurasian Bronze and Iron Age* (Oxford, 2000) at p 110.

25 Barber, *Textiles* at pp 316–319, 328.

(impressions on ceramics) which are also first-millennium[26] — and the distribution of different types of loom.

To create this map Barber has ignored facts which were available to her: she does not tell us that twill-weaving is not found in central Europe prior to 1300 BCE, i.e. at about the time when the Hallstatt salt mines were first opened. The textiles from Hallstatt date no earlier than 800 BCE, by which time 'textile production had changed from a purely domestic craft to something that can only be regarded as industrial production'.[27] Neither does she give the correct date for the Hami plaid (c700 BCE), which she herself published elsewhere.[28] Why does Barber do this? Because she apparently sincerely believes that the plaid pattern was diffused in some early stage of PIE dispersal — i.e. about 3000 BCE in her chronology.[29] This would be quite extraordinarily conservative: everything we know about ancient crafts tells us that craftsmen tend to continually modify their designs, be they for stone axes, clay pots or weaving. Archaeological typologies are in fact predicated on this observation.

If Indo-Europeans were atavistically inclined to plaids, one would expect that plaids would show up everywhere, but they do not. They are not found with the earliest Europoids in Xinjiang, nor in the Hallstatt-period burial at Hochdorf (Baden-Württemberg,

---

26 Barber, *Mummies* at pp 166 and 223. Date given in Barber, *Textiles* at p 212.

27 L B Jørgensen, *North European Textiles until AD 1000* (Aarhus, 1992), dates for twill at p 120, quote at p 126. Hallstatt dates in F E Barth, 'The Hallstatt Salt Mines', 191–194 and F Moosleitner, 'The Dürrnberg near Hallein', 195–203 in V Kruta (ed), *The Celts* (New York, 1999) at pp 193–194 and 197.

28 Barber, *Mummies*, caption to figure 7.2 at p 133: 'this cemetery, like that at Cherchen, dates to c1000 BC'; date of 700 BCE in E J W Barber, 'Bronze Age Cloth and Clothing of the Tarim Basin: the Kroran (Loulan) and Qumul (Hami) Evidence', 647–655, and I Good, 'Bronze Age Cloth and Clothing of the Tarim Basin: the Chärchän Evidence', 656–668 in Mair (ed), *Bronze Age*, volume II at pp 651 and 661.

29 PIE dispersal is dated somewhat earlier, around 3500 BCE, by Anthony, *Horse* at pp 56–57.

Germany), c520 BCE, even though it produced elaborately woven twills with colourful patterns.[30] The only possibly early European plaid, from Gerumsberg, Sweden, is also late bronze age, i.e. first-millennium BCE.[31]

It is however possible to conjecture ways of transmitting textile-patterns between east Asia and central Europe which do not rely on genetics or migrations. Commerce is a great transmitter of ideas and there is plenty of evidence for trade across the ancient world. [32] At Lattes (Hérault), an iron age port in southern France had yielded pieces of cashmere cloth, dated to the end of the sixth century BCE, and probably brought in with the Etruscan goods that made up the bulk of the imports.[33] In her *Mummies* book Barber fails to mention that Chinese long-fibre silk was used to embroider a locally-made woollen cloth found in Hohmichele grave 6 (Baden-Württemberg, Germany, early sixth century BCE), even though she has written about it elsewhere.[34] This is accepted by everybody (including Barber) as an indication of contact with the east.

There are many possible scenarios. Here is one, based on the vigorous salt-export trade, with reciprocal imports, that is

---

30 H-J Hundt, 'Die Textilien im Grab von Hochdorf — hervorragende Zeugnisse frühen Kunsthandwerks', 106–115 in *Der Keltenfürst von Hochdorf: Methoden und Ergebnisse der Landesarchäologie* (Stuttgart, 1985).

31 Barber, *Textiles* at pp 192–193; A F Harding, *European Societies in the Bronze Age* (Cambridge, 2000) at p 263.

32 Trade in rare and durable substances such as amber, lapis, jade, and some minerals is archaeologically well-documented from at least the third millennium BCE; see e.g. maps in Bahn, *Atlas*, pp 70–80.

33 Photograph published by J-M Lamblard, 'Les Étrusques de Gênes à Ampurias', *L'Archéologue* 64 février-mars (2003), 32–36 at p 36.

34 The silk-embroidered wool is illustrated and described in J V S Megaw, *Art of the European Iron Age: A Study of the Elusive Image* (Bath, 1970) at p 45 and plate 7; and also in Barber, *Textiles* at pp 189–190 and 203–204. Its context is discussed by O H Frey '"Celtic Princes" in the Sixth Century BC', 80–102 in Kruta (ed) *Celts* at pp 86–87.

well evidenced in both the Hallstatt and Dürrnberg cemeteries.[35] Salt-traders, or their middlemen, could have acquired or seen foreign cloth in chequered patterns — e.g. used for clothing, as a saddle blanket, or for wrapping other things — and then their own weavers could have adapted some designs that they liked. Barber's notion of chequered patterns being transmitted in either direction from a mid-point, as shown on her map, is acceptable, but of course by the first millennium BCE there would be more than one centre of diffusion.

Returning to Barber's work, we see that her map also shows differences in looms: vertical in the west, horizontal in the east. To me this fundamental difference in manufacturing technique greatly outweighs the superficial resemblance between plaids (having now seen both the Hallstatt and the Hami plaids I can state quite categorically that the resemblances are slight). But enough has been said to show that Barber is guilty of the archaeological sin of 'hyper-diffusionism'. Hyper-diffusionism denies the possibility of independent invention. A product of nineteenth-century colonialism, it assumes that 'others' are incapable of inventing anything for themselves. Its best-known exponent was the distinguished anatomist Sir Grafton Elliot Smith (1871–1937), who was convinced that all forms of mummification came from Egypt.[36]

Mallory and Mair's archaeological sin is that of 'ethnogenesis',

---

35 The Dürrnberg, after 600 BCE, is particularly rich in imports, see Moosleitner, 'Dürrnberg', at pp 201–202; it has yielded good evidence for Mediterranean *kermes* dyes, see T Stöllner, 'More than Old Rags: Textiles from the Iron Age Salt-Mine at the Dürrnberg', 161–174 in P Bichler, K Gromer, R Hoffmann-de Keijzer, A Kern and H Reschrieter (eds), *Hallstatt Textiles: Technical Analysis, Scientific Investigation and Experiment on Iron Age Textiles* (Oxford, 2005) at pp 167–169.

36 eg G E Smith, *The Migrations of Early Culture: A Study of the Significance of the Geographical Distribution of the Practice of Mummification as Evidence of the Migrations of People and the Spread of Certain Customs and Beliefs* (Manchester, 1915). It is not a coincidence that Smith, born in Grafton, NSW, and a graduate of the University of Sydney, was educated when Australian racism was at its peak — see A Cremin (ed), *1901: Australian Life at Federation* (Sydney, 2001) at pp vii, 17, 29–35.

a common failing among twentieth-century archaeologists, deriving from nationalism and hypernationalism. Most Western archaeologists have given it up as an exercise in futility, because it depends upon Fallacies 1 and 2. But Mallory and Mair are so determined to claim that the Europoid mummies are Tocharian-speakers that they have even revived the *kulturkreis* expression first applied to archaeology in 1911 by Gustav Kossinna (1858–1931).[37] This suggested that a consistent assemblage of material culture (houses, clothes, food) in any one area corresponded to a genuine social group. The notion of a culture-territory is a very useful tool and basically ethnographic. But whereas ethnographers can ask informants about their world-views, religion, marriage customs, kinship systems, etc, this sort of information cannot be derived from material remains only, for it goes beyond the evidence. The logical error is the use of the part (material culture) for the whole (social culture).

Why do Mallory and Mair choose Tocharian, as opposed to any of the other Indo-European languages which were also used in Tarim documents? Because they are powerfully impressed by the 'European' appearance of 'Ur-David' and his fellows and because Tocharian is the most 'western' of the Asian Indo-European languages. As Pinault puts it: 'phonetic, morphological and lexical isoglosses attest the affinity of Tocharian with "Western" Indo-European (in a broad sense of the term): Celtic, Italic, Latin, Germanic , Baltic and Slavic, i.e. the "Northwestern group" to which we should add Greek'.[38]

Like Hittite and the Italo-Celtic group, Tocharian has retained archaic traits. These languages have all retained a hard sound for e.g. the word 100 (Latin *centum*, with hard initial k sound) while less conservative Indo-European languages — the majority — have

37 Summed up as 'Our principle: territories of culture are territories of peoples' and 'My equation: a cultural group=a people' cited and analysed by T Scott, 'From Kossinna to Complexity: Excavating Germanic Antiquity' *Journal of the Australian Early Medieval Association* 3 (2007) 289–306, at pp 298–300.

38 Pinault, 'Tocharian' at pp 244–245.

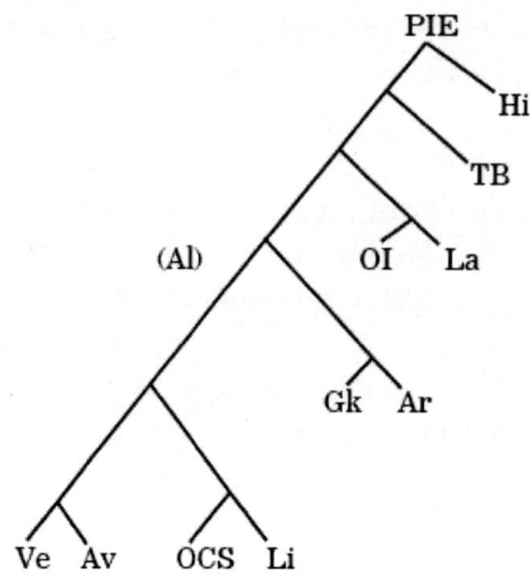

Figure 4: *Cladistic family tree, showing known Indo-European languages arranged by degree of difference from the reconstructed original (PIE). The more conservative languages (**centum** group) are towards the top, while the others (**satem** group) are below. This is not a chronological sequence, as can be seen from the dates in brackets — the times at which these languages are well attested. From top to bottom: Hi=Hittite (1400 BCE), TB=Tocharian B (800 CE), OI=Old Irish (800 CE), La=Latin (classical, 100 BCE), Al=Albanian (position uncertain, modern), Gk=Greek (classical, 400 BCE), Ar=Armenian (classical, 500 CE), Ve=Vedic (Sanskrit, 1000 BCE), Av=Avestan (Iranian, 500 BCE), OCS=Old Church Slavonic (1000 CE), Li=Lithuanian (modern).* Reproduced *from Ringe et al, figure 8.*

D Ringe, T Warnow, A Taylor, A Michailov, L Levison, 'Computational Cladistics and the Position of Tocharian' 391-414 in Mair (ed), Bronze Age, volume I, figure 8 at p. 405; Germanic is included in their figure 10 at p 408, reproduced in Anthony, Horse at p 57.

---

softened it (Avestan *satem,* with soft initial). Linguists think that the '*centum* languages' are fairly close to Proto-Indo-European (PIE), as shown in the table at *Figure 4.* They do not explain why these languages are conservative, but we can discount isolation as an explanation, for Latin was certainly never isolated.

Pinault makes no particular connection of Tocharian with Celtic. But such a connection could be inferred by the wishful thinker. Coonan wrote: 'The eastern Celts spoke a now-dead language called Tocharian, which is related to Celtic languages and part of the Indo-European group'. True and not true: Tocharian is an Indo-European language, but it was by definition not spoken by 'eastern Celts'. It will be remembered that these people moved down the Danube in the third century, attacked Delphi and after their defeat at Pergamon in 241 BCE established the kingdoms of Galatia, in Phrygia (Turkey). They appear to have spoken a form of Gaulish.

Mallory and Mair specifically link Tocharian with the third-millennium BCE Afasanievo *kulturkreis* of the Altai region, about 1000 km north of the Tarim.[39] This hypothesis is accepted by Edwin Pulleyblank, a linguist, who thinks that Tocharian speakers moved south-east towards Gansu and had by the third century BCE encountered Chinese-speakers to whom they gave the words for honey (*mi* from Toch.=mit) and lion (*shizi*, Toch.=şecake).[40] This may explain Tocharian but it makes no link at all with the Tarim, except as a potential throughway from north to south and then east to west, when the Tocharians, now reconfigured as Yuezhi, moved to Bactria.

We should be aware that while connecting Afanasievo with Tocharian appears to make sense geographically (up to a point), this is not supported by any evidence, but is only a hypothesis yet to be tested. Anthony, in 2007, says that 'if Mallory and Mair were right, as seems likely, the Afanasievo pastoralists were among the first to take their herds from the Altai southwards into the Tien Shan; and after 2200 BCE their descendants crossed the Tien Shan into the northern oases of the Tarim basin'.[41] Connoisseurs of archaeological writing will know that the word 'likely' is code for 'there is no evidence'. The Mallory-Mair-Anthony model is *not* likely or even plausible — as Thornton and Schurr have already pointed out.[42]

We should also be clear that the presence of Tocharian

39 Mallory and Mair, *Tarim* at pp 294–296.

40 Pulleyblank, 'Why Tocharians' at pp 416–417, 427–228.

41 Anthony, *Horse* at p 311.

42 '[T]hat the famous mummies are the progeny of "proto-Celtic" "Europeans" from the Pontic Steppes who migrated thousands of kilometres across two vast mountain ranges and the entire Eurasian steppe just to settle on the outskirts of one of the most inhospitable deserts in the world, is not the only interpretation for these data', Thornton and Schurr, 'Genes' at p 100.

inscriptions of the sixth to eighth centuries CE tells us nothing about what languages were spoken in the second and first millennia BCE. This is precisely the same fallacy as suggesting that Roman inscriptions in south England show that the builders of Stonehenge spoke Latin (Fallacy 3). I actually have no objection to the notion that the people buried at Cherchen might have spoken Tocharian; what I am saying is that the case is by no means proven. They may have spoken another language entirely and *assuming* they spoke one rather than another language simply closes off an avenue of research. Compounding the possibility of oversimplification is Mallory and Mair's map of Central Asia which shows only Indo-European languages, ignoring other local language-families, such as Altaic or Tibetan. This seems unkind to the general reader who is ignorant of the potential number of languages spoken along the Silk Road.[43]

While Barber appears to have withheld information, Mallory and Mair appear to glide over inconvenient facts, such as tattooing, on which they are curiously discreet.[44] Perhaps they do not wish to draw undue attention to the fairly obvious parallels with the somewhat later burials in the Altai, where there are well-preserved frozen bodies with conspicuous tattoos.[45] However, that population is routinely described as 'Scythian', i.e. not Tocharian, which certainly does not suit our authors. They also refuse to discuss the Sampul (Lop) and Niya mummies, on the slightly bizarre grounds that 'many

43 Mallory and Mair, *Tarim* at p 119. List of Altaic languages in D Sinor, *Inner Asia: History–Civilization–Languages. A Syllabus* (Bloominton, 1969) at pp 20–25.

44 Mallory and Mair, *Tarim* at pp 203–206, with minimal referencing.

45 The basic text is S I Rudenko, *Frozen Tombs of Siberia: The Pazyryk Burials of Iron Age Horsemen* [1953], trans M W Thompson (London, 1970) at pp 109–114 and 260–266. For more recent work see N V Polosmak, 'The First Report on a Burial of Noble Pazyryk Woman on the Ukok Plateau', *Archaeology, Ethnology and Anthropology of Eurasia* 4 (2000), on web, no page numbers [June 2007]; see also website of Hermitage museum, St Petersburg 'Discovery of Tattoos on Ancient Mummies from Siberia', report on conference paper of 15 February 2005, by L L Barkov and S V Pankova [June 2007].

of them date after the Early Iron Age (post Han dynasty) our cut-off point for trying to understand the movements and positioning of the peoples of East Central Asia' although they happily spend no less than 53 pages on the historical (documentary) evidence for 'movements and positionings' up to the tenth century CE.[46]

As with textiles, we can present other scenarios. Here is one: people had moved into the Tarim basin towards the end of the ice age, 10,000 years ago, speaking whatever language/s they did. As hunter-gatherers they would know how to make stone and wooden tools and also basketry and fishing nets. They would have developed their own styles of rock art, body-painting, dance, music, poetry and religious practices. As the climate changed, these people adapted. In addition, since *Homo sapiens* moves around a lot, other people arrived from time to time, bringing with them the knowledge of crops, ceramics, domesticated animals, weaving and metallurgy. Different customs and languages will inevitably have appeared, of which some were adopted, and others not.

We currently know far too little about the early settlement of Xinjiang — particularly in the neolithic — to make any more definite statements, but the increasing evidence about the early bronze age implies that the east-west routes were already active by the second millennium BCE.[47] During the lifetime of the mummies, there would have been complex and ongoing interactions in both material and social cultures, far from the unilinear situations described by the works under review.

In the Tarim basin, burial rite, costume and grave-goods differ from oasis to oasis. This implies that each group wished to distinguish itself from the others, as in today's south-east Asia where ethnic minorities define themselves by their jewellery, hairstyle and

46 Mallory and Mair, *Tarim*, at pp 64–117, quote at p 300.

47 Summarised in P L Kohl, *The Making of Bronze Age Eurasia* (Cambridge, 2007) at pp 235–241. I am pleased to report that Alison Betts and Peter Jia, from the University of Sydney, are currently working on the neolithic in Xinjiang, with promising results.

clothing.[48] What these differences mean for the Tarim, we cannot at this point say, but we *can* say that if we lump all the mummies together as one entity, we are certainly eliding distinctions which were meaningful to them in life. We have a duty of respect to these people and this includes paying careful attention to the choices that they themselves made.

Some of the points made in this paper might seem petty, but they are worth dwelling on because they show how insidiously some fallacious ideas can continue to be promulgated. This is particularly dangerous in interdisciplinary studies such as Celtic Studies, where it very hard for scholars in any one discipline to keep track of, or even to understand, what is happening in the others. Rather than accepting simplistic and Eurocentric views of Xinjiang — 'Celtic mummies in China' — we should take note of what the excavator Wang Binghua says: 'different groups of inhabitants either came and went in a rush, becoming transitory guests and leaving only slight traces of themselves or they chose to settle down on the land, mutually contacting and mingling with each other, and developed into the indigenes of Xinjiang who cannot be ignored'.[49] Australians, aware of the varieties of indigenous experience within their own arid land over the past millennia, are well placed to understand that Xinjiang should not be seen as just an eastern outpost of Indo-Europeans, with lowest-common-denominator culture, but rather as a region with its own archaeological trajectories and distinctive cultural practices.

48 P and E Lewis, *Peoples of the Golden Triangle: Six Tribes in Thailand* (London, 1984) *passim*.

49 *Ancient Corpses* at p 8.

Celts in History

Gendering the foundation myths of Scotland in the fifteenth and sixteenth centuries

Michelle Smith ⊕

If the medieval period in Scotland was one of violence, bloodshed and war, I propose it was also a time when Scotland began to emerge as an independent nation. Maintaining the freedom of both land and people became paramount, particularly when faced with constant threats of overlordship from England. The late-thirteenth and early-fourteenth centuries were dominated by the Wars of Independence, and continued Anglo-Scottish antagonisms resulted in anti-English sentiment and nationalistic rhetoric. Out of this arose the legendary literature which became part of Scotland's political propaganda and historical fabric between the late-fourteenth and mid-sixteenth centuries. In this paper I discuss the legends of Scota and Saint Andrew and argue that Scota was replaced by Andrew as the leading figure in Scotland's foundation myths. Moreover, I suggest the reasons for this lay in both medieval and sixteenth-century gender ideologies, and Scotland's developing sense of national identity.

Myths helped explain inexplicable phenomena and situations, allowing people to 'find their place in the world' and understand why certain propositions were regarded as normal and natural, and others as perverse and alien.[1] A myth's goal was the present and the future; for a Scotland under threat the persistence of a problem-

---

⊕ The University of Auckland.

This paper has been developed from chapter two of my unpublished thesis 'Assessing Gender in the Construction of Scottish Identity, c1286–c1586' (The University of Auckland, 2010).

1 K Armstrong, *A Short History of Myth* (Melbourne, 2005) 6; also see S Reynolds, 'Medieval *Origines Gentium* and the Community of the Realm', *History* 68 (1983) 375–391, at p 375.

solving myth resulted from sheer necessity, not only for the political present, but also for the future of the nation's independence.[2] The depth afforded to both Scota and Andrew as 'historical' characters by Scottish chroniclers is as varied as the versions themselves.[3] Scota was a pagan Egyptian princess who married the Greek prince, Gaythelos. After the expulsion of the Israelites, they fled Egypt and sailed the world, stopping in Spain before their descendants travelled to Ireland and subsequently Scotland. All the various versions (many repetitious and contradictory) of the myth promoted an independent and ancient Scottish race with a noble genealogy. For the Scottish chroniclers it was important to establish Scotland as an independent kingdom with a legitimate and continuous royal line. Walter Bower's *Scotichronicon* (c1440) concludes Scota's story with the claim that 'the whole of Scotland is named after the woman Scota'.[4] His narrative is the only one to include the two 1301 Papal Submissions written by the lawyer, Baldred Bisset. These documents used Scota as the main tool in the arguments against Edward I's quest for overlordship by providing Scotland with 'a long independent history and a direct classical link.'[5]

In the second submission, *The Pleadings of Baldred Bisset*, Bisset argued Scotland was governed by a common law whereby no king, kingdom, or bishopric was subject to another; in fact, he found it 'astonishing for someone who enjoys legal independence to be subjected to the authority of someone else'. Importantly, he

2 P Geary, *Women at the Beginning: Origin Myths from the Amazons to the Virgin Mary* (Princeton and Oxford, 2006) 10.

3 In *A Short History of Myth*, Armstrong argues, '[t]here is never a single, orthodox version of a myth.' As circumstances change there is a need to tell the story differently. See 11.

4 W Bower, *Scotichronicon*, D E R Watt (ed), 9 volumes (Aberdeen and Edinburgh 1987–1998) vi, 143, 183.

5 *Vita Edwardi Secundi*, W Childs (ed), (Oxford, 2005) 225. Bisset was careful to point out that the Scota legend occurred before the Incarnation, thereby making the Scottish nation '*antiquissimus*'. Avoiding any actual dating of events created a smooth chronological narrative. See Watt, i, xx.

claimed the Scots converted to Christianity 500 years before the English, with 36 Christian kings reigning freely in the Scottish kingdom before English conversion.[6] As a result, a natural hatred arose between the Scots and English 'since the converted were odious to the unconverted and vice versa'.[7] The *Pleadings* also vociferously denied the existence of Brutus' ancient division of Britain, which theoretically allowed England to subject Scotland. The main argument of Bisset's documents pivoted on Scotland's ancient lineage, despite many details being historically inaccurate; fabrications based on classical or biblical events employed to dispel any claims of English suzerainty. Having poked holes in Edward's superiority, Bisset moved on to his story of Scota.

Both submissions presented an independent, dominant Scota; Gaythelos becomes the marginalised and passive spouse. In a powerful eight lines Bisset gave Scota the masculine attributes of a soldier: Scota with 'an armed force and a very large fleet of ships ... took over that kingdom', single-handedly conquering the Picts.[8] In the *Pleadings*, Scota did not arrive in Scotland via lengthy periods spent in Spain or Ireland as in other versions. As Wendy Childs suggests, the legend was adapted to allow Scota, rather than her ancestors, direct 'landing-rights' in Scotland. The perception that the Scots were 'a wholly individual and distinct people' was clever political rhetoric employed to keep Scotland free from interference from others.[9] Scota became the coloniser, taking on the masculine role which usually subjugated the feminine, as well as the land. Furthermore, he made it clear the whole of Scotland was named after Scota, 'the lady of the Scots'.[10] While Scota named a

---

6 Bower, vi, 171. Watt notes this dating is implausible, being long before Saint Augustine's conversion of the pagan king, Aethelberht of Kent, to Christianity in 597 CE. See vi, 269.

7 Bower, vi, 173.

8 Bower, vi, 181, 183.

9 Childs, 225. In Bisset's *Pleadings*, Scota briefly stops in Ireland to pick up men to join her fleet. See Bower, vi, 14.

10 Bower, vi, 143.

whole country and its people, Gaythelos was reduced to the role of husband and of jointly naming a smaller area of Scotland with his son; the masculine was given a small integrated part, the feminine encompassed the whole. This parallels the process of procreation, especially of birth and nursing; functions inextricably linked with the feminine. Bisset also credited Scota with bringing the *sedile regium* (the Stone of Scone) to Scotland, suggesting she was not just mother of the nation, but also the mother of kings.[11] Scottish kingship was validated by a new monarch sitting on the ancient seat; an action which underlined the king's ancient lineage and cemented Scottish royal identity. I argue that Scota's independence from male authority paralleled Scotland's independence from English authority. Yet Scota's independent, warrior persona of 1301 is at odds with the feminised stereotypes of wife, mother and daughter typically found in fifteenth- and sixteenth-century chronicles.

Eighty years later, John Major's *History of Greater Britain* (1521) discounts the originary myth as mere fable, although it concedes naming rights to Scota. Major has the Scots descend from the Irish and Spanish, disputing any claim of a direct journey to Scotland. Why? Major felt the myth was simply a way for the Scots to claim a superior lineage over the English through political gamesmanship. He was happy to attribute an Irish descent to the Scots because 'he had no desire to attenuate the lineage of his kingdom'.[12] As a conservative theologian, the myth did not stand up to Major's reasoning; as an advocate for a union of the Scottish and English crowns he could not be seen as favouring one country over the other. Hector Boece's *Chronicles of Scotland* (1526) proudly embellished

11 A Bernau, 'Myths of Origin and The Struggle over Nationhood in Medieval and Early Modern England', 106–118 in G McMullan and D Matthews (eds), *Reading the Medieval in Early Modern England* (Cambridge, 2007) at p 109. Stones in myth emphasised the sacred. If Scotland's Stone was sacred it would emphasise the legitimation of the kings who sat on it. See P Gerber, *Stone of Destiny* (Edinburgh, 1997) 32–34.

12 *John Major's A Greater History of Britain*, trans A Constable (Scottish Historical Society, 1892) 50.

Scotland's origins, his patriotic and political hyperbole opposing Major's history. Put into context, one can see these two authors addressing the foreign policy debate facing James V: should he keep his alliance with France or should he put aside anti-English sentiment and ally with England? In light of Henry VIII's desire for overlordship of Scotland, and the hostility shown against the English by the Scots since the annihilation of their king and nobility at the battle of Flodden (1513), freedom had to be maintained. Boece's narrative, translated for James V by John Bellenden (1531), would have been more favourable than Major's work to those promoting Scottish independence.[13]

The earlier verse chronicler, Andrew of Wyntoun, had spared all of five lines in his *Original Chronicle of Scotland* (c1420) to outlining Scota's three most important and gendered roles in life: those of passive daughter, wife and mother.[14] Similarly, in Boece's narrative, Scota and her ancient lineage are valuable but her wifely and motherly duties are more important. Her success in these roles leads Gaythelos to reward her by calling Scotland and his subjects after her.[15] For these chroniclers, Gaythelos is the hero who becomes Scotland's first king, and who brings the coronation stone to Scotland. By the mid-sixteenth century the tradition of using myths to 'establish continuity with a suitable historic past' had waned.[16] Writing his *History of Scotland* in the 1570s, Bishop John Leslie promoted parts of the Scottish myth as 'truth', taking the lineage back to Gaythelos and Scota. He claimed the Scots

---

13 A Thomas, *Princelie Majestie: The Court of James V of Scotland* (Edinburgh, 2005) 4, 7, 135; M Drexler, 'Fluid Prejudice: Origin Myths in the Later Middle Ages', 61–75 in J Rosenthal and C Richmond (eds), *People, Politics and Community in the Later Middle Ages* (New York, 1987), at p 75.

14 *Wyntoun's Original Chronicle*, F J Amours (ed), volumes i-vi (Edinburgh and London, 1903–1914) ii, 190.

15 H Boece, *Chronicles of Scotland*, J Bellenden (trans), R W Chambers and E C Batho (eds), (Edinburgh and London, 1938) i, 21–24.

16 E Hobsbawm and T Ranger (eds), *The Invention of Tradition* (Cambridge, 1983: reprint 2004) 1.

were divinely blessed but drew the line at any mention of giants.[17] Leslie placed the expulsion of the Israelites from Egypt firmly at the feet of another Pharaoh, not Scota's father; Scottish lineage therefore remained unblemished.[18] Antiquity of ancestors was still the most desirable asset in the war of the pen. However, like those authors before him, Leslie pushed Gaythelos and his heritage to prominence, overshadowing Scota and giving the Greek prince a clear and coherent identity as a leader, husband, father and hero.[19] That Gaythelos had to be successful in all of these roles shows how sexuality and gender were important in the construction of Scottish identity. His actions, good or bad, would have repercussions for his country and future generations.[20] Once more Scota ceased to exist in any form except as wife and mother. Leslie mentions her status as a label, but only through her relationship with her husband, who called his people 'al Scottish fra the name of his Wyfe'; she was denied the autonomous identity briefly given to her by Bisset.[21] As Tamara Agha-Jaffar argues,

> [t]he power to name holds a special significance. Naming delineates, categorises, defines and imposes meaning and order … it also establishes hierarchy: the one being named is subordinate to the one doing the naming.[22]

---

17 J Leslie, Bishop of Ross, *The Historie of Scotland*, Father J Dalrymple (trans), Rev Father E G Cody (ed), (Edinburgh and London, 1888) i, 68–70.

18 Leslie, i, 71.

19 Leslie, i, 70–73.

20 L Racioppi and K O'Sullivan, 'Engendering Nation and National Identity', 18–34 in S Ranchod-Nilssen and M A Tetreault (eds), *Women, States and Nationalism: At Home in the Nation?* (London and New York, 2000), at pp 18–20.

21 Leslie, i, 70–73.

22 T Agha-Jaffar, *Women and Goddesses in Myth and Sacred Text, An Anthology* (New York, 2004) 205.

Therefore, if naming establishes hierarchy and subordination the reader can be certain that the political act of naming, and therefore legitimising, was solely a masculine action.

George Buchanan, who completed his *History of Scotland* in 1582, wanted to establish the historicity of an ancient, independent and properly constitutional Scottish monarchy, arguing ancient writers never wrote of heroes who undertook impossible and implausible journeys. He questioned why such heroes would leave their lands of plenty to become refugees, incredulous that people of great nations associated their forged ancestors with the refuse of other nations in order to give themselves an indigenous pedigree.[23] Understanding that uncovering a nation's origins was important, he nevertheless argued such fables obscured the truth and diminished the nation's credibility.[24] In Buchanan's narrative, an unnamed protagonist married 'Scota, the daughter of the King of Egypt', before sailing about the 'whole shores of Europe' stopping at some desolate place or inhabited by a few, before arriving at a country 'much more barren'.[25] Being the 'first of all men … who adventured into the ocean with a navy of ships' (the now named) Gaythelos landed and built 'a brave town … before being forced to pass into Galaecia where he built Brigantia'.[26] This language and imagery of the barren (empty) country emphasised its physical conquest by Gaythelos, paralleling the passive position of Scota as daughter and wife. In a masculine and colonial society, only a man could dominate the land in such a manner. However, Buchanan was still critical of the gallant and martial Gaythelos whom he claimed had been the leader of a band of criminals. Incredulous, Buchanan asked why the fablers picked out such an 'ignoble person for their

---

23 G Buchanan, *Buchanan's History of Scotland. In twenty books …*, W Bond (ed), 2nd Edition, 2 volumes (London, 1722) Eighteenth-Century Collections Online, i, 63–73; *Rerum Scoticarum historia auctore Georgio Buchanano Scoto, 1582*, STC/181:13, EEBO, f.14r–15r, (ll.35–36).

24 Buchanan, i, 64; *Rerum*, f.14v (ll.28–32).

25 Buchanan, i, 72–73; *Rerum*, f.17r (ll.8–12).

26 Buchanan, i, 73; *Rerum*, f.17r (ll.12–18).

founder … for the original of their race?'[27] While Buchanan briefly discusses the story of Gaythelos, there is nothing to associate Scota's name with Scotland. Using Scota as the more glorious origin story was out of the question for Buchanan, whose writings demonstrate he, like his contemporary John Knox, was uncomfortable with the idea of a woman with authority.[28] Feminine origin myths were moralistic narratives reinforcing gendered prescriptions of the roles to be played in the past, present and future, demonstrating that 'without lords, societies, like women without husbands, are prey to their own weaknesses. Even the best woman must cede power to men'.[29] Scota disappeared because she had 'limited resonance', becoming unappealing to 'an obvious political constituency', unlike the stories of Brutus, Arthur, Saint George, and Saint Andrew.[30]

Saint Andrew is the second foundation myth to be examined here; a legend, like that of Scota, which appeared in a number of chronicles in varying detail. Each version seeks to 'demonstrate the close ties of [the bishopric of] St Andrews with the apostle, and with kingship, thereby laying claim to special favours and generous endowments'.[31] After Christ's death, Andrew became a missionary who wandered the East spreading the word of God. After Andrew's martyrdom, his body apparently lay at Patras for 300 years before being removed to Constantinople. From there, Saint Regulus

---

27 Buchanan, i, 72, 74; *Rerum*, f.17r (ll.5–6), f.17v (ll.1–4).

28 It must be noted that while John Knox found Catholic women in authority abhorrent we cannot use this as a blanket statement for his opinions of women in general. See M Meikle, 'John Knox and Womankind: A Reappraisal', *Historian* 79 (Autumn 2003), 9–14. The same could be said about Buchanan, although no detailed exploration of his attitudes toward women has been undertaken.

29 Geary, 41.

30 Dr J Crick, 'Albion Before Albina: The Scottish Question', (Unpublished Paper, The University of York, 28 October 2006) 2.

31 M Ash and D Broun, 'The Adoption of St Andrew as Patron Saint of Scotland,' 16–24 in J Higgitt (ed), *Medieval Art and Architecture in the Diocese of St Andrew*, British Archaelogical Association (1994) at pp 16–18.

brought some of Andrew's bones to Scotland in 820 CE, and Hungus was the first king of Scotland to pay reverence to Andrew after the saint gave him spiritual assistance in battle.[32] Andrew was seen as pious, just and gentle; attributes that certainly appealed to the religiously-minded chroniclers, and probably appealed to those Scots seeking a virtuous patron saint. Moreover, his brother Peter held the keys of Rome and was the ancestor of popes.[33] The *Declaration of Arbroath* (1320) highlighted the link with Scottish identity and freedom because 'even though the Scots existed "at the uttermost ends of the earth" they were singled out among the first for salvation through the medium of St Andrew, the first-called of all the disciples'.[34]

The masculine and apostolic Andrew represented a higher, god-given nationhood. He was praised by Bower for allowing the Scots to become one kingdom under Kenneth (c852). He had moral superiority resulting from his chastity and his martyrdom. He did not need military prowess to make him manly, but his support in military ventures in keeping Scotland free was enough to keep his masculinity intact.[35] As a saintly and historical figure Andrew commanded more authority than any mythical figure could. He could be labelled as a chivalric knight; a spiritual protector who left the justified violence to his people to protect and defend his lady love, Scotland. As a knight of the realm he defended the land and Christianity. Although martyred through violent means, Andrew refrained from violent acts, balancing out the aggressiveness and bloodshed of war by his compassionate nature. Manliness did not

---

32 Confusion surrounds the dating of this set of events.

33 Bower, i, 311; *Declaration of Arbroath*, National Archives of Scotland (Edinburgh); Wyntoun, iii, 234–235.

34 E J Cowan, 'Identity, Freedom and the Declaration of Arbroath,' 38–68 in D Broun, R J Finlay and M Lynch (eds), *Image and Identity: The Making and Re-Making of Scotland Through the Ages* (Edinburgh, 1998) at p 39; *Declaration of Arbroath*.

35 Bower, ii, 305. Also see D M Hadley, 'Introduction: Medieval Masculinities', 1-18 in D M Hadley (ed), *Masculinity in Medieval Europe* (London and New York, 1999), at p 11.

automatically suggest sexual or military aggression; self-control and control of others could also enhance one's masculinity.[36] Andrew epitomised everything a pious man, and a Christian nation, should be; his Christianity was probably one reason the pagan Scota was dropped. His image was sustained because he left the pages of the histories and became physically tangible through political, religious and military symbolism.

Andrew and his X-shaped cross appeared on the great seal of the Guardians of the Realm in 1286 accompanied by the words '*Andrea Scotis dux esto coompatriotis*'.[37] Ursula Hall argues the seal identifies the earliest use of Saint Andrew and his cross in a Scottish national context, and for Andrew as the pre-eminent patron of the Scottish people.[38] His cross was used to link him to the freedom of the nation and to those fighting for that freedom. In 1385 an Act of Parliament ruled that '[e]very man shall have a sign before and behind, namely a white St Andrew's cross', signalling the saltire was the national symbol of freedom.[39] A tradition, begun at the battle of Bannockburn (1314), was now legally established as an identifying marker of the Scots; something theorists of nationalism, such as Eric Hobsbawm and Benedict Anderson, would see as invented or imagined. Nonetheless, this 'invention' developed Scottish identity through literary and symbolic forms which outlasted the medieval period.[40] In 1512, it was formally declared that Andrew's cross was to be put on all the standards of the *Margaret,* thus displaying the national symbol of Scotland's patron and protector to the wider naval

---

36 R M Karras, *Sexuality in Medieval Europe: Doing Unto Others* (New York and Abingdon, 2005) 37.

37 'Andrew, be thou the leader of the Scots, thy compatriots.' See C J Smith, *Saint Andrew: Patron Saint of Scotland* (1971) 33.

38 U Hall, *St Andrew and Scotland* (St Andrews, 1994) 107–108.

39 C Smith, 35; M Turnbull, *Saint Andrew: Scotland's Myth and Identity* (Edinburgh, 1997) 75. A similar statute was drawn up in England (1388) whereby the Saint George Cross had to be worn by English soldiers. See S Riches, *St George: Hero, Myth and Martyr* (Stroud, 2000) 110.

40 Hobsbawm, 4.

community.[41] The commander of the *Lion* apparently encouraged his men with the following words: 'Fight on my men ... stand fast by St Andrew's Cross'.[42] Banners displaying the Saltire were used at the battles of Flodden (1513) and Pinkie (1547). In 1523 it was specifically noted that every man taking part in an expedition against the English had to 'wear a St Andrews Cross on his tunic ... on pain of death'.[43] Despite the carnage at Flodden and the apparent lack of saintly protection, Andrew obviously had not lost his appeal, at least for those in charge. It is certainly suggestive that through the high visibility of Andrew's symbols, naval and military men understood the underlying patriotism which was being visually conveyed.

Pope Boniface VIII saw Andrew as important to the Scottish nation, a belief outlined in a letter to Edward I in 1300. Because the relics of Andrew influenced conversion to Christianity, the Pope argued Scotland was under the protection of the Holy See, and therefore could not be tampered with. Andrew was also linked to military victories and this was expounded upon by the Scottish historians. Bower attributed the continuation of freedom after the disastrous Battle of Dunbar (1296) to the saint's mediation, and the mercy of God. Andrew supposedly tended to, and healed, the injuries of the Scots by spiritually governing the actions of Edward I, prohibiting him from conquering Scotland.[44] After the English defeat at Stirling Bridge (1297), Scottish soldiers apparently dismounted, threw themselves to the ground and 'glorified God and St Andrew' through whom 'the valour and power of their enemies withered away and ... Scotland won the distinction of a famous victory with everlasting renown'.[45] The defeat of the English at Bannockburn was also attributed to Andrew after Robert Bruce had called upon

---

41 *Accounts of the Lord High Treasurer of Scotland 1507–1513*, Sir J B Paul (ed), (Edinburgh, 1902) vi, 297.

42 Turnbull, 80.

43 *ALHT*, v, 227. Also see *Pictures of the Battle of Pinkie*, c 1550, Bodleian Library, MSEng.Misc.c.13(R).

44 Bower, vi, 291–293.

45 Bower, vi, 91.

the saint to 'deliver the wretched people of Scotland from under bondage'.[46] Highlighting the independence of the Scottish church from the English, and the wider considerations of the kingdom's freedom from English overlordship, chroniclers implied the whole nation believed their survival was due to Andrew's especial care.[47] Therefore, the use of Andrew as the symbol of Scottish identity and freedom during times of uncertainty indicates a need for rationality and stability, which could only be represented by a man, not the distant, pagan and untouchable figure of Scota who was unlikely to unite the people.

Andrew appeared on Scottish coins in the reigns of Robert III, James II and James IV. Scottish kings 'had much to gain from the development of a national identity' and Andrew, used as a display of power and divine blessing, was central to that development. Scottish identity was therefore often synonymous with royal identity.[48] By giving thanks, and consecrating the cathedral at St Andrews, Robert Bruce publicly showed his veneration for the saint who had protected the Scots in battle. James III and James IV had their portraits painted with clear references to Andrew, making explicit use of the symbolism.[49] James IV used Andrew as the symbol on his livery badge. Livery collars, heavily featuring the saint and his cross, were also used by the earlier Stewart kings.[50] Leslie specifically noted that the 'ornamentis of S. Andro' were put above the gates at Linlithgow Palace, because they were 'the proper

---

46 *Liber Pluscardensis,* F J H Skene (ed), (Edinburgh, 1877) x, 183.

47 Ash and Broun, 16.

48 F Watson, 'The Enigmatic Lion: Scotland, Kingship and National Identity in the Wars of Independence', 18–37 in Broun, Finlay and Lynch, at p 20.

49 The Trinity Altarpiece was created for James III and a miniature painting was done of James IV. See T Tolley, 'Hugo van der Goes's Altarpiece for Trinity College Church in Edinburgh and Mary of Guelders, Queen of Scotland', 213–231 in Higgitt, *Medieval Art,* at pp 216–217.

50 K Stevenson, 'The Unicorn, St Andrew and the Thistle: Was There an Order of Chivalry in Late Medieval Scotland?' *Scottish Historical Review,* 83, 1 (2004) 3–22, at pp 20, 22.

armes of our natioune'.[51] Such representations certainly had political meaning, but as official images they would have been recognised by many members of Scottish society.[52] By the reign of Mary Stewart, Andrew rarely featured in a symbolic or literary sense, although the Saltire was used by the Queen's forces at the battle of Carberry Hill (1567) and on her funerary banners.[53] This was partly due to the Reformation and Protestant dismissal of saints and icons, and partly because of the increasing insecurity surrounding Mary's queenship. Militarily, the link with Andrew was fixed by acts of Parliament but only a tenuous link appears to have existed between Andrew and Mary, testifying to male tensions surrounding the governance of women. In my opinion, the above examples point to a self-consciousness on the part of the Scots as a people and as a nation. Certainly, the elite of the nation were well aware of the value of an apostolic saint as their protector, although it is harder to make concrete assertions about the lower classes.

Having identified the traditions surrounding Scota and Andrew during the fifteenth and sixteenth centuries, I now wish to consider in more depth the reasons why the masculine figure displaced the feminine as the symbol of Scottish nationhood. By specifically articulating that '[t]he whole of Scotland is named after the woman Scota', Bisset feminises the land which could then be occupied and ruled by men.[54] Scota may have conquered, yet there is no mention of her becoming queen, governing her people, or making laws. By reducing any authority she may have had, the leadership role was kept free for a man. So why did Bisset write about Scota in this way? Political use of Scota proudly defined the national collective of Scotland, a collective that was free and independent from English overlordship. I believe the Scota myth emphasised

---

51 Leslie, ii, 230.

52 J Higgitt, *'Imageis Maid with Mennis Hand': Saints, Images, Belief and Identity in Later Medieval Scotland* (Whithorn, 2003) 14.

53 Turnbull, 80; *Funeral Banners of Mary Queen of Scots*, British Library, Eg.3510 f.57b.

54 Bower, vi, 143.

a matrilineal beginning ensuring the legitimacy of a long line of Scottish kings. Once established, the feminine was removed to the narrative periphery, just as mothers were removed from the care of their sons after the initial years of nurturing. As an outsider Scota was accepted because 'in a patrilinear and virilocal society, mothers usually came from somewhere else ... the *genetrix* was *alienigena*'.[55] Moreover, fighting women belonging to a distinct ethnic group, such as Amazons, were contained and confined to a distant space and time. As Sandy Bardsley suggests, 'attitudes to female warriors changed over the course of the Middle Ages ... in the early Middle Ages direct participation did not seem to be particularly unusual'.[56] Bisset may well have been of the generation that still saw value in women's roles and, by using the literary examples of Scota in the early fourteenth century, can be seen to be encouraging feminine participation in the struggle for freedom. The different variations of the Scota-Gaythelos myth highlight the 'complex process of inclusion and exclusion, of self-identification and new prejudice in which social boundaries ... were redrawn' by medieval authors in order to establish a distinctly gendered Scottish identity.[57] Scota served her biological role and provided Scotland with future leaders; her displacement from the masculine narrative is a necessary and normal part of the social process. For later Christian writers, paganism was condemned from a safe distance of a few hundred years, and associated with the feminine.[58] Scota was therefore used as the boundary of femininity, while Gaythelos highlighted the range of masculinities that allowed him to grow from bandit to rational governor.

Juxtaposing the manly roles of conquest and provision with

55 W Pohl, 'Gender and Ethnicity in the Early Middle Ages', 23–43 in L Brubaker and J H Smith (eds), *Gender in the Medieval World East and West 300–900* (Cambridge, 2004) at pp 37–41.

56 S Bardsley, *Women's Roles in the Middle Ages* (Westport, 2007) 205.

57 Pohl, 40–42.

58 L M Bitel, *Women in Early Medieval Europe 400–1100* (Cambridge, 2002) 38.

the feminine nurturing and reproductive roles suggests Scota was viewed by some Scottish chroniclers as superior to the English founding father, Brutus. Bower emphasised her feminine qualities as wife and mother but also used Bisset's papal submissions to highlight her manly qualities in the fight for ancient lineage. As a woman, Scota would have been easy to dismiss once the ancient line of Scottish kings was established; being pagan meant she was no threat to Scotland's Christianity. As a patriot, Bower would have been only too happy to diminish the warrior status of the English under a superior, and feminine, Scottish origin legend. Other contemporary historians placed Scota firmly in the bounds of her gender as daughter, wife and mother. From being Bisset's active participant in discovering the Scottish nation, she is reduced to a label of the land and its people. Further reasons for Scota's relegation are found in the attitudes of the celibate male clerics who wrote the chronicles. Scota's ancestry as the daughter of a Pharaoh, and more importantly as mother of the Scots, was proudly written about; perhaps her antiquity was what really mattered in the war of words with England. What is intriguing is that Bower not only included Bisset's independent Scota, he outlined the short narrative of the thirteenth-century English statesman, Grosseteste, who also gave a leadership role to Scota.[59] Perhaps he was fascinated with Bisset's use of a 'manly' and 'motherly' woman who was the progenitor of the Scots despite marginalising her elsewhere. Overall, it suited Bower's nationalistic purpose to include Bisset's documents because they were part of a major event in Scotland's political history and fight for freedom, and consequently important to the national narrative. Whatever the reason, the link between memory and origins was recreated to suit the current political situation.[60] Scota's re-construction in the histories should be read as a marker of changes in the perception of the feminine. By the mid-fifteenth century, any place accorded women in the textual picture was diminishing. In the sixteenth century the question of

59 Bower, i, 37. Bower also quotes the *Historia Scholastica*.

60 Bower, vi, 143. Also see Bitel, 53.

woman's governance caused considerable angst, as demonstrated by the writings of Buchanan, and the Protestant reformer John Knox.[61] Therefore, the fact Scota features in the narratives at all testifies to her importance.

Andrew, like Scota, was employed as a discourse 'to assert legitimacy and strengthen authority', necessary in a parental figure required as a forebear.[62] Was it his excellent credentials or his unassuming and malleable nature that allowed him to become the protector of Scottish political and military society? After all, Andrew was not a strong warrior who slew dragons like England's Saint George. According to Vern Bullough, medieval masculinity was defined by 'the threefold activities of impregnating women, protecting dependents and serving as a provider to one's family'.[63] Where does this leave the celibate and saintly Andrew? While Andrew did not engage in impregnation, he certainly protected his Scottish family, provided his ecclesiastical family with offerings and riches through patronage, provided his military family with victories, and gave his political family a powerful unifying force. In contrast to Gaythelos, Andrew displayed a more humane and pious type of masculinity, while at the same time protecting and encouraging the male right to violence in order to specifically defend the realm. Politics, warfare and religion were the nurturing factors in the growth of Andrew as protector and 'father' of the Scottish people. Andrew was more malleable, and more useful, than Scota could ever be. Being a man meant he fitted the masculine identity of the nation, especially as he was seen by the Scots to have the necessary

61 By 1561 queens regnant ruled both Scotland and England. Strong female regents such as Marie de Guise in Scotland prior to 1560 and Catherine de Medici in France after 1560 also contributed to the women-in-rule debate.

62 G Schopflin, 'The Functions of Myth and a Taxonomy of Myth', 19–35 in G Hosking and G Schopflin (eds), *Myths and Nationhood* (London, 1997), at p 27.

63 V L Bullough, 'On Being a Male in the Middle Ages', 31–45 in C A Lees (ed), *Medieval Masculinities: Regarding Men in the Middle Ages* (Minneapolis and London, 1994), at p 34.

manly, heroic qualities and other appropriate virtues. The legendary figure epitomised the virtues and hopes of the nation, and Andrew was easier to follow into battle, despite the warrior qualities Bisset gave Scota in his *Pleadings*.[64] The use of Andrew demonstrates that piety and patriotism could easily be intertwined. Scota, however, was an allegorical and representative role model for the women of Scotland who were to bear continuous lines of male children — the future defenders of the Scottish nation.[65] Andrew, through his masculinity, piety and protector-status was already superior; as a disciple of Christ he furthered his superiority. Scota, as a woman, a princess and a pagan was never going to be a successful rival, instead ending up a hazy but politicised personality enclosed in the parliamentary cupboard or monastic library, and easily banished to the sidelines of Scottish history.

Patriarchy was not only about subordination of women by men, it 'involved proving oneself superior to other men'.[66] With women marginalised and relegated to their feminine roles, we cannot begin to understand what Scottish identity meant to them through the use of the origin myths, although we can presume they shared the same status and preoccupations of the men with whom they were associated. By acknowledging the roles of Gaythelos and Andrew, the educated elite showed an unquestioned acceptance of the patriarchal system which was of political and religious benefit in maintaining Scottish freedom. Myths continually changed their symbolic form and content in relation to the varying degrees of conflict or competition with those from outside a specific community.[67] Unchanging, women were always reproducers of the

64 A D Smith, *Chosen Peoples: Sacred Sources of National Identity* (Oxford and New York, 2003) 41.

65 N Yuval-Davis argues women are 'required to carry the "burden of representation" because they are constructed as the symbolic bearers of the collectivity's identity and honour,' *Gender and Nation* (London, Thousand Oaks and New Dehli, 1997) 45.

66 R M Karras, *From Boys to Men: Formations of Masculinity in Late Medieval Europe* (Philadelphia, 2003) 10.

67 A Smith, *Myths and Memories of the Nation* (Oxford, 1999) 57.

nation who were required to carry the 'burden of representation', and constructed as the symbolic bearers of the nation's identity and honour, both personally and collectively.[68] Paradoxically, women had to preserve the nation's uncontaminated purity through their own chastity before and during marriage, while at the same time sexually serving their men, assuring them of legitimate paternity and lineage. Scota determined the boundary of the national group through her marriage to Gaythelos, and her womb — her body — served as a symbol of national virtue and martial potency by being the figural mother of the nation and the biological mother of two sons.[69] Through Bisset she became an active participant in the national struggle, albeit briefly. However, if we look at the other ways Nira Yuval-Davis has shown how women were implicated in the construction of nationalism, I argue it was Andrew who became prominent as the 'active transmitter of national culture', the 'symbolic signifier of national difference' and the 'active participant in national struggles'.[70] Andrew took on these feminine roles and integrated them with the masculine. By having Scota abdicate her warrior role, Bower and his peers stabilised the social and political equilibrium which she had disrupted by being a manly woman. Medieval and sixteenth-century writers therefore promoted an elite hegemonic masculinity which spilled over into the construction of Scottish identity.

The narratives, written by celibate male clerics, were manipulated and coloured by their political, moral, and religious prejudices. Moreover, conflicting variations of the origin myths accentuate the tensions experienced by pre-modern historians who try to make pagan women and saintly men fit with specific events, and the ideologies of society. Even as a mythical figure, Scota's

---

68 Yuval-Davis, 45.

69 K Wilson, 'Empire, Gender and Modernity in the Eighteenth Century', 14–20 in P Levine (ed), *Gender and Empire* (Oxford, 2004) at pp 19–20.

70 F Anthias and N Yuval-Davis, *Racialised Boundaries: Race, Nation, Gender, Colour and Class and the Anti-Racial Struggle* (London and New York, 1992) 7–10.

sexuality was regulated and controlled by those who wrote about her. With Andrew, there were relics, pilgrimages, churches, his cross on banners and clothing, and reverence by royalty and ecclesiastical institutions; he was the perfect legendary figure. Since church and crown relied heavily on each other, it was sensible to promote an identity that suited both political and ecclesiastical agendas, and which subsequently controlled femininity. Nationalist discourse reconstituted the male as the national subject who was reborn at the expense of women's sacrifice. As Fiona Downie argues, '[p]aternal imagery embraced authority and leadership, while its maternal counterpart emphasised an emotional influence and pre-eminence'.[71] This was reinforced by the fact that '[m]aternal political imagery lacked the resonance of paternal metaphors because the image of the mother had been divested of any political power by the fifteenth century, as indicated by changes in Marian iconography'.[72]

What this paper has also shown is that 'one national narrative' has the 'possibility of multiple beginnings, narratives and omissions', and such remembering and forgetting underpins the formation of national identity.[73] Identity cannot be made up of heroic deeds and conquests alone. The reproductive faculties of women were required to ensure dynastic and cultural continuity, although these were often of momentary importance. By looking at the margins we realise Scotland's identity was made up of more than just masculine ideology, although it simultaneously reflects uneven power relations.[74] Scota's authenticity lay in her natural connection with the land and her natural role as mother. Andrew was forward-thrusting in his protection and promotion of the Scottish people and their independence. However, using a feminine national discourse

---

71 F Downie, *She is But a Woman: Queenship in Scotland 1424–1463* (Edinburgh, 2006) 23.

72 Downie, 43.

73 C A Lees and G R Overing, 'Signifying Gender and Empire', *Journal of Medieval and Early Modern Studies* 34 (Winter 2004) 1–16, at p 6.

74 E Fox-Genovese, 'Placing Women's History in History', *New Left Review* 133 (1982) 5–29, at p 29.

supplanted by a masculine one highlights the 'patriarchal desire to define and control national territory, history and identity'.[75] A female origin figure such as Scota, who at times appeared savage, opened the way for Andrew as the Christianising and civilising foundation of the Scots; a male who corrected the gendered order of society. The political, ecclesiastical, and literary contexts included women only when necessary; as essentially passive beings in a world promoting Scotland's origins as actively masculine in text and context. After all, Scottish lineage had to be masculine for '[p]ride in one's lineage [and] country ... were essential buttresses of a man's valour'.[76]

75 J Mikalachki, *The Legacy of Boadicea: Gender and Nation in Early Modern England* (London and New York, 1998) 33.

76 M Bennett, 'Military Masculinity in England and Northern France', 71–88 in Hadley, at p 86.

Edmund Burke and Mary Wollstonecraft's Irish education

Mary Spongberg ⊕

The question of Edmund Burke's 'Irishness' has been consistently debated among scholars of Burke since the first biographies appeared in the early nineteenth century, and even recent attempts to analyse Burke's Irish identities have achieved little consensus.[1] Contemporaries of Burke felt no such confusion, measuring his Irishness in direct correlation to his popularity, or, as was more often the case, his unpopularity. From the time Burke first established himself as a public figure, some reference to his Irish heritage was usually made by the caricaturists, satirists and journalists: indeed, anyone who sought to question his authority.

In this paper I want to analyse one such attack on Burke's Irishness, Mary Wollstonecraft's first *Vindication, of the Rights of Men.* While scholars have long recognised Wollstonecraft's reaction to Burke's *Reflections on the Revolution in France* as one of the more vehement responses, they have tended to overlook her snide remarks regarding his Irishness and his Catholic sympathies. Reading Wollstonecraft's *Rights of Men*, within the context of a tradition of attacks on Burke's Irishness, I hope to demonstrate that Ireland forms a critical subtext to her first *Vindication.* I want to suggest that the vehemence of Wollstonecraft's attack on Burke was part of a complex reaction to her experiences in Ireland, particularly

---

⊕ Mary Spongberg is Head of the Department of Modern History, Politics and International Relations at Macquarie University. She is the author of *Writing Women's History since the Renaissance* and has recently edited the *Companion to Women's Historical Writing* (2005).

1 For a recent discussion of this highly contested area of scholarship, see S P Donlan, 'Introduction' in *Edmund Burke's Irish Identities* (Dublin, 2006) 1–15.

her relationship with Lady Kingsborough, nee Fitzgerald, Caroline King, wife of Robert King, second Earl of Kingston and heir to the Mitcheltown Estates in Cork, who had employed Wollstonecraft as a governess in 1786. While other scholars have suggested that Wollstonecraft herself identified with Burke, I believe that Wollstonecraft identified Edmund Burke with Lady Kingsborough, whom she represented, in both her political writing and her novels, as the worst type of womanhood the courtly system could produce.

Attacks on Burke's Irishness surfaced almost inevitably in the second half of the eighteenth century, whenever he clashed with other political figures, or when his influence appeared to be becoming too great. When he fell out with Sir William Hamilton, Chief Secretary for Ireland, in the early 1760s, insinuations were made, alleging Burke's involvement with Catholic subversion. When Burke became the Marquis of Rockingham's personal secretary in the mid-1760s, Rockingham was warned that he was an 'Irish adventurer', a Crypto-Catholic, educated by the Jesuits at St Omer's. In the 1770s as his influence as a Rockingham Whig was on the rise, elements of the English press began to campaign against him. The *Public Advertiser* dubbed him 'Edmund Bonnyclabber' (a Gaelic term, denoting milk naturally clotted on souring) and 'Whiteboy', in reference to Burke's maternal relatives, who were involved with that secret agrarian association.[2] When he was campaigning for the seat of Bristol, broadsides were published condemning Burke as 'One, who if not a *Papist*, can have no dislike to *Popery*, as he cannot deny, he married a rigid Roman Catholic'.[3] During the Gordon Riots in 1780, Burke was repeatedly identified as the chief enemy of the 'Protestant Cause', and Matthew Darley, print publisher for the Protestant Association, inaugurated the caricature tradition of Burke as a secret Jesuit with cross and biretta.[4] It was James Gillray

---

2 N Robinson, *Edmund Burke: A Life in Caricature* (New Haven, 1996) 11–12.

3 F P Lock, *Edmund Burke, Vol 1, 1730–1784* (Oxford, 1998) 375.

4 I McCalman, 'Mad Lord George and Madame La Motte: Riot and Sexuality in the Genesis of Burke's *Reflections on the Revolution in*

however, who made such an image of Burke famous, and for the rest of his life, Burke appeared in caricatures dressed in monkish garb, armed with a biretta, a rosary and sometimes a poor box, a stock-in-trade 'Arrah' preceding any phrase he was heard to utter. During his prosecution of Warren Hastings in the mid-1780s, Burke began to appear as a confessor, seeking to save Hastings' soul. Occasionally he was depicted riding an ass engraved with the face of Pius VI or playing an Irish harp with a similar physiognomy.

Although his opponents had long charged that Burke's 'wild Irish eloquence' was fuelled by 'potatoes and whisky',[5] in the early stages of his career, his speeches in Parliament had been greeted with respect and admiration. This changed dramatically, however, during the impeachment of Warren Hastings, Governor General of Bengal. The manner in which Burke and Richard Brinsley Sheridan, his co-prosecutor, managed the case against Hastings functioned in ways that achieved public notoriety for him, and public odium for themselves. So overblown was their performance that some contemporary observers believed that they 'threatened to transform the House of Lords from a "vast stage of Justice [...] into a theatre of pleasure"'.[6] Burke particularly earned scorn in Parliament, as his speeches, once met with awed silence, were now greeted with hoots and jeers. Sir Philip Magnus has observed that Burke's pronounced brogue added emphasis to 'his strangeness', and this signifier of his Irishness underpinned the disdain that accompanied many of the speeches towards the end of his career.[7] The eroticism of Burke and Sheridan's oriental fantasies did little to impress the Lords, but reinforced the sense of Burke's otherness; even years later, Matthew Arnold could complain of his 'Asiatic style'. Satirists, as

France', Journal of British Studies 35.3 (1996) 355.

5 Lock, *Edmund Burke*, 516.

6 A Clark, *Scandal: The Sexual Politics of the British Constitution* (Princeton, 2004) 106.

7 K O'Donnell, '"To Love the Little Platoon" – Edmund Burke's Jacobite Heritage', 16–27 in S P Donlan (ed), *Edmund Burke's Irish Identities* (Dublin, 2006) 17.

well as caricaturists, had a field day with Burke during this period, contrasting his accented brogue with the accent of the Indian witnesses, who it was claimed, 'spoke in broad English [...] without false delicacy or circumlocution'.[8] Even Jane Austen's usually polite cousin Philadelphia Walters, who accompanied Hasting's putative daughter Eliza de Feuillide to his trial, made the common complaint of Burke, that his orations were 'so hot and hasty' she could not understand what was being said.[9]

By the time Burke published his *Reflections on the Revolution in France* in November 1790, satirists and caricaturists were well schooled in making a mockery of his Irishness. Indeed the canonical apostrophe to Marie Antoinette in this text drew together many separate strands of Burke satire, seeming to confirm, in the one instance, his Crypto-Catholicism, his Jesuitical nature and his covert support for aristocratic tyranny. Even for a monarchist, Burke's adulation of Marie Antoinette in the *Reflections* seemed excessive. At a time when the queen was subject to vile rumours regarding her political machinations in the French court, Burke chose to depict her as an ethereal, almost fairy-like creature. He waxed lyrical about his memories of 'the dauphiness' when he had visited Versailles some 17 years earlier, in tones that seemed destined to be satirised: 'surely never lighted on this orb, which she hardly seemed to touch, a more delightful vision [...]'.[10]

His friend Sir Philip Francis had warned Burke, before he published the *Reflections*, that what he had written in Marie Antoinette's defence was 'pure foppery'.[11] His decision 'to place her personal charms in opposition to her crimes' confounded Francis,

8 See *Begum Burke to Begum Bow: A Poetical Rhapsody on Comtemporary Characters [Dedicated to Lord G—rge Gordon, in Newgate]* (London1789) 4.

9 D Le Faye, *Jane Austen's Outlandish Cousin: The Life and Letters of Eliza de Feuillide* (London, 2002) 84.

10 L G Mitchell, *The Writings and Speeches of Edmund Burke Vol VIII The French Revolution* (Oxford, 1989) 126.

11 A Cobban and R A Smith, *Correspondence of Edmund Burke Vol VI* (Cambridge, 1967) 86.

and his drivelling admiration for her person earned him much scorn among radicals and the Jacobin press. On the day after the publication of the *Reflections,* a *Frontispiece* appeared, with Burke dressed as a French courtier, his brain inflamed by a cherub, worshipping at the feet of a celestial Marie Antoinette, draped in blue, like the Virgin Mary. Several weeks later *Don Dismallo, After an Absence of Sixteen Years, Embracing his Beautiful Vision* appeared, depicting Burke in Quixotic garb, embracing Marie Antoinette, proposing 'a more intimate, if less chivalrous encounter', than the one he depicted in the *Reflections.* In the background Mrs Burke, dressed as a keening Irish widow, weeps as she hears her husband's ecstatic response to the queen 'Christ Jesus, what an ass I have been a number of years; to have doted on an old woman — Heaven! what's her bacon and eggs to the delicious dairy of this celestial vision'.[12]

Such coarse humour hinted at the darker stories that had swirled around the French queen since the arrival of the self-styled Contesse de Valoise de la Motte in London. Jeanne de La Motte was one of a pair of seedy swindlers, who had duped the ambitious Louis René Édouard, cardinal de Rohan, into purchasing a fabulously expensive diamond necklace, so that he might court favour with the queen. La Motte was imprisoned and branded on the body with a V for *voleuse* as a result of her crimes, escaping to England in 1788.[13] Marie Antoinette had no part in this affair; she was inevitably drawn into the scandal by La Motte, who had written a series of memoirs, produced by the Radical publisher James Ridgway 'that advanced a remorseless and increasingly lurid attack on the political and sexual morals of the queen'.[14] Britons came to imagine this as yet another example of the vile corruption of the *ancien regime* in France. Pornography depicting Marie Antoinette became voluminous in Britain during the early stages of the Revolution, framing discussion

12 Robinson, *A Life in Caricature,* 143.

13 For a detailed discussion of this see S Maza, 'The Diamond Necklace Affair Revisited: The Case of the Missing Queen', 63–89 in L Hunt (ed), *Eroticism and the Body Politic* (Baltimore, 1991).

14 McCalman, 'Mad Lord George and Madam La Motte', 363.

of the Revolution around the body of the Queen, and forming part of a broader campaign attacking aristocratic manners and excess.[15] Thus Burke was tainted by association, and the chaste image of Marie Antoinette he had produced in the *Reflections* fuelled rumours that he had indeed gone mad.

The connection that this political pornography made between Dissent and libertinism ensured that serious respondents to Burke, such as Thomas Paine, Catharine Sawbridge Macaulay and James Macintosh, steered away from such discussion when they penned their replies. For the most part, such scholarly responses to the *Reflections* focussed on depicting the faultiness of Burke's understanding of English history, his failure to correctly read 'the Glorious Revolution' and the paucity (and indeed veracity) of his sources relating to France. The usual barbs aimed at Burke by satirists and caricaturists are not to be found in these works, although neither Paine nor Macintosh could help mocking Burke's recourse to chivalry and both sought to 'unmask his private motive for publishing, so late in life, a work of aristocratic propaganda'.[16] While clearly angered by his opinions, such respondents resisted the temptation to personally attack Burke, and little mention was made of his Irishness in such accounts.

Of the serious respondents, then, Mary Wollstonecraft is perhaps unique in her vituperative reply to Burke. Contemporary observers recognised immediately that the substance of Wollstonecraft's first *Vindication* was 'a violent attack' on Mr Burke, while Barbara Taylor has recently called this work a 'rather nasty text' that holds up for 'relentless scorn, Burke's Irishness, his Catholic background, his parliamentary pension and his unsympathetic attitude to the madness of King George'.[17] Published anonymously, several weeks

15 K Binhammer, 'Marie Antoinette was "One of Us": British Accounts of the Martyred Wicked Queen', *Eighteenth Century*, 44.2–3 (2002) 233.

16 D Bromwich, 'Wollstonecraft as Critic of Burke', *Political Theory* 23:4 (1995) 617.

17 B Taylor, *Mary Wollstonecraft and the Feminist Imagination* (Cambridge, 2002) 65.

after the appearance of Burke's *Reflections*, this *Vindication*, unlike its sister text, the *Rights of Woman*, is frequently referred to, but seldom analysed.

For the most part scholars have followed the lead of her husband William Godwin, who discounted the force of Wollstonecraft's prose, suggesting that the text was marked by its rapid composition and the 'vehemence and impetuousness of its eloquence'.[18] Godwin thought so little of the text that Wollstonecraft could joke with him that she would make him read it as an '*amende honarable*' after a tiff.[19] Published shortly after the deaths of Wollstonecraft and Burke, Godwin's *Memoirs* romanticised his wife's feminism, describing her political education, more in terms of her romantic relationships (with the artist Henry Fuseli, American adventurer Gilbert Imlay, and himself) than her involvement with the French Revolution and English Radicalism. Underpinning Godwin's analysis was a desire to represent their relationship as an attraction of opposites, with Wollstonecraft playing the passionate, intuitive ingénue to his rational materialist philosopher. Because of this romantic trajectory, Godwin viewed Wollstonecraft's experiences on the Continent as her most formative. His attempts to discover anything about her life in Ireland were patchy, and in any case, were thwarted by her spiky sisters, who were living there at the time of her death. Upon discovering that Godwin was applying to an old acquaintance, Hugh Skeys in Dublin, for information regarding the life of their sister, Everina Wollstonecraft wrote tartly to her brother-in-law that 'I am sorry to perceive that you are inclined to be minute, when I think it is impossible for you to be even tolerably accurate'.[20]

Godwin did not engage with the arguments Wollstonecraft makes in the first *Vindication*, and really only offers an apologia

18 W Godwin, *Memoirs of the Author of the Vindication of the Rights of Woman,* P Clemit and G L Walker (eds), (Ontario, 2001) 73.

19 R Wardle, *Godwin and Mary: Letters of William Godwin and Mary Wollstonecraft* (Lawrence, 1967) 44.

20 L Gordon, *Vindication: A Life of Mary Wollstonecraft* (London, 2005) 368.

for her 'too contemptuous and intemperate treatment of the great man'.[21] Early biographers and critics have followed Godwin, in depicting Wollstonecraft's *Rights of Men* as a work 'dashed off in angry haste' and lacking the orderliness of later replies.[22] Such discussion reflected Godwin's image of Wollstonecraft as passionate, but lacking in method, undermining her credibility as a political writer. Later scholars have offered varying and contradictory perspectives on her treatment of Burke. Virginia Sapiro has asked scholars of Wollstonecraft to consider the appropriate 'historical contextualisation' for these two figures, reminding us that at the time of this exchange 'Burke was widely regarded as an over-the-hill windbag'.[23] Thus Wollstonecraft might be forgiven for her patronising tone and lack of respect. David Bromwich, on the other hand, suggests that Wollstonecraft is in fact more respectful of Burke than her contemporaries in the pamphlet war. Ignoring the trenchantly sarcastic tone of Wollstonecraft's observations on Burke, Bromwich suggests that 'the steadiness of her engagement with [his work] gives her book its special authority as an act of moral indignation'.[24] James Conniff has characterised her response as mirroring Burke's treatment of the Reverend Price, suggesting that she viewed Burke as a 'basically good man [...] corrupted by the patronage and praise of the English political establishment'.[25] Certainly Wollstonecraft's snide insinuations about his Catholicism, his 'reverence for the rust of antiquity' and his superstition amply countered Burke's equally scathing comments aligning Dissenters with the Pope. Conniff's reading radicalises Burke and anticipates Wollstonecraft's revised position on the Revolution following her

---

21 Godwin, *Memoirs*, 73.

22 J T Boulton, *The Language of Politics in the Age of Burke and Wilkes* (London, 1963) 168.

23 V Sapiro, *A Vindication of Political Virtue: The Political Theory of Mary Wollstonecraft* (Chicago, 1992) 187.

24 Bromwich, 'Mary Wollstonecraft as a Critic', 619.

25 J Conniff, 'Edmund Burke and His Critics: The Case of Mary Wollstonecraft', *Journal of the History of Ideas* 60:2 (1999) 305.

visit to France.

Where there has been consensus regarding Wollstonecraft's response to Burke is in the suggestion that she herself identified with him, and that the strategies she used to attack Burke functioned to obscure the similarities between their positions. Critical to such discussion is an analysis of the way in which Wollstonecraft draws upon Burke's earlier work, *A Philosophic Enquiry into the Origin of Our Ideas of the Sublime and the Beautiful* (1757) to feminise him, and thus undermine his political authority by associating him with all that is beautiful according to his definition: smallness, smoothness, grace and weakness. In his book *Intertextual War*, Steven Blakemore provides the most extended discussion of this position. He argues that Wollstonecraft subverts Burke's authority by describing him in the language of the beautiful, and herself in the 'masculine language' of the sublime.[26] Such subversion is, however, muted, he argues, as she enacts linguistically the very criticisms she ascribes to him. Blakemore maintains that Wollstonecraft's attempts to feminise Burke are undermined because much of what she despises in Burke are in fact sites of her own self-loathing. For Blakemore, Wollstonecraft cannot transcend her own identification with Burke, and consequently she endorses the gendered distinction he has celebrated in the *Enquiry*. Similarly James Conniff has suggested that while Wollstonecraft's attempt to contrast Burke's purported femininity with her own essentially masculine intellect 'effectively neutralized the issue of gender as a qualification for political writing', it also functioned primarily to obscure her identification with him.[27] Other scholars such as Barbara Taylor have made similar observations. Such insights complicate any discussion of the *Rights of Men* as a feminist text, by asserting that Wollstonecraft identifies with Burke.[28]

26 S Blakemore, *Intertextual War: Edmund Burke and the French Revolution in the Writings of Mary Wollstonecraft, Thomas Paine and James Mackintosh* (New Jersey, 1997) 26–39.

27 Conniff, 'Edmund Burke and His Critics', 306.

28 Taylor, *Mary Wollstonecraft*, 64–71.

Focusing on Burke as a feminised object of scorn has to a large extent diminished the very real power of the political arguments condemning the relation between heredity and good government that Wollstonecraft makes in the *Rights of Men*, and her powerful indictment of the sexual politics that underpin Burke's chivalric understanding of class relations. Such psychoanalytic readings of Wollstonecraft's text have, however, also obscured Wollstonecraft's more obvious object of identification with Burke, the Irish aristocrat, Caroline King, Lady Kingsborough. Wollstonecraft identified the system Burke was celebrating explicitly with the morbid femininity she despised in her employer Lady Kingsborough, thus creating a certain conflation between the pair in the *Rights of Men*, that has been previously overlooked.

Wollstonecraft's sojourn in Ireland has rarely been considered as critical to the development of her feminism. William Godwin barely mentions the year she spent in the service of the Kingsboroughs, suggesting rather disingenuously that she 'left behind with them and their connections, a very advantageous impression'.[29] Such a statement was doubtlessly meant to counter the vicious rumours that had surfaced following Wollstonecraft's death, attributing the elopement of Mary King with her married cousin to the baneful influence of her former governess. Indeed such rumours were frequently accompanied by the tale that her employment with the Kings ended abruptly, due to an illicit affair between Wollstonecraft and Lord Kingsborough. Later biographers have tended to view her time in Ireland as formative only as it has related to this possible affair with Robert King.[30] Such accounts mimic Godwin's tendency to frame Wollstonecraft's politics around her relationships with men. Such a tendency, combined with Wollstonecraft's own aggrandising sense of self, has ensured that her relations with other women have received little attention in terms of her politics.

29 Godwin, *Memoirs*, 64.

30 See for instance her principal biographers C Tomalin, *The Life and Death of Mary Wollstonecraft* (London, 1974) and J Todd, *Mary Wollstonecraft: A Revolutionary Life* (London, 2000).

For all this speculation, Robert King is barely mentioned in Wollstonecraft's correspondence during her time in Ireland, while his wife is referred to frequently in Wollstonecraft's letters to her sisters and friends. Wollstonecraft had come to Ireland bereft, following the death of her friend Fanny Blood. Her feelings about her destination were certainly mixed, as she knew from the sermons of the Reverend Richard Price to expect 'aristocratical tyranny and human debasement'.[31] But her heart also yearned for female community and fellowship among the women of the Kingsborough household. Before destined to live in Ireland, she had spoken fondly of 'the dear County Clare' with her friends the Bloods. But the Kingsboroughs' estate at Mitcheltown she imagined as 'the Bastile' (*sic*), an idea no doubt enhanced by the reception that awaited her.[32]

She found Caroline King to be a pretty but vacuous woman, and by Wollstonecraft's forbidding standards, an unfit and uncaring mother. Her letters home are framed by the highs and lows of the awkward relationship she formed with Lady Kingsborough. Wollstonecraft is here at her most self-contradictory, on the one hand desperately seeking the approval of the great lady of the house, while on the other viciously critical of the sexual and class politics that privileged Lady Kingsborough over her governess. Wollstonecraft's letters are full of details about Caroline King, whom she described as always pretty, but overly rouged, concerned only with appearance, and more interested in her dogs than in her children. Even when she left her service, Wollstonecraft continued to write about Caroline King, really only stopping in the last year of her life. As well as regaling her relatives and friends with harsh criticisms of her mistress, Wollstonecraft used Lady Kingsborough as a model for her heroine's distant and beautiful mother in her novel *Mary*, published the year after she left her service. It is easy to recognise Lady Kingsborough, too, in Wollstonecraft's descriptions of the dog-loving lady of fashion who appears in her second *Vindication*.

31 L Gordon, *Vindication*, 83.

32 *Ibid*, 84.

Yet she is also there in the *Rights of Men*, as Wollstonecraft borrows the language she used to depict Lady Kingsborough in her letters to home, to describe Edmund Burke. Her arguments throughout the *Rights of Men* imply that at the heart of Burke's conservatism 'is a psychic femininity — a corrupt feminine eroticism',[33] that in other works she applies explicitly to Caroline King. Her comparison of Burke to a 'celebrated beauty', 'anxious to raise admiration on every occasion' through a display of 'witty arguments and ornamental feelings'[34] clearly recalls Wollstonecraft's description of her experience with Lady Kingsborough, as they competed for the attention of the politician and poet George Ogle. Indeed the barely suppressed indignation Wollstonecraft felt toward Caroline King spews forth in her assault on Burke, as she likens him to the 'fair ladies', who order their slaves to be whipped and who 'compose their ruffled spirits and exercise their tender feelings by the perusal of the last imported novel'.[35] There is a real sense in which Wollstonecraft's correspondence from Ireland might be read as a dress rehearsal for her engagement with Burke. The words she used to describe relations between the sexes among the upper and lower classes in Ireland, appear almost exactly in the more general arguments she makes against Burke and the class system he defends. It is entirely predictable then that her first hope for the Revolution is that it will alter the behaviour of women of fashion, who, unlike her employer, will become true mothers to their children.

Reading Wollstonecraft's reaction to Burke in the *Reflections* as part of a more complex response to her time in Ireland, particularly her failure to form a serious and meaningful connection with Caroline King, allows us considerable insight into what feminists have understood as the underlying misogyny that has shaped much of Wollstonecraft's writing.[36] Wollstonecraft was one of the only

---

33 Taylor, *Mary Wollstonecraft*, 69.

34 M Wollstonecraft, *A Vindication of the Rights of Men*, D L Macdonald and K Scherf (eds), (Ontario, 2001) 36.

35 Wollstonecraft, *A Vindication of the Rights of Men*, 79.

36 On Wollstonecraft's misogyny see S Gubar, 'Feminist Misogyny: Mary

female writer-observers of the French Revolution who steadfastly condemned Marie Antoinette, and had little good to say about the working-class women who engaged in political activity in the early stages of the Revolution. I believe this strand in her work was the result of the sexual politics she witnessed in the Kingsborough household, and the hideous poverty and immorality she experienced on their Mitcheltown estate. While she 'pitied' both the 'great and small vulgar', she nonetheless found both morally repugnant and sought to exclude them from her political system. It was her political education in Ireland that framed both *Vindications,* and informed the revolutionary nature of her feminism for almost a decade.

Wollstonecraft and the Paradox of "It Takes One to Know One"', *Feminist Studies* 20.3 (1994) 453–473.

Eamhain Mhacha in this world and in the otherworld

Penny Pollard ⊕

> 'The spirit of a place may be held to reside in a landscape'.[1]

Places have biographies. Legends acquire part of their mythic value and historical significance when they are anchored to monuments that inhabit the landscape, monuments that can be visited, seen and touched.[2] Eamhain Mhacha was the focus for the sense of place and identity for the early people of Ulster.[3] At Eamhain Mhacha it is possible to construct credible links between the physical remains and the fragments of history, myth and legend that survive in the written record.[4] The events that occurred at Eamhain Mhacha, which are mirrored in some aspects of *Táin Bó Cúailnge* and in the archaeological record, reflect some of the main tenets of shamanism.

From liminal locations such as hilltops or shore margins, the ecstatic shaman believes that he can move between each of the different worlds and their different levels.[5] By engaging with his spirit helpers, such as the friendly dead and animal guides, the

---

⊕ Whatawhata Road, Dinsdale, Hamilton, 3204, New Zealand.

1 C Tilley, *A Phenomenology of Landscape: Places, Paths and Monuments* (Oxford, 1994) 26.

2 *Ibid*, 33.

3 F Pryor, *Britain BC: Life in Britain and Ireland before the Romans, New Edition* (London, 2006) 370.

4 *Ibid*, 370.

5 P Jordan, *Material Culture and Sacred Landscape: The Anthropology of the Siberian Khanty* (California, c2003) 146.

shaman secures otherworld knowledge.[6] This knowledge enables the shaman or the druid to achieve power in the corporeal world.[7]

Shamanic beliefs and beliefs about the lunar goddess and her cult influenced the choice and maintenance of the site at Eamhain Mhacha, its ritual uses and its depiction in the Ulster Cycle. Echoes of the Celts' approach to life are also evident. At Eamhain Mhacha and in Irish myth there were feasting, druids' involvement in divination, tribal structures and belief in the otherworld.

Eamhain Mhacha is named after a triple lunar goddess. Eamhain Mhacha has stood as a symbol of psychic influence and of corporeal power for thousands of years. Sovereignty, kingship, the inauguration of a new king, war, and the seasonal round were thought to be under the influence of the otherworld. At Eamhain Mhacha the goddess was believed to be present and influential. The Irish used a shamanic way of viewing the landscape and perceived that this world and the otherworld were each divided into three co-extensive levels. The Khanty conceived of a three-layered vertical cosmos present on the horizontal plane simultaneously: an upper world, a middle world where humans reside, and the lower world of the dead; three zones which correspond to air, land and water.[8]

Eamhain Mhacha was identified at an early stage as a place that belonged to the moon goddess and to the otherworld. 'Recent research on the Palaeolithic and Neolithic eras supports Briffault's argument, suggesting that the Moon's role in the evolution of the human mind was older and more pervasive than anyone had imagined'.[9] A Cogul painting that dates to c30,000 BCE featured nine women who collectively formed a crescent while dancing around a young ithyphallic male. The nine figures symbolised the three distinct visible lunar phases. The oldest woman had a full moon face. The image was perhaps the first documented image

---

6 M Eliade, *Shamanism: Archaic Techniques of Ecstasy* (Princeton, 1972) 95.

7 M J Harner, *The Way of the Shaman* (San Francisco, 1990) 21.

8 Jordon, 'Material culture and Landscape', 99–100.

9 J Cashford, *The Moon: Myth and Image* (London, 2003) 16.

of the infinite cosmic dance. The moon circuits the earth nine times during each phase,[10] which may explain the later religious importance of the numbers three and nine. 'The moon became the prime symbol of the Mother Goddess everywhere'.[11]

Early moon lore, seemingly, became part of Ireland's ancient spiritual traditions. Many Irish goddesses appear to have displayed lunar characteristics. The *Mór-Ríoghan*'s facets may well be Macha, Nemain, and Badbh.[12] The *Mór-Ríoghan* was a triple goddess, whose relationship to death, prophesy, fate[13] and fecundity[14] indicated her moon status. 'The moon, however, simply because she is mistress of all living things and sure guise of the dead, has 'woven' all destinies [...] And the moon is the inexhaustible creator of all living forms'.[15] In primordial times, religious values were placed on the moon's course.[16] Women's special relationship with the moon mysteries[17] meant that early matriarchal societies revered the great moon goddess.[18] 'The Palaeolithic Goddess of Laussel, whose waxing crescent horn matching her waxing womb',[19] implied a relationship between this deity's fertility and the moon. The moon's cycle displayed the universal law of birth and death. The constant return to its beginnings and its rhythmic cycle meant that the moon was

---

10 B Johnson, *Lady of the Beasts: Ancient Images of the Goddess and her Sacred Animals* (Cambridge, 1988) 322.

11 B G Walker, *The Woman's Dictionary of Symbols and Sacred Objects* (New York, 1988) 344.

12 J MacKillop, *Dictionary of Celtic Mythology* (Oxford, 1998) 297.

13 M Gimbutas, *The Living Goddesses*, M R Dexter (ed), (Berkeley, 1999) 186.

14 M J Green, *Celtic Goddesses: Warriors, Virgins and Mothers* (London, 1995) 79.

15 M Eliade, *Patterns in Comparative Religion* (Lincoln, 1996) 181.

16 *Ibid*, 154.

17 Johnson, *Lady of the Beasts*, 87.

18 Cashford, *The Moon*, 20.

19 *Ibid*, 202.

the definitive heavenly body aligned with the phases of life.[20]

The *Mór-Ríoghan*'s alteration from radiant young woman to hag[21] reflected the maiden, mother and crone, a triad of many Irish goddesses.[22] The *Mór-Ríoghan*'s powers of prediction[23] allied her to lunar fate goddesses.[24] The *Mór-Ríoghan*'s title 'Great Queen'[25] may relate to her role as queen of heaven. Inanna was described as queen of heaven and earth; as the former she was the moon.[26] The fundamental harmony between the moon and the earth was envisaged during the palaeolithic era.[27] Once the powers of the moon were established in the human mind, links were made between all the moon-influenced phenomena.[28] 'It would seem that the Moon was expected to provide rain, dew, fertilization, conception, easy childbirth, growth for children, animals, and plants, food from hunting, long life, inspiration for poets, immortality [...]'.[29] Particular feminine deities, such as the *Mór-Ríoghan*, possessed enormous power in pre-Christian times,[30] possibly due to the moon's perceived great influence upon the landscape. The *Mór-Ríoghain* was the most fully developed of the Irish goddesses both in the Ulster Cycle and in the Mythological Cycle. This 'phantom queen'[31] was poised between the world of humans and the world of

---

20 Eliade, *Patterns in Comparative Religion*, 154.

21 J MacKillop, *Dictionary of Celtic Mythology* (Oxford, 1998) 297.

22 D Ó hÓgáin, *Myth, Legend and Romance: An Encyclopaedia of the Irish Folk Tradition* (London, 1990) 60.

23 P G Jestice, *Encyclopaedia of Irish Spirituality* (Santa Barbara, 2000) 239.

24 Cashford, *The Moon*, 256.

25 MacKillop, *Dictionary of Celtic Mythology*, 297.

26 *Ibid*, 25.

27 *Ibid*, 20–21.

28 *Ibid*, 9.

29 *Ibid*, 274.

30 R Clark, *The Great Queens: Irish Goddesses from the Morrígan to Cathleen Ní Houlihan* (Gerrards Cross, 1991) 193.

31 Green, *Celtic Goddesses*, 43.

spirits,[32] just as the shaman stood between the physical and psyschic worlds.

The *Mór-Ríoghan*'s partner, the *Daghdha*,[33] was a triple deity,[34] and a god of the otherworld.[35] The *Daghdha*'s partnership with a lunar goddess, the *Mór-Ríoghan*, implied that the *Daghdha* was also a divinity of the moon, hence the horned god. The horned god personified regeneration,[36] as did the moon.[37] The *Daghdha* was an underworld deity.[38] Death, the dead and fertility had previously been under the moon's sway.[39] 'Even in the Ice Age the meaning of the moon's phases and their magic powers were clearly known'.[40]

Originally, shamanism was a moon-centred system that focused on the moon goddess[41] and a horned figure. Such themes were apparent in pre-historic times. The 'sorcerer' from Trois-Frères in France is an upright character with legs and hands that appear human, the back and ears of a herbivore, reindeer antlers and a horse-tail.[42] The Chauvet cave, also in France, contains images that are 30,000 years old. One work portrays a figure with a bison head and torso and the legs of a human.[43] Later, the horned god paralleled the European Cernunnos, a human figure wearing

---

32 *Ibid*, 77.

33 Ó hÓgáin, *Myth, Legend and Romance*, 307.

34 *Ibid*, 146.

35 T F O'Rahilly, *Early Irish History and Mythology* (Dublin, 1946) 470.

36 Gimbutas, *The Living Goddesses*, 181–182.

37 Cashford, *The Moon*, 15.

38 M Dillon and N K Chadwick, *The Celtic Realms*, 2nd edn (London, 1972) 139.

39 Cashford, *The Moon*, 8.

40 Eliade, *Patterns in Comparative Religion*, 154.

41 J Maringer, *The Gods of Prehistoric Man* (London, 1960) 113.

42 S J Mithen, *The Prehistory of the Mind: A Search for the Origins of Art, Religion, and Science* (London, 1998) 186.

43 *Ibid*, 187.

antlers, with a stag nearby.[44] There are fragmented hints that the early Irish revered the fertility god, Cernunnos, whose cult was well established on the Continent.[45] A triple Cernunnos figure was identified in Romania.[46] Abundant evidence of the horned god appeared in early Irish sculpture.[47]

Shamanic ecstasy was documented in the palaeolithic era.[48] 'Shamanism is a general term that refers to a complex set of beliefs, practices, institutions, objects etc. associated with religious specialists who control techniques of ecstasy and trance'.[49] The moon was used by shamans as an ecstatic agent.[50] The *Fianna* navigated with ease through the natural and the supernatural worlds, engaging constantly with the underground realm; their marginal status promoted their communion with the paranormal, presumably through ecstatic means.[51] An altered state of consciousness that was related to vision, prophecy or madness was called in Irish *baile*, or *buile*.[52]

Spirituality that was allied to the invisible worlds almost certainly has been present as long as there have been communities of humans.[53] Shamanic methods are at least 20,000 – 30,000 years

---

44 Ó hÓgáin, *Myth, Legend and Romance*, 155.

45 Jestice, *Encyclopaedia of Irish Spirituality*, 137.

46 A Ross, *Pagan Celtic Britain: Studies in Iconography and Tradition*, Rev. edn (London, 1992) 133.

47 B Smith, *The Horse in Ireland* (Dublin,1991) 43.

48 M Eliade, *A History of Religious Ideas. Volume One, From the Stone Age to the Eleusinian Mysteries* (London, 1979) 24.

49 J G Oosten, 'The Diary of Therkel Mathiassen [1922–1923]', 377–390 in M Hoppál (ed), *Shamanism in Eurasia, Part 2* (Göttingen, c1984) at p 377.

50 Cashford, *The Moon*, 287.

51 P MacCana, *Celtic Mythology* (Feltham, 1970) 109.

52 B Maier, *Dictionary of Celtic Religion and Culture* (Woodbridge, 1997) 30.

53 Eliade, *History of Religious Ideas*, Volume One, 9.

old.[54] In Ireland, various hallowed sites were identified by mesolithic hunter-gather communities,[55] tribes who probably utilised a form of shamanism.[56] The moon's cycles must have been implicated in early Irish mesolithic mythic ceremony.[57] Many monuments in Ireland are located in exactly the same general areas that must have been habitually exploited by the mesolithic populations.[58] 'The overall distribution of Mesolithic sites and Neolithic burial chambers is complementary rather than exclusive'.[59] The close association of royal sites with neolithic burial mounds was a notable feature and this argues for a strong continuity within the native Irish tradition. Megaliths[60] and natural hills[61] were regarded by the Irish as otherworld dwellings.

Shamanism involves a spiritual interactive communication between the practitioner and the environment,[62] based on the belief that there is another reality apart from this one,[63] with the belief that the psychic three worlds, upper, middle and lower, exist in partnership.[64] The early Irish shared these sentiments. In the neolithic phase, liminal sites, spiritual locales, lakes, rivers, mountain summits and caverns were where otherworld encounters occurred:[65] locations that could be allied to the three shamanic zones.

---

54 Harner, *Way of the Shaman*, 40.

55 Tilley, *A Phenomenology of Landscape*, 87.

56 S Piggott, *The Druids* (London, 1968) 184–185.

57 D Ó hÓgáin, *The Sacred Isle: Belief and Religion in Early Ireland* (Cork, 1999) 6.

58 Tilley, *A Phenomenology of Landscape*, 87.

59 *Ibid*, 87.

60 Mac Cana, *Celtic Mythology*, 64.

61 Ó hÓgáin, *Myth, Legend and Romance*, 206.

62 Harner, *Way of the Shaman*, XIII.

63 F Huxley, *The Way of the Sacred* (London, 1974) 253.

64 Jordan, *Material Culture and Sacred Landscape*, 100.

65 G Cooney, *Landscapes of Neolithic Ireland* (London, 2000) 89.

The three ages of woman equated to the three visible phases of the moon, phases identified in the sovereignty goddess, the feminine element in Irish mythology, who personified Ireland, as either a beautiful young girl or an ugly hag.[66] The *Mór-Rhíoghan* was a sovereignty goddess,[67] a war goddess,[68] and a liminal figure.[69] One of the enormous critical themes of the Irish past was the sovereignty goddess.[70] Sacred marriage was a neolithic practice.[71] In preliminary myths, the sovereignty goddess assumed the primordial place as the goddess of the island, the spirit of the land.[72] '[I]n the West the Palaeolithic, Neolithic and Bronze Age Mother goddesses are all Moon goddesses as well as Earth goddesses'.[73] Where the realm was envisaged anthropomorphically as a female deity, she represented the earth and the matter of the region, and the religious and lawful authority which the monarch ruled over: his dominion.[74] 'The land remained sacred and inalienable, and the dominance of the Sovereignty, a territorial goddess, is seen in this attachment to the land itself'.[75] The first existing redactions of Niall of the Nine Hostages and the sovereignty goddess were associated with the early fifth century,[76] a concept that endured in Ireland until the sixteenth century.[77]

---

66 P Mac Cana, 'Mythology in Early Irish Literature', 143–154 in R O'Driscoll (ed), *The Celtic Consciousness* (Portlaoise, 1982) at p 152–153.

67 MacKillop, *Dictionary of Celtic Mythology*, 345.

68 Green, *Celtic Goddesses*, 79.

69 *Ibid*, 41.

70 G Ó Crualaoich, *The Book of the Cailleach: Stories of the Wise-Woman Healer* (Cork, 2003) 87.

71 Gimbutas, *Living Goddesses*, 18.

72 Green, *Celtic Goddesses*, 70.

73 Cashford, *The Moon*, 152.

74 Mac Cana, *Celtic Mythology*, 94.

75 Clark, *The Great Queens*, 200.

76 Green, *Celtic Goddesses*, 84.

77 Clark, *The Great Queens*, 5.

The goddess and the spirit-world influence upon the physical world, fertility and abundance were highlighted by the rite of sacred marriage.[78] The union of the female spirit of a territory and the human ruler was believed to bring prosperity to the land.[79] 'The idea that Ireland is a goddess, and is wedded to the king of the country, is of hoary antiquity; yet it has preserved its vitality down, one might almost say, to our own day'.[80] Macha was an aspect of the *Mór-Rhíoghan*,[81] a triple lunar deity.[82] Macha presided over life, fertility, death, rebirth, war, prophecy and sovereignty.[83] Kings as sacred individuals, holding a sacred position,[84] were traditionally inaugurated on mounds. In various cosmologies, the mountain that was in the hub of the earth was viewed as the font of the world's rivers. The centre was represented by a mountain, a pillar, a fire-altar, a tree, and the well of life.[85] The centre played a crucial role in the ideology and the techniques of shamanism. Hubs were formerly thought to have potent supernatural forces. Centres were aligned with a primeval time; a time when communication between earth and heaven, humans and the divinities was easy and accessible to all.[86] If worship involved the three shamanic worlds that were represented by a sacred hill, a ritual lake and an oak post, then it is suggested that a shamanic model once operated at Eamhain Mhacha. An otherworld locale, Eamhain Mhacha was almost certainly used to engage divine forces. The shamans believed that

78 Ó hÓgáin, *The Sacred Isle*, 157.

79 D A Binchy, 'The Fair of Tailtiu and the Feast of Tara', *Ériu* 18 (1958) 113–138, at p 134–135.

80 T F O'Rahilly, 'On the Origin of the Names Érainn and Ériu', *Ériu* 14 (1946) 7–28, at p 14.

81 Green, *Celtic Goddesses*, 69–70.

82 *Ibid*, 42.

83 *Ibid*, 79.

84 G MacNiocaill, *Ireland Before the Vikings* (Dublin, 1972) 44.

85 A D Rees, and B Rees, *Celtic Heritage: Ancient Tradition in Ireland and Wales* (London, 1961) 160.

86 Eliade, *Shamanism*, 492.

they could enter the otherworld by attaining an ecstatic state, then climbing a pole to the otherworld.[87] The pillar was a sign of the great mother.[88] The moon could be linked to the world tree.[89] Shamanic funerary beliefs involve the mountain, the tree of life, the island paradise with the cosmology relating to the three cosmic zones, the world axis, the cosmic tree, and the seven heavens.[90] Sacred space acts as the hub of the world, a special locale which allows human communication with the upper and lower worlds, the divinities, underworld goddesses, and the spirits of the dead.[91]

Ceremonial enclosures such as Eamhain Mhacha were the settings for supernatural encounters. These places were otherworld hubs, where the psychic and human worlds converged. Despite the diverse designations and locations that were attributed to the pagan Irish otherworld, there was but one ultimate otherworld realm.[92] The normal site for the revelation of wisdom, so the poets thought, was the water's edge.[93] Eamhain Mhacha was another liminal place of revelation.

Eamhain Mhacha is encircled by a single ditch and a bank: that is where any superficial resemblance to a standard iron age hill-fort ends. The bank is outside and below the ditch. This makes no defensive sense.[94] The ditch that encircled Eamhain Mhacha formed an island-like supernatural space.[95] Virtually all the ceremonial monuments constructed in Ireland between 3000 and 1500 BCE

---

87 P Jordon, 'The Materiality of Shamanism as a "world-view": Praxis, Artefacts and Landscape', 87–104 in N S Price (ed), *The Archaeology of Shamanism* (London, 2001) at pp 101–102.

88 E Neumann, *The Great Mother: An Analysis of the Archetype* (Princeton,1991) 49.

89 Cashford, *The Moon*, 227.

90 Eliade, *Shamanism*, 283.

91 Eliade, *A History of Religious Ideas*, 117–118.

92 O'Rahilly, *Early Irish History*, 481.

93 Ó hÓgáin, *The Sacred Isle*, 76.

94 Pryor, *Britain BC*, 371.

95 *Ibid*, 373.

were circles of one kind or another.[96] The circle was a symbol of the moon.[97] 'Circles appear to be intended to mark off a sacred area or area of power'.[98] Tara, Eamhain Mhacha, and Dún Ailinne, all with an internal ditch and earthen ramparts, were sites of pre-Christian ritual.[99] Dún Ailinne, Rathgall and Eamhain Mhacha all offer evidence of great wooded circular buildings, extending over 30 metres in span. These sites were doubtless ceremonial, temples rather than dwellings.[100] Tara, Knockaulin in County Kildare, and other locales were not protective, but instead ritual in character. Tara over many centuries acted as a ceremonial hub, and into historical times its iconic import remained, hosting royal inaugurations. Eamhain Mhacha and Tara were both sites that were allied with an important mythological cycle.[101] 'The sacred place was a way of entry into that world, by a descent into the earth, an ascent into the sky, or a journey beneath the water.'[102] '[A] shaman typically has a special hole or entrance into the Lowerworld, that exists in ordinary and non-ordinary reality'.[103]

Sacred venues hosted sacred assemblies at sacred times of the annual wheel. The rituals that were conducted at such places were preformed for the benefit of the whole society.[104] Ireland's major assemblies were held at different seasons of the agrarian round, at sites of confirmed holiness. Assemblies were among the most

---

96 R Bradley, *The Significance of Monuments: on the Shaping of Human Experience in Neolithic and Bronze Age Europe* (London, 1998) 132.

97 Walker, *The Woman's Dictionary*, 4.

98 W L Brenneman Jr and M G Brenneman, *Crossing the Circle at the Holy Wells of Ireland* (Charlottesville, 1995) 67.

99 Jestice, *Encyclopaedia of Irish Spirituality*, 298–299.

100 M Herity, *Studies in the Layout, Buildings and Art in Stone of Early Irish Monasteries* (London, 1995) 171.

101 F Mitchell and M Ryan, *Reading the Irish Landscape* (Dublin, 1997) 241.

102 H R Ellis Davidson, *Myths and Symbols in Pagan Europe: Early Scandinavian and Celtic Religions* (Manchester, 1988) 224.

103 Harner, *The Way of the Shaman*, 24–25.

104 Rees, *Celtic Heritage*, 168.

crucial aspects of the spiritual and the secular life of early Ireland.[105] Eamhain Mhacha was the seat of the kings of the *Ulaidh*, modern Ulster, and the centre of the province.[106] Cosmic renewal, rebirth, was a theme that lay behind these Irish holy festivals.[107] The festival of renewal was thought to provide a break with the existing order, interrupting profane, historical time so that primordial mythic time was restored.[108]

The *Daghdha* and the *Mór-Rhíoghan* shared the symbolism of *Samhain*, the meeting of order and chaos which lead to the rebirth of order.[109] The union, at *Samhain*, of the *Mór-Rhíohgan* and the *Daghdha* mirrored the actual king's sacred marriage with the goddess,[110] an act that occurred at Eamhain Mhacha[111] during this festival,[112] with a white horse;[113] the horse personified the feminine divine. The shaman, too, had a spirit wife and a semi-divine status. Spirit helpers were allied with shamans as were their spirit wives.[114] The ruler and the shaman both married in an otherworld tree top, or temple, with the powers of earth and heaven forming a unity.[115] In contemporary Siberian shamanism, the tutelary spirit, who is also considered to be a divine wife or husband, performs a crucial

105 R A S MacAlister, *The Secret Languages of Ireland: With Special Reference to the Origin and Nature of the Shelta Language* (Armagh, 1997) 13.

106 A Ross, 'Ritual and the Druids' 423–444 in M J Green (ed), *The Celtic World* (London, 1995) at p 435.

107 P MacCana, 'The Sinless Otherworld of Immram Brain', *Ériu* 27 (1976) 95–115, at p 109.

108 *Ibid*, 27–28.

109 A Gray, 'Cath Maige Tuired: Myth and Structure [84–93, 120–67]', *Éigse* 19 (1982–83) 230–262, at p 239.

110 J Davies, *The Celts* (London, 2000) 86.

111 MacNiocaill, *Ireland Before the Vikings*, 44.

112 Ross, *Ritual and the Druids*, 435.

113 Giraldus Cambrensis, *Topographia Hiberniae* trans J J O'Meara, '*The History and Topography of Ireland*' rev ed (Portlaoise, 1982) 93–94.

114 Ross, *Ritual and the Druids*, 435.

115 Huxley, *The Way of the Sacred*, 259.

function. The 'feminine' tutelary spirits provide the helping-spirits who are so essential to the human's ecstatic voyages.[116] Irish kings' origin was thought to be of divine descent. The shaman is a semi-divine figure, an individual who can reputedly ecstatically access the realm of the divinities, and while in that world, share the deities' powers, such as flying.[117]

The Irish delineated the festivals by their eves,[118] hence echoing matriarchal time. Time duration was established by nights.[119] In measuring time, the early Irish gave primacy to the night. The darkness of the night preceded the light of the day: this order reflected an important idea for the early Irish, that the light of day succeeds the darkness and the night in taking possession of the world, and that this order is eternally ordained.[120] The goddess in Irish tradition was the otherworld sentinel.[121] *Samhain*, strongly death-aligned, was especially liminal, being placed between the old and the new year, at a moment outside of time, when the barriers between the spiritual and the earthly worlds were absent.[122] For all primal communities, the purpose of creating a calendar was sacred. Eventually calendars allowed for the delineation of hallowed points of the year and festivals.[123] *Samhain*, for the Irish, was a time of divination, inauguration, public assembly and feasting.[124] *Samhain* was a time when deities and humans could easily move between the worlds.[125] In shamanism, the seasonal festivals honoured the deities

116 Eliade, *Shamanism*, 80–81.

117 Harner, *Way of the Shaman*, 47.

118 A Ross, *Everyday Life of the Pagan Celts* (London, 1970) 153.

119 Cashford, *The Moon*, 42.

120 Ó hÓgáin, *The Sacred Isle*, 109.

121 Green, *Celtic Goddesses*, 85.

122 Jestice, *Encyclopaedia of Irish Spirituality*, 312.

123 Cashford, *The Moon*, 44.

124 K Danaher, 'Irish Folk Tradition and the Celtic Calendar', 217–242 in R O'Driscoll (ed), *The Celtic Consciousness* (Portlaoise, 1982) at p 219.

125 Ross, *Ritual and the Druids*, 434.

by the sacrifice of animals, and honoured the unseen world with gifts.[126] Such activities seemingly occurred at Eamhain Mhacha.

The old Irish goddesses were tied to particular places.[127] In the pre-Christian phase, each tribe had a goddess who was the partner to the clan king, such as Macha in Ulster. The sovereignty goddess and the ancestral goddess were one.[128] Macha was the patron of Ulster kingship,[129] and she gave her name to present day Armagh, *Ard Mhacha*.[130] Macha's name is thought to mean a field or a plain.[131] This name emphasised Macha's role of embodying the land. Macha forged the boundaries of her fort with a pin taken from her brooch,[132] established the Ulster royal seat of Eamhain Mhacha and died at Eamhain Mhacha.[133] The goddess Macha had equine aspects and she raced the king's horses, and in doing so she died, in childbirth, giving birth to twins.[134] The *óenach* at Eamhain Mhacha was reputedly established in Macha's honour.[135] Just prior to the historical period *óenach n-Emna* [or O Macha], the great fair of the *Ulaidh*, was possibly the most significant assembly of its kind.[136]

Most of the female founders of Ireland, Macha, Cessair, Tailtiu, Carmun and Tlachtga, all met untimely or disturbing deaths,[137]

---

126 Jordan, *Material Culture and Sacred Landscape*, 145.

127 M Condren, *The Serpent and the Goddess: Women, Religion, and Power in Celtic Ireland* (New York, 1989) 50.

128 Clark, *The Great Queens*, 149.

129 D Ó hÓgáin, *Myth, Legend and Romance: An Encyclopaedia of the Irish Folk Tradition* (London, 1990) 284.

130 Condren, *The Serpent and the Goddess*, 30.

131 Jestice, *Encyclopaedia of Irish Spirituality*, 215.

132 Condren, *The Serpent and the Goddess*, 67.

133 Green, *Celtic Goddesses*, 41.

134 Ó hÓgáin, *Myth, Legend and Romance*, 326.

135 Ross, *Ritual and the Druids*, 435.

136 D A Binchy, 'The Fair of Tailtiu and the Feast of Tara', *Ériu* 18 (1958) 113–138, at p 126.

137 Rees and Rees, *Celtic Heritage*, 167.

which may suggest that there had been in early Ireland a clash of cultures, with patriarchy ultimately triumphing over matriarchy. In the *Lebor Gabála*, the landscape, mounds, promontories, lakes, hills and plains acquired names and importance through links with the lives, deaths and interments of mythical figures. An emphasis was placed on the initial event that occurred at a site, such as the first death.[138] The goddesses as implied by the place-names were more intimately aligned with the landscape than were the gods. Names of locations, usually ancient and infrequently altered, were often conserved from primal times, and even from earlier cultures.[139] Female deities may originally have been paramount in Ireland.[140] The mythic Ulster king, Conchobhar, was called by the name of his mother, mac Neasa.[141]

The shaman and the druid were seemingly sacred figures, with sacred roles which operated in the sacred landscape, as did the king. In shamanism, 'Karjalinen described how the terms assigned to holy places were made up of the place itself [eg land, place, lake, river, hill, etc], and a term best translated as *heilig* [German: holy/ sacred]'.[142] The word used by the Gauls for a centre of druidic ritual was *nemeton*, a word that appears in Irish in the form *neimheadh* and had the meaning 'sacred place'.[143] 'Religious belief is enacted through rituals'.[144]

Hill-top enclosures had a ceremonial role in early Ireland.[145] Eamhain Mhacha, the early capital of Ulster,[146] was primarily a

---

138 *Ibid*, 105.

139 Clark, *The Great Queens*, 190–191.

140 J Davies, *The Celts*, 82.

141 T P Cross and C H Slover (eds), *Ancient Irish Tales* (Dublin, 1973) 132.

142 Jordan, *Material Culture and Sacred Landscape*, 145.

143 Ó hÓgáin, *Myth, Legend and Romance*, 169.

144 G Cooney, *Landscapes of Neolithic Ireland* (London, 2000) 88.

145 Pryor, *Britain BC*, 366.

146 B Raftery, *Pagan Celtic Ireland: the Enigma of the Irish Iron Age* (London, 1994) 14.

ritual site. Located upon a drumlin in County Armagh,[147] and inhabited during the neolithic era,[148] Eamhain Mhacha was possibly considered sacred at an earlier time.

For the early Irish, the physical liminal landscape was alive with spirits, and embodied the creator, the great moon mother.[149] The early Irish thought that female powers resided in ponds, springs, streams, swamps, earth, hills, mountains and cliffs, and the dead in the underworld.[150] Every significant area in pagan Ireland possessed its own otherworld hill.[151] Liminal places were associated with pagan supernatural beings,[152] sites where humans could, through ritual specialists, contact and commune with the divine forces.[153] In Ireland, an engagement of the human imagination with the geography occurred.[154] In Irish myth, gods live individually either underground or on distant islands across the sea, occasionally in caves or more often in the prehistoric tombs of the ancient dead chieftains.[155] The most famous of these tombs is *Bruig na Bóinne.*[156]

Early accounts of mortal visits to otherworld places are fairly plentiful. Otherworld beings are depicted as living within hills beneath lakes or under the sea or on islands in lakes, or off the coast. There are also tales of halls chanced upon in the night which

---

147 C J Lynn, 'Navan Fort', in S Moscati, E A Arslan and D Vitali (eds),*The Celts* (London, 1991) at p 610.

148 Jestice, *Encyclopaedia of Irish Spirituality*, 123.

149 *Ibid*, 14.

150 Neumann, *The Great Mother*, 259.

151 O'Rahilly, *Early Irish History and Mythology*, 290.

152 Green, *Celtic Goddesses*, 199.

153 Ó hÓgáin, *The Sacred Isle*, 76.

154 G Ó Crualaoich, *The Book of the Cailleach: Stories of the Wise-Woman Healer* (Cork, 2003) 3.

155 M Dillon and N K Chadwick, *The Celtic Realms,* 2nd edn (London, 1972) 137.

156 *Ibid*, 138.

vanish with the coming of day.[157] 'It is this underlying belief in the unity of the otherworld and the world of the dead that connects the various magical powers such as clairvoyance, healing, spell-casting associated with female power-figures'.[158] In the minds of the Irish, the paranormal sphere was a sacred realm manifested in the physical world. Knowledge, fecundity and rebirth were all sourced in the mystical, and its fundamental feminine force was identified with the land.[159]

For the Khanty, '[o]bjects thought to be animate include people, animals, trees, water [flowing in the river], falling snow, fire, wind, and thunder as well as supernatural beings, even though they are not visible'.[160] For the Hopi, all of nature was a hidden non-ordinary reality.[161] For the early Irish, the otherworld was the psychic aspect of this world, the unseen dimension that was present in all nature. The sacred was ever-present. The otherworld could be under the ocean or a lake, within a hill, an island, the land of the dead, the abode of the deities, or a mystical realm with a great tree. The otherworld could be located in *sídh* [mounds], within a well, beneath pools or in rivers.[162] 'Thus, the surface world is a reflection of the otherworld.'[163] The landscape, animate with the unseen world of spirit virtually imperceptible to mortals, was a constant presence in the life of the tribe.[164] Eamhain Mhacha was an otherworld site.

The oak was regarded as a protector of all that inhabited it, a

---

157 J Carey, 'The Location of the Otherworld in Irish Tradition', *Éigse* 19 (1982–83) 36–43, at p 39–41.

158 W J Mahon, 'The *Aisling* Elegy and the Poets' Appropriation of the Feminine', *Studia Celtica* 34 (2000) 249–270, at p 264.

159 Brenneman and Brenneman, *Crossing the Circle at the Holy Wells of Ireland*, 25.

160 Jordan, *Material Culture and Sacred Landscape*, 103.

161 Harner, *The Way of the Shaman*, 54–55.

162 Ross, *Ritual and the Druids*, 441.

163 Brenneman and Brenneman, *Crossing the Circle at the Holy Wells of Ireland*, 25.

164 Jestice, *Encyclopaedia of Irish Spirituality*, 14.

tree that symbolised the rightful king's rule. The legitimate king would enable the terrain to flourish.[165] The oak was also sacred to the *Daghdha*,[166] and the oak was a tree that was associated with the druids.[167] The druids, priests or wise men of ancient times, believed that trees were sources of sacred wisdom. The religious leaders believed that sacred trees were no longer just trees. Trees became the embodiment of spirit.[168] The druids controlled the boundaries between the physical world and the spiritual world, and this role gave the druids a central position.[169]

At the beginning of a new phase at Eamhain Mhacha in 94 BCE, a large oak post was erected in the centre of an area that was enclosed by the outer ring-ditch and earlier ring-ditch. Around the post were six concentric rings that were arranged at intervals of around two meters and joined by lengths of planking. This edifice may or may not have been roofed.[170] Two hundred and seventy-five timber posts formed the concentric rings that surrounded this oak.[171] The central post was around 13 meters in height, and two rows of posts outlined the track towards it. This place was certainly a temple.[172] The great 40-metre round wooden structure at Eamhain Mhacha, destroyed by burning in 95 or 94 BCE, suggested druidic activity and ritual on an unprecedented scale. The oak post was the last item to be erected and it was aligned to the aisle of the great wooden edifice. The post acted as a world tree at the sacred heart of Ulster around which the universe turned.[173] The tree can be

165 N MacCoiter, *Irish Trees: Myths, Legends and Folklore* (Cork, 2003) 195.

166 *Ibid*, 65.

167 Ó hÓgáin, *The Sacred Isle*, 93.

168 D Hickie, *Native Trees and Forests of Ireland* (Dublin, 2002) 31.

169 Ó hÓgáin, *The Sacred Isle*, 111.

170 Pryor, *Britain BC*, 374.

171 Jestice, *Encyclopaedia of Irish Spirituality*, 123.

172 Mitchell and Ryan, *Reading the Irish Landscape*, 241.

173 J Campbell, 'The Aesthetic and Intellectual Foundations of the Celtic Literary Revival in Ireland', 401–426 in R O'Driscoll (ed), *The Celtic*

imagined as a symbol of the universe.[174]

Since the palaeolithic phase, the oak has been considered a sacred life-giving tree.[175] The moon was allied with trees, including the tree of life.[176] The cosmic pillar, the tree of life,[177] and the mound were all icons of the moon goddess,[178] and each personified the three shamanic worlds. The ceremonial post or tree was perhaps used by ecstatic experts as a vehicle to reach and to influence the divine forces. The most potent icon, lasting over a great period of time, appeared to be that of a huge tree or pillar joining the upper and lower worlds. A recognition that the way to access the otherworld was through the landscape's natural features was a foundation of religious conviction.[179] To create a sanctuary, an enormous amount of human effort was required.[180] On all matters of importance, those professionally trained in the conduct of religious affairs, the druids, were consulted.[181]

Chris Lynn stated that this structure at Eamhain Mhacha was laid out so as to equate the spaces between the rings with the spaces between the posts of the outer wall, and the width of each of the three aisles of the ambulatory. The design paralleled the precision in alignment and layout of Newgrange. Shortly after the erection of the structure at Eamhain Mhacha, the timbers were buried beneath a stone cairn which was constructed in segments that radiated from the central post, deliberately. The wheel of stones was white and it was buried under a mound of earth. There probably were never any

---

Consciousness (Portlaoise, 1982) at p 406.

174 M Eliade, *Patterns in Comparative Religion*, 269.

175 Ó hÓgáin, *The Sacred Isle*, 93.

176 Cashford, *The Moon*, 226–227.

177 Neumann, *The Great Mother*, 49.

178 *Ibid*, 260.

179 Ellis Davidson, *Myths and Symbols in Pagan Europe*, 224.

180 Green, *Dying for the Gods*, 71.

181 Raftery, *Pagan Celtic Ireland*, 179.

dwellings of the rich and powerful at Eamhain Mhacha.[182]

Ancient burial mounds retained their status as places of inauguration and ceremony into the medieval period.[183] The names of royal sanctified hilltops used feminine nouns.[184] The corporeal heart of a *tuath* was often centred around a mound, with a *bile* (sacred tree), a holy stone and a revered well, all aspects that formed the overall complex.[185] Continuity is one of the striking features of Irish prehistory in some aspects of the archaeological record,[186] and over long periods of time. Eamhain Mhacha showed the involvement of myth with the ritual landscape.[187] There were links between the sacred space of the monuments and the landscape features.[188] 'Sacred landscape is the term to describe an apparent closeness between the spheres of sacred and profane, or spiritual and mundane. It is an all-pervading sense of sacred presence – a sense that the divine is near to everyday lives and actions'.[189] The entire surrounding land of Eamhain Mhacha was devoted to ceremony. This locale hosted cult activities that occurred outdoors at liminal places: rivers, lakes and bogs figuring prominently in the ritual complex.[190]

Shamanic beliefs influenced the monuments that were created in Ireland, and why they were created. Near Eamhain Mhacha there are two destroyed stone circles or megalithic tombs, Loughnashade

182 Pryor, *Britain BC*, 376–377.

183 Raftery, *Pagan Celtic Ireland*, 180.

184 H Wagner, 'Studies in the Origins of Early Celtic Traditions', *Ériu*, 26 (1975) 1–26, at p 19.

185 Brenneman, *Crossing the Circle*, 24.

186 G Cooney, and E Grogan, *Irish Prehistory: A Social Perspective,* 2nd edn (Dublin, 1999) 207.

187 Pryor, *Britain BC*, 380.

188 R Bradley, *The Significance of Monuments: on the Shaping of Human Experience in Neolithic and Bronze Age Europe* (London, 1998) 145.

189 Jestice, *Encyclopaedia of Irish Spirituality*, 306.

190 B Raftery, 'The Island Celts', 555–572 in Moscati, Arslan and Vitali, *The Celts*, at p 559.

and The King's Stables, all ceremonial otherworld sites.[191] 'A votive and, perhaps, sacrificial deposit, comprising four magnificent horns decorated with late La Téne patterns and accompanied by human skulls, was recovered from Loughnashade, a lough which in all probability was connected with the nearby royal and sacred stronghold of Emain Macha'.[192] A partial human skull was formally placed in the King's Stables, a late bronze-age ceremonial pool,[193] along with bones such as dog[194] and stag antlers,[195] both moon-aligned animals.[196]

The symbolism of the deer stretched deep into the upper palaeolithic period. Antlers held iconic power, for they epitomised renewal.[197] The moon and the deer formed a relationship of reciprocal symbolism.[198] 'Animals can stand as metaphors for aspects of the human condition and can be used by people both as symbolic negotiators with the spirit world and as a means of expressing the relationship between earthly and otherworld dimensions'.[199]

The ancestors' cult possibly inspired the votive deposits at the Eamhain Mhacha complex, with the dead launched into the otherworld via liminal locations. Assemblies at the top of hills that hosted burial sites were partly influenced by the draw of ancestral spirits.[200] In early Ireland, there was a strong tradition of people attempting to contact the dead by entering an ecstatic state or going

---

191 Lynn, *Navan Fort*, 610.

192 Ross, *Ritual and the Druids*, 441.

193 Cooney and Grogan, *Irish Prehistory*, 214.

194 Johnson, *Lady of the Beasts*, 114.

195 *Ibid*, 218.

196 Cashford, *The Moon*, 98.

197 Gimbutas, *The Living Goddesses*, 13.

198 M Gimbutas, *The Civilization of the Goddess: the World of Old Europe* (San Francisco, 1991) 172–4.

199 Green, *Dying for the Gods*, 41.

200 E E Evans, *Irish Folkways* (London, 1957) 283.

to tombs,[201] such as Eamhain Mhacha, that represented the ancestors. '[R]espect for the dead as sources of otherworld knowledge is found in Irish sources.'[202] The Irish druid-poets willingly continued the reverence that had been accorded, over hundreds of years, to the outstanding funerary monuments, such as Knowth and Eamhain Mhacha. These important religious sites were afforded the same celebrated status that they had enjoyed since the tumuli were first erected.[203] 'A sanctuary was first and foremost a sacred place set apart from the rest of the world.'[204] Sacred hubs such as a mountain, pillar, stone, cave or rock were believed to be the abode of the great mother goddess and her incarnation.[205] 'A tomb, seen as a point of contact between the world of the dead and the living, and of the gods, can also be a "centre", an "*omphalos*" of the earth.'[206]

In Ireland there are indications of the existence of a cult of the ancestors. Sacred places were often set up where early graves had existed, as at Tara.[207] The *Daghdha* was an ancestor divinity for the early Irish,[208] 'The Mighty One of Great Knowledge.'[209] Early Irish myth contained the notion that divinities could travel in deer form.[210] Deer were constantly allied to otherworld beings,[211]

---

201 Ó hÓgáin, *The Sacred Isle*, 106–107.

202 *Ibid*, 106.

203 *Ibid*, 107.

204 J L Brunaux, *The Celtic Gauls: Gods, Rites and Sanctuaries* (London, 1988) 10.

205 Neumann, *The Great Mother*, 260.

206 Eliade, *Patterns in Comparative Religion*, 233.

207 Ellis Davidson, *Myths and Symbols in Pagan Europe*, 127.

208 Ó hÓgáin, *Myth, Legend and Romance*, 145–146.

209 Mac Cana, *Celtic Mythology*, 66.

210 D Ó hÓgáin, *Fionn mac Cumhaill: Images of the Gaelic Hero* (Dublin, 1988) 77.

211 *Ibid*, 80.

such as the *Mór-Ríoghan*,[212] and the *Daghdha*.[213] *Táin Bó Cúailgne* makes mention of deer-priests, which may mirror the mythical significance of the horned stag.[214] In Ireland, the horned god's cult was based in ancient Ulster, ranging from Armagh to Lough Erne. Representational proof for the Irish horned god cult includes the Tanderagee statue.[215] The horned god, deity of the shamans, was the Irish god of druidry. The Munster word for sorcerer means Ulsterman. Shamanism, it seems, is always to the north.[216]

Cathbhadh was the best known of the druids and the myths about him give certain clues about the position of druids in Irish society. Cathbhadh appears in tales of the Ulster Cycle as the court druid of Conchobhar mac Neasa. In the early accounts, Cathbhadh is Conchobhar's father. Cathbhadh was, above all, a seer who foretold the fate of infants. Legends depict Cathbhadh as the head of a druid school, which may reflect actual druidic practices.[217] In *Táin Bó Cúailgne*, there was a mystical school based near Eamhain Mhacha that was run by Cathbhad the druid. 'There were with him a hundred active men learning the druid's art — that was the number that Cathbad used to instruct':[218] '*Cét fer ndéinmech dó oc foglaim druídechta úad, is é lín doninchoisced Cathbad*.'[219]

The system of druidic schools in Irish literature was paralleled by the medieval poetic schools, where full training occupied 21 years.[220] The pre-Christian druids were also trained in schools.[221]

212 T P Cross and C H Slover (eds), *Ancient Irish Tales* (Dublin, 1973) 168.

213 MacKillop, *Dictionary of Celtic Mythology*, 63–64.

214 Davies, *The Celts*, 81.

215 Ross, *Pagan Celtic Britain*, 191–192.

216 M C O'Brien, 'The Role of the Poet in Gaelic Society', 243–254 in O'Driscoll, *The Celtic Consciousness*, at p 245.

217 Jestice, *Encyclopaedia of Irish Spirituality*, 56.

218 C O'Rahilly (ed), *Táin bó Cúailnge*, Recension 1 (Dublin, 1976) 19.

219 *Ibid*, 142.

220 Ó hÓgáin, *Myth, Legend and Romance*, 365.

221 A Ross, *Everyday Life of the Pagan Celts* (London, 1970) 127.

An early Irish tradition was the transference of knowledge between sage and student, elder and youth, and the wisdom-bestowing ancestor.[222] For the Kets, a whole initiation cycle of a 'big' shaman is 21 years, composed of three seven-year stages.[223] Shamanic training is protracted and potentially assumes the form of an apprenticeship that lasts for many years under an elder's guidance.[224]

A number of Irish women, mentioned frequently and casually in the early literature, demonstrate that their involvement with poetry and druidry was not unaccustomed, even portrayed like their male counterparts as operating in triads.[225] 'Female practitioners of druidry may have had a separate institutional structure corresponding to priestesses in other ancient traditions.'[226] 'Almost everywhere in Siberia we hear of female shamans [...] Very often [...] in myths the first shaman is a woman or at least is the first human being to receive shamanistic powers.'[227] The female druids of Ireland as portrayed in mythic literature were skilled in the art of prophecy.[228]

Ravens, sacred to the *Mór-Ríoghan* were used by the druids as birds of omen.[229] In shamanism, the raven and the wren were birds of prophecy and augury.[230] The Irish believed that ravens could predict the future, hence the phrase 'the knowledge of the raven's

222 Ó hÓgáin, *The Sacred Isle*, 124.

223 M Hoppál (ed), *Shamanism in Eurasia, Part 1* (Göttingen, 1984) at p 88.

224 R Gilberg, 'How to Recognize a Shaman among Other Religious Specialists?' 21–27 in Hoppál, *Shamanism in Eurasia, Part 1*, at p 25.

225 Ó hÓgáin, *The Sacred Isle*, 96–97.

226 *Ibid*, 97.

227 H Hamayon, 'Is there a Typically Female Exercise of Shamanism in Patrilinear Societies Such as the Buryat?', 307–318 in Hoppál, *Shamanism in Eurasia, Part 2*, at p 307.

228 Green, *Celtic Goddesses*, 140.

229 Ó hÓgáin, *The Sacred Isle*, 75.

230 U Marazzi, 'Remarks on the Siberian Turkic Shaman's Secret Language', 280–285 in Hoppál, *Shamanism in Eurasia, Part 2*, at p 281.

head'.[231] The Irish goddesses shape-shifted at will between raven and female form.[232] The *Mór-Ríoghan* and Badbh could shape-shift into raven form.[233] Cú Chulainn evidently received druidic mysteries from two speaking ravens,[234] birds that may have acted as his spirit guides. Carrion birds appear to have been allied to the lunar deities of divination, death and fate.

The Irish deities, the kings, the druids and the shamans allegedly could shape-shift, influence the physical world through their words, journey to the otherworld, heal, predict the future, and use totemism. All of these aspects can be identified in the Ulster Cycle and in the activities that occurred at the Eamhain Mhacha complex. There were also taboos. '"Your name shall be Cú Chulainn [the Hound of Culann] then", said Cathbad':[235] '"*Bid Cú C[h]ulaind t'ainm-siu íarom," or Cathbad*'.[236] Cú Chulainn's taboo was not to eat his totem animal.[237] Totemism existed in the upper palaeolithic era.[238] In the earliest times, the totem's association with fecundity, food and food taboos signified that this practice initially had belonged to the realm of women.[239] Totem animals were sometimes avoided as fare. The totem animal always personified the divinity, and was acknowledged as taboo.[240] Not only was Cú Chulainn's *geis* regarding consuming dog flesh related to his personal totem animal and spiritual life, but

---

231 W G Wood-Martin, *Pagan Ireland – An Archaeological Sketch: a Handbook of Irish Pre-Christian Antiquities* (London, 1895) 175.

232 Green, *Celtic Goddesses*, 163.

233 M J Green, *Animals in Celtic Life and Myth* (London, 1992) 178.

234 Cross and Slover (eds), *Ancient Irish*, 191.

235 O'Rahilly, *Táin bó Cúailnge, Recension 1*, 19.

236 *Ibid*, 142.

237 Ó hÓgáin, *Myth, Legend and Romance*, 136.

238 S J Mithen, *The Prehistory of the Mind: A Search for the Origins of Art, Religion, and Science* (London, 1998) 188–189.

239 Neumann, *The Great Mother*, 270.

240 B G Walker, *The Woman's Dictionary of Symbols and Sacred Objects* (New York, 1988) 360.

its contravention led to his death.[241] 'Several *gessi* have often been classified as totemic in nature.'[242] Various scholars have felt that fate was allied to the *geis* concept.[243]

Kings or great heroes are often, in myths, described as being able to shape-shift, or alter their own shape or the form of another person. There was an ancient belief that heroes and kings were the incarnation and reincarnation of the *Tuatha Dé Danann*, beings who formed the supreme fairy hierarchy. These figures were exercising, in a human body, powers which their divine race exercise over humans in the fairy world.[244] 'A related power attributed to Irish druids is that of shapeshifting.'[245] The divinities were considered to be ancient spirits, existing invisibly in the world.[246] In Ireland, the king was supposed to be descended from a god. The rituals that the ruler endured bestowed a semi-divine status upon the king.[247] This status was bestowed upon the regent by the goddess, when the king encountered her while he was in an altered state, a state which was considered to be the otherworld.

The shamans, the druids, and the tales of Ireland, all demonstrate a belief in reincarnation.[248] Respect for ancestors is one of the most viable Khanty values and is linked to ideas about the soul and reincarnation. Cemeteries are connected to the spirit world and dead relatives are thought able to have an effect on the living.[249] 'The old pagans imagined existence after death as a

241 Ó hÓgáin, *Myth, Legend and Romance*, 136.

242 P Leary, 'Honour-bound: The social context of Early Irish Heroic Geis', *Celtica* 20 (1988) 85–107, at p 90.

243 T Sjöblom, 'Before *geis* Became Magical: A Study of the Evolution of an Early Irish Religious Concept', *Studia Celtica* 32 (1998) 85–94, at p 89.

244 W Y E Wentz, *The Fairy-Faith in Celtic Countries* (New York, 1973) 260.

245 Ó hÓgáin, *The Sacred Isle*, 117.

246 Dillon and Chadwick, *Celtic Realms*, 140.

247 M Dillon, 'The Consecration of Irish Kings', *Celtica* 10 (1973) 1–8, at p 1.

248 Wood-Martin, *Pagan Ireland*, 84.

249 P Jordan, *Material Culture and Sacred Landscape*, 216.

mere slightly differentiated prolongation of earthly life'.[250] Strabo commented in 35 BCE that the druids believed that men's souls and the cosmos were immortal, although in the future fire and water may triumph.[251] The druids' teachings involved the immortality of the soul.[252] The Archdruid rowed out annually onto a lake or pond near a stone circle, to demonstrate how life ebbed away, and his return indicated that existence continued after death.[253] The druids claimed that their profession was a balance between the world of the dead and that of the living.[254] 'This is the intermingling of the living and dead, which we can take to have been an essential part of actual pre-Christian belief in Ireland'.[255] There are various texts that describe the ancient Irish poets relaying the history of mounds and naming mythical and semi-historical figures who were buried at the mounds.[256]

For the Irish, the cult of the head,[257] the cult of the dead,[258] and the creation and preservation of sacred religious sites equated with shamanic tradition.[259] With the Yuka-Gir, the shaman's cranium plays a role in prediction and prophecy.[260] In early Ireland, '[t]he

250 W G Wood-Martin, *Traces of the Elder Faiths of Ireland – A Folklore Sketch: A Handbook of Irish Pre-Christian Traditions*, 2 vols (London, 1902) Vol 2 302.

251 W Sayers, 'Mani Maidi an Nem: Ringing-Changes on a Cosmic Motif', *Ériu* 37 (1986) 99–117, at p 99.

252 MacAlister, *Secret Languages of Ireland*, 2.

253 A MacGregor, *Highland Superstitions: Connected with the Druids, Fairies, Witchcraft, Second-Sight, Hallowe'en, Sacred Wells and Lochs, with Several Curious Instances of Highland Customs and Beliefs* (Stirling, 1922) ix.

254 Ó hÓgáin, *The Sacred Isle*, 12.

255 *Ibid*, 102.

256 *Ibid*, 106.

257 Ó hÓgáin, *Fionn mac Cumhaill*, 64.

258 Ó hÓgáin, *Myth, Legend and Romance*, 403.

259 Eliade, *Shamanism*, 324.

260 *Ibid*, 391.

seers' purpose [...] was to gain knowledge, and so a severed head, having access to the world of the dead, could be seen as an ideal oracle'.[261] Eamhain Mhacha, an otherworld place, was naturally allied to the spirits of the dead, and to Macha's grave. The Irish held that the dead could grant insight. This conviction reinforced the tomb's religious importance.

The Irish sources mention the establishment at Eamhain Mhacha of Ireland's first hospital by the semi-legendary queen of Ireland, Macha Mong Ruadh, c377 BCE. Healing originated in the otherworld. The birds' songs in the otherworld reputedly healed all grief and pain, cured and revived those people who had died.[262]

The magical powers of mythical leeches were stressed in Irish literature, with the description of the leeches resembling that of the druids. The chief healer in the Ulster Cycle, Fínahein *faíhliag* ('prophetic leech'), could, by glancing at a wound, recount who had caused the injury and how the injury had occurred.[263] The shamans and healers accompany the dead on their journey to the otherworld.[264] Shamans are believed to be capable of journeying to the otherworld, returning the souls of the sick who have strayed, as well as restoring life to the deceased.[265] 'Healer and psychopomp, the shaman is these because he commands the techniques of ecstasy'.[266] The shaman has the purpose of helping others.[267] The druids were healers in numerous accounts.[268]

Understanding shamanism enables us to understand the ritual activity of Eamhain Mhacha, the themes and activities of the Ulster

---

261 Ó hÓgáin, *Fionn mac Cumhaill*, 66.

262 Ross, *Pagan Celtic Britain*, 340.

263 Ó hÓgáin, *The Sacred Isle*, 87.

264 M Low, *Celtic Christianity and Nature: Early Irish and Hebridean Traditions* (Edinburgh, 1996) 110.

265 Eliade, *Shamanism*, 313.

266 *Ibid*, 182.

267 J Achterberg, *Imagery in Healing: Shamanism and Modern Medicine* (Boston, 1985) 13.

268 Jestice, *Encyclopaedia of Irish Spirituality*, 166–167.

Cycle, the archaeology of Ireland and explains why the early Irish viewed the landscape as divine and of the otherworld. The moon goddess was an underlying theme in the early spiritual landscape of Ireland. Irish tribes and individuals seemed to develop a relationship with the hallowed environment as part of a wider system of belief. The moon goddess was thought to rule the cycle of life, death, renewal and fertility. 'In a larger sense the past never wholly dies: it lives on buried in the minds of men and in the landscapes they have fashioned'.[269]

Eamhain Mhacha has a rich biography and legendary tradition and still has a great influence upon the psyche of the Irish people. Eamhain Mhacha is an otherworld place, even today. 'Landscape is not all external, it has crept inside the soul'.[270]

---

269 Evans, *Irish Folkways*, 306.

270 J O'Donohue, *Anam Cara, Spiritual Wisdom from the Celtic World* (London, 1999) 127.

Myth and legend in the landscape of the Rhondda Valley, south Wales, as a source of cultural identity

Graham Aubrey ⊕

I believe that most people are aware of the importance and influence of the more common carriers of culture in society. These include things like traditional music, nearly always in the form of melody and verse, and dance. Then there are also various literary forms, especially poetry, which is extremely adept at asserting those uniquely cultural aspects and perceptions which are common to people who form the fundamental constituent group at the core of most societies. Cultural expression might be national, or it might support a cultural minority within a clearly defined geographical boundary. This is certainly the case in Celtic lands, subsequent to their inclusion in the United Kingdom. Here, we see clearly defined subcultures of Celtic origin, coexisting with the dominant English culture.

Language also plays a major part in preserving culture, but despite the strong revival taking place in the Celtic languages, I feel that, for the majority of people, even those within the Celtic countries themselves, English is, and is destined to remain, the dominant mode of expression, and interpretation of Celtic thought, for the foreseeable future. However, there is little doubt that there will always be those who will have a strong enough interest and commitment to preserve the Celtic languages and all that they have to offer: the leaven in the cultural loaf, as it were.

It is possible to understand why occupying forces have for centuries been aware that to eliminate culture, one has first to eliminate the carriers. For instance, it is reported that in Tudor

⊕ MA, BA (Hons), AFAIM, D.Urr.

Ireland, harpers were hanged on sight.[1] They were rightly seen as instigating subversive elements to rebel, or at least to forge some sort of material resistance to the English occupation.

Then there is the story of the 'Welsh Not'. This was a flat piece of wood, which was hung around a schoolboy's neck if he was caught speaking Welsh in school. If he could find another boy speaking Welsh, he could dob him in, and pass the Not on to him.[2] Those who were furthering the principle of Welsh nationalism had a field day attacking this form of punishment. They still do, when they refer to the period in retrospect. They stressed the unfairness of the punishment, and promoted the view that it was a deliberate attack by the English establishment on both the Welsh language and the Welsh people.

The reality, however, was somewhat different, certainly as far as the Rhondda Valley was concerned. I have chosen the Rhondda deliberately, since it was arguably one of the major centres of political and social influences in the south Wales coalfield, and much of what applies to the Rhondda applies to the region in general. Life in the pits was hard, dangerous, and at times financially uncertain due to adverse economic conditions. There was very little employment available other than in the mines. Parents were acutely aware that, if their children were to have a better future than that offered by the mines, they would have to master the English language. Two of the most common paths out of the Valley were to find employment in the teaching profession, or as a minister of religion. Those who succeeded were highly respected, and held up as fine examples of what education could do, if one was prepared to work. So the Welsh Not was condoned by most parents as a necessary evil in order to improve the learning of the English language, especially where Welsh was the language of the home.

I have introduced the above points, and there are many more to

---

1 G Ó hAllmhuráin, *A Pocket History of Irish Traditional Music* (Dublin, 1998) 25.

2 J Morris, *The Matter of Wales* (Penguin Books, 1986) 239; and A H Dodd, *A Short History: Wales* (London, 1987) 161.

which I could refer, that would indicate some of the pressures which can and do occur on carriers of cultural identity. In the instance of the Irish harper, there was a clear attempt by the forces of English occupation to eliminate what was perceived as a very real threat. Nevertheless, it was still an attack on cultural identity, given the importance of harpers and bards as carriers and custodians of Irish culture in Tudor Ireland.

The Welsh Not illustrates the willing acquiescence of the general population in an action which was clearly detrimental to their culture, even if it was perceived by the majority as having a distinct social benefit. In this particular instance, it can be considered as pressure for change exerted from within the culture itself.

Having briefly considered how pressure can be exerted to modify or eliminate the carriers of culture, I would like to draw attention to a less obvious and, paradoxically, one of the most difficult of all cultural focal points to eliminate. This is the names found embedded throughout the landscape, and the stories, legends and mythology associated with them. Let us pause to consider the difficulty of redefining or changing the names of places and features in the landscape. Existing maps would become defunct; it would take years to change existing names to something even remotely acceptable. Then, I suggest, it would be nearly impossible to force a new naming structure onto the elderly, or the less well-educated members of society. In practical terms it would be far more likely that the existing names would survive. In the instance of foreign occupation, it stands to reason that there would be much more pressing demands than that of renaming the landscape.

Focus for a moment on the landscape itself, via a British ordinance survey map, say three miles to the inch. Most of the current topographical names will be displayed thereon. It will also be clear that most regions will have an historically stratified society, with changes over time becoming enshrined in names which remain current in the landscape. Perhaps a small example will suffice to illustrate this point. In ancient times, transhumance was the normal lifestyle in the hill zones. The winter months were spent in the farm on the valley floor known as the *hendre*, or 'old farm'. Come springtime, the flocks were taken to the high pastures, known as the *hafod* or 'summer dwelling'. A quick perusal of the ordinance survey map will indicate the prevalence of these names, which are often prefixed by a person's or a chieftain's name. All have stories behind them.

By Tudor times, things had changed a little, as settlement became permanent. Most landholdings were forced to obtain written title, since the law demanded their registration for administrative purposes. Now, the lower farm became *isaf*, and the upper farm, now permanently settled as a mountain farm, became *uchaf*. In districts where the hill farm was some distance from the lowland farm, and where in past times it had been normal to camp the night, this now became the middle area or farm, called *gannol*. All three instances usually had a personal name prefix, similar to that stated in the previous examples, which gave some indication of ownership, and therefore a degree of information with respect to the history of the farm. So do field names, which are another fine source of historical information.

It is not difficult to see, from the examples given, that historical stratification is clearly embedded in the topography and nomenclature of the landscape, which also clearly reflects economic and cultural evolution.

It is not my intention to enter into an academic assessment of the development of the coal and iron industries, or their influence and effect on the industrial revolution in Wales. There are those more capable of presenting this material than I, such as Professor KO Morgan, or John Davies with his superb history of Wales, *Hannes Cymry*. Rather I wish to present the view from the inside: that of a young person growing up in the Rhondda Valley. As we travel through life we all carry invisible baggage, usually derived from the accepted values of the society we are brought up in. Naturally, this is modified by our experiences as we move through life, but it is mainly childhood memories and experiences which set in place the social code by which we live.

Since the focus of this paper is culture in the landscape of the Rhondda Valley, the first question to ask is why the Rhondda.

The answer lies in the fact that the Rhondda was a product of the second phase of the industrial revolution in south Wales. The valley consisted of very little other than a few isolated farms prior to 1807, when Walter Coffin commenced mining coal at Dinas.[3] The evolution of the coal industry determined that the Rhondda developed as a series of frontier townships. One point in which it differed considerably from the earlier phase of industrialisation in south Wales was the higher standard of urban development. Town planning, though in its infancy, began to show some effect.[4] This contrasts considerably with the earlier establishment of the iron industry. Many people moved into Merthyr Tydfil and Dowlais, where the iron industry was concentrated, obviously, in order to benefit from the employment opportunities which the new industry presented. A major problem was that there was very little urban organisation at that time. Where the worker dropped his bundle, somewhere in the vicinity he built his house, however primitive it might be. There was no provision for running water or sewerage, with the result that from time to time typhoid and cholera decimated the population.[5] An important point to stress, however, is that the workforce was mostly drawn from the surrounding districts. It could be said that, at that time, much of the population of rural Wales was moving by creepage. Clearly, one important long-term result of this was that employment in the iron industry was mainly a Welsh affair. The novel *Off to Philadelphia in the Morning*, by the Rhondda author Jack Jones, gives a creditable account of those times. The novel also shows how Welsh institutions, such as choral singing and the nonconformist revival, were in place, fortunately in time to give a definitive Welsh ethos to the newly emergent industrial society.

The Welsh population at the beginning of the industrial revolution was around 650,000: culturally, the country was in good shape. By 1850, with the initial development of the coal industry in

3 J Davies, *A History of Wales* (London, 2007) 389.

4 *Ibid*, 392.

5 *Ibid*, 339; and Dodd, *A Short History*, 139.

the western valleys, the Rhondda in particular, the Welsh population had risen to 1,630,000. By the end of the century, the population had increased to well over 2,000,000, with a disproportionate number domiciled in the industrial south, amounting to something like 60 per cent of the total population of Wales.[6] Whilst the first phase of the industrial revolution was clearly Welsh, the workforce of the second phase, dominated by the coal industry, comprised a large number of workers from outside the principality.[7] Very few of these immigrants were Welsh-speaking, yet their grandchildren are proud to call themselves Welsh, and strongly identify with all things Welsh. Yet logic tells us it did not have to happen this way. Surely, the predominant use of the English language, and the overall ubiquity of English in the social and political administration of the valley, would be enough to convince many people that south Wales would soon become, at least in cultural terms, just another Anglican provincial district.

It is against this background that I would to like portray the cultural influences on a boy growing up in the Rhondda. Although we all had Welsh accents, only a small proportion of us spoke Welsh. In school, singing was our main cultural activity, with a large percentage of the songs sung in the Welsh language. Most of us had little, if any, idea of what we were singing about. Many of the traditional folk songs were based on important Welsh events, most of which portrayed historical and legendary people from the past. The events so portrayed were located in various geographical locations throughout the principality. These, and their importance, were carefully explained to us. Saint David, as the patron saint of Wales, was acknowledged every year on 1 March, and we all sang the Welsh national anthem, in the Welsh language, whenever the opportunity presented itself. Even so, many myths were without foundation, although as children we didn't know this, and I suppose in many ways neither did it matter. Take the legend of the dog, Gelert, supposedly buried at Beddgelert in north Wales. As children

---

6 Dodd, *A Short History*, 150.

7 *Ibid*, 150.

we all loved that story. It revolved around Prince Llewellyn, who went hunting in the hills leaving his baby son in the charge of a nurse, and his favourite wolfhound Gelert. The prince returned to find everything in the nursery smashed and the dog covered in blood. The prince assumed that the dog had killed the baby and, in anger, promptly plunged a spear into Gelert, who howled as he died. This woke the baby, who cried on the other side of the damaged crib, with a dead wolf close to him. Llewellyn, in remorse, took the dog and buried him with full honours, and caused a cairn to be erected to the dog's memory. It makes a lovely story, and many a mongrel in the valley was given the name Gelert, and an extra bone now and again, on the strength of that story. The reality was somewhat different: Beddgelert is where an Irish monk, who lived and ministered to that district many centuries ago, lies buried.[8] The village, by the eighteenth century, was on the main route from London to Holyhead. The cairn was in fact constructed by the innkeeper; it turns out that the whole story was fictitious, and was created to encourage the London coaches to stop at the inn. There was no truth in the legend whatsoever, but once it appeared in print,[9] romantics perpetuated the story and it became a traditional Welsh legend. One has to be very careful with myth and legend.

To return to the immediate past (50 years ago), places of worship played an important part in the everyday life of the Rhondda communities, both in social terms, and in promoting moral standards. To some extent, the nonconformist denominations, in particular, promoted a Welsh ethos. The ministers of religion were, almost to a man, Welsh-speaking, and it would be difficult to overestimate the huge moral force they represented in the social life of the Rhondda. The mining unions also played a major part in the running of the valley. They provided good health cover, and hospitals, and, above all, the miners' institutes, where there was a library, and often a concert hall. Here, world-class performers were

---

8 Automobile Association, *Touring Guide to Wales* (Automobile Association, 1975) 156.

9 Morris, *Matter of Wales*, 34.

engaged to perform at certain times of the year, such as the Easter concerts. In political terms, there was great solidarity in the mining communities, but its major focus was on social justice rather than Welsh nationalism.

Was this enough to reinforce non-Welsh speakers in their Welsh identity, and was it enough to convert immigrants and their descedents to espousing a Welsh identity? Given that the influence of the Welsh language in the mining districts was on the decline, due mainly to the increasing proportion of the non-Welsh speaking element in the population, and that English was the modus operandi of the civil administration, the question remains, how did the people of the Rhondda maintain their Welsh identity and culture. Why did the area not become just another English provincial region, especially in the light of the dilution of the Welsh portion of the population? I think that the answer to this is to be found in three interactive elements. The first is that there was little or no indigenous population, therefore there was no minority group there to claim prior rights or ownership. That being the case, more was to be gained, especially in a frontier area, by cooperation and a common concept of destiny and purpose. The second element is the topography of the valley itself, and the third is the ethnology built into the landscape.

The topography of the valleys on the whole consisted of upland moorland and, as such, formed an ideal playground for children. The mountains were crown land, there were no fences, and one could walk as far as one's legs could carry one. They engendered a tremendous feeling of freedom. Surely the sprit of Wales is at its strongest in the solitude of the mountains. To climb the mountain, leaving the valley far below, was to enter a different world. The tops of the mountains formed an upland plateau, with peaks such as the Brecon Beacons rising from it. We children were in a world of our own; the houses were far below, if they could be seen at all. The air was pure and sweet, with none of the acrid smell of the coal fires of the terraced houses. We could drink from the streams, play hide and seek in the wooded glens, and let our imagination run riot. We would build little huts of stone, and roll boulders down the mountainside, giving ourselves a fright when they went too far. We cut clods of earth and, with a reinforcing of stones, built dams in the streams, where we could swim in the summer months. We could tickle for trout in those streams, and dig groundnuts in the late spring on the richer parts of the hillside, and pick whinberries on the rocky slopes in the late summer. Goodness knows how many hundreds of these were needed to make just one tart. As we grew older, only some of us climbed the high mountains: most played football or rugby on the lower slopes. Some of the old, and not so old, men played pontoon in some concealed site, far away from the prying eyes of what little law-enforcement there was, but there was still that same sense of freedom and independence we enjoyed as children. We were ourselves, and there by no one's grace or favour. We were still lords of all we surveyed and it was something we never forgot, even when we were too old or too dusted to climb the mountains any more. Two fundamental Celtic philosophies are, firstly, that in nature we see the mirror of god and, secondly, that everyone has the right to fulfil their own destiny, or to put it another way, a right to be themselves. For us children, the mountains more than adequately fulfilled both these requirements.

I look back now with amusement at our ignorance, when as youths we walked the mountain roads of a fine summer evening, often with a girlfriend. The motor car was just becoming commonplace, and it was not unusual to find the remains of a condom on some of the vehicle lay-bys. It was obvious to us that the people responsible were not up there to admire the view, beautiful though it might be. In the conceit of youth, it never crossed our minds that the culprits were in all probability our parents, desperate to get away from us.

If the mountains and moorland were an essential part of our being, that leads to the last element mentioned, culture in the landscape. The names and stories associated with features inherent in the landscape gave an added dimension to it. It was this knowledge which gave us a claim to all it represented. As I stepped out of the house and looked south, I saw the Maindy mountain, a corruption of the Welsh words *Maen Ddu*, or 'black stone'. The stone was in all probability once located in or near the ancient Celtic camp, on the crest of the hill, whose ruins still exist. Ancient trackways radiate from this point, one in particular leading to a pass at the head of the valley, called simply *The Bwlch*. From there, it proceeds on to the adjoining valleys. The track, as it descends into the Ogmore valley, passes a prominent rock formation known as the Devil's Chimney, if you were from the Rhondda, or the Devil's Table, if you were a native of the Ogmore valley. All of these features point to a probable pre-Christian period in the valley's history, though it is clear that the tracks were used until comparatively recent times. Another of the ancient roads which climbed the mountain and led to the Bwlch was known locally as the Parc-cachan, probably derived from the Welsh *ParcYechian*, meaning 'the field of the oxen'. It is highly likely that oxen were to be hired at this point, to assist in carrying loads over the mountain tracks between the Rhondda and the adjacent valleys. Once again, the truth is lost in pre-industrial history. Ancient trackways fell out of use with the advent of the railways, and the coming of better roads and wheeled transport, but they still exist, for those who have sufficient stamina and sense of adventure to follow them.

Looking east, I saw *Moel Cadogan*, named after a Welsh chieftain who fell there whilst fighting for his land. Lower down the valley was *Pen Rhys*, where another chieftain fell, also fighting for his land. You will find little evidence of these chieftains in the historical record. However, they have certainly survived in folk memory, and because of their names being enshrined in the landscape. Another point of interest is that a holy well once existed on Pen Rhys, despite its remoteness, and a small monastic cell existed there until the dissolution of the monasteries.[10] There are, of course, many other places of historical interest which could be mentioned, and still others which refer to otherworldly places, like the Fairy Glen.

I would like to reaffirm my belief that it was primarily the culture built into the landscape that created a fierce and undying love of Welshness in us all, be we of Welsh or English extraction. It is culture in the landscape which is largely at the root of folk memory

10 C Batstone, *Rhondda Remembered* (Glamorgan, 1983) photo 158.

and tradition. It was this which drew us into itself; it invited us to become an integral part of its persona. In that way, we became its future, and therefore its continuity. It also, by some alchemy, confirmed us in our love of Wales, and in so doing confirmed in us our right as inheritors of Welsh culture. Dylan Thomas' radio play *Under Milk Wood* and Richard Llewellyn's *How Green Was My Valley* are two of the most enduring and popular works which reflect the ethos of south Wales. Both authors clearly derive much of their inspiration from aspects of culture inherent in the landscape.

'And anyway she was always going about with the Mother of God': the Brigid and Mary stories in Gaelic culture

Mary O'Connell ⊕

> And there are some say Brigit fostered the holy Child, and kept an account of every drop of blood he lost through his lifetime, and anyway she was always going about with the Mother of God.[1]

It is now widely — although not universally — accepted that Saint Brigid[2] (c450–c523), miracle worker, founder and abbess of Kildare, patron saint of Leinster and Ireland, is a Christianised version of an earlier Celtic goddess of the same or a similar name.[3] The goddess Brigid was a corn mother or triple goddess also associated with healing, sacred knowledge, poetry and smithcraft. Like the saint, she is also associated with a sacred and eternal fire. The eternal flame which the saint is said to have established at her double monastery in Kildare, tended only by women, survived for hundreds of years, at least until the twelfth century. Gerald of Wales (Giraldus

⊕ University of New South Wales.

1 Lady Gregory, *A Book of Saints and Wonders* (1906) 3rd ed (Bucks, 1971) 20.

2 Brigid is also known as Bridget, Brigit and Bride.

3 eg P Berger, *The Goddess Obscured: Transformation of the Grain Protectress from Goddess to Saint* (Boston, 1995); A Bourke, 'Irish Stories of Weather, Time and Gender: Saint Brigid', 13–31 in M Cohen and N Curtin (eds), *Reclaiming Gender: Transgressive Identities in Modern Ireland* (New York, 1999), at p 16; J Campbell, *Primitive Mythology: the Masks of God* (New York, 1959) 431–2; J G Frazer, *The Golden Bough* 1922 (London, 1978) 177–8; R Willis (ed), *World Mythology: the Illustrated Guide* (London, 1993) 186.

Cambrensis) who visited Ireland in the twelfth century attested to the flame's existence. His text has added weight to the concept of Brigid as pagan goddess, with the idea of vestal virgins in a pre-Christian sacred community of women.[4]

Like the goddess, Brigid the saint has a very large portfolio. As well as being patron saint of Leinster and Ireland she is the patron saint for 'babies and infants, blacksmiths, boatmen, cattle, chicken farmers, children whose parents are not married, dairy maids, dairy workers, fugitives, mariners, midwives, nuns, poets, poultry, printing presses, sailors, scholars, travellers, and watermen'.[5] Nor is Saint Brigid confined to Ireland. In Scotland she is known as Bride, in Wales as Ffraid and in England both as Brigid and Bride.[6]

Despite the current scholarly and popular consensus that an earlier goddess metamorphosed into saint, there are other views. Lisa Bitel inverts the goddess-precedes-saint thesis with her argument that in fact it was the historical Brigid's various seventh- to ninth-century hagiographers who 'gave us the goddess Brigit'.[7] That is, in order to boost Brigid's — and their — status they used 'local literary traditions and heroic history' in order to cast their saint as 'a mistress of the animals, territory and landscape'.[8]

Whether she be human or divine, Brigid has lived now for centuries within Irish and Scots cultural texts and practices: in walking rituals and pilgrimages, in place-names and women's names, in sacred and magical symbols, in prayers, poetry and invocations, and in dramatic, magical and often humorous stories.

---

4 The Celtic goddess Brigid has also been associated with the Roman goddess Minerva who was also commemorated with an eternal flame. Willis (ed), *World Mythology*, 186.

5 Catholic Forum Online www.catholic-forum.com/saints/saintb)3.htm [2 July 2007].

6 D Attwater, *The Penguin Dictionary of Saints*, 2nd ed (Harmondsworth, 1983) 71–72.

7 L M Bitel, 'Body of a saint, story of a goddess: origins of the Brigidine tradition', in *Textual Practice* 16(2) (2002) 209–228, at p 211. Available online at www.tandf.co.uk/journals [1 Feb 2008].

8 *Ibid*, 225.

Saint Brigid's Feast day is 1 February, the same date as the pre-Christian Celtic early Spring festival of *Imbolc*.[9] To this day, in many parts of Ireland, her special cross is woven from rushes on the eve of her feast day — a time when the saint is understood to spiritually traverse the countryside — and hung above the front door for protection against fire, storm and disease throughout the year. Brigid still has holy wells in her name scattered throughout Ireland. Moreover, in recent years, the saint has seen a resurgence of devotion in both new age and Catholic cultures, in Ireland and beyond.[10] In 1993, the flame of Saint Brigid was rekindled at Kildare by a community of Brigidine sisters. The restoration of Brigid's flame in contemporary Kildare is acknowledged as a flame for both goddess and saint.[11] Then on Saint Brigid's feast day in 2006 President Mary

9 The etymology of the word *Imbolc* itself, which has not survived into modern Irish, is still disputed. *Imbolc* is often said to be a festival related to lambing, and lactation of ewes, although 1 February is very early for any lambing. Thomas Torma points out, however, that in the centuries before a major calendar revision in 1752 cut 11 days, *Imbolc* was celebrated in what is now mid-February — a time more suited to lambing. T Torma, 'Milk Symbolism in the "Bethu Brigte"', *The Heroic Age* 7 (Spring 2004) 3: available online at www. heroicage.org/issues/7/torma.html [20 Feb 2008]. Angela Bourke also indicates a connection with cereal rather than milk in that Brigid's feast marks the beginning of spring sowing, while Lughnasa, the festival named after the Irish god Lugh (and possibly Brigid's masculine counterpart) marks the beginning of harvest. A Bourke, 'Irish Stories of Weather, Time and Gender: Saint Brigid', 19–21.

10 Marion Bowman discusses the renewal of Brigid rituals in modern Glastonbury, where she is celebrated as both goddess and saint. M Bowman, 'Arthur and Bridget in Avalon: Celtic Myth, Vernacular Religion and Contemporary Spirituality in Glastonbury', *Fabula* 48, 1/2 (2007) 16–32.

11 Interestingly, earlier writers record that the flame was suppressed by Henry Launders, Archbishop of Dublin in 1220. See D P Conyngham, *Lives of the Irish Saints and Martyrs* (New York, 1871) 175, also J S P Tatlock, 'Greater Irish Saints in Lawman and in England', *Modern Philology* 42/4 (1945) 72–76, at p 73. Tatlock does not state who or what ended the flame but gives the same date of suppression as Conyngham, 1220. Yet the twentieth-century revivalists of the flame claim it was the

McAleese visited Kildare to officially present the sacred flame 'to the People of Ireland and beyond'. In her speech, the Irish president spoke of 'the sheer power' of the saint's continuing presence, and of Brigid as the point of intersection between the Irish Christian and Irish Celtic pagan worlds, in an address which indicated the new politically correct Ireland, including both protestant and pagan histories into the national story.[12]

The early medieval stories indicate a woman marked from birth as both special and marginal. Brigid was a love child, born at dawn over a threshold, reared for some years in the household of a druid. Her pregnant mother, Broicsech, had been sold as a slave by her father Dubhtach, under pressure, so the stories say, from his jealous principal wife. Growing up, Brigid worked willingly as sheep minder, pig and cow herder, cook and dairy maid but her constant giving away of food, ale and goods to the poor annoyed both her foster and biological kin. She eventually so wore out the patience of her father Dubthach that he tried to sell her as a slave to the King of Leinster.

> 'What cause of annoyance has she given?' said the king. 'Not hard,' said Dubthach. 'She acts without asking permission; whatever she sees, her hand takes'.[13]

While waiting in her father's chariot as this exchange was taking place, Brigid gave his sword away to a passing beggar. When her father demanded what she had done with his sword, she replied, 'Christ has taken it'. As the admiring king told Dubthach, 'Truly,

---

Tudor invasions and the suppression of the monasteries. *Solas Bhride*, Christian Community Centre for Celtic Spirituality, available online at www.solasbhride.ie/flame-of-brigid.htm [2 July 2007].

12 *Solas Bhride, Ibid.*

13 *Bethu Brigte*, 13, trans D Ó hAodha (Dublin, 1978). Available online at www.ucc.ie/celt/published/G201002/index.html [3 March 2008].

this girl can neither be sold nor bought'.[14]

The story of Brigid crosses gender boundaries as well. Many of the texts assert that she had been consecrated as a bishop, instead of as a nun, by her bishop Mel, he being 'intoxicated with the grace of God'.[15] In another version of this story, the young cleric MacCaille protests at Bishop Mel's act, to which Mel replies, 'No power have I in this matter.'[16]

Many aspects of her Christian legend link Brigid to fertility, fecundity and abundance. She could churn limitless amounts of butter out of small supplies of milk. When guests came unexpectedly to her monastery she went out to milk the community's cows and their milk flooded the plains and created a lake of milk in Leinster. But the generous saint was not above a little bit of cheating. She famously obtained her lands from the king of Leinster when he granted her as much land for her cows as her cloak could cover. Her magical cloak spread out for miles on every side until he begged her to stop.[17]

Generous beyond fault, the saint was often tough on the mean and niggardly. She cursed the fruit trees of a woman who had given apples to her community but had then protested when she heard the saint had given them away to lepers. The ninth-century *Bethu Brigte* records with satisfaction that that orchard 'remains barren forever'.[18]

Regardless of the occasional attempts to confine the figure of Brigid into more patriarchal models of womanhood — as when the

---

14 *Bethu Brigte*, 13.

15 *Bethu Brigte*, 19.

16 *Leabhar Breac*, trans W Stokes, 69. Available online at www.ucc.ie/celt/published/T201010/text001.html [18 Feb 2008].

17 P Kennedy, *Legendary Fictions of the Irish Celts* (1866) (London, 1969) 334.

18 *Bethu Brigte*, 32. There are other examples of saintly cursing in the various medieval *Vitae*. These aspects of her story do not necessarily reflect a pagan origin; Christ also cursed a fig tree into barrenness, as well as famously whipping the money lenders out of the temple.

later medieval text in *Leabhar Breac* asserts that she never looked a male person in the eye, and never spoke without blushing![19] — the medieval texts, early and late, describe a dynamic, bold and essentially libertarian figure, travelling widely through much of Ireland, friends with kings, bishops and lepers, reckless in her generosity, almost relentless in her miracle-working.

Centuries later, faith in Brigid's powers of healing remained strong in Ireland. Lady Gregory tells of a local woman's story of being healed of an eye affliction by seeing the miraculous fish in the local Saint Brigid's well, which 'was surely Saint Brigit I saw that time; who else would it be?'[20] Here the shape-shifting saint and the supernaturally powerful fish are pure Celtic inventions. While the fish is certainly also a Christian symbol, miraculous salmon and trout dwelling in sacred waters form no part of Roman Catholicism, but instead hark back to the earliest sagas of Finn, the salmon of wisdom and the well of Seaghais, the spring of the otherworld.[21]

Like the Celtic faery people Brigid has an element of caprice in the bestowing of any favours. The healed woman wondered to Lady Gregory why she had been so honoured with a miraculous cure. 'Did I say more prayers than the rest? Not a prayer. I was young in those days. I suppose she took a liking to me, maybe because of my name Brigit the same as her own.'[22]

Lady Gregory recorded many Brigid stories, both from oral and from textual sources, and placed them first in her published work, *A Book of Saints and Wonders: according to the old writings and the memory of the people of Ireland.* We can be grateful for Augusta Gregory's fondness for Brigid, because many other Gaelic revivalists were not interested.[23] The non-Irish-speaking Yeats was

19 Possibly a later gloss, in *Leabhar Breac*, 85.

20 Gregory, *A Book of Saints and Wonders*, 21.

21 Willis (ed), *World Mythology*, 185.

22 Gregory, *A Book of Saints and Wonders*, 21.

23 Indeed, Sean O'Casey referred to Lady Gregory as 'Blessed Bridget O'Coole.' O'Casey thought Lady Gregory looked 'like an old, elegant nun of a new order, a blend of the Lord Jesus Christ and of Puck', C Toibin,

of course more interested in Celtic myth than the embarrassment of Catholicism, while Douglas Hyde, who also published a work on Irish 'legends of saints and sinners' claimed that he heard no stories at all about St Brigid.[24] The folklorist Patrick Kennedy did however record five stories of Brigid in his 1866 publication, *Legendary Fictions of the Irish Celts.* But Lady Gregory repeats the *Leabhar Breac* claim that Brigid was 'the queen of the south, she is the mother of the flocks, she is the Mary of the Gael'.[25]

In Scotland's Hebrides, in the last half of the nineteenth century, Alexander Carmichael recorded many rituals, ceremonies, chants, invocations and images used to honour Bride, 'the beauteous, the shepherdess of the flocks', and commented that in some areas Bride was more important to the people than the figure of Mary.[26]

Yet a love of Brigid did not prevent an affectionate popular engagement with Mary. Devotion to the virgin mother by the Gaelic-speaking Catholic communities of Ireland and Scotland is embedded in the language of poetry, invocations, prayers and — in

---

Lady Gregory's Toothbrush (Madison, 2002) 105. The description may encompass the saint herself, if Puck means mischief, faery, the natural world.

24 D Hyde, *Legends of Saints and Sinners: Collected and Translated from the Irish* (Dublin, 1916) ix. Hyde makes one passing reference to Bridget's Well at Kilbride at p 11. Ignoring or simply not seeing the divine feminine in action is not confined to nineteenth-century researchers. In his book written to accompany a ten-part TV series made for Scottish television in the 1990s, Alistair Moffat fails to mention the goddess or saint or any vernacular traditions and practices involving her at all. A Moffat, *The Sea Kingdoms: the History of Celtic Britain and Ireland* (London, 2001). Likewise Ken Loach in his 2006 film on the Irish War of Independence and Civil War, *The Wind that Shakes the Barley*, depicts a devout rural Ireland completely devoid of Marian images.

25 Gregory, *A Book of Saints and Wonders*, 22. The lines are from *Leabhar Breac.*

26 A Carmichael, *Carmina Gadelica: Hymns and Incantations with illustrative notes on words, rites, and customs, dying and obsolete/orally collected in the highlands and islands of Scotland,* 2nd edition (Edinburgh, 1928) 173.

the Irish language — in the very greeting, '*Dia duit*' (God be with you), and its response, '*Dia 's Muire duit*' (God and Mary be with you). While scholars dispute how widespread Marianism actually was in Ireland before the massive explosion in Marian devotion in the embattled nineteenth century, it is known that Marian prayers, poems and even moving statues existed in Ireland from at least the thirteenth century.[27] Interestingly, one of the first Irish textual references to Mary is in the ninth-century *Bethu Brigte*, where Bishop Ibor dreams of the virgin Mary and then the next day recognises the young Brigid as the woman he saw in his dream vision.[28]

Certainly by the nineteenth century, Mary was the official Church favourite, within Europe and the Catholic diaspora in the new worlds. With an increasingly dominant middle-class ideology constructing femininity as essentially passive and fragile, Mary — her traditional blood-red dress replaced by virginal white — was undergoing a reduction in height, age and breast size.[29] Her obedience and meekness were stressed. It could never be said about Mary as it was of Brigid, 'She acts without asking permission; whatever she sees, her hand takes'.[30] Yet for many of the faithful, Mary was still a powerful regal figure, a dealer in miracles and capable of transforming and healing human lives and hearts. She was the Mother of Sorrows, Star of the Sea and Queen of Heaven, hardly bourgeois occupations.

The powerful presence of the divine mother in nineteenth-century Catholic spirituality was not just an Irish phenomenon.

---

27 Annals stated that the statue of Mary spoke miraculously at Cell Mór in Tír Briúin in 1381. P O'Dwyer, *Mary: a history of devotion in Ireland*, (Dublin, 1988) 98–99.

28 *Bethu Brigte*, 11.

29 Medieval and renaissance images show the Madonna almost always in a blood red dress with dark blue cloak, but the royal blue had faded to baby blue in the nineteenth century and the virginal white dress become de rigeur, leaving Mary, Charlene Spretnak notes, 'with no hint of maternal potency'. Charlene Spretnak, *Missing Mary: the Queen of Heaven and her re-emergence in the modern church* (New York, 2004) 221.

30 *Bethu Brigte*, 13.

Apparitions of Mary had been recorded all over nineteenth-century Europe, the most famous ones being in La Salette, France, in 1846; Lourdes in 1858; Marpingen, Germany, 1876; as well as at Knock, Ireland in 1879. The visions provoked massive gatherings of people, and prompted pilgrimages. While many contemporary commentators and later historians of these gatherings and pilgrimages saw them as essentially conservative, new readings are emerging. Instead, the persistence of Marianism within Catholicism, despite outside opposition and internal ambivalence, may indicate a powerful psychic drive for wholeness in a one-sided masculinist system.

David Blackbourn, in his study of the conflict between rationalism and religion in nineteenth-century Germany, feels that Our Lady was a potent religious symbol to be used against controlling civil authority.[31] He draws comparisons between nineteenth-century Marian pilgrims and contemporary political forms of passive resistance. For one thing, Marian pilgrims continued singing and carrying flowers and candles in the face of police and military hostility to their gatherings. These pilgrims in their heightened emotional states threatened a social order based on work and obedience to the machine. It was a form of cultural and often gendered resistance to modernity, sometimes diffuse and inchoate, sometimes more sharply and locally focussed.

That Marian visionaries themselves were mainly women or children further indicates the liminal and oppositional nature of Marian Christianity in the new age of reason. Traditionally, Mary appears most often to the 'have-nots', the divine mother making common cause with the poor, the oppressed, women and children. The Virgin of Guadalupe said to Juan Diego, the Aztec Indian who met her on the road in 1531, 'am I not of your kind?'[32] Likewise, Ruth Harris noted that the Lourdes pilgrimage movement became

31 D Blackbourn, *The Marpingen Visions: rationalism, religion and the rise of Modern Germany* (London, 1995) 42.

32 *Abundant Life*, Catholic Pregnancy Assistance Newsletter, East Perth, WA (March 2001) 2. See also Spretnak, *Missing Mary*, 186–92.

the leading spiritual event 'of a Catholic counter culture' in an aggressively secular state.[33] Certainly throughout the nineteenth century in Europe, Marian sites 'attracted large numbers of those whose mobility was least expected or desired: women, children, the poor'.[34]

In nineteenth-century Ireland, where Catholicism and nationalist identity became inextricably intertwined, Mary had become a political as well as cultural and spiritual figure. When Daniel O'Connell held his largest 'monster meeting' in the campaign to repeal the Act of Union at the ancient Celtic royal site of Tara in 1843, he deliberately chose a Marian date: August 15, the feast day of the Assumption of the Blessed Virgin Mary. Thirty-six years later, many people believed that the appearance of the Virgin at Knock 'was a sign of divine support for the Land League'.[35] Indeed, one of the first cures there involved the daughter of a well-known Fenian and Land League activist. The rosary itself had become such a symbol of both Marian devotion and Irish resistance that the Irish Volunteers were reciting it in the Dublin GPO and Boland's Mill in the armed Easter uprising of 1916.[36] Padraig Pearse's poem, *Mise Eire* ('I am Ireland'), links the sorrowful maternal figures of Mary, Ireland and Pearse's own mother, soon to be bereft of her executed son.[37]

Mother Mary had merged with Mother Church and Mother Ireland. She was the weeping mother at the grave of a crucified Ireland: *Mater Dolorosa*, the Mother of Sorrows. In fact, Mary is a

---

33 R Harris, *Lourdes: Body and Spirit in the Secular Age* (London, 1999) 17.

34 Blackbourn, *The Marpingen Visions*, 40.

35 P Bew, 'A Vision to the Dispossessed? Popular piety and revolutionary politics in the Irish Land War, 1879–82', 137–151 in J Devlin and R Fanning (eds), *Religion and Rebellion, Historical Studies XX, Papers read before the 22nd conference of Irish historians, UCD May 1995* (Dublin, 1997), at p 138.

36 O'Dwyer, *Mary*, 297–9.

37 Interestingly, it was Lady Gregory who translated Pearse's poem from the Irish. C I Innes, *Woman and Nation in Irish Literature and Society, 1880–1935* (Athens, USA, 1993) 160–2.

much sadder woman than Brigid can ever be. There is a liveliness about the figure of Brigid, an eternal youthfulness, the archetypal pattern of one the most popular motifs in Irish storytelling, the clever country girl.[38] Mary, for all her beauty and kindness, has no such wit. It could be said that, while Brigid was the maiden, Mother Mary had become the *Cailleach* aspect of the Goddess, the portal of death, reflected in the oft-repeated Marian prayer: 'pray for us sinners, now and at the hour of our death.'

Outside of official church texts, but in stories told throughout Scotland, Ireland and some parts of the diaspora, the earthly Mary was very often joined by a brave, resourceful, loyal and spirited companion. In these tales, Brigid has far more divine powers than Mary, and it is a wonder how the holy family got on at all without her.

Lady Gregory retells a story where the pregnant Mary is halted by crowds admiring her radiant beauty. This, however, distresses Mary and prevents her from moving on. Luckily, she then meets Brigid:

> They met then with Brigit, and the Mother of God said to her, 'What can we do to make these crowds leave following us?'
> 'I will do that for you', said Brigit, 'for I will show them a greater wonder.'

The greater wonder is the agricultural implement, the harrow, used for ploughing the earth. In Brigid's upraised hands, however, the humble harrow blazes forth and 'every one of the pins gave out a flame like a candle', thus diverting the attention of the crowd and enabling Mary to make her escape. The grateful Mary then asks what she can do for the saint as a reward. '"Put my day before your own day," said Brigit. So she did that, and St Brigit's Day is kept before her own day ever since.'[39]

As noted, St Brigid's Day is 1 February, and Candlemas (Mary's

38 S Ó Súilleabháin, *Storytelling in Irish Tradition* (Cork, 1973) 20.

39 Gregory, *A Book of Saints and Wonders*, 19–20.

Day) is 2 February.[40] Candlemas was also known as the Feast of the Purification of the Virgin Mary, according to the Judaeo-Christian law that women, being unclean after childbirth (of sons), had to wait 40 days before returning to the temple, to be ritually purified.[41] In Christianity, this practice was called 'being churched'. In Willeen Keough's research on the lives of women of the Irish diaspora of Southern Avalon in Newfoundland (1750–1860), she describes how women treasured the blessed candles from the church given out on Candlemas Day. The candles were associated with Mary and her power to ward off evil.[42] But Candlemas also included Brigid, again as friendly supporter and protector of Mary. According to Newfoundland versions, Mary was on her way to be 'churched', and Brigid went ahead of her, with 'rays of light pouring from her head to distract attention from Mary's shame'.[43]

This sisterly intervention by Brigid to protect and support a more tentative Mary is, according to Angela Bourke, one of the most common stories told about her feast day in both Irish- and English-language sources. Bourke relays a further version of this story from Cork, where Brigid lit a candle and put it in the tail of her own dress, 'and she was so holy that the candle didn't burn the dress and while they were all looking at St Brigid, the Blessed Virgin

---

40 The candles used in Candlemas may originally have derived from an earlier Roman pre-Christian festival of the same date sacred to women and to the Goddess of Love (Walker, *The Woman's Encyclopedia,* 134–5). The candles are also associated with Brigid: in all of the Brigid and Mary stories, it is Brigid who holds them.

41 Bourke, 'Irish Stories', at p 26.

42 Women dripped blessed candle wax at the windowsills of their homes, praying to Mary for protection of these homes, and dabbed the wax into their children's shoes, for Mary to guide their children's footsteps. Willeen Keough, *The Slender Thread, Irish Women on the Southern Avalon 1750–1860* (Columbia University Press, e-books). Available online at www.gutenberg-e.org/keough 2006 ch 5, p 13.

43 Here the harrow of Lady Gregory's story is now St Brigid's miraculous rays of light. Keough notes the goddess Brigid was sometimes portrayed with rays of light pouring from a headress of candles. Keough, *The Slender Thread*, ch 5, p 14.

slipped into the church and no-one noticed her'.[44]

In Alexander Carmichael's outer Hebrides, the Candlemas story says that Bride lit the way for Mary when she went up to the temple. Bride's candles shone on through a fierce wind, and did not flicker or fall.[45] In a story from Valentia Island, off Kerry, the irrepressible saint wore a hoop with lighted candles around her waist as she 'danced up the aisle before the Virgin and down again'.[46]

None of these stories in the oral tradition about Brigid and Mary feel the need to explain or explain away Brigid's presence in the Holy Land, a presence which breaches both temporal and spatial laws. They are, as Shirley Toulson notes, 'a venture into the spiritual, timeless world that makes nonsense of chronology'.[47] Keough also notes a Newfoundland story that the ever-helpful and resourceful Brigid wove a woollen web from her ewes to protect the infant Jesus from harm during the flight into Egypt.[48] Such stories are part of a deeper mythological and spiritual storytelling tradition, which, as Keough notes, 'wreaks havoc with history's love of time lines'.[49]

Other Irish stories on occasion combined the heroes of the Ulster Cycle with Christian figures. Some accounts placed Cú Chulainn at Calvary, and other versions told how King Conchobar died as a result of rage at the news of Christ's crucifixion. News, interestingly enough, told him by a druid, when the king asked why the day had suddenly turned very dark.[50] Sometimes an explanation — of sorts

---

44 Story from Irish Folklore Collection (IFC 900:16–17) quoted in Bourke, 'Irish Stories of Weather, Time and Gender', at p 27.

45 Carmichael, *Carmina Gadelica*, 169.

46 E Andrews, 'A Legend of St Brigid,' *Man* 22 (1922) 187.

47 S Toulson, *The Celtic Year: a Month-by-Month Celebration of Celtic Christian Festivals and Sites* (Shaftesbury, 1996) 80.

48 Keough, *The Slender Thread*, ch 5, 14–15. The association of cloth with Brigid is strong, with much folklore asserting that Saint Brigid wove the first piece of cloth in Ireland (Gregory, *A Book of Saints and Wonders*, 15) and that she wove the shroud of Saint Patrick, as he had requested.

49 Keough, *The Slender Thread*, ch 5, p 15.

50 Ó Súilleabháin, *Storytelling in Irish Tradition*, 27.

— was given to reconcile time and place. In County Galway, local women told Lady Gregory that a heavenly messenger brought both Mary and Jesus over to Ireland to escape the persecutions of Herod, and to place them under the care and protection of Brigid.[51]

A story reported in the *Carmina Gadelica* places Brigid as serving maid in the inn at Bethlehem. She was unable to give the old man and his beautiful pregnant wife any shelter, but characteristically she gave them her own last piece of bread. When she returned to the kitchen to find the bannock of bread still there, the young saint knew she had met no ordinary woman. She ran out and, following a golden light, arrived at the stable in time to assist Mary in her birthing. Brigid then blessed the baby with three drops of water from a nearby spring.[52]

Alexander Carmichael also recorded a beautiful Scottish Gaelic prayer for women in labour, calling on Bride's midwifery skills:

'S mar a chòmhn' thu Òigh an t-solais,
Gun òr, gun odh, gun ni,
Còmhn' orm-sa, 's mór m'òthrais,
Còmhn' orm a Bhrìde!

(And as thou didst aid the Virgin of joy,
without gold, without corn, without kine,
Aid thou me, great is my sickness,
Aid me, O Bride!)[53]

The tradition that Brigid was Mary's midwife is also well known in Ireland. In certain areas women hung out a piece of cloth on Saint Brigid's Eve hoping that the saint would touch it, and infuse it with her healing powers, giving it power to relieve the pain of their own

51 Irish Theatre Institute, play listing. Available online at www.irishplayography.com/search/play.asp?play_ID=2076 [28 February 2008].

52 Carmichael, *Carmina Gadelica*, 164.

53 *Ibid*, 177.

childbirth. The cloth varied in colour from region to region, and was called *brat Bhríde*, Brigid's cloak.[54] In Donegal, oral folklore tradition states that women sometimes used the *brat Bhríde* to ease the pain of calving cows.[55] The tradition of Brigid as midwife to Mary reveals an integrative and inclusive spirituality, whereby the old goddess is the first to assist the new. Brigid is also the first person to hold the Christ child in her arms, and with the water from a sacred spring she is his baptiser. Thus not only is she Mary's midwife, she is also the midwife of Christianity.

The stories of Brigid and the Holy Family attracted the attention of Celtic revivalists and artists in the late nineteenth and early twentieth centuries, and the story was re-performed in new cultural texts and contexts. Lady Gregory wrote a play which was performed by the Abbey Theatre at Easter 1924, called 'The Story Brought by Brigit', in which Lady Gregory extended the oral tradition of Brigid's presence at the birth of Christ to place her also at the scene of his death.[56] In England in 1914, a pageant play was staged in Glastonbury, which also has an oral tradition of Saint Brigid, as well as a chapel and well in her name.[57] *The Coming of Bride* showed Brigid taking care of the weary and frightened holy family in a saintly dream vision. When Brigid woke, she was still in her fields in Ireland, but Saint Joseph had kindly left her a bejewelled cloak as proof of their visit.[58]

In Scotland in 1913, the painter John Duncan, one of the leading representatives of the Celtic Revival, created a luminous

54 Bourke, 'Irish Stories', 22–23.

55 Bitel, 'St Brigit of Ireland: From Virgin Saint to Fertility Goddess', paper presented at Fordham University, Feb 2001. Available online at monasticmatrix.org/commentaria/article.php?textId=6 [14 Feb 2008].

56 Irish Theatre Institute, play listing. The play drew upon the popular connection between 'the Easter Rising and the martyrdom of Christ.' C I Innes, *Woman and Nation*, 161.

57 There is also an image of Saint Bride with a cow on the fourteenth-century Saint Michael's Tower on the Glastonbury Tor. Bowman, 'Arthur and Bridget in Avalon,' 24.

58 *Ibid*, 24–25.

canvas now held in the National Galleries of Scotland which depicts angels carrying a sleeping Saint Bride to Bethlehem, to be present at the birth of Christ.[59] A seal accompanies them over the seas. The white-gowned saint, lying stiffly between the two magnificent and richly robed angels, is golden-haired as Bride is in Scottish lore, but also rather thin and frail: a girl much like the scared and skinny Mary in Dante Gabriel Rossetti's 1850 *Annunciation*, and nothing like the energetic self-willed saint of the medieval texts.

Not only was Brigid Mary's midwife, she was also honoured in Gaelic oral and written culture as Christ's foster-mother, which meant — as in Celtic cultural practice — that she also breastfed him.[60] As noted, the figure of Brigid is often associated with milk, a nurturing and life-giving substance.[61] Though virginal, she is also a fertile and fecund personage, and suckling the Christ child was just one more of her 'greater wonders'.

Another Irish female saint also said to have shared in this cosmic mothering of Christ was the sixth century saint of Limerick, Saint Ita, teacher of Saint Brendan the Voyager. An early Irish poem in Ita's voice says:

> I nurse him in my lonely place
> though a priest have stores of wealth,
> all is lies save Ísucán [The Christ Child]
> [...]

59 Even the inclusion of angels indicates a rational element when so many of the stories offered no such 'logical' explanation for Brigid's presence at Christ's birth. Duncan's painting is viewable online at www.nationalgalleries.org/collection/online_az/4:322/result/0/17484?artistId-3210&artistName=John%20Duncan&initial=D&submit=1 [12 December 2007]

60 From Peter Parkes, 'Celtic Fosterage: Adoptive Kinship and Clientage in Northwest Europe', *Comparative Studies in Society and History*, 48 (2006), 359–395, at p 362.

61 Thomas Torma notes that not only were dairy products and cattle a crucial part of the early and medieval Irish economy, milk was also biologically vital, the vitamin D in milk making up for the lack of sunlight in Ireland. Torma, 'Milk Symbolism in the *Bethu Brigte*', 2.

> in his dwelling high above,
> though at my breast, is Ísucán.[62]

There is an erotic sweetness to the breastfeeding maternal figure, which even warrior or monastic cultures, or perhaps especially such masculinist cultures, would find comfort and sustenance in.

The Celtic practice of fostering out babies born into leading families to be raised by relatives or clients increased social cohesion within the *tuath* or clan. It forged, as Alistair Moffat notes, 'two sets of social bonds of immense intensity'.[63] Indeed, as the twelfth-century visitor, Gerald of Wales, and other later commentators would note, the milk connection in Irish society was often stronger than blood. Gerald complained of the warring Irish: 'If they have any love or loyalty, it is only for their foster-sons and foster-brothers'.[64] Thus, with Brigid as his foster-mother, Christ enters the Celtic world as a milk-son to the Celtic divine feminine, and a milk-sibling to the Celtic community — a bond as strong as blood.

Sometimes within the medieval Irish texts there was also a total merging of Mary and Brigid. In one example, a hymn attributed to the seventh-century Ultán of Ardbraccan conflates the two figures:

> Brigit, excellent woman, sudden flame [...] May she do away with the rent sin has put upon us; the blossomed branch; the Mother of Jesus; the dear young woman greatly looked up to. That I may be safe in every place with my saint of Leinster![65]

As one mother or as joint mothers of Christ, it is clear that Mary and her divine sister Bride formed a powerful protective and nurturing spiritual force constantly invoked in prayers and poetry,

---

62 J Carney, *Early Irish Poetry* (Cork, 1969) 51.

63 Moffat, *The Sea Kingdoms*, 167.

64 P Parkes, 'Celtic Fosterage: Adoptive Kinship and Clientage in Northwest Europe,' *Comparative Studies in Society and History* 48/2 (2006) 359–395.

65 Gregory, *A Book of Saints and Wonders*, 19.

and especially within women's devotional practices and stories in Irish and Scottish Gaelic cultures. Their invocations and prayers sometimes put Mary first and sometimes Brigid, but there is no sense of rivalry or competition, just two lovely women taking care of us all. One Irish prayer that was said over smooring the hearth fire goes: 'I save this fire as holy Christ saves, may Mary be on the roof of the house and Brigid within it'.[66]

Brigid and Mary, then, lived together within Gaelic oral traditions, in creative works by Celtic revivalists, as well as within at least one diasporic community, that of Newfoundland. But it is important to note that the southern Avalon community was established before the catastrophe of the potato famines, *An Gorta Mór*, the Great Hunger of 1846–1850 which swept away millions of the Irish rural poor, by death or emigration. It was this class which had held onto the language and the older traditions of Gaelic Ireland.

As Angela Bourke notes, 'rich resources of imagination, memory, creativity and communication were jettisoned' when the Irish language and its worldview and traditions, including its awesomely rich, varied and layered oral narratives, were discarded and even denigrated throughout Ireland.[67] Without the labouring and landless poor, their language and their narratives, the nineteenth-century 'ideology of rationality',[68] in both its imperial/colonial and its episcopal forms made deeper inroads into the cultural landscapes of Ireland and Scotland. The increasing standardisation and ultramontanism of the Catholic church would also assist in drying up the local verdant landscape, with its standardised saints for a new globalised spiritual economy.

To some extent, the cult of Brigid in Ireland has — at least partially — survived these grinding down processes, possibly because

66 O'Dwyer, *Mary*, 277.

67 A Bourke, 'The Baby and the Bathwater: Cultural Loss in Nineteenth-Century Ireland,' 79–92 in T Foley and S Ryder (eds), *Ideology and Ireland in the Nineteenth Century* (Dublin, 1998), at p 79.

68 *Ibid.*

her cult was wedded to physical landscape and seasonal rituals — of cloth, pilgrimage, holy wells, feast day bread baking, and of course the making of her cross — as much as it was embedded in story and language. And partly because, in the early twentieth century, the Irish state embarked on a recovery process, 'setting seriously about the task of cultural decolonisation by investing heavily in the reprivileging of native tradition'.[69] The old stories of Brigid were told again, this time for children through the official school system, including the tale of the magical cloak spreading over the lands of Kildare, and also how Brigid once hung her wet cloak upon a sunbeam to dry.

For the Catholic children of the Irish diaspora, there were no such beautiful, mythopoetic tales. As Patrick O'Farrell notes of the Irish in Australasia, they had come to lands 'whose antiquity was not Christian, whose sentiment and disposition was secular, and whose politics were British'.[70] In the absence of a known, beloved and spiritualised physical landscape, Catholic Irish emigrants came to rely more heavily, says O'Farrell, 'on the institutional machinery of formal religion'.[71] Locked out of her originary landscape and language, the Brigid of the diaspora is — like the sleeping girl in John Duncan's painting — a lovely but lesser woman.

The statues churned out in Italy for numerous Catholic parishes worldwide privileged the holy family, leaving out their midwife, Herod rescuer, web weaver and Candlemas dancer. Brigid, when she was represented in diasporic churches, was never accompanied by anything so heathen and so rural as a cow: she was now the abbess, the church builder. Although still the female patron saint of Ireland, and still often wielding a bishop's crozier, she was increasingly elided by her male counterpart, the glorious Saint Patrick. By the mid-twentieth century, in the ubiquitous 'Lives of the Saints' picture books for children, Church orthodoxy had dried up

69 Bourke, 'Irish Stories', 18.

70 P O'Farrell, *Through Irish Eyes: Australian and New Zealand Images of the Irish 1788–1948* (Melbourne, 1994) 61.

71 *Ibid.*

Brigid's lakes of milk and ale, and made no mention of any runaway cloak, as they presented a woman whose only power was in prayer. The grandeur of her establishment and church at Kildare which so impressed the eighth-century hagiographer Cogitosus becomes 'a lovely little convent'.[72] Even the eye which, in the medieval texts and persisting oral tradition, she famously plucked out of her own face — to successfully put an end to familial pressure on her to get married — has become God making her ugly in answer to her prayer, and of course restoring her beauty once she became a nun.[73]

The 'most powerful of Irish women saints — a figure of the feminine in all its aspect'[74] became in the diaspora just one amongst many, left behind not just by Mary but also by Catherine, Therese, Margaret, Anne, Clare, Bernadette, etc. Katherine Massam has noted how, while Catholicism in Australia was dominated numerically and administratively by the Irish, Mary was increasingly used as the unifying symbol to gather and unite Irish and Italian, Polish and Yugoslav immigrants to Catholic Australia.[75] Even as early as the mid-nineteenth century, Irish women were beginning to drop the name which had once clearly identified them as Irish.[76] Of over

---

72 D A Lord, 'St Brigid of Ireland' in *Miniature Lives of the Saints, Book IV*, (New York, 1946).

73 *Ibid.* By contrast in both the *Bethu Brigte* and the *Leabhar Breac*, Brigid pokes her own eye out, and offers it to her irritating brother Beccán. In the *Bethu Brigte* it is not stated if her eye is restored but in the *Leabhar Breac* Brigid 'puts her palm to her eye and it was quite whole at once.' Her brother was less fortunate. In the *Bethu Brigte*, Brigid curses her brother and he loses the sight in both eyes. In the *Leabhar Breac* she has slightly more compassion, and Beccán loses only one eye. *Bethu Brigte*, 15 and *Leabhar Breac*, trans W Stokes, 65. Angela Bourke also notes how the folk tradition differs from literary accounts, in that in many of the oral tales, Brigid's eye is not restored. Bourke, 'Irish stories', 26.

74 Bourke, 'Irish Stories', 28.

75 K Massam, *Sacred Threads: Catholic Spirituality in Australia 1922–1962* (Sydney, 1996) 20. Interestingly, the cover of *Sacred Threads* is adorned by Therese of Lisieux.

76 Of the 400 women and girls who were sent from Irish workhouses to Sydney immediately following the Great Famine, one quarter were called

140 parishes established in Sydney, NSW, since 1800, only two bear Brigid's name.[77] Of over 550 Catholic schools now operating in all of NSW, Brigid can only count nine in her protective care.[78] Mary has 100; Saint Joseph, a popular diasporic saint, has 80.

Perhaps it was not possible for Mary's sister Bride, the free-wheeling saint of the fields and the sacred waters, to leave her homeland. But traces of her, surely, must survive, even in the dry rational colonial realm. Indeed, in the recent (2006) Australian film *Jindabyne*, a scene showed a Saint Brigid's protective cross put up in a contemporary Australian home (albeit by a controlling interfering Irish mother-in-law) with an Irish-language prayer said.

As Brigid is re-emerging in Ireland, and even in England, so too the fuller figure of the archaic and anarchic Brigid may yet enliven the spiritual landscapes of the diasporic and descendant communities with her boldness and magic. For we need her qualities, that woman who could be neither bought nor sold.

Mary. Brigid did come in third, as 44 (approximately ten percent) were called Bridget or Biddy. The second most popular name was Catherine (50 girls). After Bridget came Anne (32), Margaret (28) and Ellen (19). Irish Famine Memorial, 'Australian Monument Lists Four Hundred Names: Girls orphaned by the Irish Famine'. Available online at http://irishfaminememorial.org/orphans/names_monument.htm [20 June 2007].

77 Saint Patrick has seven, the largest number outside of the Holy Family, and just beating Saint Therese of Lisieux (6) and the Archangel Michael (6), but the biggest winners are of course Mary (29 parishes), Joseph (14) and Christ (8). Archdiocese of Sydney, Parish register. Available online at www.sydney.catholic.org.au/Parishes/parishMassTimes.asp [29 Jan 2008].

78 List of non-government schools in New South Wales, NSW Board of Studies, October 2007. Available online at Wikipedia. http://en.wikipedia.org/wiki/List_of_non-governmental_schools_in_New_South_Wales [29 January 2008].

CELTS IN LAW

The idea of continuation and extinguishment of 'Welsh' customary land law in the face of Norman-English conquest and legal regime change

Michael Stuckey ⊕

In the setting of military conquest and revolutionary change, and the consequent resolution of legalities, lawmakers will often attempt to articulate very selective distinctions about the past and the present and about continuities and transformations. The idea of the continuation, or conversely the extinguishment, of customary law is of course a concept which has attracted the attention of historians of the common law, and in the context of land law there has been a particular concern in recent years relating to native title claims in 'settled colonies', principally in the United States of America, Australia, Canada and New Zealand. In line with common law methodology, precedents endow this discourse; and the Welsh case which is cited in this context as the exemplar of the survival of indigenous laws in a post-conquest settlement is *Witrong v Blaney* (1674) 3 Keeble 401 [84 ER 789]. It has been by way of cases like *Witrong v Blaney* that Sir Edward Coke's analysis of the legalities of conquest informed the Blackstonian declaration of the colonies, establishing the paradigm within which we still largely function. However, a close reading of *Witrong v Blaney* reveals an indistinct and possibly hesitant judicial position in relation to the effects of the (apparently) crucial piece of legislation, the 1535 Act (27 Henry VIII cap 26), possibly indicating that at its heart this piece of legislation had an inherent ambiguity so far as the idea of

⊕ B.A.(Hons), LL.B., LL.M.(Hons), Ph.D. (Syd.), Grad.Dip.Prac.Leg. Training (UTS), Professor of Law and Head of the School of Law, The University of Glamorgan (Wales).

continuation or extinguishment of Welsh law was concerned. It is argued, accordingly, that one must be very cautious, and very critical, about the use to which the history of conquest is put.

In the watershed Australian native title case *Mabo v Queensland (No 2)*, Justice Brennan cited two cases which, his Honour held, represented authority for the proposition that there was ancient common law precedent for the survival of indigenous laws in post-conquest or feudal circumstances.[1] Of the two paradigms his Honour selected for treatment, the Irish and the Welsh experiences were exemplified (respectively) in the cases of *The Tanistry* and *Witrong v Blaney*.[2] The Irish example has been subjected to the greatest level of scrutiny and investigation by far: indeed there have been, both before and after *Mabo*, extensive considerations of the meaning and implications of *The Tanistry*, from as early as Sir John Davies' own *A Discovery of the True Causes Why Ireland was Never Entirely Subdued …*, which was published in 1612, to a very recent and penetrating article by Shaunnagh Dorsett.[3] The wider impact of

1 (1992) 175 CLR 1 at p 49.

2 (1608) Dav 28 [80 ER 516] and (1674) 3 Keeble 401 [84 ER 789].

3 Sir J Davies, *A Discovery of the True Causes Why Ireland was Never Entirely Subdued [And] Brought Under Obedience Until the Beginning of His Majesty's Happy Reign*, J P Myers (ed), (Washington DC, 1988) and S Dorsett, 'Since Time Immemorial: A Story of Common Law Jurisdiction, Native Title and the Case of Tanistry', *Melbourne University Law Review* 26 (2002) 32–59. See also Sir H Maine, *Lectures on the Early History of Institutions* (London, 1875) 98–208; *Moore & Ors. v. A-G (Saorstat Eireann), Goan & Ors.* [1934] IR 44 at 62–64 and 87–89; K S Bottigheimer, 'Kingdom and Colony: Ireland in the Westward Enterprise 1536–1660' and B Bradshaw, 'Native Reaction to the Westward Enterprise: a Case-study in Gaelic Ideology', 45–64 and 64–80 respectively in K R Andrews, N P Canny and P E H Hair (eds), *The Westward Enterprise: English Activities in Ireland, the Atlantic and America 1480–1650* (Liverpool, 1978); Sir H S Pawlisch, *Sir John Davies and the Conquest of Ireland* (Cambridge, 1985); J P Myers, 'Early English Colonial Experiences in Ireland: Captain Thomas Lee and Sir John Davies', *Eire – Ireland* 23 (1988) 8–21; B Bradshaw, 'Robe and Sword in the Conquest of Ireland', 139–162 in C Cross, D Loades and J J Scarisbrick (eds), *Law and Government Under the Tudors* (Cambridge, 1988).

these researches, and the historical (or possibly it is more accurate to say 'historicist') methodology of the common law courts which have considered the question of the legal systems of the successor states to the aforementioned 'settled colonies', has been extensive and profound,[4] but regrettably it is an impact which is beyond the scope of this article to treat in any way other than with some brief and sweeping remarks towards its conclusion.

The idea of the survival of Welsh customary laws (including, critically, land laws), contrary to the legal effects of Norman and English military triumph and legal reorganisation, is one which has attracted rather less attention from scholars than has the Irish experience. The Welsh case, which is cited as the exemplar of the survival of indigenous laws in post-conquest or feudal circumstances by Justice Brennan in *Mabo*, is the 1674 decision in *Witrong v Blaney*. The case ostensibly concerned the issuing of process, specifically the *scire facias*, into Wales. The issues for determination were divided by the court between a narrow and technical point concerning the availability of the procedural response from the defendant to the sheriff, and a wider and more decisive jurisdictional point about whether the *testatum scire facias* could issue into Wales. All of the judges in the case, Justices Ellis, Atkins and Windham, agreed all of the points unanimously, but it is with the second and more all-embracing point with which we are concerned: because it was in relation to this point that there was some explicit and extensive consideration of the historical basis of the jurisdiction exercised by royal courts over and in Wales.

Justice Ellis delivered the leading judgment in *Witrong v Blaney*, and in relation to what his Honour referred to as 'the main point' his Honour articulated an apparently robust statement as to the basis of royal jurisdiction in Wales. His Honour stated:

> 9 Ed. 1, by conquest and attainder of David and lluellin Slaine, he had *vitae & necis potestatum*, and

4 see M Stuckey, 'Not by Discovery but by Conquest: The Use of History and the Meaning of 'Justice' in Australian Native Title Cases', *Common Law World Review* 34,1 (2005) 19–38.

> as 7 Co. 17, he might alter laws or dispose the lands as he pleases 2 Inst. 195, but there needs no new grant for admitting parties to continue in possession this of itself is a sufficient title to Christians but infidel kingdoms having laws against the Decalogue, they are abolished by conquest, till new established. And all lands by conquest are held mediately or immediately of him, but need no new conveiance from the Crown [...]

His Honour, in a pithy judicial style, thus encapsulated the legal effects of the conquest of Wales by Edward I: but for our purposes it is worth expanding on this terse account (if only a little). In 1255 Llywelyn ap Gruffydd ruled north and mid-Wales solely, although from this year until 1282 a drawn-out battle with the English occurred over the sovereignty of Wales. Notwithstanding the truces of 1267 and 1276, Edward's unrelenting strategy of subjugation was ultimately successful with his acquisition of the possessions of Llywelyn when the latter was killed in battle in December 1282. Two years later the *Statutum Walliæ*[5] was enacted at Rhuddlan. The statute was drafted consequent to the report of a commission (which was actually instituted before Llywelyn's death), and in fact was not a parliamentary statute: it was the king's own 'enactment' as the edict of a conqueror of a rebellious and (at least) autonomous country. Edward's intentions, from the first words of the statute, were patent. The statute commenced with a preamble which recited the political realities extant: stating that Wales, with its inhabitants, had hitherto been subject to the king by feudal right, but that divine providence, amongst other gifts, had 'wholly and entirely transferred the land of Wales with its inhabitants' to the king's domain. It was furthermore stated that the king having diligently heard, and fully understood, 'the laws and customs of those parts hitherto in use,

5 12 Ed I cap 1. See Ll B Smith, 'The Statute of Wales, 1284', *Welsh History Review* 10, 2 (1980–1) 127–54 and W H Waters, 'The First Draft of the Statute of Rhuddlan', *Bulletin of the Board of Celtic Studies* 4, 4 (1929) 345–8.

had abolished some of them, allowed some, corrected some, and commanded certain others to be added thereto' and that the country was annexed and united unto the crown of the realm of England as a member of the same body.[6] Under the statute of Rhuddlan trials relating to real property were always to be conducted before a jury selected by the parties, and those relating to personal actions were to apply Welsh law. In criminal cases English laws were to be followed. Most importantly, the thirteenth section of the statute, demonstrating Edward's policy of maintaining certain Welsh laws, regulated succession to landed property upon death. It recognised the Welsh custom of inheritance by the equal division of real property amongst male heirs, thus, and expressly, differing from English primogeniture.[7]

The references in Justice Ellis' judgment to Sir Edward Coke were specifically and respectively to *Calvin's Case* (1608) 7 Co 17, and to its discussion by Coke in his *Institutes*, particularly on the issue of the legal consequences of military conquest. Gavin Laughton has lately shown how the gradual judicial acceptance of Coke's analysis of 'conquest' in *Calvin's Case* in the seventeenth century occurred, and how that slow but sure curial acceptance created a distinct legal rule about the effects of conquest which was suited to the acquisition of empire.[8] Of course, as Laughton shows, the chief illustrations of this new rule were to be found in Ireland and America. Eventually, and without a doubt by way of

---

6 *Ibid.* See I Bowen, *The Statutes of Wales* (London, 1908) xxviii–xxxii and 2–3.

7 On the eventual introduction of primogeniture, a process which was (in fact) far less controversial than might be anticipated owing to differential effects of the *Statute of Uses* (1536) on the practice of the circumvention of the common law rules by granting land *inter vivos* to feoffees to uses in Wales: see T G Watkin, *The Legal History of Wales* (Cardiff, 2007) 136–7. Cf. S E Thorne, 'English Feudalism and Estates in Land', *Cambridge Law Journal* [1959] 193–209, at p 202–204.

8 G Laughton, 'Calvin's Case and the Origins of the Rule Governing 'Conquest' in English Law', *Australian Journal of Legal History* 8 (2004), 143–80.

the incremental effects of precedent in cases like *Witrong v Blaney* and others, Coke's analysis of conquest informed the Blackstonian declaration of the colonies rule with which we are most familiar today. Thus was the common law discourse of the legal effects of conquest created, nourished and established.

In the course of his judgment Justice Ellis also referred to the 1535 Act (27 Henry VIII cap 26), although not in the same crucial and defining way as his Honour had cited the effects of the conquest and legal actions of Edward I. The 1535 Act (sometimes known as the Welsh Act of Union), according to its preamble, recognised that Wales: 'justly and rightly is, and ever hath been incorporated annexed and united and subject to and under the Imperial Crown of this Realm'. His Honour, although declaring that the Henrician Act 'made the great alteration', then in descriptive and exemplary forms, expressly narrowed the effect of this ostensibly fundamental legislation to a mere clarification of discrepancies and a systematising of process. Given the precise legal question before the court in this instance (the technical point concerning the availability of the procedural response from the defendant to the sheriff) why did his Honour not place heavier reliance on this Act?

The answer, it is submitted, may lie in an understanding of the more sophisticated and multi-layered, if untidy, canvas upon which the Act of 1535 was superimposed. The late thirteenth-century Edwardian 'settlement' was, as we know, actually far from tidy. Even before the 'conquest' of Edward I, Norman barons had embarked on hostile operations into Wales. Between 1066 and the 1130s in the south of Wales these lords established domains out of what had previously been Welsh kingdoms. The extraordinary claims to the holding of regalities by right of conquest and not by grant of the crown advanced by the Marcher lords is a telling indication of the complexities of the legal effects of military conquest. According to Cam, the historical evidence underlying the assertion was that Anglo-Norman Marcher lords had succeeded, directly, to the rights of their Celtic antecedents. Cam further notes that these rights were pre-feudal but post-(1066)-conquest, and citing the earlier work of Rees, that as such the first Marcher lords were 'conquerors in their own right of lands which had never been within the allegiance of the king'.[9] All the same, this indistinct admixture existed for centuries. As is often the case, it may well be that it is the exceptions to accepted or supposedly well-understood rules which elucidate and make comprehensible their forms and operations. As we have seen, by the time of Edward I's Statute of Wales in 1284,[10] after the subjugation of 'the Principality' (essentially in the north and centre of Wales), the Welsh nation became 'annexed and united' to the Crown of England. What is significant to note here is that Welsh law, albeit in such diverse conditions as it existed in the Marches and the Principality, then survived until Henry VIII's legislative measure in 1535. This new statute was for this reason a measure, notwithstanding the linguistic pacifiers contained in the first few words of the preamble (previously cited), whose intention was also plainly stated later in the same preamble: 'utterly to extirpe all and singular the senister usages and customes' in Wales that varied from English law.

In this context, it is submitted that Justice Ellis' indistinct and possibly hesitant position on the effects of the 1535 Act (27 Henry VIII cap 26) discloses, possibly, that his Honour understood that at its heart this piece of legislation was based upon an intrinsic and deliberate vagueness so far as the idea of continuation

---

9 H M Cam, *Liberties and Communities in Medieval England* (Cambridge, 1944) 211, citing W Rees, *South Wales and the March: 1284–1415 – A Social and Agrarian Study* (London, 1924) 23–26 and quote at p 43. See also J Otway-Ruthven, 'The Constitutional Position of the Great Lordships of South Wales', *Transactions of the Royal Historical Society*, 5th ser. 8 (1958) 1–20, the numerous works of Rees Davies, including 'The Twilight of Welsh Law 1284–1536' *History* 51 (1966) 143–164; 'The Law of the March', *Welsh History Review*, 5 (1970–71) 1, 'Colonial Wales', *Past and Present*, 65 (1974) 3–23 and 'Law and National Identity in Thirteenth-century Wales' 52–69 in his and others (eds) *Welsh Society and Nationhood: Historical Essays Presented to Glanmor Williams* (Cardiff, 1984); J Cook, 'Hywel Dda's Law Books and the Welsh Legal Tradition', *Ius Commune*, 18 (1991) 195–205 and D Jenkins, 'The Medieval Welsh Idea of Law', *Legal History Review*, 49 (1981) 323–348.

10 12 Ed I cap 1.

or extinguishment of Welsh law was concerned. It reveals, at least implicitly, that his Honour comprehended the multi-jural environment which the 1284 statute of Rhuddlan had allowed and which the 1535 statute sought to terminate.

Returning to the remainder of the court in *Witrong v Blaney*, Justice Atkins agreed with what Justice Ellis described as the 'main' point: the principal basis for this was, his Honour stated, that '[o]riginally Wales and England were but one nation, so the union is but a restitution [...]'. Justice Atkins further explained that, while there was some separation consequent to what he (to our sensibilities somewhat unusually) termed the 'Saxons successes', it was ultimately Edward I who 'changed [Wales] from a dominion of tenure and right to a dominion of propriety on attainder of David'. Although the Act of Henry VIII referred to Wales as always having been a part of England, Justice Atkins reaffirmed his view that it was in fact Edward I who put this question beyond doubt in so far as the legal effects of union were concerned. One can notice, therefore, that Justice Atkins' construction of the issue was slightly and subtly different from, and closer to the precise wording of the 1535 Act (27 Henry VIII cap 26) than the more equivocal reasoning of Justice Ellis.

Justice Windham also agreed as to the 'main' issue for determination, also adopting the union-as-restitution posture. His Honour went perhaps further than Justice Atkins by stating that while the effects of conquest were even more pronounced in Ireland (indeed Windham J cited *The Tanistry* as authority for describing Ireland as a place, according to Windham J, 'gained meerly by conquest, which shews what may be done for execution of justice, much stronger than here'). In the case of Wales — a place, according to Windham J (and to our sensibilities even more extraordinarily) 'anciently part of England' — the issue could not be in doubt. Again, like Justice Atkins, Justice Windham elected to keep closer to the Henrician orthodoxy, as expressed in the 1535 legislation, rather than to lift the veil on the potential ambiguities of continuity and extinguishment to which Justice Ellis had adverted.

Of course it is understandable that in 1674 the court in *Witrong v Blaney* would adhere reasonably closely to the 1535 Welsh Act of Union in determining the matters in issue. The legislation, at least superficially, provided a plain and virtually prêt-à-porter answer to the question about jurisdiction, which was (after all) the matter in dispute before the court and which called for direct resolution. None of the members of the court, however, confined their reasoning solely to this (permissibly) narrow approach. Instead, as has been demonstrated, all the judges also chose to address the broader question as they saw it. This was because, it has been proposed here, the legislation which purported to provide the court with a straightforward answer to the issue at hand in fact released a hidden truth about the continuity of a jurisdictionally multi-faceted environment, where indigenous law survived the post-conquest settlement. The case called for a different style of judicial approach, which their Honours palpably adopted in order to reach the required outcome without upsetting certain politically determined givens. This style of reasoning is interestingly redolent of a modern style of appellate judicial historicism which can be seen in cases like *Mabo*,[11] which sometimes overtly pursues a 'feudal' basis for the contemporary discourse of common law native title. It is important to note that while *Witrong v Blaney* has been wrapped up in these treatise-like handlings of the foundations of a feudal basis of the absolute and beneficial crown land ownership, at no point in the judgment in *Witrong v Blaney* is the word 'feudal' used by the judges. Even though the expression had been in use in the English legal vocabulary since the early part of the seventeenth century, it has been demonstrated that the term had not yet in 1674 gained the degree of judicial acceptance and quasi-mythical and ideological reverberations that it would in the post-Blackstone era.[12]

---

11 M Stuckey, 'Feudalism and Australian Land Laws: 'A Shadowy Ghostlike Survival'?', *University of Tasmania Law Review* 13 (1994) 102–115.

12 See J G A Pocock, *The Ancient Constitution and the Feudal Law: A Study of English Historical Thought in the Seventeenth Century: A Reissue with a Retrospect* (Cambridge, 1987) 91 and J W Cairns and G McLeod, 'Thomas Craig, Sir Martin Wright, and Sir Williams Blackstone: The English Discovery of Feudalism', *Legal History* 21,3 (2000) 54–66.

That said, traces (at least) of a feudal idea certainly do infuse the judgments delivered by the court, as is evidenced in particular by Justice Ellis' statement that 'all lands by conquest are held mediately or immediately of him'.

It is also understandable, in the circumstances of military conquest and revolutionary change, and (critically) the consequent resolution of legalities, that lawmakers will attempt to articulate very discriminating distinctions about the past and the present and about continuities and transformations. One frequently exploited expedient is the presentation of the changed reality as a restoration of a venerable *status quo ante bellum*. There are, of course, circumstances or conditions where such a stratagem is either impossible (perhaps because the device represents too great a stretch of the imagination) or unwanted (perhaps because a more direct message about change is preferred). However, in many situations where there has been the political necessity to re-present the present, lawmakers resort to a schema of continuity and permanence to disguise the actualities of radical change.

This tendency extends, I would argue, to include modern common law appellate judicial application of precedent in native title cases in the settled colonies, such as *Mabo*. *Witrong v Blaney*, as exposed, exemplifies the ultimately unsure and unsatisfying approach of modern common law appellate courts in their understanding and treatment of historical lineages and historiographical perspectives. It is an approach which, I have argued elsewhere, is inherently incongruous because, at one and the same time, it indicates that it is proper, functional and desirable to utilise historical materials in an evidentiary sense to provide a 'context' but that it is not permissible (again in an evidentiary sense) to 'generalise upon the broad sweep of history': a distinction which is plainly unsustainable.[13] So, for example, in the Australian setting, where it has been conventionally thought that the first expression of feudalism by the courts was the decision of *Attorney-General v Brown*[14] in 1847, it has now been

13 Stuckey, 'Not by Discovery but by Conquest'.

14 (1847) 2 Legge 312.

discovered that the lineages of the feudal idea in judicial thinking about land tenure in Australia can be traced back to at least as early as 1834 in the decision of Sir Francis Forbes in *R v Steele* – or possibly even earlier.[15] Conversely, while there had for centuries been a developing discourse of the common law in relation to the effects of conquest, with its genesis in *The Tanistry* (a discourse actually cited by Justice Windham in *Witrong v Blaney*), no such lineage has existed in relation to *Witrong v Blaney* itself prior to *Mabo*.

The legal history of the common law in the 'settled colonies' abounds with instances of the elimination of indigenous property by politico-military acts. However, while it may be one thing to say, in the vernacular of the American courts, that when the conqueror engages in conquest, relief to the victims is not available in 'the courts of the conqueror',[16] it must be an entirely different thing to say that the conquest itself may occur (at least in the legal sense) by the operation of those courts in 'finding', as it were, a constructive conquest. While in the Welsh context this might be seen as an ancient wrong and the result of battles fought so very long ago, in other places these memories and these acts are comparatively fresh and the attendant wrongs are not beyond practical redress. We must be very careful, and very critical, about the use to which we put the history of conquest, especially before today's courts.

---

15 Supreme Court of New South Wales, Forbes C J, Dowling and Burton J J, 18 October 1834, reported in the *Sydney Herald*, 20 October 1834; B Kercher and J Young, 'Formal and Informal Law in Two New Lands: Land Law in Newfoundland and New South Wales under Francis Forbes', 147–191 in C English (ed), *Essays in the History of Canadian Law, Two Islands: Newfoundland and Prince Edward Island* (Toronto, 2005) at pp 172–3. The authors suggest, while acknowledging that such a proposition is subject to a contrary but equally valid construction of the dicta in question, that this lineage may indeed be pushed back to Forbes' judgment in *R v Cooper* (1825) Supreme Court of New South Wales, Forbes C J, 12 February 1825 reported in the *Australian*, 17 February 1825.

16 *Johnson* v *M'Intosh* (1823) 21 US (8 Wheat) 543 at 588.

The Welsh laws of women

Gwenyth Richards ⊕

Following his final conquest of the Welsh in 1284, Edward I issued the 'Statute of Wales'. Clause XII of that statute proclaimed that '… whereas heretofore women have not been endowed in Wales, the king granteth that they shall be endowed'.[1] Edward I was apparently redressing a perceived anomaly, and thereby giving Welsh women some parity in respect to landholding with their English sisters. Before this time, strict observance of Welsh native law meant that women could not inherit land, nor could land be inherited through women. Consequently, a Welsh widow could not inherit a third share of her husband's lands in dower, which was the case under English common law. I will argue, however, that while the native Welsh laws ostensibly stood as barriers to women owning land and influencing political affairs in Wales in the thirteenth century, in reality, during the thirteenth century itself, many Welsh noblewomen owned land and received dower from their husbands. I will also explore the paradox that despite Edward I's proclamation of 1284, the situation for Welsh noblewomen owning land in the following centuries did not improve, and in fact actually declined from what it had been in the century leading up to the conquest.

While there is evidence to support the persistence of many Welsh native laws in many areas of Wales from 1284 through until

---

⊕ The University of Sydney.

This paper is based on a chapter of the same title in my PhD thesis, published as G Richards, *Welsh Noblewomen in the Thirteenth Century: An Historical Study of Medieval Welsh Law and Gender Roles* (Edwin Mellin, 2005).

1 I Bowen, *The Statutes of Wales* (London, 1908) 24. For valuable analysis of the strengths and limitations of the Statute of Wales see L B Smith 'The Statute of Wales, 1284', *The Welsh History Review* 10 (1980) 127–54.

the Act of Union in 1536, in practice, by the thirteenth century, English laws and customs were gradually being adopted, especially among the Welsh nobility. During the greater part of the thirteenth century itself, up until the final conquest, these native laws were being actively rationalised and brought to a prominence that had not really been sustained continuously from the time of Hywel Dda, the tenth century, when the laws are believed to have been collected and assembled. As part of a concerted effort to make Wales a separate state, thirteenth-century Welsh rulers manipulated and managed the native laws to suit this end. They were not bound by ancient law; this was the exercise by Welsh rulers of power over the law, as distinct from the exercise of power bound by law. In effect, the ruling group could use what they pleased to establish the state.

The thirteenth century was a time of great change in western Europe, particularly in relation to the laws of the land. The common law of England had its genesis in the twelfth century and came firmly into being by the middle of the thirteenth century. The political climate in Wales during the thirteenth century also saw many changes, as during this century Wales was dominated by two strong Welsh rulers, both of whom sought to rule a united Wales or Welsh 'nation'. Previously even strong Welsh rulers, although they may have increased the area over which they dominated, did not really seek to unite Wales.[2] At the same time, two of the Anglo-Norman rulers of the thirteenth century, Kings John and Henry III, are considered to have been weak kings, who were ultimately faced with rebellion and political dissent. This uncertainty produced a climate in Wales where strong native rulers could expand and consolidate their position with regard to their ambitions to govern a Welsh nation, without interference from Anglo-Norman kings who had to deal with far greater problems in their own personal domains.[3]

---

2 For example, another great Welsh leader, Rhys ap Gruffudd (the Lord Rhys), who presided over Deheubarth in the twelfth century, appeared content to be a vassal of Henry II. He was certainly a willing ally. See D Walker, *Medieval Wales* (Cambridge, 1990) 50.

3 King John and his son Henry III both faced the rebellion of their greatest barons and magnates.

While they remained vassals of the kings of England, both Llywelyn ab Iorwerth (later known as Llywelyn Fawr) and his grandson, Llywelyn ap Gruffudd, were able to expand their domination of native rulers and make inroads into Marcher lordships.

The legal environment for noblewomen in Wales at this time was also determined by the political ascendency of their marriage-partners of similar hereditary rank. Politically advantageous marriages with the Anglo-Norman nobility had been common since the coming of the Normans, and were a feature of the rise of both Llywelyn Fawr and Llywelyn ap Gruffudd. Indeed both of these Welsh rulers married Anglo-Normans. As a consequence, Welsh noblewomen who married Anglo-Norman lords received land in marriage settlements and in dower, which was the custom under English common law, despite the prohibition on women owning land under Welsh native law. Moreover, even some marriages between the noble Welsh included dower in land.

Wales had gradually become a feudal society as a consequence of the coming of the Normans, who brought with them new laws and customs, but many of the ancient native Welsh laws and traditions continued to be applied and upheld. Indeed in small pockets of Wales they were still in use until the fifteenth century.[4] Primogeniture for example, where the eldest male was the heir, was the form of inheritance brought to Britain by the Normans, but in Wales partible inheritance among male heirs was the custom and 'title to land depended on membership of a patrilineage and was restricted to the male members of a four-generation agnatic group'.[5] It should be noted, however, that dynastic succession in

---

4 R R Davies gives many examples of the Welsh adopting English land practices when it proved to their advantage, and conversely, of the English settlers adopting Welsh tenurial and inheritance customs when those practices suited them. Indeed according to Davies, a hybrid system of dividing land held by English tenure between male heirs in the Welsh way "survived in Pembrokeshire into the sixteenth century and beyond". R R Davies, *Conquest, Co-existence and Change, Wales 1063–1415* (Oxford, 1987) 448–456.

5 R R Davies, 'The Status of Women and the Practice of Marriage in Late

Wales was quite different from the inheritance of a patrimony and that, in principle, kingship could not be divided.[6] For example, the succession to the rulership of Gwynedd, or Powys, or Deheubarth, would fall to one man, usually the eldest son of the ruler. Another difference was that illegitimacy was no bar to either dynastic succession or inheritance of a patrimony.

For the past ten years or so I have been researching noblewomen who lived in Wales in the thirteenth century. The noblewomen whom I have studied were at the uppermost level of Welsh society and in many cases would have ranked among the highest level of Anglo-Norman society as well.[7] Consequently, a great deal of landed territory and power was at stake when it came to considerations of marriage among this group. Marriage contracts with Anglo-Norman noblewomen would have included dowry in the form of land and the acquisition of this land would have been the prime consideration in the choice of the marriage partner. If the bride were an heiress, the prospective husband could look forward to controlling his wife's landed interests during the period of the union, as well as having it for their offspring. Similarly marriages were sought by Anglo-Norman lords among the Welsh noblewomen as a means of forming political alliances, and these would also have included marriage contracts involving landed territory. Noblewomen in both Welsh and Anglo-Norman societies would therefore have been highly valued and sought after as marriage partners and we must explore the legal position as it related to women holding land in this period both in Wales and in England.

The extant copies of the ancient Welsh native laws, the

Medieval Wales' in D Jenkins and M E Owen (eds), *The Welsh Law of Women* (Cardiff, 1980) at p 101.

6 P I Lynch, 'Court Poetry, Power and Politics' 167–190 in T M Charles-Edwards, Morfydd E Owen and Paul Russell (eds), *The Welsh King and his Court* (Cardiff, 2000) at p 175. In actual practice, however, disputes among family members over succession were common.

7 For example, the women studied include wives and daughters of Welsh princes, the daughter of one English king and the niece of another English king.

so-called *Law of Hywel Dda*, which were redacted in the late twelfth and thirteenth centuries, contain specific 'Laws of Women' which outline the status of women and their place in Welsh society.[8] There were several versions of the native Welsh laws and some of them are thought to have been of earlier provenance than the Iorwerth version, which is believed to have been compiled in the early thirteenth century.[9] As R R Davies has said, native Welsh law was not a corpus of law issued by or in the name of a sovereign ruler and 'enforced by the machinery of state authority'. It was customary law which was 'an assemblage of legal lore transmitted largely by memory and arranged, glossed and expounded by a class of quasi-professional jurists'.[10] The laws as they exist in their extant redactions, and as they are pertinent to the thirteenth century, were probably not all in use at any one specific time. Rather they are collections of laws which had developed before, during and after the rule of Hywel Dda, who was said to have ruled all of Wales, except the south-east, in the tenth century, up until the time they were redacted in the late twelfth and thirteenth centuries. Indeed the laws continued to be further developed up until the Act of Union of 1536 when all of Wales came under English law.[11]

This was not a formal set of laws and statutes which were designed to be enforced by the state. The extant law books were for

8 For translation of the law, see D Jenkins, *The Law of Hywel Dda* (Llandysul, 1986). The law was divided into three books. Book I dealt with 'The Laws of Court', Book II 'The Laws of the Country' and Book III 'The Justices' Test Book'. 'The Laws of Women' are in Book I, pp 45–61. Other sections of interest are 'The Royal Family', 'The Queen's Officers', 'Women and Land', 'Aliens' and 'Family Law'. For specific and comprehensive studies of the 'Laws of Women' see Jenkins and Owen (eds), *The Welsh Law of Women*, and for similarly detailed studies of 'The Laws of Court' see Charles-Edwards, Owen and Russell (eds), *The Welsh King and his Court.*

9 For a brief description of each law book see T M Charles-Edwards, *The Welsh Laws* (Cardiff, 1989) 20–21.

10 R R Davies, 'Law and National Identity in Thirteenth-Century Wales' in R R Davies et al, *Welsh Society and Nationhood* (Cardiff, 1984) at p 54.

11 Jenkins, *The Law of Hywel Dda,* xvii.

the use of lawyers and others, who needed to know the traditional customs, rights and obligations of the people, and the prescribed compensation or punishment for offences, as well as guidance in the settlement of disputes. As R R Davies has pointed out, the law books were 'lawyers' manuals, not guidebooks for social observers'[12] and we may only use the information gleaned from them to help us to understand certain situations. The law books do not provide evidence or proof to support the arguments of scholars, because it is believed that many of them were probably archaic and obsolete. It is also not known which laws were in fact in use in the thirteenth century. The law books can, however, be used as a guide to support hypotheses as to what may have been behind certain decisions which were taken, and to explain certain outcomes.

As previously mentioned, during the thirteenth century both Llywelyn Fawr and Llywelyn ap Gruffudd were primarily concerned to rule a Welsh 'nation', or at least to gain independence from England, so that it is likely that they wanted many of their native laws to remain. I believe, however, that it suited both Llywelyn Fawr and Llywelyn ap Gruffudd to be seen as staunch champions of their unique and distinctive native Welsh laws and customs, but they were both extremely pragmatic when it came to their own personal interests, particularly that area of the laws concerning women and inheritance.

Earlier in the century, Llywelyn Fawr had wholeheartedly adopted the Norman custom of primogeniture where the eldest legitimate son inherits, when it came to his choice of an heir. His actions suggest that he may have been interested only in those native Welsh laws which suited him, or that he was open to the appeal of Norman customs which accorded with his political ambitions. The available evidence discloses that in Wales and the Marches in the thirteenth century, for both Welsh and Anglo-Normans, there was what might be called opportunistic borrowing of laws and customs on both sides.[13] By the thirteenth century much of

12 Davies, 'The Status of Women', 94.

13 Davies, 'Law and National Identity in Thirteenth-Century Wales', 60

Wales was becoming more and more subject to English common law. There were times when litigants appealed to the ancient Welsh laws, but these occasions were becoming less common. Native laws became entrenched in small pockets in the north-east of Wales, and it appears to have suited both the English and the Welsh for those laws to be enforced locally at times in the fourteenth and even the fifteenth centuries.[14] For the greater part of Wales, however, English common law came gradually into use from the time of its beginnings in England in the twelfth century, and was widely used in the Marches and other areas, particularly in the south, by the thirteenth century.[15] Welsh and English law seem to have co-existed in most of Wales during the 200 years of the conquest, and the Marcher lords exploited Welsh law when it suited them in much the same way as the Welsh princes exploited their native law, for political advantage and for material gain.

The thirteenth century up until 1282 was a time of resurrection of Welsh power, and consequently the territories under discussion were of greater importance strategically and in terms of the power assumed by the possession of the lands involved. The women in my study were the wives, mothers, sisters and daughters of rulers, not of members of the *uchelwyr* or middle class, and for this reason I believe they were extremely important to political outcomes in

---

and 63. See also Davies, *Conquest, Co-existence and Change*, 21 and L B Smith, 'Towards a History of Women in Late Medieval Wales' in M Roberts and S Clarke (eds), *Women and Gender in Early Modern Wales* (Cardiff, 2000) at p 23. A D Carr has stated that 'the Normans had a particular talent for adopting the customs and habits of the people among whom they settled'. A D Carr, *Medieval Wales* (New York, 1995) 37.

14 For discussion of the continued use of Welsh native laws see R R Davies, *Lordship and Society in the March of Wales 1282–1400* (Oxford, 1978) 448–456 and also Davies, 'The Status of Women', 100–103.

15 For a brief but concise outline of the development of the 'custom of the king's courts into the Common Law of England' over the period c1160–c1240 see R Frame, *The Political Development of the British Isles 1100–1400* (Oxford, 1990), esp 'English government in England and Wales', 74–85.

Welsh medieval history.

The Welsh law books contain solutions for every conceivable situation and variation with which it was thought contemporary lawyers might have been expected to deal. Welsh native law, and in particular the law relating to women, is a very large and complex area of study. The following is a discussion of those aspects of Welsh native law which pertain to the women in my study.

Under Welsh native law as it is laid down in the extant redactions, a girl remained under her father's protection and responsibility until she reached puberty between the ages of 12 and 14 and a marriage was arranged for her. The marriage involved a complicated exchange of wealth in which the prime commodity to change hands was the girl herself.[16] The girl's family would usually give a gift of money or movable goods with the girl as her dowry or *argyfrau.* Immediately upon her marriage a payment known as *amobr*, which was similar to *merchet* or *leyrwite*, became due and payable, usually by the girl's family, to the feudal lord. After the girl had shared her husband's bed for the first time and provided he was satisfied that his wife was a virgin, he would give her a gift known as *cowyll*, which is said to correspond to the morning-gift of Germanic society.[17] The value of the gift was evidently based on the status of the wife. D Jenkins states that in the Iorwerth text the amount was £8 for a king's daughter, £1 for the daughter of a *gŵrda* (nobleman) and 80d for a villein's daughter, although these amounts could change through a process of bargaining.[18] In order for her to receive her *cowyll* the bride was obliged to specify what she wanted the *cowyll* to consist of before she left the marriage bed the morning following the marriage. Failure to make specific choices meant that she would forfeit exclusive rights to the *cowyll*, and the *cowyll* would

16 C McAll, 'The Normal Paradigms of a Woman's Life in the Irish and Welsh Law Texts' in *The Welsh Law of Women,* 8–9.

17 D Jenkins, 'Property Interests in the Classical Welsh Law of Women' in *The Welsh Law of Women,* 76.

18 Jenkins, 'Property Interests in the Classical Welsh Law of Women', 76–77.

become part of the common household pool of wealth.[19]

Since, according to native law, no Welsh woman could inherit land, the gifts exchanged as *argyfrau* and *cowyll* usually took the form of movable commodities, such as household utensils and other portable items, and often included livestock. It should be noted that although women did not own land, they did own livestock such as cattle, pigs and horses, and these animals would have been very valuable in this society. Vast landholdings would not be of much use without the means of production, namely cattle. Men needed women's *argyfrau,* especially when it included cattle, and this would have placed such women in a position of power in the relationship.

There are many variations in the redactions of the Welsh laws and while it is generally held that no woman could inherit land, nor could title to land be claimed through a woman, the laws relating to the Welsh king in the Cyfnerth version (Cyfn §73/2) state that land is paid as *cowyll* to a king's daughter.[20] This exception in the laws also provides evidence that in the thirteenth century Welsh noblewomen could and did own land. When Llywelyn Fawr gave land with his daughters for their marriages, under native law this was *argyfrau.* Welsh native law apparently did not make an exception for royal *argyfrau* as it did for *cowyll.*

Many other entitlements and benefits, as well as forfeitures, pertained to the practice of marriage in the Welsh Laws of Women, some of which were designed to govern contingencies which might arise in the future of the union, such as separation before and after seven years, adultery by one or other partner, and so forth. The Laws of Women commence with the rights of each partner in the event of separation.[21] There is a seeming irony here in the fact that the text foregrounds what happened in the event of the failure of a union, rather than stressing the entitlements which accrued for

19 McAll, 'The Normal Paradigms of a Woman's Life', 10. See also Jenkins, *The Law of Hywel Dda,* 58.

20 Jenkins, 'Property Interests in the Classical Welsh Law of Women', *The Welsh Law of Women,* 76 n 33.

21 Jenkins, *The Law of Hywel Dda,* 45.

a successful partnership, but these are, after all, 'lawyers manuals' which would have been designed to deal with variations from the norm. At the expiration of seven years of marriage, the husband and wife were entitled to equal shares of the marriage wealth. The wife was entitled to a payment which was known as *agweddi* if she separated from her husband for a valid reason before the expiration of seven years, or if he abandoned her for an invalid reason during the same seven-year period. If the marriage lasted for seven years then no *agweddi* was payable and the wife was entitled to a half share of the marriage-wealth even if they now separated or if the husband died.[22] Thomas Charles-Edwards equates *agweddi* with English dower (and the Irish *coibche*) because it is a payment from man to woman.[23] In a successful union, the *agweddi* presumably was never paid. This is different though from the English common law dower which stipulates that the husband bestows on his wife one third of the lands which he holds at the time of their marriage for her use if she survives him.[24]

Following the death of her husband the wife was allowed to stay in the home for nine days, but at the end of that time she was to take her half share of the household goods and animals and leave. As Dafydd Jenkins has said, 'while the English widow took her dower as an interest in land, […] she at least ensured that she had somewhere to lay her head'. The Welsh widow, who supposedly could not inherit land, had to rely on her children, if she had any, or perhaps her family of origin, to provide a home for her.[25] Hopefully because of the movable assets she could contribute she would be welcome. Provided the widow in question had been given to the

---

22 Jenkins, *The Law of Hywel Dda,* 46–7. For discussion see McAll, 'The Normal Paridigms of a Woman's Life', 16.

23 T M Charles-Edwards, *Early Irish and Welsh Kinship* (Oxford, 1993) 469.

24 *The Treatise on the Laws and Customs of the Realm of England commonly called Glanvill*, G D G Hall (ed), (London, 1965) Book VI, 58–60.

25 Jenkins, 'Property Interests in the Classical Welsh Law of Women', 85–86.

man by her family with the gift of *argyfrau*, and then proved to be a virgin and received *cowyll*, she was entitled to retain what remained of both of these payments for herself and when added to the half-share of her husband's wealth, excluding land, she may have been in a comfortable position financially. Another factor which may have influenced outcomes, but of which there would be no evidence, would be the effect of relationships within the family, such as affection for the woman by her family, for example, as mother or daughter. For the women in my study however, there are examples of sons contesting their mothers' rights to dower lands so that family affection is not a reliable indicator.

The Welsh laws mention several grounds on which a woman could validly divorce her husband before the expiry of seven years and keep her *argyfrau*, *cowyll* and *agweddi*. These included the husband's impotence, if he was 'leprous' or had 'stinking breath' and if the wife discovered the husband on three occasions with another woman.[26] It is also thought that a couple could separate by mutual agreement and that the wife would retain her entitlements.[27] Both impotence and leprosy appear to me to be valid reasons for divorce and I would suggest that the term 'stinking breath' very probably related to a symptom of serious physical ill health. By today's standards this seems to be a very civilised and sensible way of dealing with failed marriages and could be seen as giving Welsh women a higher legal status.

The majority of the women in my study, which concentrates on the thirteenth century, either held lands or expected to receive lands as part of marriage settlements or in dower. In their efforts to gain autonomy for Wales, both Llywelyn Fawr and Llywelyn ap Gruffudd were anxious to restore native Welsh law and custom, which involved the non-ownership of land by women, but when it came to their own personal familial situation, English common law practices concerning bestowing of land were apparently more attractive. Llinos Beverley Smith believes that by the fourteenth

---

26 Jenkins, *The Law of Hywel Dda*, 46 and 53.

27 Jenkins, 'Property Interests in the Classical Welsh Law of Women', 79.

and fifteenth centuries Welsh society which was 'once resolutely patrilineal in its stance towards land slowly but inexorably came to accept the rights of women to a share of the patrimony'.[28]

Llywelyn Fawr gave his mistress Tangwystl, the mother of his illegitimate children Gruffudd and Gwenllian, a portion of land in Dincadfel, Llanafydd as a gage, which he had received from Hoedlyw ab Ithel. Tangwystl in turn is said to have 'sold the land to Cynon ap Llywarch in whose family it remained'.[29] The reason for the gift of the land is not known. As pointed out before, the bestowing of land on a woman was contrary to Welsh native law but perhaps, even though Tangwystl was not Llywelyn's legal wife, she received the land as *cowyll*. As Llywelyn's concubine she would not have been entitled to dowry in land under English common law. On the other hand, perhaps it was a parting gift from Llywelyn when he married Joan, the illegitimate daughter of King John. The liaison with Tangwystl must have lasted for some time as she gave birth to two of Llywelyn's children. A portion of land seems a suitable settlement in the circumstances, but this is speculation. Four of Llywelyn ab Iorwerth's daughters married Anglo-Norman lords and he gave them Welsh lands as part of their marriage settlements. There is clear evidence that all four daughters also received dower in

28 Smith 'Towards a History of Women in Late Medieval Wales', 36.

29 *Survey of the Honour of Denbigh, 1334*, P Vinogradoff and F Morgan (eds), (London, 1914) 127–128. Hoedlyw ab Ithel mortgaged his rights to this land to Llywelyn ab Iorwerth, who in turn gave the mortgage to Tangwystl ferch Llywarch Goch. See also P C Bartrum, *Welsh Genealogies AD 300–1400*, (Cardiff, 1974) 634. T M Charles Edwards comments on this transaction also, in *Early Irish and Welsh Kinship*, 435–7, and he states that 'not all of this story can be true, for Cynon ap Llywarch lived at the end of the eleventh century not at the beginning of the thirteenth.' He may be right, and as he suggests the name Cynon ap Llywarch may just stand for his lineage and that it may have been his descendants who bought the land. I note, however, that Tangwystl ferch Llywarch Goch had a brother named Cynon (ap Llywarch), and in view of the importance to the Welsh of keeping land in the family, I feel that it would have made better sense for her to have sold the mortgage to her brother.

land upon the deaths of their husbands.[30] Llywelyn's fifth daughter Angharad held landed property,[31] but I do not know whether her father settled this property on her at her marriage or whether she received the lands in dower following her husband's death. I can find no evidence that she was dowered by her husband who, unlike the husbands of her sisters, was a Welsh nobleman, but that does not mean that she did not receive dower, it may be that I have just not found any evidence.

Although the laws stated that women could not inherit land, nor was it possible to inherit land through a woman, under the heading 'Women and Land' the Blegywryd redaction of the Laws of Women states that 'if an owner of land has no other heir than a daughter, the daughter will be heir of all the land'.[32] Huw Pryce believes that this 'represents the intrusion of English law, upheld against local custom by the church of St. Asaph in the late thirteenth century' and that it was later confirmed by the Statute of Wales in 1284.[33] At this point in the law book there is a section concerning the property rights of the sons of women who were conceived as the result of liaisons with aliens,[34] and this section would be relevant to many of the Welsh noblewomen studied.

Most of the evidence cited in support of the argument that 'land could only be inherited through males' in Wales in the later Middle Ages comes from the north-east March, in particular the court rolls of Dyffryn Clwyd. Llinos Beverley Smith has stated that the 'conclusions drawn on the basis of the experiences of the north-east march [...] may not necessarily apply to the country in

---

30 Details of the endowments of Llywelyn's daughters may be found in Richards, *From Footnotes to Narrative,* 46–76.

31 See letter from Rhys Fychan ap Rhys ap Maelgwn which refers to the vills of Angharad the daughter of Llywelyn, dated 23 Feb 1260 in *Littere Wallie*, J G Edwards (ed), (Cardiff, 1940) 26.

32 Jenkins, *The Law of Hywel Dda,* 107.

33 H Pryce, *Native Law and the Church in Medieval Wales* (Oxford, 1993) 107–8.

34 Jenkins, *The Law of Hywel Dda,* 107.

its entirety.[35] R R Davies drew our attention to the resilience of Welsh law in the north-eastern March and to 'the firm insistence that land could only be inherited by or through males', but for the Welsh noblewomen in my study inheritance through females was possible, including women from the north-eastern March. Davies did concede that although in some areas such as Dyffryn Clwyd the rules of inheritance by and through males were strictly adhered to, elsewhere the rules were often relaxed.[36]

An example of where land was expected to be inherited through a female is the case of Gwenllian de Lacy, one of the daughters of Llywelyn Fawr. Curiously, in light of Davies' emphasis on the resilience of Welsh law in the north-eastern March, this land was in Dyffryn Clwyd. This particular case could be viewed both as an argument against the theory of the son of an alien inheriting through his mother under Welsh law, and as an argument for the view that land could be inherited through a woman. Dafydd ap Gruffudd (ob1283) was Gwenllian's nephew. His father Gruffudd and Gwenllian de Lacy were the son and daughter of Llywelyn Fawr and Llywelyn's mistress Tangwystl. Gwenllian was given the land in Dyffryn Clwyd by her father on her marriage to William de Lacy, an alien, and she had held the land for approximately 60 years. At her death, although she had at least one son, Dafydd ap Gruffudd expected to inherit the three townships which were held by his aunt. Dafydd did not inherit the lands as expected because the king had taken possession of them, and this particular issue was one of the grievances cited by Dafydd ap Gruffudd as among the reasons for the outbreak of the war of 1282, a significant political event.[37] Even though Gwenllian had at least one son, when she died it was not her son, by an alien, but her Welsh nephew, who expected to inherit her Welsh lands. Similarly, Roger Mortimer, the son of Gwladus

---

35 Smith, 'Towards a History of Women in Late Medieval Wales', 16.

36 Davies, 'The Status of Women and the Practice of Marriage', 101.

37 A D Carr, '"The Last and Weakest of His Line": Dafydd ap Gruffydd, the Last Prince of Wales', *The Welsh History Review* 19 (June, 1999) 375–399 at p 390.

ferch Llywelyn Fawr, inherited the lands which Gwladus received from her father on her marriage to the Anglo-Norman lord Ralph Mortimer, and although this could be viewed as the son of an alien inheriting his mother's lands, it had also been part of a marriage contract between an Anglo-Norman lord and a Welsh noblewoman under English common law.[38]

There were also instances where Welsh noblewomen received dower from their noble Welsh husbands. Maredudd ab Owain of Ceredigion, who was a great-grandson of the Lord Rhys of Deheubarth, had dowered his wife Elen 'at the church door when he married her' and on 27 August 1246 Henry III ratified the 'assignment of that dower'.[39] The dower comprised 'Gwonhonith' (Gwynionydd), so that in native Wales in 1246 a Welsh nobleman of a prominent Welsh lineage did provide dower for his wife in land. Admittedly Elen was the daughter of Sir Gilbert de Valle, an Anglo-Norman nobleman,[40] and also Maredudd ab Owain had transferred his allegiance from Dafydd ap Llywelyn to the king at the time the dower was ratified,[41] so that these two factors would almost certainly have influenced this transaction. A further example whereby a Welsh nobleman dowered his wife in the thirteenth century is the charter sealed by Owain ap Maredudd of Ceredigion, the son of Maredudd ab Owain mentioned above, on 24 January 1273 which provided dower of the commote of Anhuniog for Angharad his wife.[42] This time Ceredigion was under the control of Llywelyn ap Gruffudd, and he confirmed the transaction by adding his

---

38 Richards, 'From Footnotes to Narrative', 58–65.

39 *Calendar of Patent Rolls of Henry III, AD 1232–1247* (London, 1906) 487.

40 P C Bartrum, *Welsh Genealogies, AD 300–1400* (Cardiff, 1974) Vol 4, 781.

41 Smith, *Llywelyn ap Gruffudd,* 55.

42 For discussion of this particular grant see J B Smith, 'Dower in Thirteenth-Century Wales: a Grant of the Commote of Anhuniog, 1273', *Bulletin of theBoard of Celtic Studies* 3 (1983) 348–355.

seal to the document.[43] Angharad was the daughter of Owain ap Maredudd of Cydewain and she also held lands in Cydewain by the gift of her father. The legal record also shows that she enfeoffed her grandmother of a manor in Cydewain. Angharad had previously held Dolforwyn and I believe that Llywelyn ap Gruffudd in fact exchanged the commote of Anhuniog, subject of the above charter, for Dolforwyn so that he could build a castle there.[44] Llywelyn ap Gruffudd's sister, Margaret, is highly visible in the legal record of the thirteenth century contesting her dower rights. She was the widow of the ruler of Northern Powys, Madog ap Gruffudd.[45]

It would seem that in those parts of Wales under Llywelyn ap Gruffudd's rule in 1273 Welsh noblewomen could hold land, despite the strictures of native Welsh laws and also in spite of Llywelyn's determination to retain those laws. In January 1278, Edward I sent some of his nobles to inspect the lands which Llywelyn ap Gruffudd was proposing to assign in dower to Eleanor de Montfort, consequent upon their marriage,[46] so that Welsh native law notwithstanding, Llywelyn ap Gruffudd also dowered his own wife.

It is interesting to note that the sons of Meredudd ab Owain of Ceredigion, mentioned above, who were allies of Llywelyn ap Gruffudd, also complained to Archbishop Pecham about the loss of their native laws. Gruffudd ap Maredudd and Cynan ap Maredudd complained to Pecham that

> All Christian men have their own laws and customs in their own lands, the Jews living among the English have their laws, they themselves [the Welsh] and their ancestors in their lands had their immutable

---

43 Smith, 'Dower in Thirteenth-Century Wales', 351.

44 Richards, 'From Footnotes to Narrative', 247–254.

45 G Richards, 'Margaret of Bromfield', *Eras 3 (2002):* available online at http://www.arts.monash.edu.au/publications/eras/edition-3/richards.php

46 'Calendar of Welsh Rolls', *Calendar of Chancery Rolls, Various* (London, 1912) 163.

> laws and customs until the English deprived them of
> their laws after the last war.[47]

This is similar to the wording of the letter Llywelyn ap Gruffudd had sent to Archbishop Pecham.[48] I believe that the discontent of Gruffudd and Cynan ap Maredudd and their lamenting of lost native laws relates to the intrusive exercise of English royal control over their lands.[49] It is also of interest, however, that the grandsons of the abovementioned Angharad, Owain and Thomas, were later to claim that Gruffudd and Cynan ap Maredudd had 'wrested the commote [Anhuniog] from their father during the conflict of the reign of Edward I'.[50] Seizing the commote which their brother had specified as dower for his wife may show evidence that they were determined to stick strictly to the native Welsh laws when it came to women possessing rights in land, apart from the fact that they wanted the commote themselves.

From the foregoing it is clear that significant developments took place regarding Welsh laws and the related issues surrounding the position of Welsh noblewomen in the wider context of a dynamic period in Welsh history. Firstly, it would appear that while Welsh native laws may have been followed in some parts of Wales for some of the time in the thirteenth century, changes had been made to the laws themselves and Welsh and Norman rulers applied Welsh law when it suited them and English common law when that proved to their advantage, either personally or in terms of the political climate. It is equally apparent that in this century some Welsh rulers provided dowry in land to their daughters and a number of Welsh noblemen dowered their wives. Throughout these vicissitudes, Welsh noblewomen maintained their importance and status in the changing Welsh society. Through marriage, they helped provide

---

47 *Registrum Epistolarum Fratris Johannis Peckham, Archiepiscopi Cantuariensis, ii*, C T Martin (ed), (London, 1882–86) 453–4.

48 *Registrum Epistolae Peckham, ii*, 442.

49 J B Smith, *Llywelyn ap Gruffudd: Prince of Wales* (Cardiff, 1998) 458.

50 Smith, 'Dower in Thirteenth-Century Wales', 353.

political stability. They brought landed wealth and territory, as well as other wealth in the form of movable goods, to their marriages and more importantly, they provided heirs for Welsh and Anglo-Norman noblemen.

Linda Mitchell has made similar claims about the experience of English noblewomen in the thirteenth century. She argues that they were able to take advantage of increased legal status and access to power during the reigns of John, Henry III and Edward I by adapting to changing circumstances.[51] She has hypothesised also that the fourteenth century 'may have witnessed a gradual but deliberate hardening of gender categories that had a deleterious effect on women's access to power'[52] and mentions the 'legal steps taken to limit women's access to property' which came about between the fourteenth and sixteenth centuries.[53] I believe that many Welsh noblewomen were similarly able to benefit from the prevailing political circumstances during the reigns of these Plantagenet kings of the thirteenth century, and took advantage of the access to landed wealth which presented itself. For example, Welsh-born noblewomen like Gwladus ferch Llywelyn Fawr and her sisters Elen and Margaret owned lands in England which they acquired upon the deaths of their Anglo-Norman husbands. They also owned Welsh lands which were bestowed on them at the time of their marriages. During this century they and other 'Welsh' noblewomen, as defined in my study, experienced greater access to power and increased legal status than was to be available to the Welsh *uchelwyr* in the following centuries. However, the supposed benefit to be derived by Welsh women having access to dower courtesy of the Statute of Wales of 1284 did not materialise. Paradoxically, the statute, which seemed to offer improved access to property for Welsh women following the conquest, was negated by the very conquest itself.

When Edward I and his forces finally completed the conquest

---

51 L E Mitchell, *Portraits of Medieval Women: Family, Marriage, and Politics in England 1225–1350* (New York, 2003) 126–127.

52 Mitchell, *Portraits of Medieval Women,* 133.

53 Mitchell, *Portraits of Medieval Women,* 136.

of Wales by 1284, the king issued the Statute of Wales in which he declared that the Welsh were allowed to keep some of their laws, although he had abolished or amended others. As previously stated, by granting in Clause XII that Welsh women could in future be dowered like their English sisters, he was amending a perceived anomaly in Welsh native law. Clause XIII, however, which was entitled 'Inheritance by the Law of Wales', enshrined the Welsh custom of 'partible inheritance among heirs male' with the amendment that bastards were not to inherit.[54] This same clause also allowed for females to inherit in the event of the absence of a male heir, with the final comment 'although this be contrary to the custom of Wales before used'.[55] The king was prepared to allow partible inheritance to stand, but as was the case under English common law, illegitimate sons could not inherit and females could now inherit the patrimony in the event of failure in the male line.

Lest I be accused of believing that 'the emancipation of Welshwomen from the tenurial shackles of an outmoded and conservative inheritance law is attributed entirely to the liberating forces of English land law',[56] I feel I must stress that this is not what I am suggesting. My contention is that the Welsh themselves were making changes to the laws concerning inheritance throughout the thirteenth century up until 1282. The difficulty as I see it in aligning my argument with those of scholars who quote evidence from the fourteenth and fifteenth centuries is that following the defeat of the Welsh in the late thirteenth century, there were very few Welsh noblemen remaining of the status of those to whom I refer earlier in the thirteenth century. Following the conquest, the upper echelons of Welsh families were mainly comprised of the Welsh middle class, or *uchelwyr*, who had comparatively small land holdings and thus comparatively little power when contrasted with the Welsh princes and noblemen of the twelfth and thirteenth centuries. Therefore even when women were increasingly able to own land, it was

54 Bowen, *The Statutes of Wales*, 25–26.

55 Bowen, *The Statutes of Wales*, 26.

56 Smith, 'Towards a History of Women in Late Medieval Wales', 23.

territorially of less importance than the holdings under discussion in the thirteenth century.

The Scottish Highlands and the conscience of the nation, 1886 to 2003

Ewen A Cameron ◎

The problems of the Scottish Highlands have been repeatedly discussed in emotional terms by the politicians who have been challenged by them. This can be seen in three separate historical contexts, each of which will be dealt with in this paper. The impression created is that the difficulties of the Highlands are 'special' in Scottish and British politics. Another theme of recent political discussion is that the Highlands have been 'neglected' by British governments. This paper will seek to challenge both notions and will, in addition, consider the place of historical writing about the Highlands in Scottish historiography, where some have alleged that it has been overemphasised.[1] In fact, if one examines the history of government attitudes to the Highlands, there is a tendency to see the theme of special treatment and even to identify the Highlands as a 'special policy area' founded on the fact that the *Crofters Holdings (Scotland) Act* of 1886 established a separate form of land tenure in the seven crofting counties from Argyll to

---

◎ University of Edinburgh.

The author would like to record his thanks to the Sydney Society for Scottish History and the Clan Cameron Australia for financial assistance in making the trip to Australia to present this paper. The personal kindness of Mrs Val Smith, Mr Malcolm Broun and Dr Robert Cameron was much appreciated by the Camerons of Upper Stronaba during their time in Sydney.

1 R H Campbell, 'Too much on the Highlands: a plea for change', *Scottish Economic and Social History* 14 (1994) 58–75; D Scott, 'The south of Scotland – challenges and opportunities', 70–87 in D Newlands, M Danson, J McCarthy (eds), *Divided Scotland? The Nature, Causes and Consequences of Economic Disparities within Scotland* (Aldershot, 2004) at pp 71–2, 82.

Shetland. On later occasions, certainly down to the establishment of the Highlands and Islands Development Board [HIDB] in 1965, the government appeared to do distinctive things in the Highlands of Scotland. Sometimes the government even seemed to favour the area over other parts of rural Scotland or other parts of the country, such as Mid Wales, which seemed to have similar social, economic, agricultural and demographic problems.[2] In fact, if one probes beyond the apparent distinctiveness, it is notable that policy for the Highlands can be contextualised in terms of the general thinking of governments of the day, rather than identifying a continuity of special treatment, as is implied by some of the rhetoric referred to below.

Many historical studies have emphasised the distinctiveness and insularity of the Highlands, concentrating on features such as crofting, clearances, language and culture to point to the divergent nature of its historical development. Indeed, this was the view taken by the government when the Highlands impinged on their consciousness, resulting in studious non-intervention during the famine of the 1840s and active intervention in the 1880s. One result of this has been the paradoxical historiographical visibility of the Highlands. The region features disproportionately in treatments of Scotland, because of its *perceived* distinctiveness. Indeed, as Bob Morris and Graeme Morton have noted, Scottish historians tend to shelter behind the idea of a Highland/Lowland divide, partly in search of something distinctively Scottish in a nineteenth-century experience dominated by generic themes like industrialisation and urbanisation (although it can be argued that these were important driving forces of the Highlands experience in this period):

---

2 E A Cameron, 'The Scottish Highlands as a Special Policy Area, 1886 to 1965', *Rural History* 8 (1997) 195–215; E A Cameron, 'The Scottish Highlands: From Congested District to Objective One', 153–69 in T M Devine and R J Finlay (eds), *Scotland in the Twentieth Century* (Edinburgh, 1996). These essays emphasise the distinctive element of Highland policy but do not sufficiently recognise the wider context of many of the developments discussed.

> [...] all authors and editors of books covering nineteenth century Scottish history must decide if they are to include a chapter on the Highland Question/Problem, thus implicitly separating out one area of Scotland from the general economic and social processes of the nation as a whole. [...] In the second volume of the *People and Society in Scotland* series, the editors made a deliberate decision to have no chapters specifically on the Highlands. The hope was that the contributors would be moved to write about Scotland as an integrated whole. This was not really a success, despite the fact that there is considerable evidence that the Highlands were firmly tied into Scottish economy and society — that migration, ownership and trade were all bound together. None the less, few historians seem comfortable with the conception of a Highland/ Lowland Scottish whole.[3]

On a slightly wider canvas John Stevenson commented on

> [...] the subject of the Highlands, that large agricultural region which seems so different from anything that is to be found in lowland England. But the Highlands are not quite so different from what could be found in Wales, or even in parts of the South West of England.[4]

There is no mention of Ireland here, which is perhaps a little odd since so much comparative research has been devoted to finding parallels and contrasts between those two nations, but the point about Wales

---

3 R J Morris and G Morton, 'Where was nineteenth century Scotland', *Scottish Historical Review* [*SHR*] 73 (1994) 93–4.

4 J Stevenson, 'Writing Scotland's history in the twentieth century: thoughts from across the border', *SHR* 76 (1997) 109.

is a good one. The comparison between Scotland and Wales may well be a fruitful one to pursue: both nations were characterised by industrialisation and a rural hinterland with cultural and linguistic distinctiveness. An Irish historian writing a history of England took the trouble to point out, not without substance, that

> [...] the whole historiography of Victorian Scotland [...] is heavily distorted by a kind of nostalgia which sees to it that the countryside attracts more attention than the towns and the Highlands more than the Lowlands. [...] The Highlands assumed a disproportionate place in the perceptions of later generations, not only because of romantic myth, but because it has proved temptingly simple to summarise the nineteenth century experiences of their inhabitants under three highly charged headings: 'the clearances', the 'Highland Famine', the 'Crofters' War'.[5]

The first of these, the 'clearances', has even achieved visibility in a recent history of Europe. Norman Davies has argued that

> The clearances completed a purging process which was to give British society some of its most abiding characteristics. These purges deprived Great Britain of the peasants who formed the backbone of most other nations of Europe.[6]

The remainder of this paper will examine the extent to which this identifiable historiographical trend was matched in more tangible terms by politicians who influenced the shape of the modern Highland economy and society. The influence of three such figures

---

5 K T Hoppen, *The Mid-Victorian Generation, 1846–1886* (Oxford, 1998) 543, 545–6.

6 N Davies, *Europe: A History* (London, 1997) 632.

— William Gladstone, William Ross and Donald Dewar — and the contexts within which they operated will be assessed.

William Gladstone

During the 1880s, amidst the first serious debate about Highland land reform, the Prime Minister, WE Gladstone, remarked to the Home Secretary, William Harcourt, that the justification for legislating to give rights to Highland crofters was

> not because they are poor or because there are too many of them, or because they want more land to support their families, but because those whom they represent had rights of which they have been surreptitiously deprived to the injury of the community.[7]

This was his essential justification for the infringement of the rights of property-holders which were contained in the Crofters Bill of 1885 and the eventual *Crofters Holdings (Scotland) Act* of 1886. He argued that the rights of property in the Highlands were not absolute but came with engagements in the shape of history. Even if he did not go so far as to endorse the suggestions contained in the report of the Royal Commission chaired by the former Governor of Madras, Lord Napier, that the solution to the problems of the region was to recreate the traditional pre-clearance township (closely related in some Victorian minds to the village communities of India), he was impressed by the weight of history and grievance which pressed on the politics of the Highland land question.[8] The principal element of the *Crofters Act* was to provide security of tenure for crofters. The historical dimension of the debate leading up to its passage

---

7 London, The National Archives of the United Kingdom: Public Record Office [TNA: PRO], CAB37/14/173–4, Gladstone to Harcourt, 19 Jan 1885.

8 C Dewey, 'Celtic agrarian legislation and the Celtic revival: Historicist implications of Gladstone's Irish and Scottish Land Acts, 1870–1886', *Past and Present* 64 (Aug 1974) 30–70.

was tangibly reflected in its text, particularly in the stipulation that its provisions were to apply in all parishes of the seven crofting counties in which common grazing rights had been evident within 80 years prior to the passage of the act. So the strictures of political economy, sometimes thought of as rigid in Victorian Britain, were elided for Scottish crofters in 1886 as they had been for Irish small tenants in 1870 and 1881. The legislation, however, was in tune with another aspect of Victorian Liberalism: retrenchment. No landlords had to be bought out by the state, no interest had to be compensated by the Exchequer and, other than the running costs of a legal and regulatory body known as the Crofters Commission, no public expenditure was committed.

Gladstone viewed the claims of the Highland crofters in much the same way as he had viewed those of the small tenants of Ireland who had been given legislative protection by his government in 1881. This should not be viewed as evidence that there was a deep cultural link between the Scottish Highlands and Ireland. Many involved in the debate over land reform, both advocates and detractors, argued that it was the distinctions and contrasts which were more important than the similarities. The Irish were demonised in many ways in late nineteenth-century Scotland: Catholicism, disloyalty to British and imperial identities, violence, poverty and racial inferiority were among the perceived characteristics which contributed to this. Although Highland Scots were sometimes also on the receiving end of this obloquy they were also participants, and sought to distance themselves from the Irish by a warm embrace of the symbols of Britishness. This helped to keep the Highland land question within the confines of mainstream political debate in Britain, in contrast to its Irish version which was closely connected with the politics of home rule and nationalism.[9] The Highland land question was taken up by the Scottish labour movement as it evolved from the

9 J Hunter, 'The Gaelic connection: the Highlands, Ireland and Nationalism, 1873–1922', *SHR* 54 (1975) 178–204; E A Cameron, 'Communication or separation? Reactions to Irish land agitation and legislation in the Highlands of Scotland, c1870–1910', *English Historical Review* 120 (2005) 633–66.

Liberal political culture which dominated Scotland until the early 1920s. Although an emotional anti-landlordism was part of their outlook they have had little truck with nationalism at any point in their history.

This history, however, should not be seen only in a purely 'Celtic' context. The Highland land question was part of a much wider debate on the land question which spread throughout Britain in the period from the 1870s to the early 1920s. In some ways this can be divided into separate national debates, each with their own special characteristics and noted land reformers. In Scotland, the debate focused on the Highlands, with its romantic past layered with levels of rebellious Jacobitism cruelly crushed by brutal Hanoverianism; imperial tartan-clad militarism; repeated cycles of vicious and intense eviction; topped off with heart-wrenching emigration. Over the course of the nineteenth century the Highlands became central to symbols of Scottish identity. The starting point for this is often taken to be Scott's stage-management of George IV's visit to Edinburgh in 1822, but the role of Highland regiments in the Napoleonic wars also played a huge role, as did Queen Victoria's obsession with the Highlands, especially after her purchase of the Balmoral estate. The fact that the Highlands were becoming accessible for tourists and sportsmen added to the visibility of the region and the attraction of representations of it, for example, in paintings. Often this work presented a rather sanitised and romanticised version of the Highlands, without much place given to the people who lived there, either in terms of empty landscapes or greater prominence given to wildlife, especially deer.[10] If sport was central to the romanticisation of the Highlands, it was also important to the protests of the 1880s, which induced government to intervene on behalf of the crofters. Nothing was more controversial than the fact that huge acreages were given over to an exclusive leisure pursuit when there was great hunger for land. Although a positive employment effect was alleged

10 T R Pringle, 'The privation of history: Landseer, Victoria and the Highland myth', 142–61 in D Cosgrove and S Daniels (eds), *The Iconography of Landscape: Essays on the Symbolic Representation, Design and Use of Past Environments* (Cambridge, 1988).

in favour of commercialised sport, this does not seem to have been significant: deer forests were scarcely labour-intensive and sporting tenants had a tendency to bring luxury provisions with them rather than patronise retailers in towns like Inverness, Dingwall or Fort William. Ironically, however, deer forests had tended to displace sheep rather than people. Sheep farming – the supposedly superior economic dispensation which once displaced so many people in the late eighteenth and early nineteenth centuries – was itself in crisis by the 1880s as prices fell and tenants could not be engaged. This fact, and the series of bad seasons and difficult climatic conditions in the early 1880s and the protests which were partly a result, all contributed to the context whereby the Highlands were on the conscience of the Prime Minister in 1885.

There are, however, other dimensions to the Scottish land question which have not been so much discussed in the historiography. The tension surrounding the game laws is one example, with Highland and Lowland tenant farmers unable, for fear of eviction, to protect their crops against the depredations of ground and winged game. The position of the landlord as a privileged creditor to his tenants through the doctrine of hypothec, was another: this meant that the landlord could be fairly sure of getting his money in the event of the bankruptcy of a tenant. These were important issues in the 1860s and 1870s and stimulated the politicisation of tenant farmers, some of whom, like the famous Aberdeen Angus cattle breeder William McCombie of Tillyfour, were elected to parliament in this interest.[11]

The urban land question was another important area. This has not been neglected by historians, but the link with the rural land question, thoroughly addressed by contemporary land reformers such as Henry George and his disciples, has not been so fully discussed in a Scottish context. The Welsh land question, on the other hand, was focussed around the gap between the Anglican

11 I G C Hutchison, *A Political History of Scotland, 1832–1924: Parties, Elections and Issues* (Edinburgh, 1986) 104–9; R H Campbell, *Owners and Occupiers: Changes in Rural Society in South-West Scotland before 1914* (Aberdeen, 1991) 122–8.

landowning aristocracy and their nonconformist tenants. The grievances involved in this relationship included the exaction of tithes to support an alien church and politically-inspired evictions after the Liberal victory at the general election of 1868.[12] The English land question is more difficult to pin down, and land was not so central to the narrative of English politics in the Victorian and Edwardian period as it was in Scotland, Wales and Ireland. Nevertheless, it was there. Georgite ideas of land restoration were popular in radical circles in England; Alfred Russel Wallace advocated land nationalisation and socialist organs such as *Justice*, the newspaper of HM Hyndman's Social Democratic Federation, debated the land question, as did the more conventional Radical weekly *Reynolds's Newspaper*, both organs referring to the Highlands in broad discussions.[13] Another strand of English land reform, more conservative ultimately, was represented by Joseph Chamberlain and his acolyte Jesse Collings. Using the slogan 'Three acres and a cow' they argued that social liberation could be achieved by the creation of allotments and smallholdings.[14] Many of the land reformers discussed above visited and spoke in Scotland. Henry George, the original advocate of restoring the land to the people through his nostrum of single taxation, visited Scotland frequently and found a ready audience for his ideas in urban Scotland.[15] He debated the

12 M Cragoe, 'Conscience or coercion? Clerical influence at the General Election of 1868 in Wales', *Past and Present* 149 (Nov 1995) 140–69.

13 A R Wallace, *Land Nationalisation, Its Necessity and its Aims: Being a Comparison of the System of Landlord and Tenant with that of Occupying Ownership in their Influence on the Well-Being of the People* (3rd edition, London, 1882); *Justice*, 2 Feb, 29 Mar, 3 May 1884, 3 Jan, 28 Feb, 4 Apr 1885; *Reynolds's Newspaper*, 9 Nov 1884, 31 May, 15 Aug 1885, 24 Jan 1892, 26 Jul 1895 for a series of letters from 'Northumbrian' which set the Highland land issue in a wide context of radical causes.

14 J Chamberlain, 'Labourers' and artisans' dwellings', *Fortnightly Review* 34 (1883) 761–76; P Readman, 'Jesse Collings and land reform 1886–1914', *Historical Research* 81 (2008) 292–304; P Readman, 'Conservatives and the politics of land: Lord Winchilsea's National Agricultural Union, 1893–1901', *English Historical Review* 121 (2006) 25–69.

15 *"Thy Kingdom Come": A Sermon by Henry George in the City Hall Glasgow*

land question with the eighth duke of Argyll, that most disputatious defender of the rights of the landowning classes, and in 1884 visited the Isle of Skye, where his ideas were fairly well known, although not especially popular, through the activities of his faithful supporter Edward McHugh.[16] Michael Davitt was another frequently to be heard preaching the theology of land reform in Scotland. Most of his activities were concentrated in the urban areas of Lowland Scotland, especially in Glasgow where his associate John Ferguson was such a popular and important figure.[17] Davitt also visited the Highlands in 1882 and 1886. Chamberlain gave a famous speech in Inverness in November 1885 and visited the Highlands again the following year. By then his star had fallen somewhat in Liberal circles through his apostasy over the question of Irish home rule.[18] Although some of these figures thought of Scotland as the ultimate laboratory for land reform due to its extreme concentration of landownership and the intensity of the process of clearance in the Highlands, in truth for

---

(Glasgow, 1889); *The "Single Tax" Faith: An Address by Henry George in the Temperance Institute Bridgeton* (Glasgow, 1889); J R Frame, *America and the Scottish Left: The Impact of American Ideas on the Scottish Labour Movement from the American Civil War to World War One* (unpublished PhD thesis, University of Aberdeen) 77–118.

16 G D Campbell, 8th Duke of Argyll, 'The Prophet of San Francisco', *Nineteenth Century* 15 (1884) 537–58; H George, 'The "Reduction to Iniquity"', *Nineteenth Century* 16 (1884) 134–55; K Mulhern, *The Intellectual Duke: George Douglas Campbell, 8th Duke of Argyll, 1823–1900*, (unpublished PhD thesis, University of Edinburgh, 2006) 190–232; A Newby, 'Edward McHugh, the National Land League of Great Britain and the "Crofters' War", 1879–1882', *SHR* 82 (2003) 74–91; A Newby, '"Scotia Major and Scotia Minor": Ireland and the birth of the Scottish land agitation, 1878–82', *Irish Economic and Social History* 31 (2004) 23–40.

17 A G Newby, *Ireland, Radicalism and the Scottish Highlands, c1870–1912* (Edinburgh, 2007) 74–84; M Ó Catháin, 'Michael Davitt and Scotland', *Soathar* 25 (2000) 19–26; L Marley, *Michael Davitt: Freelance Radical and Frondeur* (Dublin, 2007) 165–82; E W McFarland, *John Ferguson, 1836–1906: Irish Issues in Scottish Politics* (East Linton, 2003) 132–8.

18 E A Cameron, '"A far cry to London", Joseph Chamberlain in Inverness, September 1885', *Innes Review* 57 (2006) 36–53.

the likes of George, Davitt, Ferguson or McHugh the land question was generic. Power lay with the owners of property, whether that was a city tenement block or a large acreage of Highland land, and it was exerted to the disadvantage of the powerless tenant. This relationship was no different in the west of Ireland or the east end of Glasgow and could be dealt with through generic solutions such as restoration or nationalisation. Such solutions were necessary, argued land reformers, because landownership was a transnational phenomenon. The duke of Sutherland may have held a million acres in the north of Scotland but he also had substantial landholdings in Nottinghamshire and Staffordshire, and most of his stupendous wealth came from his English estates. The Marquis of Bute was not an insubstantial landowner in Scotland, but most of his wealth derived from his ownership and development of the Cardiff waterfront.[19]

A further point which is relevant to the remainder of this paper is to note the survival of the land question in Scottish political culture in the period after the 1920s. The land question in a British context declined in importance from the early 1920s. This has been linked, first, to the demise of the Irish question in British politics with the creation of the Free State in 1922. A second point is the eclipse of the Liberal party in the post-war period; the Liberals had been the party of land reform in the late Victorian and Edwardian period, especially in Scotland and Ireland, but also in a wider context as their taxation policies and assaults on the House of Lords — 'House of Landlords' in Liberal propaganda — in the years before the Great War demonstrated. Indeed, as late as 1912 Lloyd George had attempted to revivify Liberalism, after disappointing election results in 1910, with an appeal to the party to rally around the traditional anti-landlord banner. Although the issue drifted down the political agenda in Scotland in the inter-war period, it remained in the bloodstream of Scottish politics. Nevertheless, the domination of the 1920s and 1930s by Conservative governments meant that it was on the backburner. Other factors which ensured

19 D Cannadine, *The Decline and Fall of the British Aristocracy* (New Haven, 1990) 710–11.

this included the desperate economic condition of Scotland for much of the period: the industrial structure based on traditional industries seemed incapable of delivering prosperity, and Scottish society was scarred by massive and persistent unemployment, mitigated only by the rearmament of the late 1930s.[20]

In this context land reform seemed a pointless irrelevance. Indeed, in the Scottish Highlands the results of the great land settlement operation seemed to have exacerbated these problems. Although by the mid 1920s nearly 1600 new crofts had been formed and a further 1200 enlarged under legislation of 1911 and 1919, this had limited impact on the overall structure of landholding in the Highlands. In 1935 very small holdings, the bane of the Highland economy in times of economic crisis such as the 1840s, the early 1880s or the 1930s, remained prevalent. In the five mainland Highland counties, 34 per cent of holdings were under five acres (over 50 per cent in Sutherland and the Isle of Harris) and nearly 70 per cent under 15 acres. In the Isle of Lewis 98.5 per cent of holdings were under 15 acres.[21] This meant that when it was no longer possible to earn money from temporary migration to the industrial economy and families were thrown back on the resources of the land, it provided little economic support. Emigration was another factor in the difficult social and economic conditions of the inter-war years. In the years between the censuses of 1921 and 1931 the Scottish population declined by about 40,000, as net emigration of 390,000 exceeded natural growth. Although the pattern of Scottish emigration throughout the nineteenth century had been dominated by skilled industrial workers, there was a substantial outflow of people from the Highlands and this continued in the 1920s. This was partly funded by the *Empire Settlement Act* of 1922, which assisted around 40 per cent of all British emigrants in the period from 1922 to 1933. Highland emigration of this period is

---

20 R J Finlay, 'National identity in crisis: politicians, intellectuals and the "End of Scotland", 1920–39' *History* 79 (1994) 242–59.

21 E A Cameron, *Land for the People? The British Government and the Scottish Highlands, c 1880–1925* (East Linton, 1996) 188–9, 201.

symbolised by the 600 Hebrideans who left their native land aboard the *Metagama*, which sailed from Stornoway, and the *Marloch*, which sailed from Lochboisdale, in April 1923.[22] These were people for whom the land settlement operation of the 1920s had not catered. Land reform, the great Highland concern of governments of both parties, had failed them and emigration provided an escape from the difficult economic conditions of the Scottish Highlands.[23] Gladstone's solution had not been effective in the long term.

Willie Ross

Reference to the Labour movement and to emigration provides the link to the second political context and another emotional reaction to Highland history and politics. In 1965, in his presentation of the Highland Development Bill to the House of Commons, Willie Ross, Labour Secretary of State for Scotland, remarked, in an oft-quoted phrase:

> For two-hundred years the Highlander has been the man on Scotland's conscience [...] no part of Scotland has been given a shabbier deal by history from the '45 onwards. Too often there has been only one way out of his troubles for the person born in the Highlands — emigration.[24]

If Gladstone's remark was very much in character for that most delphic and often contradictory figure, Ross's effusion was more

---

22 M Harper and N J Evans, 'Socio-economic dislocation and inter-war emigration to Canada and the United States: A Scottish snapshot', *Journal of Imperial and Commonwealth History* 34 (2006) 529–52; M Harper, *Emigration from Scotland Between the Wars: Opportunity or Exile?* (Manchester, 1998).

23 C Birnie, *"New Deal" or Raw Deal? Public Administration and Economic Development in the Highlands and Islands of Scotland, 1929–1939*, (unpublished MSc thesis, University of Edinburgh, 2003).

24 *Parliamentary Debates*, 5th series, vol 708 (House of Commons), col 1095, 16 Mar 1965.

surprising. Ross was the archetypal representative of the post-war west of Scotland Labour movement. Gone was the indisciplined romance and uncontrolled passion of the likes of James Maxton; in the ascendancy was a more technocratic approach. Ross was a former school teacher from Ayrshire, an elder of the presbyterian Church of Scotland and an enthusiast for the poetry of Robert Burns. He had not shown much previous interest in the Highlands, although they had not been a major political issue in the 20 years since the Second World War, a period which had been dominated by debates over the Scottish economy and industrial landscape, issues which meant that the centre of political gravity was in the central Lowlands. Less often quoted, however, is a passage which came slightly earlier in the speech. Here Ross recognised that, far from being neglected by government, the problems of the Highlands had been subjected to disproportionate scrutiny.

> There is no part of these islands of ours that has merited or received more attention from this house than the Highlands and Islands, not always with the success that the intentions deserved [...] It is regrettable that in this day and age [...] we have not faced this problem, which has been present for over eighty years, and used the powers that are in the special Scottish set-up, to experiment and to prove a successful way to do things, which could have been applied to other areas now suffering from exactly the same problems which started in the Highlands 100 years ago.[25]

The vehicle which Ross was presenting as a solution to these historic problems, with which earlier governments had not been able to deal, was a Highlands and Islands Development Board empowered to stimulate the Highland economy and, he suggested, deal with the problems of private landownership. Its success in the first area over

25 *Ibid*, cols 1079–80.

the long term (the Board was replaced by Highlands and Islands Enterprise in 1990) is far from clear, but it is abundantly clear that it had no powers to expropriate landowners. The Board became associated, perhaps unfairly, with a series of large-scale industrial enterprises which were parachuted into the Highlands — a pulp and paper mill near Fort William and an aluminium smelter at Invergordon in Easter Ross — which became high profile failures in the early 1980s, bringing a range of social problems to the communities which had become dependant on the employment associated with them. Nevertheless, the establishment of the HIDB was representative of an era, with its origins in the difficulties of the 1930s, in which the land question, prioritised by Gladstone in the 1880s, had been downgraded in favour of the idea of solving the Highland problem by means of economic development rather than land reform. This had been seen by the attempts to establish a carbide industry in the Great Glen in the 1930s, a policy which produced a classic debate between those who asserted that this would bring economic development and prosperity and others who deprecated the prospect of environmental destruction from the hydro-electric schemes associated with the demand of such an industry for electricity. When hydro-electricity was developed in the period from 1943 to the early 1960s, it was not for private enterprise but in the public service. The huge schemes which were constructed in the Highlands generated employment and power which was distributed by the North of Scotland Hydro Electric Board. The costs of distribution, very high for remote and sparsely populated areas, were not passed on to the consumers, but were charged at a flat rate across the Hydro Board's area, which covered Scotland north of Perth.[26] Thus the Board was successful in bringing about a domestic revolution in the Highlands where light, heat and power could be turned on at the flick of a switch, replacing time-consuming and dirty methods associated with lamps and ranges fuelled by paraffin, peat and coal.

26 P Payne, *The Hydro: A Study of the Development of the Major Hydro-Electric Schemes Undertaken by the North of Scotland Hydro-Electric Board* (Aberdeen, 1988).

The Hydro Board was the legacy of Thomas Johnston, Secretary of State for Scotland during Churchill's wartime coalition. Johnston had an interesting pedigree in the matter of the land reform. From 1906 he had been the editor of *Forward*, a Glasgow newspaper associated with the Independent Labour Party, an organ of great intellectual power and rich political debate encompassing radical Liberalism and socialism. In its columns, Johnston published one of the great series of polemical journalism in twentieth-century Scotland, later published as a book entitled *Our Scots Noble Families*. Johnston excoriated the leading landowning families in Scotland in a text which helped to cement the anti-landlord tradition of the Scottish Labour movement.[27] Once, however, he became an establishment figure in the post-war period in the NSHEB, the Scottish Tourist Board and the Forestry Commission, Johnston, by his own admission, attempted to buy up all the extant copies of the book, lest it embarrass him in the exalted circles in which he now moved.[28]

Johnston's political journey from Edwardian and wartime firebrand (*Forward* had been suppressed after its unexpurgated account of Lloyd George's visit to Glasgow in 1915) to the realms of officialdom via the coalition government is something of a metaphor for Labour's changing attitudes to the land question in a British context. Throughout the inter-war period the party had retained its official commitment to its traditional policy of land nationalisation, although it had not implemented this during its two periods of minority government, in 1924 and from 1929 to 1931. During the war, however, and during the period of office of Attlee's administration from 1945 to 1951, this was quietly ditched.[29] The Scottish context of this can be seen in two episodes

27 T Johnston, *Our Scots Noble Families* (Glasgow, 1909).

28 T Johnston, *Memories* (London, 1952) 35–6.

29 K Manton, 'The Labour Party and the land question, 1919–1951', *Historical Research* 79 (2006) 247–69; M Tichelar, 'The conflict over property rights during the Second World War: the Labour Party's abandonment of Land Nationalization', *Twentieth Century British History* 14 (2003) 165–88.

in the late 1940s. The first was the widely reported Knoydart land raid of 1947. This was an attempt by some workers on the estate of Lord Brocket, an exceptionally egregious landowner, to revive a tactic which had proved so important in the period from 1880 to the early 1920s. It took place on territory which had deep historical resonance. Knoydart was the archetypal cleared landscape. It had once been fairly heavily populated, but had been cleared in the 1850s and its population and agricultural vitality allowed to dwindle further since then, not least under the appalling neglect which passed for Brocket's estate management. The land raid itself, supported by the local priest, Father Colin MacPherson, later Bishop of Argyll and the Isles, was given a drama and prominence through its coverage by the populist *Scottish Daily Express* which sent a reporter to Knoydart and published evocative photographs of the raiders. In their heyday land raids had been a symbol of the power of the crofters and cottars and their use had discomfited estate managements, even governments, in the period from the 1880s to the 1920s. Knoydart revealed, however, that the land question was in abeyance. The Labour government of the day declined to intervene on behalf of the land raiders. Legislation of the inter-war period, notably the *Land Settlement (Scotland) Act* of 1919, was inoperative despite its retention on the statute book.[30] The government did concede the appointment of a Commission of Enquiry to investigate crofting conditions, but this was a fairly low-key affair chaired by the Principal of the University of Aberdeen and decidedly not a rerun of the Napier Commission of 1883–4.[31] One member of the commission did advocate land nationalisation, but the fact that she had to do so in a minority report seemed to symbolise the marginalisation of far-reaching land reform in favour of small-scale technical amendments to existing legislation

30 E A Cameron, 'The Seven Men of Knoydart and the Scottish Highlands in the 1940s', *Transactions of the Gaelic Society of Inverness* 62 (2001–3) 156–83; 'Knoydart, Seven Men of (act 1948)', *Oxford Dictionary of National Biography* [*ODNB*], (Oxford University Press, 2004).

31 Parliamentary Papers 1953–4, VIII, *Report of the Commission of Enquiry into Crofting Conditions.*

and administrative changes, both of which were represented by the crofting legislation of 1955.[32] The alternative approach in this period, ultimately seen in the establishment of the HIDB in 1965, was a bipartisan consensus on the efficacy of regional policy and economic planning.

The *Distribution of Industry Act* was an attempt to bring industry, employment and prosperity to areas of high unemployment by offering incentives and inducements to companies to set up in such areas. It was an extension of the Special Areas legislation of the 1930s, which was deemed to have been an inadequate response to the problems faced in that decade. Development Areas were identified. They were wider than the Special Areas and included a swathe of west central Scotland, the district around Dundee and, after 1948, an area around Dingwall and Inverness which was chosen for its economic potential as much as for the seriousness of the unemployment problem there.[33] Although this was welcomed by many people, there were those who regarded this form of regional policy as inappropriate for the Highlands. The Scottish Council of Industry was one such voice, as were a number of members of the Scottish Office's new Advisory Panel on the Highlands, who feared that industrial concentration in the Development Areas would drain the western Highlands of population.[34] This line of argument suggested that government policy, and in this period government was seen as a positive force, should concentrate on the traditional industries of the area, like agriculture and fishing, or industries based on readily available natural resources, like forestry. Outside the favoured localities of the eastern Highlands, the worry was about

---

32 'Note of dissent by Mrs Margaret H MacPherson in *Report of the Commission of Enquiry into Crofting Conditions*, 91.

33 G McCrone, *Regional Policy in Britain* (London, 1969) 109; A Cairncross, *Years of Recovery: British Economic Policy, 1945–51* (London, 1985).

34 Edinburgh, National Archives of Scotland [NAS], SEP12/94, Scottish Council of Industry, Highland Problems: Summarised Investigation Progress Report, no date (c1945); SEP12/2, Advisory Panel on the Highlands and Islands, Minutes of 11th Meeting, 11 Jun 1948; Minutes of 15th Meeting, 5 Nov 1948.

the collapse of community and social life. A letter of 1947 from the Secretary of the Raasay Local Development Committee indicates how the population of the island felt remote from the landowner:

> Although we number about 400 people we have not for many years been visited by any authority higher than the local representatives of the Department of Agriculture for Scotland, our landlords. We have been consistently bypassed by every authority responsible for the development of the Highlands and life on the island has come dangerously near to the point of extinction.[35]

In considering this specific example, it should be noted that the landowner was the government, which had purchased the island in 1922 after a land raid which saw cottars from the island of Rona stake a claim to land on Raasay.

Nevertheless, the principal drive of the post-war Labour government was to encourage industry to the Development Areas. This policy was conducted through the Board of Trade and the Development Areas Treasury Advisory Committee [DATAC], which had very strict rules about the potential profitability of any business to be supported, the exhaustion of other sources of funding, and the amount of data required of applicants. There were countervailing pressures, however; the lack of resources for capital investment meant that new construction projects had to be considered on their potential for contributing to the national priority for export generation and import saving.[36] This policy, whatever its success in other areas, was an almost total failure in the northern Development Areas, to which DATAC could attract

35 NAS, SEP12/7/1, Letter from the Secretary of the Raasay Local Development Committee, c 1947.

36 NAS, SEP/12/7/2, Advisory Panel on the Highlands, Highland Development, 29 Oct 1948.

no industry.[37] The policy is not, therefore, significant for its results, but reveals elements of official thinking about the Highlands which once again were characterised by the application of a nationwide policy to this particular region and were justified by vivid language. Civil servants in London did not share in the romantic view. They felt that the extension to selected areas of the Highlands of the *Distribution of Industry Act* was not justified. The view of the Board of Trade, on whose conscience the problems of the Highlands did not weigh heavily, argued that the policy was 'designed to relieve the worst cases of high unemployment [...] it is not designed to affect changes in population'.[38] The Minister concerned, Stafford Cripps, went so far as to argue that urban unemployment was a 'greater evil, particularly from a social aspect' than rural unemployment.[39] In 1948 the Scottish Office returned to this theme, that the Highlands were special and neglected, in a further effort to have the region scheduled as a development area under the *Distribution of Industry Act*.

> The whole area has suffered for generations from economic hardship, inadequate social services and constant depopulation, to a degree not paralleled elsewhere; and it is accepted by all parties as a primary obligation of the government to restore to the highlands a measure of prosperity.[40]

---

37 G C Peden, *The Treasury and British Public Policy, 1906–1959* (Oxford, 2000) 418; S N Broadberry and N F R Crafts, 'British economic policy and industrial performance in the early post-war period', *Business History* 38 (1996) 65–91; P Scott, 'British regional policy, 1945–51: a lost opportunity', *Twentieth Century British History* 8 (1997) 358–82; S Rosevear, 'Balancing business and the regions: British distribution of industry policy and the Board of Trade, 1945–51', *Business History* 40 (1998) 77–99.

38 TNA: PRO, BT106/45/25, Jay to Anderson, 19 Jun 1945.

39 TNA: PRO, BT106/45/45 and /49, Tom Fraser to Cripps, 13 Nov 1945; Cripps to Fraser, 27 Nov 1945.

40 TNA: PRO, BT177/192/2, R E C Johnson (Scottish Home Department)

A Scottish Home Department civil servant argued that distribution policy should be applied to the Highlands not only because of unemployment, but also as a response to emigration and depopulation, criteria which were not applied to any other part of Scotland.

> There can be no doubt whatever that the conditions which have led to unemployment and depopulation in the highlands will persist unless special and vigorous measures are taken to prevent them. Since it would be impossible to contemplate with equanimity the progressive depopulation of some 50 per cent of the entire area of Scotland and social and other consequences of the virtual extinction of an eminently vigorous racial stock, every effort will require to be made to provide an economic means of livelihood for the local inhabitants of the highlands areas.[41]

Thus by 1965, Willie Ross, in arguing for the highlander as the man on Scotland's conscience, was drawing on a deeply held view among his own officials. The Highlands had powerful advocates within the Scottish Office. Indeed, there was an inter-departmental 'Highlands Committee' in the Scottish Office and, although it was largely administrative rather than policy-oriented, it did much to keep the subject at the forefront of the official mind. This was in contrast to the Scottish Borders or rural Wales, and the Highlands had not lacked government initiatives: but, in Ross's view, they were not of the right kind. He aimed to put this right with his Highlands and Islands Development Board. This is not the place to conduct an assessment

to C F Monier Williams (Board of Trade), 9 Jun 1948.

41 TNA: PRO, BT106/45/11, *Legislation on balanced distribution of industry, application to selected areas in the Highlands*, (note by Scottish Home Department).

of the efficacy of the Board over the 25 years of its existence, but it is worth emphasising that Ross's uncharacteristically emotional presentation elided, perhaps for political effect, the contribution of earlier government policy on the Highlands and emphasised the novelty of his own approach. In fact the Highlands had not been ignored by twentieth-century governments. The existence of the North of Scotland Hydro Electricity Board was evidence of this, but Ross's speech became a handy cliché for subsequent aggrieved assertions of the orthodox thesis of neglect.

Donald Dewar

In most discussions of land reform in Britain, the narrative tends to run out in the aftermath of the Great War. This coincides with the disappearance of the problems of Ireland — where the land question had been especially intense — from the British political agenda. Although the Liberals tried to raise the banner of land reform in the 1920s as a means of rallying the divided party, this failed.[42] The lapsing of the land question was even evident in the context of government initiatives in the Scottish Highlands, as we have seen, where the objective shifted from tenurial reform to economic development. Nevertheless, the subject did have something of a 'half-life' in Scotland by virtue of the continuing distinctiveness of the crofting system. There was a commission of enquiry in the early 1950s, but it was followed only by a weak piece of legislation in 1955. There was an attempt by the new Crofters Commission created by that Act to initiate a debate on the nature of the crofting system, but once again this resulted in the largely inoperative Crofting Reform Act of 1976. James Hunter's 'Scottish Crofters' Union' attempted to force crofting issues back onto the agenda in the 1980s, with some success.[43] Nevertheless, the issue was conscripted as part of the critique of Westminster neglect of Scotland during a period in

---

42 M Dawson, 'The Liberal land policy, 1924–1929: electoral strategy and internal division', *Twentieth Century British History* 2 (1991) 272–90.

43 J Hunter, *The Claim of Crofting: The Scottish Highlands and Islands, 1930–1990* (Edinburgh, 1991).

which nationalism became an important actor in Scottish politics from the late 1960s. A land reform tradition also survived in the Labour party and to a certain extent in Scottish culture.[44] This history ensured that when Labour returned to power in 1997 with a commitment to implementing Scottish devolution, land reform was back on the political agenda.

In September 1998, a point at which it was clear that the Scottish parliament, which had been his long-held objective, was to be created, Donald Dewar, the then Secretary of State for Scotland and future First Minister in the Scottish Executive created by his *Scotland Act* of 1998, delivered the annual John McEwan Lecture. He used the occasion to argue:

> The creation of the Scottish parliament is a huge step forward for Scotland. But it is only a means to an end; and it is what the parliament will do rather than what it will be that matters [...] It is clear that we need an integrated programme of land reform legislation — sweeping away outdated land laws, properly securing the public interest in land use and land ownership, increasing local involvement and accountability — to fit Scotland for the 21st century. Such a programme needs to deal, not just with the highly publicised circumstances of the big Highland estates, but with land related problems in all their diversity throughout Scotland.[45]

This seemed to have a different emphasis. If Gladstone and Ross had looked back into Highland history for their justifications, then Dewar seemed to be looking to the future. Scottish land reform was one of the main issues debated by the Scottish parliament in its

44 E A Cameron, '"Unfinished business": the land question and the Scottish Parliament', *Contemporary British History* 15 (2001) 83–114.

45 D Dewar, *Land Reform for the 21st Century*, The fifth John McEwan Memorial Lecture on land tenure in Scotland (Perth and Kinross Archives, John McEwan Collection, MS174/2/5).

early years, not only resulting in an important piece of legislation in 2003, but also providing hints that the historical dimension of the discussion remained current. One oddity was the *Abolition of Feudal Tenure etc (Scotland) Act* of 2000 which, as the then leader of the Conservatives in the parliament noted, represented the eradication of a 'system of land tenure which — for all its faults — is distinctively Scottish', perhaps an ironic thing for the new Scottish parliament to have done.[46] Further evidence of the interconnectedness of the historical and contemporary dimensions of this aspect of Scottish politics came from a short debate in the Parliament in September 2000 when the Liberal Democrat MSP for Caithness and Sutherland presented a motion expressing the Parliament's 'deepest regrets for the occurrence of the Highland clearances and extends its hand in friendship to the descendants of the cleared people who reside outwith our shores'. Despite the fact that many, even most, victims of the clearances remained within Scotland, often close to the place of eviction, this motion is an interesting example of the collective guilty conscience which burdens Scottish politicians on the matter of the land issue. Responding for the Scottish Executive, the MSP for the Western Isles, Alasdair Morrison, asserted that, from the point of view of the victims of the clearances,

> it would have seemed inconceivable that there would one day be public funds available to help Highland communities to take on ownership and management of the land from which so many of our people had been evicted. Today, thanks to this Administration's commitment to land reform such funds are firmly in place.[47]

This statement indicates that the fact that a contemporary debate has historical resonances does not obviate it from being conducted in a historically factual vacuum. Of course, it suited Morrison to

46 *Official Report, Scottish Parliament* [*ORSP*] 15 Dec 1999, col 1580.

47 *ORSP*, 27 Sep 2000, col 700.

CELTS
IN
LITERATURE

Irish myths: fantastic nonsense or a real record of astronomical catastrophes?

Patrick McCafferty ⊕

Irish myths have inspired a range of responses, from belief to disbelief. Today, these tales are generally viewed as literary fiction, too fantastic to be of value to archaeologists or historians. A new theory suggests that perhaps we should not be so dismissive: the myths may contain a real, but poorly understood, record of forgotten astronomical events.

It is clear that the action in some myths takes place in the sky. Furthermore, that many of the motifs in myths can be interpreted as comets.[1] If this is true, then these tales of catastrophe, involving sky-gods and superheroes, appear to describe events caused by a busy sky and suggest that our planet was blasted by cometary debris a few millennia ago. In particular, the Irish Mythological and Ulster Cycles of tales can be read as a fascinating, and surprisingly detailed, record of violent cometary encounters befalling Ireland in the twelfth and first centuries BCE.

This observation finds support in the work of astronomers, who suspect that the sky was busier two millennia ago, as earth

---

⊕ Irish and Celtic Studies – Queens University Belfast, Belfast BT7 1NN, Northern Ireland and Armagh Observatory, College Hill, Armagh BT61 9DG, Northern Ireland.

I would like to express my thanks to the organisers of the Sixth Australian Conference of Celtic Studies; to Northern Ireland's Department of Employment and Learning for funding my studies; to my supervisors, Professor Dónall Ó Baoill of Queens University Belfast and Professor Mark Bailey MBE of Armagh Observatory; and to Professor Mike Baillie of Queens University Belfast for his encouragement.

1 P McCafferty and M Baillie, *The Celtic Gods: Comets in Irish Mythology* (Stroud, 2005) 82.

repeatedly encountered debris from a large, fragmenting comet. This theory finds further support in environmental events recorded in tree rings, in the onset of the so-called dark ages, and in Roman history. If substantiated, this cometary theory may help to synthesise mythology and archaeology into a unified narrative that is slower to dismiss Irish mythology as fiction.

This paper attempts to address a key question: are Irish myths merely a collection of fictional narratives invented by monks and storytellers, or might they have some basis in history?

Attitudes to Irish myths

The corpus of Irish mythology contains hundreds of tales of courtship, adventures, voyages, cattle-raids, battles, feasts, visions, boyhood deeds, and so on. These are usually divided into cycles: the Mythological Cycle, with tales of Lugh and Balar and the Tuatha Dé Danann; the Ulster Cycle, with stories of Cú Chulainn and the *Táin Bó Cúailnge*; the Finn Cycle, with its adventures of Finn mac Cumall and his warrior *fianna*; the Saints' Cycle, with hagiographical accounts of the lives of Saints Patrick, Brigit, Columcille, et al; and the Kings' Cycle, with legendary exploits of historical kings such as Niall Noígiallach.

Attitudes to these tales have varied through the centuries. It is possible that people once believed these stories. To believers, events had occurred just as described in the tales, no matter how magical or unlikely these seemed. Modern attitudes to this material are much less credulous, but can depend on which cycle a tale belongs to. The Saints' Cycle is treated as hagiography, and although it is widely appreciated that some of the miraculous deeds of the saints are unlikely to have occurred exactly as described, nobody would ever doubt that Columcille and his contemporaries had existed: after all, somebody founded Irish monasteries. Similarly, the Kings' Cycle, despite the implausibility of certain battles, is perceived to be quite historical: unreliable perhaps, but with a core of truth.

At the beginning of the twentieth century, the Finn Cycle was thought to be just as historical as it was mythical. It was felt that a warrior chief called Finn had once existed, but that his deeds were exaggerated after his death until he became quite legendary. Thus, to ascertain from the tales who Finn was, one must merely reverse this process by peeling away the layers of exaggeration to reveal the historical core. Finn's death is recorded in the Annals of the Four Masters at 283 CE.[2] Keating, writing in the seventeenth century, accepted that many of the tales were incredible, but regarded Finn as a real figure.[3] O'Curry also maintained that behind the mythical exterior, there lay an historical figure:

> It is quite a mistake to suppose him to have been a merely mythical character. Much that has been narrated of his exploits is, no doubt, apocryphal enough; but Finn himself is an undoubtedly historical personage.[4]

The Ulster Cycle was not widely treated as history. The authors of the Annals of Ulster, who were content to enter Finn's death as an historical event, ignored Cú Chulainn when compiling their chronicles (although the Annals of Tigernach have Cú Chulainn dying c10 CE).[5] Kenneth Jackson argued that although he was not

2 M Ó Cléirigh et al, *Annala Rioghachta Eireann*, trans and ed J O'Donovan, *Annala Rioghachta Eireann: Annals of the Kingdom of Ireland by the Four Masters, from the earliest period to the year 1616. Edited from MSS in the Library of the Royal Irish Academy and of Trinity College Dublin with a translation and copious notes* (Dublin, 1848–51) 3rd edition (Dublin, 1990) Vol 1, 118–121; D Hyde, *The Story of Early Gaelic Literature* (London, 1895) 102.

3 G Keating, *The general history of Ireland... / collected by the learned Jeoffry Keating; faithfully translated from the original Irish language, with many curious amendments, taken from the Psalters of Tara and Cashel, and other authentic records, by Derm'd O'Connor* (Dublin, 1809) 268.

4 E O'Curry, *Lectures on the manuscript materials of ancient Irish history / Delivered at the Catholic University of Ireland, during the sessions of 1855 and 1856* (Dublin and London, 1861) 303.

5 Tigernach, *Annales Tigernachi* trans W Stokes, *The Annals of Tigernach Vol 1* (Lampeter, 1993) 37 (reprint of 'The Annals of Tigernach', 374–479 in *Revue Celtique* 16 (Paris, 1895), at p 407).

suggesting that 'any of the people who act in them or any of the events described are historical, and indeed some of them are much too unreal for this to be possible',[6] nevertheless the Ulster Cycle could provide a 'window on the iron age': 'If we want to know what it was like to be a late La Tène Celt, and what life in the early iron age was like, we can get some notion of it by reading the Irish Ulster cycle of hero stories'.[7]

This was disputed by the work of Mallory, who showed that the material culture of the tales was later than the iron age. For example, Cú Chulainn's long slashing sword was more like a Viking sword and unlike the short stubby sword from the iron age. He concluded that the tales dated to the early medieval period and that the authors of the *Táin* 'were engaged in producing an historical fiction'.[8]

The Mythological Cycle, set farther back in time, was thought to represent an ancient pantheon of gods, representing various cosmic bodies, with Lugh as the sun god fighting Balar, who represents the forces of night. Hyde maintained that much of the mythical character had been lost from most Irish literature:

> It is in [the Mythological Cycle] that we find the clearest traces of the old Irish pantheon. We might read through Irish literature and scarcely see that it contained a mythology at all. At a very early period the Irish forgot that these beings and races, of whom they still continued to tell, were the gods and demi-gods of their ancestors, until at last their historians came to speak of them as though they were ordinary

6 K H Jackson, *The Oldest Irish Tradition: A Window on the Iron Age* (Cambridge, 1964) 3.

7 *Ibid*, 55.

8 J P Mallory, 'The world of Cú Chulainn: The archaeology of Táin Bó Cúailnge' 103–159 in J P Mallory (ed), *Aspects of the Táin* (Belfast, 1992) 153.

tribes and ordinary men (Euhemerism).[9]

Just a decade later, Mac Neill agreed that the ancient gods had been humanised:

> It is now established beyond all question that the Tuatha De Danann, of ancient tradition, were not a human race. They were the gods of ancient Ireland. The old Christian historians could not accept the tradition that this race was divine and immortal. They could not obliterate the tradition of their existence, for it pervaded all the early literature. They accordingly deprived the Tuatha De Danann of immortality and made them human.[10]

With this attitude in mind, one could treat characters in these myths as the personifications of physical forces or even abstract qualities, and see their battles as analogies of the natural world. This led Arbois de Jubainville to proclaim that:

> Lug is the Celtic Hermes: like the Greek Hermes, he personifies the dawn, and like him also, slays his adversary with a stone. He casts the stone from a sling, mortally wounding the eye of Balor, who is the Celtic Argos, that is to say, a personification of the powers of evil, foremost among which is the night, and also, according to the Celtic idea, the thunderbolt and Death.[11]

Other approaches to myths were developed during the

---

9 D Hyde, *The Story of Early Gaelic Literature* (London, 1895) 60.

10 E Mac Neill, *Celtic Ireland* (Dublin and London, 1921) 46.

11 H d'Arbois de Jubainville, *Le Cycle Mythologique Irlandais et la Mythologie Celtique* trans R I Best, *The Irish Mythological Cycle and Celtic Mythology* (Dublin, 1903) 113–114.

twentieth century. With the development of Indo-European theory, it was hoped that myths would provide an insight into the world-view of those leaving the Indo-European homeland. Thus Irish tales were compared to myths from Scandinavia, India and Greece. For example, Dumézil's theory that Indo-European myths fitted a tripartite template was found to apply to many Irish tales, with their triple goddesses or triple aspects of their heroes.[12] It was also noted that certain passages in Irish myths sounded similar to passages in the Iliad, although it was unclear whether this was the result of an ancient Indo-European structure or plagiarism by monks. After all, we know that Irish monasteries had access to a copy of Homer's *Iliad*, since they translated it into Irish.[13]

In the later twentieth century, myths were analysed from a psychological perspective: in Jung's work, the images of myth mirror the immensely old psyche of man;[14] in Joseph Campbell's model, the journey of the mythical hero was a narrative constructed to aid humans in negotiating difficult rites of passage in their lives.[15] Thus myths are full of images that originate in our dreams, and many myths fit a similar pattern, in which the hero is given some magical implements by an old sage, then propelled on a dangerous quest to vanquish the evil forces (such as a dragon) and is finally anointed the rightful king. Campbell's model of the monomyth has influenced the development of modern fantastic narratives such as the 'Star Wars' films.[16]

Today, few people consider the issue of a possible historical reality of Irish tales. When Hollywood depicts myths in film, as in

---

12 G Dumézil, *Mythe et épopée: l'idéologie des trois fonctions dans les épopées des peuples indo-européens* (Paris, 1968) Vol 2, 331–353.

13 'Togail Troí. The Destruction of Troy', 1063–1117 in R I Best and M A O'Brien (eds), *The Book of Leinster: formerly Lebar na Núachongbála* (Dublin, 1965).

14 C G Jung, *Man and His Symbols* (London, 1964) 67.

15 J Campbell, *The Hero with a Thousand Faces* (London, 1993).

16 *Star Wars Episode IV: A New Hope*, directed and written by G Lucas (1977).

the recent version of *Troy* starring Brad Pitt,[17] all fantastic elements are stripped from the tale. The film removed all references to the gods, and presented us with an exclusively human narrative.

It was once believed that druids or poets transmitted Irish myths orally, until monks wrote them down. Although some Christian elements were evident in the tales, it was generally accepted that the tales were primarily pagan in origin. The work of Carney[18] and McCone[19] has led to a radical shift from this view, and Irish tales are now seen primarily as a literary product of the medieval period: narrative tales, rather than myths. It is taken as a given that the myths are primarily a body of literary fiction, 'obviously without any historicity',[20] of little or no relevance to historians or archaeologists, and of use only as entertaining tales for children or as material to be dissected by scholars of literature. The myths are thus subjected to a variety of literary and textual analyses — structural, character, gender, etc — and are seen as relevant only in the way they influence modern political identities of the Irish and other Celts.

Myths based on the sky

I would like for a moment to focus on the cosmic interpretations of myths. I first became interested in myths through archaeology. At Newgrange, Ireland's best-known passage tomb in County Meath, built over 5000 years ago, the rising sun enters the passage at the winter solstice to light up the inner chamber. Standing at Newgrange, or at Stonehenge or indeed any of the hundreds of stone circles scattered throughout Britain and Ireland, one is aware that people expended tremendous effort building monuments that are aligned to the movement of the sun and moon. With this in mind, it is but

17 *Troy*, directed by W Petersen (2004).

18 J Carney, *Studies in Irish Literature and History* (Dublin, 1955) 79.

19 K McCone, *Pagan Past and Christian Present in Early Irish Literature* (Maynooth, 1991) 5.

20 C Vielle, 'The oldest narrative attestations of a Celtic mythical and traditional heroic cycle', 217–227 in J P Mallory and G Stockman (eds), *Ulidia* (Belfast, 1994) 217.

a brief logical jump to the idea that people may have once worshipped the sun as a god. And when one sees depictions of the Aten, worshipped in ancient Egypt as the one true god, the idea of a sun god makes some sense.

This model of a sun god was developed by Max Müller[21] and Alvin Boyd Kuhn.[22] They were able to show that the sun god explained many mythical heroes across different cultures: after all, many mythical gods shine brightly and fly through the sky. For Müller, who maintained that myth was a disease of language, 'gods' were originally words used to express abstract ideas, but transformed into imagined personalities. Thus an Indo-European word *dyaus*, meaning 'shining', had become transformed into the father-god Dyaus Pita, Zeus, and Jupiter. Müller believed that this deity, and indeed many others, had stemmed from primitive worship of the sun.[23]

For scholars of Irish mythology, it appeared that Lugh provided the best evidence of a sun god, since he is described as 'rising in the west, with his facing shining like the sun'.[24] However, Cú Chulainn, the son of Lugh, was another possible solar deity, since he too is bright.[25] O'Rahilly listed Goll,[26] Eochaid,[27] Dian Cécht,[28] Áine,[29]

---

21 F M Müller, *Physical Religion* (London, 1891) 179.

22 A B Kuhn, *The Lost Light: An Interpretation of Ancient Scriptures* (New York, 1940) 497.

23 *Ibid*, 179.

24 E O'Curry, 'The "Tri Thruaighe na Scealaigheachta" (the "Three Most Sorrowful Tales") of Erinn', *The Atlantis: or register of Literature and Science of the Catholic University of Ireland* 4 (1863) 113–240, at p 177.

25 R S Loomis, *Celtic Myth and Arthurian Romance* (New York, 1927) 51.

26 T F O'Rahilly, *Early Irish History and Mythology* (Dublin, 1946) 58.

27 *Ibid*, 59.

28 *Ibid*, 66.

29 *Ibid*, 290; 304–7.

Grian,[30] Macha[31] and Ériu[32] as other possible solar gods. There just seemed to be too many solar deities, and this prevalence proved the undoing of the theory when Littledale demonstrated that, according to his own criteria, Max Müller himself was a solar myth.[33]

Among other difficulties with the idea was the fact that it did not help to clarify myths: thinking of Apollo as a solar deity does not really help to explain his role in the destruction of Troy. Many solar deities such as Jupiter also had other characteristics that made them gods of thunder, a concept difficult to reconcile with the sun. From an Irish perspective, although Lugh's shining face makes him a solar deity, the fact that he has a long hand and rises in the west causes problems: the sun does not rise in the west and does not have a long hand.

Myths and comets

There is one way of resolving all of these difficulties, and in many ways it is surprising that Müller and others never realised this. Only one type of astronomical body can shine with a bright light, can rise in the west, can throw destructive thunderbolts, can have a long hand, and can even appear with long hair: that body is a comet. In *The Celtic Gods: Comets in Irish Mythology*,[34] Mike Baillie and I have demonstrated that many supernatural elements and motifs in myths can be understood in cometary terms. We showed that, just like comets, many mythical heroes were bright, shining, fast, destructive, and shape-shifting. We even went so far as to suggest that characters such as Lugh and Cú Chulainn might be comets, and that tales such as *Táin Bó Cúailnge* provide a record of a time when earth had a catastrophic encounter with a comet and its debris. This proposal flies in the face of the general consensus that myths are

30 *Ibid*, 290.

31 *Ibid*, 293.

32 *Ibid*, 297.

33 R F Littledale, 'The Oxford Solar Myth' 279–290 in R Y Tyrrell and Sir E Sullivan (eds), *Echoes from Kottabos* (London, 1906).

34 McCafferty and Baillie, *Celtic Gods*, 15.

Figure 1: *Comet Donati, 1858, with two straight gas tails and a curved dust tail.*[35]

primarily works of fiction, but it is an idea that makes sense when one explores myths with comets in mind.

The possibility that Cú Chulainn or Lugh could be comets must come as a shock to anyone familiar with these characters from childhood tales, in which they are depicted as sporting warriors, the ultimate hurling heroes. So, to overcome this surprise somewhat, let us take a brief look at comets.

At its heart, a comet consists of a nucleus, typically 10km in diameter, made of ices and dust. It spends most of the time in cold regions remote from the sun. On its orbit around the sun, lasting from 3.3 to millions of years, it periodically travels closer to the sun. As it does so, the nucleus heats up, and the ices vaporise, forming a cloudy coma. The material ejected from the nucleus forms tails: a yellow dust tail and a fluorescent blue gas tail. The gas tail always points away from the sun, due to the solar wind, and can be hundreds of millions of kilometres long (*Figure 1*).

Comets can appear in a variety of shapes, some like the standard schoolbook model and others that are much more dramatic and unexpected. One document that shows the incredible variety of shapes is the Mawangdui Silk (*Figure 2*) from Han, China (c third century BCE), which depicts 29 different types of comets, and documents their effects.[36] We can see comets that look like a pagoda, or like a stag. On the bottom right, the 'long-tailed pheasant star' has a shape we recognise today as the swastika. Carl Sagan suggested that a rotating comet with four jets could appear as a swastika in the sky, and that this would explain its prevalence throughout the entire northern hemisphere.[37]

Comets can rotate. The Roman writer Pliny referred to a comet he called 'Hippeus' or the 'Horse-star': 'horses' manes in very rapid motion and revolving in a circle'.[38] This has a remarkable parallel

---

35 A Guillemin, *Les Comètes* (Paris, 1875) plate 9.

36 X Ze-Zong, 'The cometary atlas in the silk book of the Han tomb at Mawangdui', *Chinese Astronomy and Astrophysics* 8 (1984) 1–7.

37 C Sagan and A Druyan, *Comet* (London, 1997) 184–194.

38 C Plinius Secundus, *Naturalis Historia Liber II* trans H Rackham

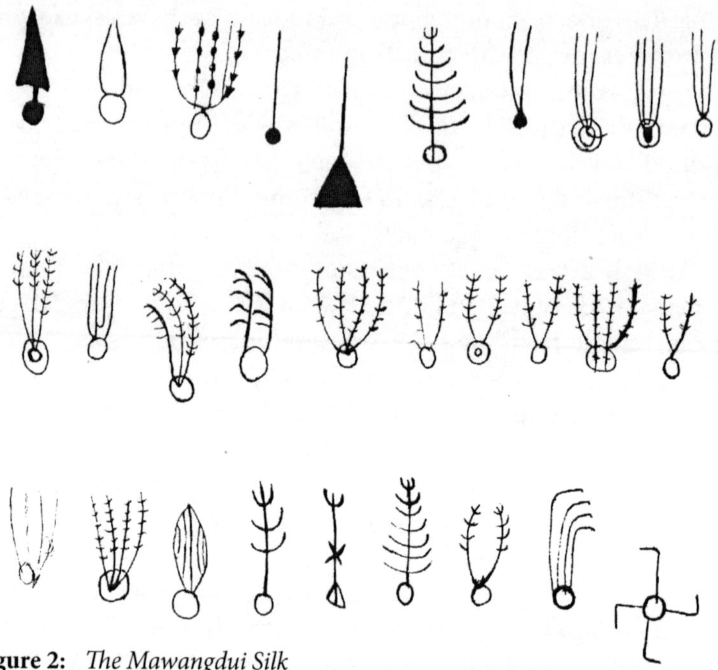

Figure 2: *The Mawangdui Silk*

to Manannán mac Lir, who rolled down from the mountain-top on three fiery legs.[39] So here we see that a three-legged comet could have formed the basis of a Celtic god.[40] The appearance of the triskele on coins from the third century BCE may thus be depicting a comet. Again, in the Finn Cycle, there is a tale in which the *bodach*, or giant, sets a pig on a self-rotating spit in front of the bonfire.[41] Needless to say, no self-rotating spits have ever been found in Irish archaeological sites.

(London, 1938) 233.

39 S Morrison, *Manx Fairy Tales* (London, 1911) 181–182.

40 McCafferty and Baillie, 84–85; P McCafferty, 'Cult in Cometary Context', 229–233 in D A Barrowclough and C Malone (eds), *Cult in Context* (Oxford, 2007) 230.

41 S H O'Grady, *Silva gadelica (I–XXXI): a collection of tales in Irish with extracts illustrating persons and places*, trans and ed S H O'Grady (London, 1892) i: 292–293; ii: 238.

Elsewhere, Baillie and I have drawn attention to other motifs from Irish myths that could have been based on the appearances of comets. For example, Comet West in 1976 looked remarkably like a fish, and could have inspired tales of the Salmon of Knowledge.[42] Similarly, in 1858, Comet Donati sometimes looked remarkably like Cú Chulainn's three layers of hair — as one might expect from the word comet, which means 'long-haired'.[43] Even more convincingly, a comet referred to by Pliny makes it apparent that people in the past once saw an anthropomorphic comet in the sky: 'a shining comet whose silvery tresses glow so brightly that it is scarcely possible to look at it, and which displays within it a shape in the likeness of a man's countenance'.[44] This reminds one of Cú Chulainn, who 'wore at his white clear breast ... a brooch of light-gold and silver [...] — a shining source of light too bright in its blinding brilliance for men to look at'.[45]

Comets and destruction

One aspect common to many myths is their sheer destructiveness, as the thunderbolts of the gods strike at random with devastating effect. Cú Chulainn gives a thunder feat that injures two out of three people in Ireland. The dead at the Battle of Moytura are too many to count. This raises the issue of the violence of an interaction with a comet.

In November 1799, 1833 and 1866, Earth experienced major meteor showers when it passed through a trail of dust left behind by Comet Tempel-Tuttle. So, when Earth goes through the path of a comet, we know that one can expect major meteor showers. These are caused by tiny pieces of dust striking the Earth's atmosphere at tremendous speed. But what if the pieces of the comet are not tiny? In this case, events can be much more destructive. A piece of

---

42 McCafferty and Baillie, *Celtic Gods*, 58.

43 *Ibid*, 28–29.

44 *Pliny Natural History*, 233.

45 T Kinsella, *The Tain – From the Irish Epic 'Táin Bo Cuailnge'* (Oxford, 1969) 158.

comet, c50m in diameter, is thought to have caused the Tunguska event, in which 2000km^2 of Siberian forest were flattened by an atmospheric explosion on 30 June 1908.[46] Could such an event lie behind the destructive events in the *Táin*? Could this be the origin of the Twrch Trwyth, the mythical pig in Welsh Arthurian legend[47] that destroyed an entire province in Ireland before making its way over Wales, the Bristol Channel, Cornwall and the ocean, with pieces falling into the Severn Estuary en route?[48]

The Tunguska Event on 30 June 1908, and a bombardment of the Moon in late June 1974–1975,[49] drew attention to the Taurid meteors. These are unusual in that they travel around the sun on a 3.3-year orbit, just like Comet Encke. They are also remarkably spread out, suggesting that the parent comet has been travelling on this orbit for many thousands of years. In the 1980s, astronomers in England realised that many asteroids had similar orbits to the Taurids. They postulated that a very large comet had broken up in the inner solar system thousands of years ago, forming the Taurid complex of dust, comet, debris and asteroids.[50] Most of the time, earth would not have intercepted this material, but on occasions the orbits of our planet and this debris stream would have coincided, leading to destructive Tunguska-like events — and hence tales of dragons; Arthurian swords that strike dolorous blows; mythical pigs that fly through the air leaving a path of destruction; and giants whose shouts can flatten forests.

We see here that myths may not simply be fictional narratives

---

46 L Kresák, 'The Tunguska object: a fragment of Comet Encke?' *Bulletin of the Astronomical Institutes of Czechoslovakia* (1978) 129–134.

47 G Jones and T Jones, *The Mabinogion* (London, 1993) 109–112.

48 McCafferty and Baillie, *Celtic Gods*, 98.

49 J Dorman, S Evans, Y Nakamura and G Latham, 'On the time-varying properties of the lunar seismic meteoroid population', *Proceedings of the Lunar Planetary Science Conference* 9 (1978) 3615–3626, at p 3621.

50 S V M Clube and W M Napier, *The Cosmic Serpent: A Catastrophist View of Earth History* (London, 1982) 153; Clube and Napier, *The Cosmic Winter* (Oxford, 1990) 147–154.

designed to express abstract concepts. Instead, they may represent an attempt to explain, in human terms, real, destructive events to a pre-scientific society. If that is the case, myths would be a form of history — a narrative describing events as they occurred, with deeds attributed to the forces participating. Of course, myths have a magical character that is absent from conventional historical narratives, but that may have arisen simply because they are describing powerful events outside the everyday human experience. Also, like all forms of history, myths can gain and lose in their retelling: but at their core may lie a real record of astronomical events.

There is one aspect of myths that marks them clearly as a form of history. That is their attempt to relate events to the passage of time. Myths are full of details of dating: for example, 'seven years to the day', 'one year and one day later', 'when Cú Chulainn was just 17', etc. And most convincingly, these dates match the return time of Comet Encke and the Taurid meteors. Comet Encke is on a 3.3 year orbit, and one can expect events to occur after 4, 7, 10, 14, 17, 20, 24, 27, 30 and 33 years. The main events in the *Táin* seem to match this pattern, occurring when Cú Chulainn is 4, 7, 14 and 17 years old. Similarly, one finds that King Conchobar spends three years and three months in his mother's womb, a pattern shared by mythical kings in China and in Mali.

Again and again, one finds that the authors of many myths resisted the temptation to let their imaginations roam. They refused to fill in the gaps in the narratives, and instead presented us with what seem to be incomplete accounts, focusing only on a few days. A good example of this is to be seen in the *Iliad*, in which Homer does not describe what happened during the ten years of war after the abduction of Helen, but instead focuses on just five days of battle. This is exactly the pattern one might expect from a meteor shower on a Taurid orbit: a major event followed by ten years of peace ended by another major event on the third reappearance of the comet, ten years after the first event. The *Iliad* has not strayed beyond this account: and this suggests that many mythical narratives are more trustworthy than hitherto suspected.

Myths as a record of global events

One of the main repercussions of this idea is that myths from around the world may in fact be describing events on the same day. In the Battle of Moytura, it is said that 'these events happened at the same time as the War at Troy'. At Moytura, Lugh of the Long Hand rises in the early morning in the west, his face shining as bright as the sun.[51] He can only be a comet or large meteor, and the fact that his appearance is followed by three days of destructive activity by god-like warriors suggests that Ireland was hit by a major meteor shower and fireball storm at this time.[52] In the story, Lugh uses his spear to kill his grandfather Balar: otherwise Balar would have opened his evil eye and all of Ireland would have been burned in a flash.[53]

When we compare this event with Homer's description of Troy, we find an interesting parallel. During Homer's war, which takes place over five days in the tenth year after the abduction of Helen, exactly as one might expect from three periods of Comet Encke, the gods intervene from above in human affairs: 'Athena came swooping down from the heights of Olympus like a meteor […] blazing, it shoots out a mass of sparks' striking everyone with awe.[54] We also find that 'at dawn [...] Thetis emerged in the morning from the waves of the sea, rose into the broad sky and reached Olympus [...] Thetis plunged down from glittering Olympus into the salt-sea depths'.[55] Since the sea lies to the west of Hisarlik, or Troy, we realise that this event may be describing the rising of Lugh in the west — except that in Greece, which is 1–2 hours ahead of Ireland, Thetis rises after dawn, while in Ireland, Lugh rises before the sun.

The possibility that one can compare myths from different

---

51 Lady A Gregory, *Gods and Fighting Men: the story of the Tuatha de Danaan and of the Fianna of Ireland*, ed and trans Lady A Gregory (Coole, 1970) 45.

52 McCafferty and Baillie, *Celtic Gods*, 63.

53 Gregory, *Gods and Fighting Men*, 66.

54 Homer, *Iliad* ed and trans D C H Jones and E V Rieu, *The Iliad / Homer* (London, 2003) 50.

55 *Ibid*, 14–15.

parts of the world, to see if they are recounting the same events, raises an awkward issue for the Ulster Cycle. If the interpretation of the Ulster Cycle as an encounter with a comet is correct, then this means that, during the first century BCE, Ireland was bombarded from space by cometary debris. But the Romans, who were writing history at this point, must have witnessed similar events. Why do they not record these? Well, it turns out that they do, especially in 49 BCE, when the city of Alba Longa was struck by a thunderbolt from a clear sky on the night that Caesar crossed the Rubicon and a comet was seen in the sky.[56] Unfortunately, since most historians are not familiar with the potential significance of this event, they have written it out of all interpretations of the past.

The conclusion from an analysis of the *Táin* and *Cath Muighe Tuired* (the Battle of Moytura) is that Ireland experienced debris falling from the sky, at the same time that comets appeared there. The myths make sense as a narrative of something in the sky; they make little sense otherwise. This has interesting implications for archaeology. Mike Baillie, who constructed Ireland's oak-tree-ring record in Belfast, realised that there were some years when Irish oak trees were suffering. These years coincided with clusters of myths, when characters such as King Arthur were at their most active. He concluded that comet dust might have blocked sunlight from earth, resulting in famines and plagues, and the downturn of human civilisations and the descent into dark ages.[57]

Conclusion

To conclude, myths have always seemed too fantastic to be of any use in understanding prehistory. Full of magical powers and impossible deeds, the temptation to reject myth has always been strong: it is too fantastic and suspicious to allow us to trust anything it says. Instead, we have relied on archaeology for our understanding of

---

56 Lucan, *Pharsalia*, ed and trans J D Duff, *Lucan / The Civil War (Pharsalia)* (Cambridge, MA and London, 1977) 43–45.

57 M G L Baillie, *Exodus to Arthur: Catastrophic Encounters with Comets* (London, 1999) 88.

prehistory, and when we depict myths in film, we strip away all of the silly nonsense to get a sense of the deeds of the humans at the heart of the tales.

By assuming that myths are describing earthly events, and then dismissing the tales as nonsense, we have missed a vital point: many of the impossible deeds can in fact be understood as astronomical events. They tell a fascinating story: they suggest that our planet was occasionally subjected to debris from comets over the past 5000 years, and these events influenced culture, adversely affected human lives and perhaps even destroyed civilisations. As a result, we are at the beginning of a new understanding of the past: one that will require a combined understanding of archaeology and comets and mythology — and one that does not simply reject these fascinating tales from our past as literary invention.

Imperial Roman elements in the architecture of the city in *Saltair na Rann*

Tessa Morrison ⊕

Saltair na Rann, or 'psalter of the verses', is considered one of the most important religious poems of early Ireland.[1] There is only one early copy of the poem, held at Oxford Bodleian Library (MS Rawlinson B502: *The Book of Glendalough*) in a manuscript which was written c1130. The poem has been stylistically dated to the tenth century, the author is anonymous and it appears that the poem was not known outside of Ireland.

The description of the cosmos in Canto I parallels that of Genesis 1, but also contains a collection of Irish and classical cosmological lore. The emphasis is on the measurements of this cosmos. The distances between the seven heavens are multiples of 126 miles, a distance that comes directly from Pliny's *Natural History*.[2] Although the geometry of this universe appears to be an attempt at creating a perfect mathematical model of the universe in concentric spheres, the measurements do not comply to a spherical cosmos.[3] The geometry is muddled, and it can only work in a two-dimensional plane. The *Ríched*, or abode of the noble king, described in Canto II appears, at first, to be equally confused in its design elements.

The description of the celestial city of the seventh heaven is detailed, and the structure of the city is unique. The celestial city

⊕ University of Newcastle.

1 E Hull, 'The Saltair Na Rann, or Psalter of the Verses', 1–50 in E Hull (ed), *The Poem-Book of the Gael* (London, 1913), at p 3.

2 Pliny, *Natural History*, trans D E Eichholz (London, 1962), at 2.19.

3 The distance of the earth's surface to the depths of hell is 3024 miles, the same as from the earth to the *Ríched* or the abode of God.

is ten times the size of the earth.[4] It is perfectly symmetrical, with four chief doorways, each a mile wide[5] and connected by a long path.[6] Each one of the chief doorways has a lawn; each lawn is the size of the earth and is enclosed by a wall of silver.[7] There are eight porches set side by side around the stronghold.[8] The porches and the walls of each of the lawns have three doorways; these doorways with the addition of the four chief doorways make 40 doorways in the abode of the *Ríched*.[9] Furthermore, there are 12 walls of the porches and the lawns.[10] The entire city is encircled by three walls: the outer wall is of green glass, the middle wall is of purple glass and the inner wall that surrounds the stronghold is made of gold.[11] The width of the ramparts is the distance of the earth to the moon, 126 miles, and the height of the walls of the lawns is the distance from the earth to the sun, 378 miles. The height of the inner wall is the distance from the earth to the firmament, 1512 miles, and each of the walls surpasses the next by a third, the middle wall being 3024 miles in height and the outer wall 4536 miles in height.[12] Although these measurements may be an attempt to show the grandeur of the celestial city, they are disproportionate to the scale of the rest of the cosmos that was described in Canto I. In fact, the city of the seventh heaven is larger than the entire seventh heaven itself — this perhaps indicating a lack of either understanding of or regard for geometry by the author of the poem.

The geometry of the city is far more complex than the plan

---

4 'Saltair Na Rann, Cantos I–III', 75–124 in J Carey (ed), *King of Mysteries: Early Irish Religious Writing* (Dublin, 1998), at line 344.

5 *Ibid*, lines 357–360.

6 *Ibid*, line 356.

7 *Ibid*, lines 373–384.

8 *Ibid*, line 389.

9 *Ibid*, line 401.

10 *Ibid*, line 405.

11 *Ibid*, lines 345–352.

12 *Ibid*, lines 427–428.

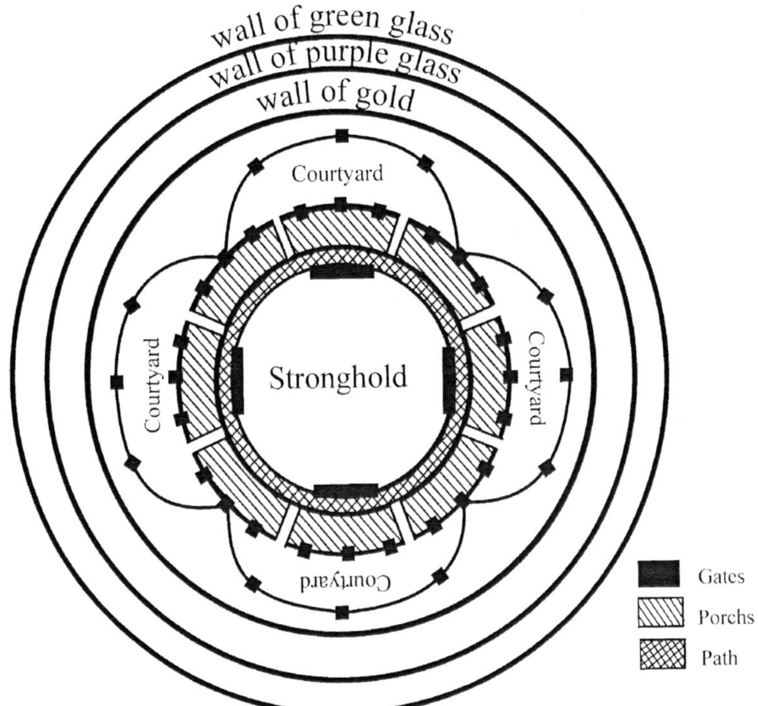

Figure 1: *The plan of the city of the* ***Ríched*** *in* ***Saltair na Rann****, drawn and interpreted by the author from the description in Saltair na Rann Canto II.*

---

of the cosmos. In the plan of this city, the number of walls and doorways is clearly specified. However, the four chief doorways are described as being 'side by side'[13] and each lawn as being the size of the Earth.[14] Since the entire city is ten times the size of the Earth, this makes the total area of the lawns 40 per cent of the area of the city. The only possible placement of the chief doorways side by side is around the stronghold like the eight porches, which are described as having been 'set side by side, until they meet going around the stronghold'. With this interpretation, the city's plan falls into place

13 *Ibid*, line 359.

14 *Ibid*, lines 374–376.

(*Figure 1*), with the one curiosity that the three outer walls have no entrances. Although the main gates to the city might have been assumed, the author failed to mention any.

This plan of the city bears no resemblance to the new Jerusalem in *Revelation*. Although there are clear references to *Revelation* at the end of the Canto, including to the Tree of Life,[15] the author has ignored the description of the city in *Revelation* and planned a unique celestial city. Not only was this celestial city unlike the city of *Revelation*, with which the author was familiar, it was also unlike any tenth-century Irish ecclesiastical architecture.

There is very little existing evidence of early Irish Christian architecture. Circular banks of earth are often the only surviving feature of early Irish Christian monasteries, which has led to the assumption that early churches were made of wood.[16] A law text refers to 'dimensions of and payment for church building'[17] and in a commentary on the old Irish Brehon laws, dated to c1000, it is suggested that the normal wooden church's ground plan was 4.6 x 3 metres, or 10 x 15 feet.[18] There is one early account of a church on a much grander scale: Cogitosus, a seventh-century biographer of Saint Brigid, described the saint's monastery in Kildare. The church covered a large area, had many windows, was decorated with frescoes and was of 'a dizzy height'. However, it was probably made of wood, despite the 'dizzy height'.[19] Monastic communities

---

15 Lines 518–620 parallel *Revelation*: the 24 white saints are taken from *Revelation* 4:4, the Lamb with his flock upon the mountain from *Revelation* 14:1–2 and the Tree of Life from *Revelation* 22:2.

16 C B McClendon, *The Origins of Medieval Architecture* (New Haven and London, 2005) 69; M Hare and A Hamlin, 'The study of early church Architecture in Ireland: an Anglo-Saxon viewpoint', 131–145 in L Butler and R K Morris (eds), *The Anglo Saxon Church* (London: 1986), at p 131.

17 L Breatnach, *A Companion to the Corpus Iuris Hibernici* (Dublin, 2005) 84.

18 P Harbison, H Potterton and J Sheehy, *Irish Art and Architecture* (London, 1978).

19 Cogitosus, 'Vita Sanctae Brididae virginis,' in T Messingham (trans), *Florilegium Insulae sanctorum* (1624) unpaginated.

were sometimes built on prehistoric ring-forts, which consisted of dry stone masonry or earthen ramparts. They sometimes featured circular beehive huts such as those found on Skellig Michael, a form of building with ancient precedents. Skellig Michael was known to have been inhabited in 823 and the beehive huts that survive are thought to date to the twelfth century. However, their form is unlikely to have changed since the island was originally settled.[20] Folio 202v of the Book of Kells, from the eighth or early ninth century, shows Christ on the pinnacle of the temple being tempted by the devil; the rectangular building has a single story with a steep shingled roof. Although the exterior of the building is ornately decorated and has dragon-head finials, the structure of the building is very minimal and is in a style that was repeated in later simple stone churches dotted around the Irish countryside. From the evidence of early Irish ecclesiastical architecture, it would appear that the author of *Saltair na Rann* was influenced by an exterior source in the architecture for the abode of the noble king.

Although there are individual elements in *Saltair na Rann* that have some similarity to the *Apocalypse of Paul*, Adomnán's *De locis Sanctis*, Bede's *Historia ecclesiatica* and *Fis Adamnán*,[21] it is questionable that these are the direct sources of the city plan of the *Ríched*: the similarities in the mentioned texts are in only some individual elements, which are not measured and lack design details. The city appears to have no literary precedent.[22] With the exception of the few references to *Revelation* near the end of the canto, the second canto stands out from the others in the poem

---

20 W Horn, J W Marshall and G D Rourke, *The forgotten heritage of Skellig Michael* (Berkeley, 1990).

21 J N Bremmer and I Czachesz (eds), *The Visio Pauli and the Gnostic Apocalypse of Paul* (Leuven, 2007); Bede, *The Ecclesiastical History of the English People*, J McClure and R Collins (ed) (Oxford, 1999); Anonymous, 'Fis Adamnáin' 28–36 in C S Boswell, *An Irish precursor of Dante; a study on the Vision of heaven and hell, ascribed to the eighth-century Irish saint, Adamnán, with translation of the Irish text by C S Boswell* (New York, 1972 [1908]).

22 T Morrison, 'Celestial Differences and Similarities' (forthcoming).

because of its lack of biblical references. That the plan was not the author's invention is suggested by the city walls having no gates — a strange oversight to omit a major design element from such a highly detailed plan. The city is a complex product of sophisticated geometry, while the plan of the cosmos has disproportionate ratios. Furthermore, the scale of the celestial city is disproportionate to that of the cosmos, and this suggests that the designs of the city and the cosmos were designed by two different geometric 'hands'.

Without any surviving architectural precedent in Ireland for the celestial city, or any clear influence in the literature that would have been available in the tenth century in Ireland,[23] it must be presumed that the designer of the celestial city of *Saltair na Rann* was influenced by the architecture of the continent, perhaps directly whilst on pilgrimage, or indirectly from descriptions by other pilgrims. The floor plan in *Figure 1* was developed from the description in Canto II. However, the overall plan could be round, square, octagonal or a mixture of round, square and octagonal. The canto only states that it is perfectly symmetrical.[24] Figure 1 has been drawn as circular because it is the simplest and the most perfectly symmetrical form from which to consider the overall plan.

The geometry of the celestial city in *Saltair na Rann* fits together through the numbers of the elements. The four walls of the lawn and the eight porches that surround the central stronghold create the 12 divisions of porch and lawns; there are also three surrounding walls and a total of 40 doorways. These are all numbers that have significance in pagan and early Christian numerology.[25] The number symbolism is representative of the early medieval period, where the 12 apostles bring the four gospels of the trinity to the four ends of the earth.[26] The number 40 was an important number

23 J Carey, 'Cosmology in Saltair na Rann', *Celtica* 17 (1985) 33–52, at p 36.

24 Carey, 'Saltair Na Rann Cantos I-III', 354.

25 R A Peck, 'Number as Cosmic Language', 15–64 in D L Jeffrey (ed), *By Things Seen: Reference and Recognition in Medieval Thought* (Ottawa, 1979).

26 V F Hopper, *Medieval Number Symbolism* (New York, 1969).

in Babylonian astronomy, which gained significance in the late Roman era through the astronomy of Ptolemy.[27] In the Ptolemaic system, the seven heavenly bodies required 39 epicycles to move through the sky. The addition of the outermost cycle of the fixed stars made this system an even 40 epicycles.[28] Ptolemy's universe system gained favour with astronomers, and it shaped the vision of the universe from the time that it was written in Alexandria in c130 CE up to the early seventeenth century.[29]

In early Christian architecture and art, eight was a highly significant number.[30] From the early fourth century, an octagonal structure was built and attached to the east side of the Christian basilica.[31] Eusebius praised a church called the Golden Octagon at Antioch, which had commenced construction in 327 under Constantine.[32] There were many examples of these octagonal structures from this period in Milan, Rome, Antioch and Bethlehem, with the most extraordinary surviving examples being in Ravenna.[33] These examples were primarily used as baptisteries. On the continent, the hand signal of the Christian blessing was the gesture for eight: it was also an ancient numerical gesture and was used extensively in medieval computus.[34] Eight was the number

27 A Baker, *Scientific Method in Ptolemy's 'Harmonics'* (Cambridge, 2000).

28 A Koestler, *The Sleepwalkers* (London, 1959) 66–68.

29 A Nicolson, *Power and Glory: Jacobean England and the Making of the King James Bible* (London, 2003) 164.

30 T Morrison, 'The art of early medieval number symbolism', *Journal of the Australian Early Medieval Association* 2 (2006) 174–178.

31 R Krautheimer, *Early Christian and Byzantine Architecture* (Middlesex, 1986) 60.

32 Eusebius, 'The Life of the Blessed Emperor Constantine,' 481–560 in P Schaff (ed), *Nicene and the Post-Nicene Fathers* (Grand Rapids, 1979), at III.L.

33 Examples are The Church of the Nativity, Bethlehem; San Lorenzo, Milan; the octagonal baptisteries and San Vitale, Ravenna. See Morrison, 'The Art of Early Medieval Number Symbolism', 169-181.

34 T Morrison, 'An Examination of the Blessing Hand in Insular Art', 288–300 in R Moss (ed), *Making and Meaning in Insular Art* (Dublin, 2007)

that was closely associated with baptism and the resurrection.[35] Both the octagonal baptistery and the blessing hand, as the gesture eight, were used extensively in art and architecture of the early medieval period on the continent.[36] Nevertheless, there is no existing evidence that either was used in insular architecture and art until the ninth century.[37] The central feature of the celestial city is the eight porches[38] surrounding the central stronghold, which would suggest that this central feature might be octagonal in shape. This further strengthens the argument that the design came from the continent.

There are four chief doorways to the central stronghold, which is surrounded by the eight porches. In front of each of these doorways is a lawn. The size of the lawns is described as being the size of the earth,[39] and they are of the same area and symmetrical, following the overall plan of the city. Cruciform churches had become popular in northern Italy and the alpine region in the fifth century.[40] Nevertheless, these would not be consistent with the symmetrical city, particularly since the lawns are of equal size. The Baldacchino form was the governing principle of sixth-century Christian architecture and was a prevalent style for many centuries after. The building of this style had harmonic variations on the theme of the domed image of heaven, and the ancient canopied symbol of the divine was set around a central space with radial symmetry or within a non-congruent peripheral rectangle.[41] The central space with radial symmetry is similar to the symmetry of the floor plan of

---

at pp 294–295.

35 Morrison, 'The Art of Early Medieval Number Symbolism', 174.

36 Morrison, 'Blessing Hand in Insular Art'.

37 *Ibid*, 299–300.

38 Carey, 'Saltair Na Rann, Cantos I-III,' 389.

39 *Ibid*, 376.

40 McClendon, *The Origins of Medieval Architecture*, 13.

41 W MacDonald, *Early Christian and Byzantine Architecture* (London, 1962) 33.

the celestial city of *Saltair na Rann*. An extant example of this style is the Mausoleum of Galla Placidia, Ravenna, dated to the mid-fifth century, where each of the radials is of equal size.[42] The fifth-century Saint Stefano Rotondo in Rome was originally a central core with four wings on cross axes, surrounded by a circular wall. Wilfrid of Hexham visited Rome in 655 and it is possible that Saint Stefano Rotondo influenced St Mary's church that he later built at Hexham. Although St Mary's was not as complex as Saint Stefano Rotondo, it was a combination of a rotunda and cross plan.[43]

Early Christian architecture had an entirely different meaning and purpose from the Greco-Roman architecture from which it had evolved. However, the structural solutions and elements of classical architecture remained and evolved in early Christian architecture. Two primary architectural influences on early baptisteries were the imperial Roman bath building and the Imperial mausoleum.[44] Early Christian fonts were large, often four or five metres across. A surviving example from the mid-fifth century can be found in the Neonian baptistery, Ravenna.[45] The central pattern of baptisteries from the fourth century onward is the same as the design for the imperial Roman bath building.[46] Examples of these are Badenweiler and Stabian Baths at Pompei and the Thermae of Caracalla in Rome. Prior to the sanctioning of Christianity as the official religion of the state, baptisteries were square or rectangular. The tomb of Augustus consisted of a central rotunda with a second rotunda. The tomb of Hadrian had a second, square rotunda surrounding the first. These massive buildings[47] dominated their surroundings and were a

42 *Ibid*, plate 34.

43 McClendon, *The Origins of Medieval Architecture,* 71.

44 R Krautheimer, 'Introduction to an Iconography of Medieval Architecture', *Journal of the Warburg and Courtauld Institutes* 5 (1942) 20–33.

45 Salbaroli-Ravenna, *Ravenna: City of Art* (Ravenna, 2003) 104–110.

46 *Ibid*, 21.

47 For reproductions of these buildings see C Tagell, *Imperial Space* (London, 1998) 14 and 15.

monument to the emperor and to imperial power. On the Palatine in Rome, there are the remains of the temple of Domus Augustana: the central rotunda was an octagon and at the eight sides are radials which alternate between square and semi-circular.

The Golden Octagon in Antioch adjoined the imperial palace, and it is thought that the Golden Octagon functioned as an imperial throne room and royal chapel under the emperor Constantine. Constantine moved the capital to Byzantium, renaming it Constantinople, in 326 AD. Of the many churches built by Constantine in Constantinople little evidence remains; however, Eusebius has left a description of the first Hagia Sophia, Church of Holy Wisdom. The church was a Greek cross shape. At the crossing was a conical roof and below this was the sarcophagus of Constantine surrounded by piers inscribed in honour of the twelve apostles. This mausoleum for Constantine was also dedicated to the apostles, and in the enclosure masses were read daily. The mausoleum was covered with so much gold that Eusebius claimed that it 'dazzled all eyes that beheld it and reverberated the rays of the sun'.[48] In the architecture of Constantine, the martyrium, round and octagonal, became the centre of the structure of the basilica.[49]

The imperial mausoleum and octagonal church became intertwined. The concept of divine kingship is visualised by the mosaics of the octagonal church of San Vitale, Ravenna. Two famous mosaics of Theodora and Justinian, and attendants, face each other on the apse walls. Theodora and Justinian, heavily jewelled and dressed in the royal purple, solemnly offer their Eucharistic gifts. The emphasis of the mosaics is on the connection between the heavenly and the imperial powers through the act of the Eucharist.[50]

The round or octagonal structure with four radials is the floor plan of the celestial city of *Saltair na Rann*. In the centre of the

---

48 Eusebius, 'The Life of the Blessed Emperor Constantine', 481–560 in P Schaff (ed), *Nicene and the Post-Nicene Fathers* (Grand Rapids, 1979) at IV and LVIII.

49 Krautheimer, *Early Christian and Byzantine Architecture*, 70.

50 R Milburn, *Early Christian Art and Architecture*, (Aldershot, 1988) 181.

stronghold is the 'King royally noble in his royal abode',[51] his throne made of red gold and surrounded by innumerable radiant angels.[52] The concept of imperial power and grandeur radiates from the centre of the celestial city. The numerology and the overall plan of the city mimic the floor plans of the imperial bath buildings, mausoleums and baptisteries in the Baldacchino form.

There were many examples of this style of building that would have been accessible to a pilgrim to the Holy Land, Rome, Constantinople or Ravenna. To travel from the circular beehive huts and small wooden churches of Ireland to the massive baptisteries and basilicas of the Holy Land, Rome, Ravenna and Constantinople, that were richly decorated and strongly linked to the imperial court, must have struck awe into any pilgrim. Arculf, a bishop of Gaul, had travelled to Jerusalem, Damascus, Constantinople and Alexandria in the late seventh century, and on his return he was shipwrecked at Iona. Here he met Adomnán, abbot of Iona, who listened to stories of his travels and committed to writing everything Arculf had seen in the Holy Land in his *De Locis Sanctis*.[53] Arculf described and sketched the floor plan of the buildings of the Holy Land into a wax tablet.[54] Unfortunately the recorded descriptions of the building are a bare outline, and, although a few elements are similar to those of the celestial city of *Saltair na Rann*, it is clearly not its architectural source because although there are a few minor similarities, the overall plan is significantly different.

As noted previously, the design of the city and the cosmos indicate that they were designed by two different geometric 'hands'. John Carey has examined the sources of the cosmology of *Saltair na Rann* and claims that they include a large range of material that would have been available to a tenth-century Irish author.[55] Yet

51 Carey, 'Saltair Na Rann, Cantos I-III', 568.

52 *Ibid*, 533.

53 Bede, *Ecclesiastical History*, 263.

54 Adamnán, *De Locis Sanctus*, Denis Meehan (ed) (Dublin, 1958) 2.10–15.

55 Carey, 'Cosmology in Saltair na Rann', 33–52, at p 50. Carey notes the primary source to be Pliny's *Historia naturalis*, Herodotus' *Historia*,

the celestial city's architectural detail appears to have no literary precedent; nor does it have any similarity to the architecture of tenth-century Ireland. The floor plan does strongly resemble, however, the floor plans of contemporaneous Christian architecture from the continent. This would indicate that the original plan came from a pilgrim, either directly or indirectly through a sketch into a wax tablet to be relayed by somebody else, like the one that Arculf sketched for Adomnán. That the description of the city is from a personal experience is strongly indicated by the lack of biblical references in Canto II. This also makes Canto II stand out from the other 161 cantos of the poem.

Nevertheless, I argue that the plan of the city as related in *Saltair na Rann* did not originate with the author. This is suggested by the city walls having no gates, which is a very strange oversight, and not one that would have been made by the original author of this complex plan. I argue that the plan in *Saltair na Rann* was copied from another source, possibly from a pilgrim's description or a sketched plan. *Saltair na Rann* is the most detailed plan of the celestial city in early Christianity, which makes it extremely significant; yet its source was not the Bible or the philosophies or theologies of the time, but the magnificent and earthly architecture of imperial Rome.

Macrobius' *Somniva Scipionis*, pseudo-Isidore's *De Ordine Creaturarum* and Isidore of Seville's *Etymologiarum*.

Fiction, feminism and the 'Celtic Church': the Sister Fidelma novels of Peter Tremayne

Carole Cusack ◎

Introduction

Since the 1994 publication of *Absolution by Murder* by Peter Tremayne (the pen-name of the popular Celtic Studies author and bard Peter Berresford Ellis), 16 further detective novels and two collections of short stories featuring the seventh-century Irish nun and Brehon law advocate, Sister Fidelma, have appeared. The appeal of the series is that it presents a picture of early medieval Ireland and the 'Celtic Church' that is compatible with secularised liberal modernity, while exploiting the 'otherness' and counter-cultural *mores* promoted in new age understandings of 'the Celts'. Fidelma is a feisty, professionally successful, sexually attractive (and active) young woman who challenges the traditional image of medieval nuns. The Irish church to which she belongs is free from the dogmatic and illiberal tendencies that medieval Christianity frequently manifested.

Seventh-century Ireland is depicted as a tolerant society in which Christians and those retaining the traditional polytheistic religion interact in a variety of ways; *conhospitae* (double monasteries) and love and marriage between monks and nuns are presented as part of mainstream Christianity; and the place of women within the Irish legal system is affirmed as far superior to that of any contemporary society (for example, Anglo-Saxon England or continental Italy). Tremayne has stated that the novels are based on 'fact' and has sought to authenticate this claim by several means. He regularly invokes his status as a Fellow of both the Royal Historical Society and the Royal Society of Antiquaries of Ireland, and in the 'Frequently Asked

◎ The University of Sydney.

Questions' section of the website of the International Sister Fidelma Society (previously published in their magazine *The Brehon*), he answers readers' queries with short essays that demonstrate his apparent erudition.[1] He refers to his 'academic' published works, and to the works of early medieval scholars.

This paper argues that the novels are definitely fiction, and distinctively modern in sensibility. The illusion of 'authenticity' is created in part by Tremayne's selective presentation of historical and legal sources, and in part by the readers' desire for verisimilitude (wanting the world depicted within the Sister Fidelma novels to have existed) and their willingness to believe that early medieval Ireland is at once a society that is alien or 'other' and yet also a mirror of the contemporary West (in its equality between the sexes, vibrant individualism, forthright sexuality, tolerant Christianity and freedom from restrictions). The 'evidence' Tremayne calls upon in his responses to reader queries and in other published interviews is scrutinised and material from primary sources and reputable academic publications is employed to critique Tremayne's faulty historical technique and frequent misrepresentation of evidence.[2]

Detective fiction and historical settings

The detective story was developed and became popular in the nineteenth century, and is virtually ubiquitous in the twenty-first

1 www.sisterfidelma.com (accessed 29 November 2007). The abstract of this paper appeared on the web page of the Sixth Australian Celtic Conference, 18–21 July 2007 (www.arts.usyd.edu.au/foundations/CSFoundation/conference2007/home.html). I later received e-mail from David Robert Wooten, the Society's Director, chiding me for the critical tone of the abstract and reminding me that 'many leading Celtic Scholars and experts on Early Medieval Ireland have published applauding the accuracy of the background of the books' (e-mail received 4 August 2007 from david@sisterfidelma.com).

2 My thanks are due to the School of Letters, Art and Media (SLAM) at the University of Sydney, which paid for thirty-five hours of research assistance so that I could complete this paper. The talented Dr Helen Young was the 'roving research assistant' assigned to me. Her work was exemplary and I wish her every success in her own academic career.

century. It is a quintessentially modern phenomenon. Crime has always been part of human society, but until the modern era efforts to seek out and punish perpetrators were notably unsuccessful. This is an important consideration in the assessment of contemporary detective novels set in the middle ages, as they impose a modern frame of reference that is completely foreign on a historical period where there was no police force, and the standards of proof were uncertain. Juries existed and medieval rulers were 'greatly concerned both with the public order and that state of their treasury',[3] which was relevant as an 'increasing number of different officials [...] were appointed, especially in the later Middle Ages, to see that accused criminals were brought to trial'.[4] The religious climate of the medieval era, which welcomed miracles and was inclined to attribute anomalous occurrences to demonic intervention, rendered crime-solving improbable, if not impossible. The 'watch', usually elderly men without gainful employment mustered by the parish (and who appear as minor comic characters in a number of Shakespeare's plays), were the principal means of law enforcement from the later middle ages to the early nineteenth century.[5]

An examination of the development of the genre reveals much about the social anxieties of the people who wrote and read detective fiction. One crucial social change was the retreat of institutional Christianity from the public culture of western societies. Modern methods of solving crime are the product of Enlightenment rationalism, and the first detectives in fiction were practitioners of the art of reason.[6] Detective fiction, like all cultural products,

3 R C van Caenegum, 'Public Prosecution of Crime in Twelfth-Century England' in C N L Brooke (ed), *Church and Government in the Middle Ages* (Cambridge, 1976) 50.

4 A McCall, *The Medieval Underworld* (London, 1979) 52.

5 See P D James and T A Critchley, *The Maul and the Pear Tree: The Ratcliffe Highway Murders, 1811* (London, 1987) for an indictment of the inefficiency and inadequate crime-solving skills of these ill-equipped amateurs.

6 C M Cusack, 'Scarlet and Back: Non-Mainstream Religion as "Other" in Detective Fiction' in C M Cusack, F Di Lauro and C Hartney (eds), *The*

reflects the historical and social contexts in which it is produced. The first fictional detectives — C Auguste Dupin, featured in the novellas of Edgar Allan Poe (*eg* 'The Murders in the Rue Morgue', 1841 and 'The Mystery of Marie Roget', 1850) and Arthur Conan Doyle's very similar Sherlock Holmes (who debuted in 1887) — were gentleman amateurs. The Metropolitan Police Force (the first modern, professional law-enforcement agency), was established by Sir Robert Peel in England in 1829, with an initial 1000 constables (known as 'bobbies' and 'peelers' after him). The first detective novel featuring a policeman, the formidable Sergeant Cuff, was Wilkie Collins' *The Moonstone* (1868).

The detective, in solving a puzzle that usually involved violent death, functioned as a secularised father confessor, by imparting meaning to otherwise random elements of life.[7] GK Chesterton's Father Brown married the figure of the detective with the priest of traditional Christianity; in the late twentieth century, the sub-genre of the medieval detective novel regularly featured clergy as investigating protagonists.[8] Again following broader social trends, in the twentieth century women detectives became more prevalent in fiction (initially amateurs, like Agatha Christie's Miss Jane Marple and Patricia Wentworth's Miss Maud Silver). The detective/crime genre splintered into sub-genres: police procedurals, courtroom, and 'hard-boiled'. 'Private eye' novels featured investigators who were outside the police force. Later, female police officers and then female private investigators became popular protagonists.[9]

Medieval detective fiction was born with the 1977 publication

---

Buddha of Suburbia (Sydney, 2005) 161.

7 J Wren-Lewis, 'Adam, Eve and Agatha Christie: Detective Stories as Post-Darwinian Myths of Original Sin', *Australian Religion Studies Review* 6:1 (1993) 20–24.

8 E E C B Lindsay, 'The Habit of Detection: The Medieval Monk as Detective in the Novels of Ellis Peters', 276–289 in Leslie J Workman (ed), *Medievalism in England* (Woodbridge, 1992).

9 I Maassen, 'An Unsuitable Job For A Woman? Gender, Genre and the New Detective Heroine', 152–165 in H G Klaus and S Knight (eds), *The Art of Murder: New Essays on Detective Fiction* (Tuebingen, 1998).

of Ellis Peters' (Edith Pargeter's) *A Morbid Taste for Bones*, featuring the Welsh ex-crusader Benedictine of Shrewsbury Abbey, Brother Cadfael. Brother Cadfael went on to feature in 20 novels and a collection of short stories. There was also series of made-for-television films, starring Derek Jacobi as Cadfael. The tourist industry in Shrewsbury benefited from the re-foundation of the medieval guild of Saint Winifred and the marketing of Cadfael walks in the town and driving trails in the surrounding county.[10] However, the genre might never have taken off without the success of Umberto Eco's *The Name of the Rose* (Italian 1980, English 1983), a book that has spawned a scholarly sub-industry.[11] Eco, rather than Peters, established the stereotype of the author of medieval detective fiction. An unusually large number of these writers are academics or have postgraduate training in history. Eco, an expert on Thomas Aquinas and medieval aesthetics, taught at the University of Turin. His first novel exhibited profound knowledge of the middle ages and was made into a critically acclaimed film in 1986 by director Jean-Jacques Annaud. Brother William of Baskerville, the detective who references Sherlock Holmes, was played by veteran actor Sean Connery, and his novice assistant, Adso, by Christian Slater.

Despite this remarkable start for the genre of medieval detective novels, few authors who followed Eco could match his knowledge of the period, his narrative mastery, or his ingenuity of plotting. Apart from Barry Unsworth's Booker Prize-winning *Morality Play* (1995), the literary quality of medieval detective and crime fiction is limited. These novels tend to serve a market more reminiscent

10 See R Whiteman, *Cadfael Country: Shropshire and the Welsh Borders* (London, 1990).

11 Eco himself started this with *Reflections on The Name of the Rose* (London, 1990). See L Braswell, 'Meta-psychomachia in Eco's 'The Name of the Rose', *Mosaic: A Journal for the Interdisciplinary Study of Literature* 20:2 (Spring, 1987) 1–11 and M T Inge, *Naming the Rose: Essays on Eco's The Name of the Rose* (Jackson and London, 1988), among others. Scholarly publications investigating Eco's pioneering novel is one phenomenon that clearly distinguishes him from other authors in the medieval detective fiction genre, who are rarely (if ever) the subject of academic studies.

of that established by the prolific Agatha Christie, where the reader likes a certain type of novel and reads many of them, disregarding their formulaic nature and similarities of character, setting and plot. This type of readership is also conducive to the formation of 'fan clubs' like the International Sister Fidelma Society, and Wolfe Pack, the Nero Wolfe Fan Club. The expansion of the internet has facilitated such groups, as well as increased opportunities for informal reviewing and discussions of favourite authors.[12]

Peter Tremayne and the Sister Fidelma novels

Peter Tremayne (Peter Berresford Ellis) is a well-known figure in the field of Celtic Studies, publishing in a space between genuinely academic work and unashamedly unscholarly books. He has an honorary doctorate and writes works of popular Celtic history; he is also a bard of the Gorsedd Kernow (Cornish Assembly of Bards) and a frequently used photograph shows him attired in his blue bardic robes;[13] finally, he is a prolific novelist using several *noms de plume*, and the creator of the Sister Fidelma series. To date there are 17 Fidelma novels and two collections of short stories, culminating in *Council of the Cursed* (2008). A further title is anticipated for 2009. In *Absolution by Murder* (1994), the character of Fidelma is established. She is a *dálaigh* (advocate) of the Irish Brehon law system, qualified to the second-highest level of *anruth*. The first novel is set during the Synod of Whitby of 664 CE. This was a church council presided over by King Oswy of Northumbria and hosted by the Anglo-Saxon aristocrat Hilda, abbess of the double monastery of Streoneshealh. Here Fidelma meets Brother Eadulf, an Anglo-Saxon monk (who is a hereditary magistrate of Seaxmund's Ham and thus shares her passion for solving crimes and legal puzzles), with whom she develops a close relationship over the series.

Fidelma is a young woman, still in her mid-twenties, but with

12 When researching this paper I put 'detective fiction' into Google on 29 November 2007 and got 1,640,000 hits. It is acknowledged that a substantial proportion of these are booksellers' sites.

13 This image is reproduced on the back of the dust jacket of P Berresford Ellis, *The Druids* (London, 1996).

eight years' legal training. She has 'some fluency' in Latin, Greek and Hebrew, and is as notable for her physical attractiveness as her learning. Tremayne minimises the effect of the lack of sex appeal inherent in the term 'nun' by referring to Fidelma anachronistically as a '*religieuse*' ('religious' would suffice). Abbess Hilda's first impression of Fidelma is:

> She was tall, with a well-proportioned figure which, the keen eyes of the abbess saw, vibrated youthful exuberance. Rebellious strands of red hair streaked from beneath her headdress. She had an attractive face — not beautiful, thought Hilda, but attractive. The abbess suddenly realised that her scrutiny was being returned by a pair of watchful bright eyes. She could not make out whether they were blue or green in the changing light that seemed to emanate from them.[14]

A few pages later, Fidelma runs into Brother Eadulf in a corridor and experiences a 'moment of pure chemistry'. The sexual attraction between them is an important element in the series; their wedding (after a period of temporary marriage and a child) is the subject of *A Prayer for the Damned* (2006).

The seventh century was a time of change for the Irish church, and *Absolution by Murder*'s setting furnishes Tremayne with opportunities to explain the differences between the Roman and Irish church customs that caused the synod to be called (chiefly the dating of Easter and the style of tonsure worn). The historical outcome of Whitby was that Oswy, who himself adhered to the Irish church, ruled in favour of Wilfrid of Hexham and the Frankish cleric

14 P Tremayne, *Absolution by Murder* (London, 1994) 29. It is not the purpose of this paper to castigate Tremayne on account of his writing style, but it must be noted that the description 'Rebellious strands of red hair streaked from under her headdress' is used in *Shroud for the Archbishop* (London 1995) 9 and 'red hair tumbling from beneath her headdress' in *The Spider's Web* (London, 1997) 9.

Agilbert, the representatives of Rome (who invoked the authority of Peter). He thus dismissed the claim of Colman of Lindisfarne and Cedd (who invoked the authority of Columba). The king ruled that:

> Peter is the guardian of the gates of heaven, and I shall not contradict him. I shall obey his commands in everything to the best of my knowledge and ability; otherwise, when I come to the gates of heaven, there may be no one to open them, because he who holds the keys has turned away.[15]

The second Fidelma novel, *Shroud for the Archbishop* (1995), has Fidelma and Eadulf in Rome; she to gain papal approval for the Rule of Saint Brigit of Kildare and he as part of the process of appointing the next Archbishop of Canterbury.

Marriage and sex between monks and nuns

In *Absolution by Murder*, Fidelma and Eadulf, acting at the behest of King Oswy, investigate three murders that take place during the Synod of Whitby. The motive is passion; the young Pictish nun, Sister Gwid, is in love with Abbess Étain of Kildare and cannot bear that she intends to take the Anglo-Saxon monk Aethelnoth as a husband. Gwid kills them both, and she later kills the monk Seaxwulf whom she knows to be hot on her trail.[16] This is an important plotline, as one of Tremayne's core contentions, that mixed religious houses were common and marriage between monks and nuns was perceived as one choice open to those who had taken religious vows, is given expression. Tremayne claims that:

---

15 Bede, *Ecclesiastical History of the English People*, L Sherley-Price (trans), rev ed (Harmondsworth, 1990) 192.

16 A further death takes place in *Absolution by Murder*. Deusdedit, Archbishop of Canterbury, is found dead of the Yellow Plague on p 176. This is a manipulation of the historical evidence. Deusdedit did have the plague and did not attend the Synod of Whitby. He died a few months later. See F M Stenton, *Anglo-Saxon England* 2nd ed (Oxford, 1967 [1947]) 129.

> Throughout the 7th century there is much documentary evidence showing that in Frankia and Gaul the majority of clerics, priests, abbots and bishops, were married. In the following century, St Boniface of Crediton (c AD 675–755), comments that almost no bishop or priest in Germany followed the idea of celibacy. Indeed, well into the 9th century, it was reported at the Council of Aix-la-Chapelle that the inhabitants of monasteries and convents were living together and that where the bishops and abbots were trying to enforce celibacy there were a number of abortions and infanticide taking place to cover up these relationships.[17]

There are many problems with Tremayne's explanation. The first is that he never clearly distinguishes between regular clergy (those living under a rule, *regulus*, like monks and nuns) and secular clergy (those living in the *saeculum*, 'this age', and interacting with the laity, like priests and bishops). It is true that until the eleventh century, secular clergy were permitted to marry (although, when promoted to the rank of bishop, a priest was expected to live celibately with his wife). It is thus the case that bishoprics could be passed down from father to son. Gregory of Tours, the sixth-century bishop and historian, is justifiably proud of the lineage of bishops his family has provided to the city of Tours.[18] In the eleventh century, this situation came to an end with the reforms of Pope Gregory VII (1073–1085 CE). However, from the beginnings of monasticism in the fourth century, monks and nuns took vows of poverty, chastity and obedience.[19]

---

17 P Tremayne, 'Clerical Marriages: Celibacy in Fidelma's Time', www.sisterfidelma.com (accessed 29 November 2007).

18 Gregory of Tours, *History of the Franks*, L Thorpe (ed and trans), (Harmondsworth, 1974) 7–16.

19 M Bateson, 'Origin and Early History of Double Monasteries', *Transactions of the Royal Historical Society* New Series 13 (1899) 137–198, at p 139, discusses the earliest rules for both men and women, devised by the

Further, the *conhospitae* or double monasteries to which Tremayne regularly refers were quite different institutions from what he suggests. First, it is erroneous to suggest that there were many double monasteries in Ireland. There was one, and one only, Kildare (Fidelma's own institution in the novels).[20] *Vitae* of Saint Brigit attribute this establishment jointly to her and Bishop Conlaed, which Tremayne accepts uncritically (as he does her appointment as a 'bishop'). This, however, exhibits a lack of sophistication with regard to textual criticism of early Irish saints' lives. The two seventh-century lives of Brigit, that of Cogitosus and the anonymous *Vita Prima* (so named not because of its historical primacy, but due to the Bollandists placing it first in their printed edition) are texts in which the saint raises dead animals to life, hangs her cloak upon a rainbow and, after self-mutilating to avoid marriage, miraculously heals herself. The 'history' which Tremayne selectively extracts from the *vitae* of Brigit is simply not history.[21] Second, double houses were not particular to Irish or 'Celtic' Christianity. They are commonest in Frankia and Anglo-Saxon England and represent a continuation of late antique asceticism. Third, they were institutions where men and women were strictly cordoned off from each other, often by walls dividing the men's and women's quarters. Only the church was a shared space, and that was for religious ceremonies rather than socialising. As Bateson comments, 'there is no promiscuous mixing of the sexes; the monastery is double not mixed'.[22]

In the search for evidence that Tremayne intends to mislead readers of the Sister Fidelma novels as to the 'factual' nature of the

---

Egyptian monk Pachomius.

20 G C Alston, 'Double Monasteries', in *The Catholic Encyclopedia* X (New York 1911) www.advent.org/cathen/10452a.htm (accessed 29 November 2007).

21 See S Connolly, 'Vita Prima Sanctae Brigitae: Background and Historical Value', *Journal of the Royal Society of Antiquaries of Ireland* 119 (1989) 5–49 and S Connolly and J M Picard, 'Cogitosus's Life of St Brigit: Content and Value', in *Journal of the Royal Society of Antiquaries of Ireland* 117 (1987) 5–27.

22 Bateson, 138.

setting, it can be proved that he quotes scholars out of context to make it appear that they agree with his picture of early medieval Ireland. He writes that:

> Professor Lisa M. Bitel, in spite of her later arguments, confessed in *Isle of the Saints: Monastic Settlement and Christian Community in Early Ireland* (Cornell University Press, 1990): 'Abbots and officers openly supported wives, sons and other kin. They sent their relatives to become officers in nearby monasteries, or they kept sons, brothers and nephews within their own communities to succeed to offices there. Successive generations of the Macc Cuinn na mBocht, for example, controlled major monastic offices at Cluan Moccu Nois (Clonmacnoise) for about three centuries.[23]

If Bitel, a respected scholar of women in medieval Ireland and of Irish monastic foundations, really did say this, it would represent unimpeachable academic support for Tremayne's position.

However, he takes the quotation significantly out of context. It comes from a chapter titled 'The Monastic Family', which establishes that '[i]nside their holy walls, the monks joined together, in their words, as a *familia*',[24] that '[m]onastic leaders urged monks to abandon blood kin and patrimony', that the demands of blood kin and of the spiritual family were conflicting, and that different 'issues of affection, loyalty, and property repeatedly assaulted each monk'.[25] The quotation Tremayne takes from Bitel is immediately preceded in the original by:

---

23 P Berresford Ellis, 'Celibacy in the Catholic Church', *Irish Democrat* www.irishdemocrat.co.uk/anonn-is-anall/celibacy-in-the-church/ (accessed 29 November 2007). See also Tremayne, 'Clerical Marriage', www.sisterfidelma.com (accessed 29 November 2007).

24 L Bitel, *Isle of the Saints: Monastic Settlement and Christian Community in Early Ireland* (Ithaca, 1990) 85.

25 Bitel, *Isle of the Saints*, 86–87.

> [y]et even when a core group of monks maintained themselves as a celibate elite within a community their rulers and their associated lay brothers often provided the stock from which they drew recruits. Kathleen Hughes and John Kellner have shown that major monasteries such as Slaine, Lusca, and Cluain Moccu Nois contained monastic families that were bound by blood as well as by consciously created family-style ties.[26]

The meaning is clearly quite different from what Tremayne wants it to be, particularly in the context of a chapter about the way religious communities were structured *like* a family but were often in tension with actual blood ties.

Tremayne's picture of intimate relationships between monks and nuns involves sexual intercourse. Here, he possibly misunderstands or misrepresents an important phenomenon that is well-attested in pre-reformation Christianity. This was the situation in which professed religious of both sexes cultivated intimate friendships, and were soul companions, but chastely, without sexual expression of any sort.[27] This state was known as 'spiritual marriage' or *syneisactism*. However, the practice was widely disapproved of, and Saint Patrick (and the later Irish penitentials) condemned it as courting temptation.[28] With regard to sexual sin among the clergy, Tremayne implies that clerical fornication was not taken seriously:

> For example, Dr Patrick Power, in *Sex and Marriage in Ancient Ireland*, points out that a Céili Dé 'Penitential' does not order excommunication and expulsion for

26 Bitel, *Isle of the Saints*, 105.

27 R E Reynolds, '*Virgines Subintroductae* in Celtic Christianity,' *Harvard Theological Review* 61:4 (October 1968) 547–566. See also C S Jaeger, *Ennobling Love: In Search of a Lost Sensibility* (Philadelphia, 1999).

28 N Chadwick, *The Age of the Saints in the Early Celtic Church* (London, 1961) 149.

> any monk or nun who has a sexual relationship but only prescribes a penance.[29]

What he does not mention are the details of the penance. According to the penitential of Vinian, 'a cleric who has had "fellowship" with a woman, forty days on bread and water, and expunging the friendship from his heart is ordered'.[30] A cleric who has friendships with many women and 'has given himself to [...] their lascivious embraces' must complete six months on bread and water, followed by a further six months without meat or wine. The ultimate sin, falling 'to the depths of ruin' occurs when a cleric begets a son. The sentence is 'three years on bread and water, followed by seven years' exile'.[31] These penances would suggest that sexual sin among the clergy was taken very seriously indeed.

Finally, with regard to clerical marriage, the permitted grounds for divorce initiated by the wife included if her husband 'turns out to be in Holy Orders, or is too fat or impotent, or if he persists in revealing secrets about their intimate life to third parties'.[32] This would suggest that men in holy orders were not generally husbands and the suggestion of sexual incapacity (obesity, impotence) creates the impression that male religious were either sexually incapable or should be. It must be admitted that the final condition, if the husband persists in discussing marital sex with others, does not fit neatly with either of the first two provisos.

Tremayne does acknowledge that his portrayal of a sexually liberated society in which regular clergy were allowed to marry would ultimately be overcome by the Roman church's insistence

29 Tremayne, 'Clerical Marriage', www.sisterfidelma.com (accessed 29 November 2007).

30 *The Irish Penitentials*, L Bieler (ed), (Dublin, 1963) 77–79.

31 T Newlands, 'The Changing Position of Women in Early Christian Ireland?' *Australian Celtic Journal* 3 (1990–1) 38–55, at p 43.

32 C McAll, 'The Normal Paradigms of a Woman's Life in the Irish and Welsh Texts' 7–22 in *The Welsh Law of Women*, D Jenkins and L E Owen (eds), (Cardiff, 1980), at p 20. *Ancient Laws of Ireland*, Hancock et al (eds), (Dublin, 1865) V, 132.

on celibacy for regular clergy. This is expressed in several of the novels: for example, in *The Leper's Bell* (2004), Fidelma's brother Colgú warns her and Eadulf that their son Alchú may have been kidnapped because advocates of clerical celibacy wished to punish them for their decision to marry.

The medieval Irish legal system in the Sister Fidelma novels

Tremayne's enthusiasm for Irish law, and the enlightened position that he claims it accords to women, is well-known. He has spoken in interviews and in short articles for *The Brehon* of the advantages of the system:

> [u]nder the ancient Irish law system, women occupied a unique place. Simply, the Irish laws gave more rights and protection to women than any other western law code at that time or until recent years. Women could, and did, aspire to all offices and professions as co-equal with men. They could be political leaders, command their people in battle as warriors, be physicians, poets, artisans, local magistrates, lawyers and judges. Women were protected under the law, from sexual harassment, against discrimination and against rape. They had the right of divorce on equal terms as their husbands, with equitable separation laws and could demand part of their husband's property as a divorce settlement. They had the right of inheritance of personal property and the right of sickness benefit when ill or hospitalised. They remained the owners of any wealth that they brought into a marriage. Indeed, it was automatic that on divorcing their husband, if he were at fault, they took half of all the joint property accrued during the time of the marriage. The Irish law system was very ancient and sophisticated. While we have fragmentary texts from the early period, the first complete surviving

> texts do not survive until the 11th century.[33]

It is also important to recognise that, as with historical issues, Tremayne invokes certain scholars in the field of Irish law and implies that they are in broad agreement with him. For example he remarks that

> [t]o my mind, however, one of the handiest guides to the law texts, and the best yet published is Professor Fergus Kelly's *A Guide to Early Irish Law* [...] I do not go along entirely with all Professor Kelly's interpretations.[34]

It must be presumed that Tremayne disagrees with Kelly's statement that Irish law 'reveals a society in which a woman is generally without independent legal capacity'.[35] This would appear to contradict Tremayne's picture of the liberated and egalitarian nature of early medieval Ireland. Kelly supports his conclusion with reference to primary sources, citing the Old Irish *díre*-text:

> her father has charge over her when she is a girl, her husband when she is a wife, her sons when she is a [widowed] woman with children, her kin when she is a 'woman of the kin' (*ie* with no other guardian), the Church when she is a woman of the Church (*ie* a nun). She is not capable of sale or purchase or contract or transaction without the authorization of

33 S Cuthbertson, 'The Fascination for Sister Fidelma', www.historicalnovelsociety.org/solander/fidelma.htm (accessed 30 November 2007). This is an interview with Peter Berresford Ellis.

34 P Tremayne, 'Brehon Law: The Background to the Sister Fidelma Mysteries', www.sisterfidelma.com/FAQs.htm#world (accessed 29 November 2007).

35 F Kelly, *A Guide to Early Irish Law* (Dublin, 1988) 75.

> her superior.[36]

There are certain minor exceptions noted by Kelly, but it is difficult, if not impossible, to see how his interpretation of the status of women in early Irish law could be construed as compatible with those of Tremayne.

In discussing the status of women in Ireland, Tremayne also speaks approvingly of Myles Dillon, as 'one of the great influences in my studies',[37] and refers specifically to Dillon's chapter in *Studies in Early Irish Law*. The details of Dillon's argument are complicated, but he draws four clear conclusions, all of which appear to violate Tremayne's understanding (which makes Tremayne's expressed admiration of Dillon's essay appear inexplicable):

> (i) Once a father has sons he loses his right to inherit from their mother, his share going to them [...] (ii) A woman cannot acquire as heir more than a life interest in the land [...] The only property in land she can transmit to her heirs is property acquired for services rendered [...] or by gift. (iii) A daughter may inherit as *banchomarba*, that is to say, she can acquire a life-interest in real property, including family land [...] as well as chattels, (a) from her father if there are no male heirs, (b) from her mother if there are no sons. (iv) A woman does not pass into the *fine* [family] of her husband for purposes of inheritance, but remains in the *fine* of her father.[38]

Two further matters need clearing up before concluding this

36 *Corpus Iuris Hibernici*, D A Binchy (ed), (Dublin, 1978) 443.30–444.6, cited in Kelly, 76.

37 Tremayne, 'Brehon Law', www.sisterfidelma.com (accessed 29 November 2007).

38 M Dillon, 'The Relationship of Mother and Son, of Father and Daughter, and the Law of Inheritance with regard to Women', 129–179 in *Studies in Early Irish Law*, R Thurneysen et al (eds), (Dublin, 1936) at pp 178–9.

examination of Irish law and Tremayne's general misrepresentation of it in the Sister Fidelma novels. These are the precise nature of 'Irish law' and how historically authentic Fidelma's role as *dálaigh* (advocate) of the Brehon law is. Tremayne is frequently frustratingly vague and imprecise. He rarely cites a source so that it is possible to identify exactly where it is from. Most commonly he resorts to generalisations, and 'Irish law' is one of these. Two editions of the Irish law texts are readily available: the *Ancient Laws of Ireland* (five volumes) which was edited by Hancock et al and published in Dublin from 1865 to 1901; and the *Corpus Iuris Hibernici* (six volumes) which was edited by Daniel Binchy and published in Dublin in 1978. These large collections contain a number of law codes from different time periods and regions of Ireland. Tremayne misleadingly implies that 'Irish law' is a seamless whole. In fact, the *Senchas Már* ('great tradition', sometimes identified with the Brehon laws) was probably compiled in the northern midlands and is quite different to the *Nemed* collection from the southern kingdom of Munster, which includes *Bretha Nemed Toisech* (regarding clerics, poets and other professionals) and *Uraicecht Becc* (regarding status).[39] Other important texts that fall outside these two groups include *Cáin Adomnáin* and *Críth Gablach*.

One important difference in these legal texts is how an individual's social standing is determined: *Uraicecht Becc* depicts social rank as dependent on arts and skills, whereas *Críth Gablach* and *Senchas Már* depict social rank as dependent on family and land-holdings.[40] Overwhelmingly, the social class of women is derived from that of men. The honour and standing they receive, and the price placed on that honour and standing should they be insulted, is set by the status of their male relatives and husbands.[41]

---

39 Kelly, 242 and 246. I am grateful to my former doctoral student Bridgette Slavin for her clarification of these issues for me.

40 N Power, 'Classes of women described in the *Senchas Már*', 81–108 in Thurneysen et al (eds).

41 P O'Leary, 'The Honour of Women in Early Irish Literature', 27–44 in *Eriu* XXXVIII (1987).

Regarding Fidelma's career as an advocate, despite Tremayne's assertion that women could become 'local magistrates, lawyers and judges', there is actually very little evidence that this was so. The only reference to a woman working as any kind of legal professional in the *Ancient Laws of Ireland* is to Brigh, a female brehon, who gave a judgment on female capacity to distribute land on her death:

> the mother had died and left no sons, but daughters only. And the daughters shall obtain all the land with obligation to perform service of attack and defence, or the half of it without obligation to perform service of attack and defence, and there is power over them to compel them to restore the land after their time.[42]

She is known as *Brigh Ambui*, which is glossed as 'exile' or 'pauper'. The reference to her in the *Senchas Már* says 'Brigh Ambui was a female author of wisdom and prudence among the men of Erin. From her is named Briathra Brighi'.[43] She is the only woman named in a list of brehons four pages long. She is likely to be mythical, as she is chronologically situated in the pre-Christian period according to this passage (three generations before Patrick), although how significant that is, considering that the same text spends some time establishing that the Irish law was originally written by one Cai who learned it from Moses in Egypt, is unclear. One noticeable thing about her meagre profile is that there is no mention of her lineage or where she was from, unlike the male brehons on the list.

In another text, she is also said to have been the wife of a male judge, Sencha mac Ailella. They pass one judgment 'the distress of two days' together, although in it 'the Ulstermen submitted to *his* adjudication' (my emphasis).[44] In the tract 'Of Taking Lawful Possession', she is said to be his daughter[45] and to have cured him of

---

42 *Ancient Laws of Ireland* IV, 41.

43 *Ancient Laws of Ireland* I, 21–23.

44 *Ancient Laws of Ireland* I, 155.

45 *Ancient Laws of Ireland* IV, 17.

blotches that appeared on his face when he gave a biased judgment, by herself giving a fair, lawful one:

> That is, the judgment which Sencha passed was that the female possession-taking should be like male possession taking, and blotches did rise on his cheeks; and the truth of Brigh cured him. And the judgment she passed was that the women should have a possession taking of their own [...] that which is ten days for the man is four days for the woman.'[46]

Concerns regarding her historical status are further raised by the fact that in the *Senchas Már* Brigh and Sencha are separated by three generations, and thus cannot be either a married couple, or a daughter and father. Sencha is one of the lawgivers in the time of Patrick, but Brigh is supposed to have been three generations earlier.

There are very few women mentioned in the legal texts and they tend to be identified as daughters or wives, rather than claimants in their own right. It is thus very unlikely, indeed almost impossible, that Fidelma could have practiced law as Tremayne claims in the novels. Bitel concludes that:

> [i]n almost all public legal processes, a woman needed a man to act for her [...] The assumption of the lawyers who made special provisions for women and other disenfranchised, was that free males, and particularly the heads of families [...] acted for their dependents in legal disputes.[47]

With reference to the *Cain Lánamna*, the law on marriage to which Tremayne alludes, without examining it in detail, scholarly opinion appears to indicate that most of the 'types of marriage' listed are

46 *Ancient Laws of Ireland* IV, 15.

47 Bitel, *Isle of the Saints*, 10.

forms of concubinage which function to benefit men rather than women.[48]

Further, when discussing Fidelma's unrestricted travel, Tremayne has stated unequivocally that '[i]n leaving Kildare, Fidelma was only exercising the right shared by everyone, not simply because she was the sister of the King of Muman.'[49] This is not the case; one of the *Heptads* (51) explicitly says that 'neither chieftain nor church nor *aire feibe* has any right, nor the protection of sanctuary to shield them [...] to shield a monk who elopes from his church.'[50] This may be read to suggest that certain types of travel, approved by monastic superiors, may be permitted. Nevertheless, it appears that Tremayne has exaggerated the freedom of movement that would have been available to early medieval Irish nuns.

The interaction of Christianity and paganism in the Sister Fidelma novels

Tremayne is concerned to portray seventh-century Ireland as a tolerant and open society, and readers have responded to this, as the modern liberal West assumes that freedom of religious association and personal choice are paramount values. In *The Spider's Web* (1997) Fidelma and Eadulf investigate the murder of the chieftain Eber of Araglin and his sister Teafa. Crón, the heiress to Eber's lands, believes the killer is Móen, a young man of 21 who is deaf, dumb and blind and was Teafa's adopted son. Fidelma is unconvinced and seeks to establish Móen's innocence. She and Eadulf meet the

48 N Patterson, *Cattle-Lords and Clanmen: The Social Structure of Early Ireland* (London, 1994) 288–9. This popular perception that 'the Celts' were sexually liberal and advocated equality of the sexes is found in many non-academic publications. See P Cherici, *Celtic Sexuality: Power, Paradigms and Passion* (London, 1995) and P Berresford-Ellis, *Celtic Women: Women in Celtic Society and Literature* (London, 1995). These views are comprehensively refuted by Ann Trindade in her scathing review of Cherici, *Australian Celtic Journal* 5 (1996–1997) 62–65.

49 Tremayne, 'Answer to French Fan', www.sisterfidelma.com (accessed 30 November 2007).

50 *Ancient Laws of Ireland* V, 291.

old hermit Gadra, who has remained faithful to the pagan religion. When asked by Eadulf why he did not convert, Gadra replies:

> I am an old man, brother Saxon. In me, the ancient gods and goddesses of our people take a long time a dying. Yet I do not grudge you your new ways, your new thoughts and your new hopes. It is the nature of things that the old should die and the new should live. It is also the danger of this world as well as its blessing. That is the nature of the children of Danu, the Mother Goddess. Life dies and is reborn. The old gods die, and the new are born. The time will come when they will also die and new gods will arise.[51]

On returning to Araglin, Gadra communicates with Móen by spelling ogham letters into his hands, and Fidelma and Eadulf solve the mystery of Eber's murder, of which Móen is innocent.

There is no sense in this novel that seventh-century Irish Christians might be hostile to adherents of the pagan religion of Ireland. At the novel's conclusion, Gadra has accepted the responsibility of caring for Móen and decides that the best place for them is the monastery of Lios Mhór. He needs to teach people to communicate with Móen, as he is aged and will die soon. He asks Fidelma, 'Would not an old pagan like myself be welcomed there?' and she responds, 'There is a welcome for everyone in the house of the Christ'.[52] However, scholarship suggests that relations between pagans and Christians were not so cordial. For example, the early synod known as the First Synod of Saint Patrick:

> reveals a semi-christianised Ireland in which the cleric and his flock are in regular contact with pagans and paganism. It is thus necessary for it to be stated that a Christian must not make an oath before a

51 Tremayne, *The Spider's Web*, 167–168.

52 *Ibid*, 334.

> druid in the pagan manner. Similarly, a cleric must not act as an enforcing surety for a pagan or accept alms from a pagan for his church.[53]

The seventh-century *vitae* of Saint Patrick by Muirchu and Tírechán feature the saint in confrontation with druids, the representatives of paganism. Patrick is triumphant, through the power of the Christian god.[54]

Certain scholarly authorities have, in the past decade, sought to establish that at least some of the 'specialness' accorded to the 'Celtic' or 'Irish' church is based upon fact and not merely wishful thinking or new age inclinations. Michael W Herren and Shirley Ann Brown have argued persuasively that from the fifth to the tenth centuries the Irish church's theological orientation was distinctive, combining a strong semi-Pelagianist strand and unique imagings of Christ.[55] Tremayne is aware of the importance of Pelagianism (at one point Eadulf cautions Fidelma 'lest you be accused of following the Pelagian heresy'[56]), but otherwise this fine book appears to have escaped him. Similarly, John Carey's sustained investigation of the Irish church's important contribution to the Christian understanding of polytheism, and the valuation of the natural world, are apparently unknown to Tremayne.[57]

Conclusion

In his efforts to authenticate the portrayal of early medieval Ireland found in the Sister Fidelma novels, Peter Tremayne employs several

53 Kelly, *A Guide to Early Irish Law*, 40. Kelly is citing *The Irish Penitentials*, L Bieler (ed), (Dublin, 1963) 54–56.

54 A Hopkin, *The Living Legend of St Patrick* (New York, 1989) 33–52.

55 M W Herren and S A Brown, *Christ in Celtic Christianity* (Woodbridge, 2002).

56 Tremayne, *Shroud for the Archbishop*, 29.

57 J Carey, *A Single Ray of the Sun: Religious Speculation in Early Ireland* (Andover and Aberystwyth, 1999) and Carey, *King of Mysteries: Early Irish Religious Writings* (Dublin, 2000).

strategies. He cites, though rarely exactly, certain scholars who are reputable in the fields of medieval history, Irish law and other relevant academic disciplines, presenting their views as in agreement with his. He also presents himself as a qualified scholarly authority, someone whose views should be trusted:

> I did my degrees in Celtic Studies. I am a Fellow of the Royal Historical Society and a Fellow of the Royal Society of Antiquaries of Ireland and have held various senior positions on Celtic educational bodies. I have lectured at universities in Ireland, the UK, Spain, France, Canada and the US as a 'guest lecturer' in Celtic Studies.[58]

This may be the case, but he is not a professional academic. His doctorate is honorary, and does not represent a sustained piece of research that has been examined by peers. Further, even enthusiasts on the web have noted his poor referencing and unscholarly techniques. Ralph Askin, posting to 'Amused In Review', observes that 'pilgrimages to the Shrine of St James in Santiago de Compostela did not begin until many years well after he has Sister Fidelma *en route*'[59] and Michael Martinez, posting at Andre Norton Forum, observes that '[s]ince Ellis is not an academic historian I was unsuccessful in finding any evaluation of his interpretation

58 T Racz, 'interview with P Berresford Ellis, www.sisterfidelma.com/interview.html (accessed 30 November 2007).

59 R Askin, 'Amused In Review', www.webamused.com/amusedinreview/archives/0012300.html (accessed 30 November 2007). See P Tremayne, *Act of Mercy* (London, 1999). M Dunn and L K Davidson, 'Bibliography of the Pilgrimage: The State of the Art' in M Dunn and L K Davidson (eds), *The Pilgrimage to Compostela in the Middle Ages* (London and New York, 1996) xxiv, state that although seventh-century pilgrims have been hypothesised by some, the first attested pilgrims are ninth-century and the first named pilgrim, Bishop Gotescalc of Le Puy, travelled to Compostela in 950.

by the academic community'.[60] Nettle, after reading *The Druids*, perceptively charges the author with three major faults. These are failure to cite sources, biased interpretations, and pseudo-scholarly tactics.

It has already been demonstrated that Tremayne/Berresford Ellis fails to cite sources precisely and frequently distorts sources to which he does allude. Nettle's further criticisms are also important. With regard to biased interpretations he notes:

> I found his contortions to try to explain away the Lindow Man to be kind of funny — he is so completely invested in the idea that the ancient Celts did not do human sacrifice that he cannot face the fact that human sacrifice is a [...] legitimate interpretation in that case. This particular hobby-horse of his is problematic, because it reveals his particular biases on the subject, and the reader is left to wonder about what all of the less obvious biases might be.[61]

Nettle's charge that Tremayne/Berresford Ellis engages in duplicitous positioning of himself *vis à vis* scholars and those they despise is very significant.

Celtic Studies is a field in which important but experimental scholarly work occasionally struggles to find recognition. Sub-fields such as early medieval Irish history, Irish law, pre-Christian Celtic religion and mythology and Irish church history have been divided by scholarly controversies and hard-line methodological factionalism. Tremayne has disingenuously engaged in criticism of Robert Graves, author of *The White Goddess* (1948, revised edition 1966), which is universally rejected by all Irish and Welsh

60 www.sf-fandom.com/xoa/andre_norton/archive_18/3068.htm (accessed 26 November 2007).

61 Nettle, 'All the charm of a scholarly work, with the scholarship of a popular history', nettle.wordpress.com/2007/03/06/all-the-charm-of-a-scholarship-if-a-popular-history/ (accessed 26 November 2007).

Scotland.[50]

The eventual Act had three objectives: to create right of responsible access to land; to allow rural communities to buy land when it is put on the market; and to permit crofting communities to buy land at any time.

It is not the intention of this paper to examine the potential for success or failure inherent in the 2003 Act but to note the way in which the land question has been part of Scottish political culture since the Victorian period at least, and the way in which recent debates on the land question have been conducted with reference to the historical background of the issue.[51] This point can be dealt with by reference to a debate in the Scottish Parliament in March 2002. To quote Ross Finnie again, 'whatever view is taken of the bill, the historic importance of today's debate cannot be overstated'.[52] There was a general political consensus in the Parliament about the Bill. The SNP, although wishing that the Bill had gone further in its proposals, were prepared to support the Labour/Liberal Democrat coalition. Roseanna Cunningham led for the Nationalists and began her speech with a Gaelic slogan of the Highland Land Law Reform Association's campaigns from the 1880s.[53] This left the Conservatives as isolated opponents of the Bill. They were even taunted by one Liberal Democrat MSP for having 'implemented the Irish Land Act of 1903 and empowered tenants to buy their land. Does he think that government was wrong?'[54] Surprisingly, or perhaps not, the Conservatives proved unable to provide the obvious riposte that land purchase of this kind was entirely consistent with their ideology, a classic example of what Noel Skelton defined as a property-owning democracy. Their opposition was expressed in lurid terms by Bill Aitken, who on the morning of the debate had

50 *ORSP*, 20 Mar 2002, col 10381.

51 Cameron, '"Unfinished business"', 83–114.

52 *ORSP*, 20 Mar 2002, col 10380.

53 *ORSP*, 20 Mar 2002, cols 10388–93.

54 *ORSP*, 20 Mar 2002, col 10394.

stress the novelty of the Executive's proposals, but it is striking that the legislation of the period from 1897 to 1919, which had such an important effect on the Highland landscape, creating hundreds of new holdings, enlarging hundreds of others, effectively nationalising land in some areas and effectively reversing the clearances, should not figure in the political memory bank.[48]

In 2003 the *Land Reform (Scotland) Act* was passed by the Scottish parliament, allegedly signifying the capability of the Scottish parliament to deal with outstanding grievances affecting Scotland upon which the Westminster parliament, regardless of which party was in Government, had neither the time nor, possibly, the inclination to legislate. This point was specifically referred to in the debates on the Land Reform Bill by Ross Finnie, the Liberal Democrat Minister for Environment and Rural Development:

> In the past 60 years, land reform did not get on to the Westminster Parliamentary agenda, although it has consistently been on the agenda of the people of Scotland. There is no doubt that devolution and the creation of the Scottish Parliament have brought forward land reform. The vast majority of those who voted in the Scottish parliamentary elections in 1999 did so for parties whose manifestos included a commitment to legislate on land reform.[49]

This legislation was justified by Finnie in the following terms:

> To remove land-based barriers to development. The means of achieving that are increased diversity and increased community involvement in the way in which land is owned and used. Such an approach reflects the Executive's broader priorities for economic development and social justice in rural

48 Hunter, *Crofting community*, 206.

49 *ORSP*, 20 Mar 2002, col 10380.

published a newspaper article condemning what he feared would be 'new Highland clearances' and 'a landgrab of which Robert Mugabe would be proud'. He rounded off his speech with the following peroration:

> What is being proposed is, frankly economic madness. It is ironic that, at a time when every country — with the exceptions of Cuba and North Korea — has spurned Marxism, we are attempting a bill of which Kim Jong-il or Fidel Castro would be proud [...] the bill is not so much about land reform as about a crusade by those who are fighting 200-year-old battles [...] Rather than seeking to avenge the Highland clearances, they are creating the clearances of the 21st century.[55]

For Aitken, the historical dimension was to be used as a stick with which to beat the Executive for their atavism. Many of the same historical resonances were evident in a debate at an earlier stage of the process, when the general principles of land reform were being discussed; on that occasion a number of the Labour MSPs from the Highlands made reference to the crofters' protests of the 1880s, the Highland Land League and the land raids which followed the Great War.[56] There is a certain amount of evidence, then, that the political debates on the land question are conducted with a degree of historical awareness on the part of MSPs, or at least convenient references to supposed historical positions. For the opponents of land reform, this historical perspective was seen as a cloak to mask the irrelevance of land reform to modern Scotland.

Conclusion

The shifting historical dimension has been important to considerations of the Highland land question since the 1880s,

---

55 *ORSP*, 20 Mar 2002, col 10398.

56 *ORSP*, 24 Nov 1999, cols 863, 867, 871.

although recent developments have had a wider Scottish dimension. The kind of rhetoric with which Highland land reform has been presented has masked the fact that it ought to be understood, not only in a 'Celtic' context, but also in a wider British framework, whether that was the classical Liberalism of William Gladstone, the centralist economic planning of William Ross or the patriotic unionism of Donald Dewar. It will be interesting to see whether the actions of the Scottish Executive (Government) are sufficient to salve the national conscience and to obviate the engrained perception of neglect. Whether the Highlander ought to have had such a prominent position on the national conscience, to the exclusion of other victims of the multiple traumas of Scotland's nineteenth-century social changes, is another question for another paper.

specialists as a fantastic work, uninformed by real scholarship.[62] In fact, Graves was a fine novelist (arguably better than Tremayne) and in terms of purportedly 'scholarly' output, the two men are hardly distinguishable. Nettle notes that Berresford Ellis:

> has the usual concluding chapter saying the usual ridiculous things about modern druidry. I came to the conclusion long ago that authors use this sort of thing as a shield. Certain topics are highly suspect in the academic world: Druids, witches, goddesses, drugs, the occult, and magic can ruin a scholar's reputation. By clearly indicating that they think that the vast majority of what is written on these subjects is trash, and by making fun of the people who take these things seriously, the scholar says to his peers, 'See, I'm not one of *those* people. *Those* people are nuts. I'm serious. I'm not like them, I'm like *you*.'[63]

It is unfortunate that academics do not generally believe that it is a valuable exercise to write critical appraisals of popular writers and pseudo-scholars.[64] LJ Swain of Western Michigan University has reviewed *Absolution by Murder, Shroud for the Archbishop* and *Suffer Little Children* (1995) for the online journal *The Heroic Age*, which specialises in early medieval history. He takes issue with Tremayne's uncritical use of sources, awards the books a 'B+' and advises 'that one should take the historical background Tremayne paints with

---

62 P Berresford Ellis, 'The Fabrication of "Celtic" Astrology', *The Astrological Journal* 39:4 (1997) cura.free.fr/xv/13ellis2.html (accessed 30 November 2007).

63 Nettle, 'All the charm' (accessed 26 November 2007).

64 There are a few exceptions to this rule. Jacqueline Simpson has reviewed modern Pagan books (though usually unfavourably) and her article, 'Margaret Murray: Who Believed Her and Why?', *Folklore* 105 (1994) 89–96 is a notable contribution to the investigation of modern Pagan pseudo-scholarship, offering a sceptical interpretation.

a few grains of salt'.[65] That seems to be the limit of academic or quasi-academic assessment of Tremayne's novels. One exception to this critical silence concerns the publication of his non-fiction work, *Erin's Blood Royal: The Gaelic Noble Dynasties of Ireland* in 1999. Tremayne/Berresford Ellis retracted his support for his preferred chief, Terence MacCarthy, after discovering that his pedigree was faked. This has attracted some critical comment.[66]

Tremayne states on the website of the International Sister Fidelma Society that those who insist that marriage between professed religious did not happen 'can only put forward their argument by distorting or ignoring the evidence'.[67] This paper has sought to demonstrate that actually it is Tremayne who consistently distorts evidence and ignores scholarly standards. E H Carr, author of *What is History?* (1962), advised students to:

> [s]tudy the historian before you begin to study the facts [...] you cannot fully understand or appreciate the work of the historian until you have first grasped the standpoint from which he himself approached it.[68]

Nettle did precisely that, and found Tremayne's objectivity and dedication to the historical method wanting. The Sister Fidelma novels are just that, novels, and perhaps readers should expect a certain amount of latitude in the use of historical material in fiction.

---

65 L J Swain, 'Review of Peter Tremayne', *The Heroic Age* 2 (Fall/Winter 1999), www.heroicage.org/issues/2/ha2toc.htm (accessed 30 November 2007).

66 S Murphy, 'Review of Peter Berresford Ellis, Erin's Blood Royal' at homepage.eircom.net/~seanjmurphy/chiefs/bloodroyal.htm (accessed 30 November 2007). Sean Murphy works at the Centre for Irish Genealogical and Historical Studies.

67 Tremayne, 'Clerical Marriages', www.sisterfidelma.com (accessed 29 November 2007).

68 Quoted in M A Weinstein, 'The Creative Imagination in Fiction and History', *Genre* IX (1976) 276.

However, Tremayne himself has staked the claim, by including lengthy historical notes in each book and insisting (through the International Sister Fidelma Society) that his portrayal of early medieval Ireland is the genuine article.

Receiving mail from the Society's Director, David Robert Wooten, stating that '[we] again stress that we are not arguing with your personal interpretation of the historical accuracy, or otherwise, of the Sister Fidelma books' but that '[w]e really do feel that this Society has to address these matters of inaccuracy in your presentation' inspired me to begin the process of scholarly critical appraisal of Berresford Ellis/Tremayne. This paper is hopefully the beginning of a very lengthy exercise.[69]

69 At the Australian and New Zealand Association for Medieval and Early Modern Studies (ANZAMEMS) conference at the University of Tasmania, 2–5 December 2008, I was delighted to meet Anne Louise McKendry, who is also engaged in the scholarly appraisal of the Sister Fidelma novels. I acknowledge gratefully her generosity in giving me a copy of her paper 'Celts, Saxons and Detectives: The Political Medievalism of Peter Tremayne', which she had presented at a conference at University of California, Riverside earlier in 2008.

Morgan le Fay: Celtic origins and literary images

Dominique Beth Wilson ⊕

Morgen, Morgana, Morgaine of the Fairies, the legendary Morgan le Fay is a character of innumerable traits and characteristics. She is a literary character so famous that the Fata Morgana, a mirage seen in the Straits of Messina, is named after her.[1] Since the earliest accounts of King Arthur and his knights, she has appeared in many guises: as healer, sister, lover and enchantress, to name but a few. However, it would appear that her origins go back further still, into the mythological cycles of Irish and Welsh tradition. It is from these sources that her core traits of healer, shape shifter and enchantress can be traced, along with elements of her family tree. The aim of this paper is to explore the progression and transformation of Morgan le Fay from Celtic goddess, healer, malicious sorceress and evil temptress, to her position in modern fantasy literature as a neo-pagan goddess figure and feminist role model. This paper employs Marion Zimmer Bradley's influential feminist fantasy novel, *The Mists of Avalon*, as a case study. Morgan's position in Arthurian legend as a possible sovereignty goddess, with Arthur as the land's sacred king, will also be examined.

The high medieval tales of Arthur, his deeds and knight companions can be traced back to the oral tradition found within the later Welsh mythological texts. While there is no concrete evidence that he ever existed, the figure of Arthur, like that of his sister/lover Morgan, has evolved over time. He first appears within the Welsh mythological/pseudo-historical records (such as the

---

⊕ The University of Sydney.

1 R S Loomis, 'Morgain le Fay and the Celtic Goddess,' *Speculum* 20/2, (1945) 183.

Triads and the *Historia Brittonum* which was formerly attributed to Nennius), but it was Geoffrey of Monmouth's twelfth-century epic *Historia Regum Britanniae,* that launched him in both the history books and the imagination of the British people. The earlier texts concerning Arthur contain no hint of Morgan. Geoffrey's *Historia Regum Britannie* mentions her only briefly as Arthur's sister (called Anna); however, his *Vita Merlini* (Life of Merlin) lays the foundation for the later amplification of her role.[2]

The first reference to Morgan (Morgen) by name appears in Geoffrey of Monmouth's *Vita Merlini* (c1150). She is introduced thus:

> She who is first of them is more skilled in the healing art, and excels her sisters in the beauty of her person. Morgen is her name[3]

From her initial entrance onto the literary stage, Morgan is seen as a healer, who, as the *Vita* explains, is learned in the 'useful properties all herbs contain'.[4] Geoffrey also portrays her as one trained in the arts of shape-shifting and mathematics, the latter of which she has also taught her sisters.[5] Thus, from the twelfth century, Morgan's position as a female with talents that fall outside the usual realm of womanly pursuits is cemented. However, Morgan is not named as Arthur's sister, arguably her most significant identity, until Chrétien de Troyes' Arthurian romances in the second half of the twelfth century.[6] Geoffrey introduces the figure of Arthur's sister (Morgan)

2 Geoffrey of Monmouth, *Life of Merlin – Vita Merlin,* Basil Clark (ed and trans), (Cardiff, 1973).

3 *Ibid,* 85.

4 *Ibid,* 85.

5 *Ibid,* 85. The confusion of Morgan with Arthur's 'other sister' Morgause of Orkney, sometimes asserted as the mother of his incestuously-conceived son Mordred, is a dilemma which cannot be explored within the confines of this paper.

6 Chretien de Troyes, 'Yvain', in *Arthurian Romances,* D D R Owen (trans),

in his *Historia Regum Britanniae*: he names Arthur's sister as Anna.[7]

The family tree of the Arthurian legend is a complex phenomenon, which changes with each retelling of the tale,[8] so an examination of Welsh mythology is of use here. Morgan has long been associated with the Welsh goddess Modron, meaning 'mother', who is known as the 'nurturer of the gods'.[9] Modron is best known as the mother of Mabon (the divine youth), a sun god, who is the product of a union between Modron and Urien, and who is named as one of Arthur's warriors in *The Dream of Rhonabwy*.[10] The argument for Morgan being a later incarnation of Modron is supported by this position, as both mother of Mabon and wife of Urien, within the family tree outlined in the Welsh *Triads of the Isle of Britain*. Here Modron is named as the daughter of Afallach (or Avallach, lord of the otherworld) and also as the mother of one the 'Three Fair Womb-burdens' of the Isle of Britain: Owain.[11] The interesting factor here is that, in later variations of the Arthurian cycle, Morgan is named as the mother of Owain, through some connection (usually marriage) to Urien, now presented as the king of north Wales. The connection of Modron with Urien, Owain and Annwfn within the Welsh sources and the appearance of these

(London, 1988) 321.

7 '... so are born noble Arthur and his sister Anna.' *The Historia Regum Britannie of Geoffrey of Monmouth: Cesta Regum Britannie*, N Wright (trans and ed), (Cambridge, 1991) 173.

8 For examples of the genealogy of King Arthur in various cycles of the tradition, see J Joe, 'House of King Arthur', http://www.timelessmyths.com/arthurian/housearthur.html, (26 November 2007).

9 A Ross, *Pagan Celtic Britain* (Chicago, 1967: repr 1996) 290.

10 'Arthur arose and went to take counsel ... and his counsellors were brought to him there: ... and Mabon son of Modron.' 'The Dream of Rhonabwy', in *The Mabinogion*, G Jones and T Jones (trans), (London, 2000) 125.

11 'The second, Owain and Morfudd daughter of Urien and Anarun archbishop of Llydaw, by Modron daughter of Afallach their mother.' *Trioedd Ynys Prydein: The Welsh Triads*, R Bromwich (trans and ed), (Cardiff, 1961) Triad 70, 185.

characters within the later Arthurian cycle show that Morgan is a probable reformation of Modron. It also important to note here that Mabon, who is cited as Modron's son in early Welsh sources, is the earlier incarnation for Mordred, Morgan's ill-fated son from an affair with her brother Arthur.

In Bradley's *The Mists of Avalon*, the concept of Mordred as the personification of the 'divine youth' is explored. Bradley makes use of the imagery of the stag king, who triumphs over the fading king, ruling for a time before he in turn is overthrown by the next young stag destined to become king. It is a continuous cycle, in which the king is eternally young, fertile and in his prime. Bradley sets Arthur up as the stag king early in her novel, with Morgan playing the virgin huntress, the prize and consort of the newly triumphant king.[12] It is through this ritualistic union, on the eve of Arthur's triumph and acceptance by Avalon as the chosen king, that Mordred is conceived. Ultimately, he is to become the next stag king, who will replace his father, keeping the kingship forever young: hence Mabon, 'divine youth' Morgan's dilemma, as Modron the mother, is being torn between her lover/brother and her son. The question, 'what of the Stag King, when the young stag is grown?',[13] is a continuous theme throughout *The Mists of Avalon*.

This representation of the king as the divine youth, if taken to symbolise vitality and fertility, is common within the Arthurian tradition, as well as reflecting earlier Celtic ideas of the tribal king who symbolises the unity and potency of the entire community. As the symbol of life, he must be perfect, untainted. Thus, in primitive societies, 'he is always ritually killed if he shows signs of illness or old age, so that the 'spirit' of the tribe may function better in the body of his successor'.[14] The figure of the fisher king or wounded grail

12 See chapters 14 and 15 of M Zimmer Bradley, *The Mists of Avalon* (London, 1983: repr 1993) 90–209.

13 Bradley, *Mists of Avalon*, 839.

14 E Jung and M von Franz, *The Grail Legend* (Princeton, 1998) 191–92. For a concrete example, see 'The Second Battle of Moytura' in T P Cross and C H Slover (eds), *Ancient Irish Tales* (New York, 1936: repr 1969) 28–48. In this tale Nuada loses the kingship of the Tuatha Dé Danann

king commonly embraces this notion; however, it can be argued that the fall of Camelot and the end of Arthur's golden reign are due to imperfections on Arthur's part, be it his incestuous relationship with Morgan, his refusal to acknowledge the relationship between Lancelot and Guinevere, or, in some versions, a wounding to his manhood, and ultimately his refusal to step down as king. A further consistency between the Welsh representations of Modron and Mabon mirrored as Morgan and Mordred is the idea of Mabon and Mordred as lost sons. In the Welsh traditions, Mabon is said to have been 'taken away when three nights old from his mother'.[15] For Bradley, it is arguably Morgan's abandonment of Mordred that creates his resentment and desire to destroy. Of course, Arthur, too, is a lost son, but he is 'saved' by his loving foster-father Ector and his mentor Merlin.

The figure of the war goddess, the Morrígan ('great queen') is another divine being believed to have influenced Morgan's characteristics within the Arthurian corpus. Apart from the obvious similarities between their names, the Morrígan, like Geoffrey's Morgan, is a shape-shifter who has a complex relationship with the hero Cú Chulainn, who Paton argues is an early Arthur prototype.[16] Miranda Green explains that the most important of the Irish battle-goddesses are 'the Morrígan, Badbh, Macha and Nemhain. They were simultaneously one goddess and three: the entity of the Morrígan may be triple, or Badbh, Nemhain and Morrígan may be combined to become the triadic Morrígna'.[17] Of the Morrígan herself, Green says:

> She was a goddess of victory for whichever army she chose to support, and she was fickle and capricious in her allegiences. She was a prophet of

---

when he loses his arm and is no longer whole.

15 'Culhwch and Olwen' in *The Mabinogion*, Jones and Jones (trans) 98–99.

16 See L Paton, *Studies in the Fairy Mythology of Arthurian Romance* (New York, 1903: repr 1970) 148–150.

17 M Green, *Celtic Goddesses* (London, 1995) 43.

> either death or victory; an instigator of war; she interfered with combat; changed her shape; and was closely associated with destruction, fertility and sovereignty.[18]

If the primary function of the Morrígan is to incite deeds of prowess and organise battles,[19] then it can be argued that Morgan's animosity toward her brother Arthur, even her conception of Mordred, stems from this lineage, and that her actions are an attempt to stay true to her origins as a battle goddess. This is similar to the relationship between the Morrígan and Cú Chulainn, in which she acts as both his patroness and his would-be paramour. As his patroness, she leads him to victory in numerous battles. As his paramour, her role is more intimate: she twice offers him her love, access to her physical form, only to be rejected. Her female pride hurt, her anger is roused and she withdraws her divine protection and support from his next battle, seeking to hinder him instead.

> 'Then' says she, 'if you will not have my love and help, you shall have my hatred and enmity. When you are fighting with a warrior as good as yourself, I will come against you in various shapes and hinder you, so that he shall have the advantage'.[20]

The twofold relationship as protector and would-be lover is echoed in Bradley's *The Mists of Avalon*. Morgan is initially a mother figure for Arthur, as Queen Igraine is too consumed with her love for Uther Pendragon to spend time with her children.

> I thought, *Igraine has forgotten both of us, abandoned him as she abandoned me. Now I must be his mother, I suppose* ... 'Mother's gone, she's with the King,'

18 Green, *Celtic Goddesses*, 43.

19 Paton, *Fairy Mythology*, 11.

20 C Squire, *Celtic Myth and Legend* (New York, 1905: repr 2005) 169.

> I said, 'but I'll take care of you brother.' And with his chubby hand in mine I knew what Igraine had meant: I was too big a girl to cry or whimper for my mother, because I had a little one to look after now.
>
> I think I was all of seven years old.[21]

Later, after Arthur's native kingship ritual, and his consummation of marriage with the land, with the virgin huntress, Morgan unknowingly becomes his first love, his first encounter with the female body and the female divine, thus adding an erotic element to their relationship, moving from the mother/protector role into that of lover/unrequited love. The sexual encounter between the brother and sister, with the obvious result of the conception of Mordred, adds a complexity to their relationship, as Arthur is unable to let go of his love for Morgan, As his first love, she always holds a place in his heart and mind.

> She sensed Arthur's hand was still in hers, and that troubled her: that bond would have to be broken [...] Gwenhwyfar would become the Goddess to Arthur and he would not look at Morrígan in that way that troubled her so.[22] [...]
>
> 'What is the Goddess to me?' Arthur tightened his fist on the hilt of Excalibur. 'I saw her always in your face, but you turned away from me, and when the Goddess rejected me, I sought another God [...]'[23]

As Bradley's version of the story unfolds, Arthur turns his back on the old ways, the native tribes, ruling instead under Christian morals. Morgan, as a priestess of Avalon, avatar of the goddess, feels impelled to speak out against Arthur, in an endeavor to remind him of his pledge to Avalon, and to bring him back to the

---

21 Bradley, *Mists of Avalon*, 126–7.

22 *Ibid*, 329.

23 *Ibid*, 998.

old customs of the land. Upon failing, like the Morrígan in her fit of anger, she attempts to remove his sacred backing, and take back Excalibur, the gift of Avalon, in a plan that will see him possibly killed.[24] This ties up with constant Irish references in which women (normally dressed as hags) appear and oppose the hero of myth and legend.[25] Yet when all is said and done, it is Morgan, as the maiden who summoned the king stag, as the mother who gives birth to his son, and as the crone, the queen of Northwales and the native tribes, who conveys him through the mists to Avalon, to the arms of the goddess, when he is mortally wounded.[26] Like the Morrígan and Cú Chulainn, the relationship between Morgan and Arthur traverses several dimensions — sister, lover, protector, priestess and adversary — but remains ultimately eternal.

The Morrígan is normally presented as a triple goddess, with the sisters Badb, Macha and Nemhain being most commonly named as the constituent parts.[27] With this in mind, the presence of three queens or sisters in the barge that takes Arthur away to Avalon can be seen as an echo of Morgan's previous incarnation as the Morrígan. And it is not only Bradley's *The Mists of Avalon* that describes three women on the barge; the motif occurs in various retellings of the Arthurian cycle, including Malory, who describes how:

> There [re]sceyved hym three ladyes with grete mourning. And so they sette he[m d]owne, and in one of their lapis kyng Arthure layde ys hede. And then the quene seyde,
>
> 'A, my dere brother! Why [ha]ve ye taryed so longe frome me? Alas, thys wounde on youre hede hath caught overmuch coulde!' [28]

24 *Ibid*, 838–864.

25 Ross, *Pagan Celtic Britain*, 291.

26 Bradley, *Mists of Avalon* (1983), 998–99.

27 Green, *Celtic Goddesses*, 41.

28 Malory, *Works* (Oxford, 1971) 716.

In Geoffrey of Monmouth, Morgan is said to be the first of nine sisters who dwell on the island of apples, or 'The Fortunate Isle'.[29] This use of the numbers nine and three, when placing Morgan in the wider Celtic tradition, is important, as three, and any multiples of it, were considered sacred in pre-Christian Celtic religions.[30] Throughout Celtic mythology, there are numerous examples of gods and goddesses who appear in triplicates. Obviously, the Morrígan is one of them, but others include the Irish goddess Brigid, who has two sisters of the same name, and the moon-related symbolism corresponding to the three aspects of the goddess — maiden, mother, crone — which has been embraced by contemporary paganism. As Young explains, 'In the company of two other queens [Morgan] thus form[s] a divine trinity, similar to that of Macha, Matrona and Morrigan, and echoing the trio formed with her two sisters'.[31]

The maiden-mother-crone imagery features throughout Bradley's entire Avalon series, which focuses on a 'reconstructed' following of Celtic priestesses, who worship alongside the druids in the British Isles.[32] In *The Mists of Avalon*, it is Viviane, the lady of the lake, who first introduces this triplicate imagery, when she speaks to Igraine about her forthcoming role as mother to Arthur:

> 'She is not yet a maiden, and nor I yet a wise-woman ... but we are the Three Igraine. Together we make up the Goddess, and she is present here among us.'[33]

---

29 Geoffrey of Monmouth, *Merlin*, 85.

30 D Carver, *Goddess Dethroned: The Evolution of Morgan le Fay* (Geroria, 2006) 28. There are also the nine muses of Greek mythology, of which Calliope ('lovely voice') had a son, Orpheus, with underworld connections, similar to those of Modron's father Afallach. See J March, *Cassell's Dictionary of Classical Mythology* (London, 1998) 515.

31 S Young, 'King Arthur and Morgan le Fay', 181–194 in E Bernard and B Moon (eds), *Goddesses Who Rule* (Oxford, 2000) 185.

32 The series consists of *The Mists of Avalon* (1982), *The Forest House* (1993), *Lady of Avalon* (1997), and with Diana L Paxton, published posthumously, *Priestess of Avalon* (2000) and *Ancestors of Avalon* (2004).

33 Bradley, *Mists of Avalon*, 26.

The progression of Morgan from Celtic goddess to mortal priestess, healer and sister of Arthur seems definitive, though it is fascinating that none of the sources ever competently explains how Morgan's human status, as Arthur's half-sister through Igraine, cohabits with the presentation of Morgan as 'Morgan le Fay', with her supernatural fairy nature.[34] The image of the otherworldly women appears throughout Celtic mythology. They are able to cross the boundaries between the worlds, and in turn enable chosen mortals to return to the otherworld with them.[35] Roger Loomis suggests that Morgan was originally the lady of the lake,[36] which offers a possible explanation for her title 'Morgan le Fay'. Water is often seen as a porthole to the otherworld, be it in the form of lake, pool or river, or even the great ocean to the west.[37] Thus, the lady of the lake, and her damsels, are most definitely fay creatures, who act as guardians to the otherworldly realms, taking on the role originally designated for goddesses, to bestow 'both the life giving and destructive powers of water'.[38] Even more interesting is Loomis' insight into a

> belief which dominated the imagination of their inhabitants [people of the islands of Moléne and

34 Young, 'King Arthur and Morgan le Fay', 181.

35 One such example occurs in *The Voyage of Bran*, where Bran, after being entranced by the song of a *sídhe* woman, journeys aboard a ship in search of her to the Island of Women, where they live for a year. On their return to Ireland they discover, to their dismay, that they can never set foot on the fair Isle again, as several hundred years have passed. They were offered conditional immortality by the Fay women. M Heaney, *Over Nine Waves: A book of Irish Legends* (London, 1994) 56–62.

36 R Loomis, *Celtic Myth and Arthurian Romance* (New York, 1927: repr 1967) 193.

37 J Wooding (ed), *The Otherworld Voyage in Early Irish Literature: An Anthology of Criticism* (Dublin, 2000), *passim*.

38 K Selling, 'The Locus of the Sacred in the Celtic Otherworld', *Spirit of Place: Source of the Sacred? Proceedings of the Religion, Literature and the Arts Conference* Vol 5 (Sydney, 1999) 298.

> Ouessant], a belief in sea fairies known as Morgans [...] The Morgan is a fairy eternally young, a virgin seductress whose passion, never satisfied, drives her to despair [...] Accompanied by other fairies, of whom she is in some respects the queen[39]

This fragment of folklore shows a correlation between Morgan and water, which offers evidence for her place as an otherworldly or fay figure. This, combined with the idea that the characters of Morgan and Arthur have been influenced by tales concerning the Morrígan and Cú Chulainn, suggests that Morgan was mortalised to fit within the parameters of the Arthurian tradition. She thus becomes another example of what occurs elsewhere, when an immortal woman, fae or goddess, falls in love with a human: the female may choose mortality 'in order to be with the hero that they choose' and love.[40]

From the thirteenth century, the presentation of Morgan changes. No longer is she shown as a 'possible avatar of a Celtic goddess',[41] or the famed healer spoken of in Geoffrey's *Vita Merlini*. Instead, she is heaped with possibly every negative trait associated with women. She becomes a vicious and vindictive sorceress, who openly pursues and tempts men into her bed. What are seen by Geoffrey and Chrétien de Troyes as magical and divine talents become acts of the darkest witchcraft. As Maureen Fries explains, she 'develops from an entirely wholesome [being] into a mainly maleficent presence'.[42] Several scholars, most notably Fries, have argued that this movement to such a negative portrayal of Morgan is due to the Christian moralities of the times. As Friedrich Heer

39 R Loomis, 'Breton Folklore and Arthurian Romance', *Comparative Literature* 2/4 (1950) 294–295.

40 Young, 'King Arthur and Morgan le Fay', 181.

41 M Fries, 'From the Lady to the Tramp: The Decline of Morgan le Fay in Medieval Romance', *Arthuriana* 4:1 (1994) 2.

42 M Fries, 'Female Heros, Heroines and Counter-Heroes: Images of Women in the Arthurian Tradition', 5–17 in S Slocum (ed), *Popular Arthurian Traditions* (Ohio, 1992) at p 12.

explains, '[w]itch-mania was a catching malady in a world made schizophrenic by masculine anxieties and masculine fears'.[43] Women were removed from any position of respect and power within society: healer, midwife, and even preaching roles in religious sects like the Waldensians and Cathars. What could not be explained by men and science was feared, and 'the arts of healing with herbs and other natural remedies became in the Middle Ages and early Renaissance associated with older women who were accused of witchcraft'.[44] Women were to be timid, subordinate to the rule and needs of men and God. Any woman who refused to accept this role was presented as the root of all evil, the handmaiden of the devil.[45] The literary trends of the time were concerned with images of courtly love and chivalry, where women were no more than beautiful figurines to be admired and loved from afar. Women with purpose and strategies were presented as wicked and immoral, seen as overstepping their place in society and religion. The *Vulgate Cycle* is an example of such negatively themed literature from the time. Believed to have been written and circulated by Cistercian monks,[46] it presents Morgan as a jealous enchantress, who repeatedly tries to seduce the object of her desire, is thwarted in her efforts by Lancelot, and in revenge attempts to denounce the affair between Lancelot and Gwenhwyfar.[47] Malory also joins the bandwagon, and seems unable to conceive of the idea of a positive female hero character type, instead turning Morgan into a female counter-hero,[48] whose

---

43 F Heer, *The Medieval World: Europe 1100–1350* (London, 1961: repr 1998) 254.

44 Spivack, 'Morgan le Fay', 18–23.

45 See C Rider, *Magic and Impotence in the Middle Ages* (Oxford, 2006), especially 'What adulterous women do', 29–52 and 'Herbs and Magic: Medicine, 1240–1400', 160–185, for examples of the connections the church made between women and magic.

46 Fries, 'From the Lady to the Tramp', 6.

47 See N Lacy (ed), *Lancelot-Grail: The Old French Arthurian Vulgate and Post-Vulgate in Translation* (London, 1993) 307–327.

48 For a more comprehensive exploration of female character types within

main purpose is to destroy the kingdom and peace that Arthur and his knights have wrought.

The downfall of Morgan has not gone unchallenged, as many writers of contemporary Arthurian literature and scholars have attempted to balance the scales. Numerous papers and theses have explored the varying portrayals of Morgan through her numerous guises,[49] while authors of fiction have given Morgan a voice to explain her actions.[50] This does not mean that in contemporary fantasy the image of Morgan is uniformly presented. Some texts choose to present her in the guise of an 'evil sorceress who destroys her lover, something like Circe in the *Odyssey*',[51] while in others, as mentioned above, she is given a chance to tell her story, and more often than not, the evil-step-sister-from-hell element is omitted. Mary Grey notes that 'interestingly people who are attempting to portray her in a positive light tend to refer to her as Morgaine, almost like it's an attempt to distance her from the "demonic" and evil sorceress out to kill Arthur and his knights — or even Christianity'.[52]

Bradley's *The Mists of Avalon* presents Morgan as a strong heroine figure, who can be seen as a role model for both feminist and contemporary pagan movements. Bradley's novel highlights the struggle between the purported goddess-oriented elements of pre-Christian Celtic religion and the later patriarchal Christian themes that are found within the Arthurian tradition. Essentially, Bradley's

---

Arthurian literature, see Fries, 'Images of Women in the Arthurian Tradition', 5–17.

49 Examples include D Carver; K Lievre, *Celtic Mythology and French Sources as a Background to Malory's Morgan le Fay* (unpublished thesis, Flinders University, South Australia, 1996); C Spivack and M Fries, (1994).

50 These include Bradley (1983); F Sampson, *Daughter of Tintagel Omnibus*, (London, 1996); N Springer, *I am Morgan le Fay: A Tale from Camelot*, (London, 2002).

51 Jung and von Franz, *The Grail Legend*, 393.

52 M Grey, 'The Dark Knowing of Morgan le Fay: Women, Evil and Theodicy', 111–130 in T Elwes (ed), *Women's Voices: Essays in Contemporary Feminist Theology*, (London, 1992), at p 126.

Morgan (who is a Morgaine), embraces the characteristics specified by Geoffrey in his *Merlini*, being a priestess of a sacred isle, educated in the arts of healing, reading, writing, mathematics and astrology.[53] While there is no evidence of her having any shape-shifting ability, she can create a glamour around her person, allowing her to appear larger than her true small physical stature:

> Morgaine drew a deep breath, drawing the mantle of a priestess around her again, the glamour she could summon when she would [...] she knew that suddenly she looked tall and imposing.[54]

In Bradley's work, and others, Morgan is presented as the hand of the goddess and, as such, she is linked to the land and the old ways. Her purpose is to keep these rituals and beliefs alive and not let them be lost behind the growing force that is Christianity. In *The Mists of Avalon*, she is the maiden huntress, whose embrace bestows kingship, and as such she can be seen as a representation of a Celtic sovereignty goddess, who can *choose* to bestow sovereignty and kingship on a chosen male, in this case Arthur. In Celtic mythology and society, a king, on any scale, held a sacral office. He was the protector of his people, the mediator between the secular and the supernatural world, and as such was required to uphold certain virtues in order to maintain the prosperity of his subjects and the fertility and abundance of produce in his realm.[55] A common inauguration ritual mentioned in the Irish Annals is the *Feis Temro*,

---

53 'Morgen is her name, and she has learned what useful properties all the herbs contain, so that she can cure sick bodies. She also knows an art by which to change her shape, and to cleave the air on new wings like Daedalus; when she wishes she is at Brest, Chartres, or Pavia, and when she will she slips down from the air onto your shores. And men say that she has taught mathematics to her sisters [...]', Geoffrey of Monmouth, *Merlin*, 85.

54 Bradley, *Mists of Avalon*, 183.

55 P Mac Cana, 'Celtic Goddesses of Sovereignty', 85–100 in Bernard and Moon, *Goddesses Who Rule*, 92.

or 'feast of Tara', where a king makes a 'sacred marriage' with the goddess of the land, to ensure the prosperity of the kingdom and confirm his legitimacy.[56] This idea of the sacred marriage, and gaining the blessing of the local goddess, occurs both within Celtic mythology and in other threads of the Arthurian cycle.[57] The role of the sovereignty goddess is twofold: her embrace bestows kingship and rightful accession, but she must also prevent the accession of an unworthy or unrighteous leader. This can be achieved by any force necessary, as a king must be without blemish on his physical or spiritual body to rule and ensure the prosperity of the land during his rule.[58]

With this in mind, Morgan's later animosity towards Arthur can be seen as a natural reaction, due to her position as a sovereignty goddess and Arthur's failure, as the sacred king, to serve the land and keep the religion and traditions of the old ones. His failure to support these rituals and traditions, normally illustrated by an acceptance of Christian values, make him no longer worthy of the goddess's blessing, no longer worthy to be the sacred king:

> 'When Arthur came to the throne, I heard he had the support of Avalon, that the Merlin gave him the sword of the Holy Regalia. But now he has made this so Christian a court […] my father told me that he feared Arthur would move this land back to Druid rule, but it seems he has not'[59] [...]
> 'Hear me, Arthur of Britain! As the force and power

56 D Bray, 'Sacral Elements of Irish Kingship', 105–116 in C Cusack and P Oldmedow (eds), *The Immense Panorama: Studies in Honour of Eric J Sharpe* (Sydney, 1999) at p 113.

57 These include tales such as Echtra Mac Nechach in *The Cycles of the Kings*, M Dillon (trans), (Dublin, 1946, repr 1994) 38-41. The three eponymous goddesses of Ireland – Eriu, Banbha and Fodla – give the land to Amairghin, leader of the Sons of Mil, in the Lebor Gebála Érenn. See P MacCana, *Celtic Mythology* (London, 1970) 64.

58 Mac Cana, 'Celtic Goddesses', 94.

59 Bradley, *Mists of Avalon* (1983), 643.

> of Avalon set you on your throne, so the force and power of Avalon can bring you down into ruin! Think well how you desecrate the Holy Regalia! Think never to put it to service of your Christian God, for everything of Power carries its own curse'.[60]

This being the case, Morgan is logically driven to withdraw her blessing, and even to work against him, for the good of the land. As Arthur allows himself to be courted by the Christian priests, or as portrayed in Bradley's *The Mists of Avalon*, give in to Gwenhwyfar's constant complaints and demands, Morgan can be seen as doing nothing more than her duty to the land, in her role as a sovereignty goddess.[61] Thus, her use of Accalon — a knight dedicated to the old ways and subsequently her lover — is an acceptable path, as she is the symbol of the land's sovereignty. It is within her power to bestow her blessing on him, and choose him as the new 'male hero', charging him to recover the 'Holy Regalia' (Excalibur), and renew the prosperity of the land.

Excalibur itself has obvious connections with fertility. The sword is a phallic icon which symbolises vitality and strength, which in the hands of historical figures such as Charlemagne is seen as a symbol of sovereignty in its own right.[62] As such, the function of Excalibur as Arthur's sword within Arthurian legend is to signify Arthur's place as the rightful ruler of the land. Furthermore, there is evidence in Irish tradition of an inauguration ritual where, after the performance of a '*deiseal*', the ceremonial right-hand turn made around the king to symbolise prosperity, an 'item associated with the kingship, such as a rod made from an ancient and venerated

60 *Ibid*, 825.

61 This is seen in the scene where Arthur, to placate Gwenhwyfar after she has just miscarried, agrees to carry her banner depicting the Virgin Mary, instead of the banner of Avalon, which he swore to carry at his kingmaking ritual on Avalon. See Bradley, *Mists of Avalon*, 441–458.

62 H Biedermann, *Dictionary of Symbolism: Cultural Icons and the Meanings Behind Them* (New York, 1989: repr 1994) 336.

tree (*bile*) which grew at the inauguration site'[63] is handed over. This ritual can be seen as the source for the emphasis placed on Excalibur within the Arthurian tradition. If one substitutes the 'rod' for a 'sword', then the gifting of the sword Excalibur by the lady of the lake, with the sword coming from the lake itself (water often representing the porthole to the otherworld), is arguably an example of such an inauguration ritual, placed as a major element within the Arthurian tradition. It also confirms the image of Arthur as a sacral king, who in turn is gifted with a symbol of sovereignty by a goddess-like figure, such rituals being an important mechanism that legitimises the ascension of a new ruler.[64]

However, Morgan's position as a bestower of sovereignty and legitimisation for male rule of the land has not stopped Bradley's *The Mists of Avalon* from being embraced by the feminist and neo-pagan movements. Her works, including the Darkover series, which is set on a remote planet, can be seen as vehicles that reflect what Fry calls the 'feminist religious position'.[65] Bradley has stated that she is not a feminist, but admits that novels such as *The Mists of Avalon* were her exploration of 'issues relating to female self determination and powers'.[66] Nonetheless, the series has been embraced and acclaimed by members of both feminist and neo-pagan movements, as it restructures one of the most famous legends of western society in such a manner as to support both matriarchal and non-Christian beliefs. The most prominent person on the island of Avalon is the lady of the lake. In Bradley's version of the tale, she is not an immortal being; instead, the position is passed on from generation to generation, to the most worthy and strong-willed of the priestesses. Often, it is passed on to a daughter,

---

63 B Jaski, *Early Irish Kingship and Succession* (Dublin, 2000) 59.

64 Mac Cana, 'Celtic Goddesses', 92.

65 C Fry, 'The Goddess Ascending: Feminist Neo-Pagan Witchcraft in Marion Zimmer Bradley's Novels', *Journal of Popular Culture*, 27/1, (1993) 67–80, at p 71.

66 D Paxton, 'Marion Zimmer Bradley and *The Mists of Avalon*', *Arthuriana* 9/1 (1999) 114.

granddaughter or other blood relation, echoing the mother-right of matriarchal societies. As such, Bradley has humanised what is seen as an otherworldly figure in other versions of the tale. She has re-centred the story around these passionate and empowered women, instead of focusing on the usual male-dominated themes that include 'rivalry over women and the impossible conflicting demands of church and chivalry'.[67] She has thus altered the usual roles given to women within the tradition. Morgan's acts are not presented as wicked and immoral deeds; instead, they are the product of years of training and lifelong dedication.

It is not only Morgan whose role transcends its usual position in the Arthurian literary corpus. Igraine's and Morgause's stories are expanded, as Bradley explores their motivations and actions. Even Gwenhwyfar is given the chance to vocalise her feelings and thoughts.[68] While Bradley's Gwenhwyfar is in no way what might be called a feminist or neo-pagan role model, her character is developed, and the reasons behind her actions explained. Ultimately, it is Bradley's unique blend of Celtic mythology and pagan practices, interwoven within the action of the book, that have led to its popularity within the neo-pagan community. Bradley's *The Mists of Avalon* illustrates the struggle between the pagan origins of the Arthurian tradition and its eventual Christianisation. She shows Arthur as the king stuck between the old ways and the coming of a new regime, with Morgan as the sister who endeavours to bind him to the land and the old ways. As such, Morgan becomes the heroine of the story, despite her complex relationship with, and animosity toward, Arthur. It is her struggle to keep some fragment of the old ways and the image of the goddess alive within the world that is the true theme of the story, and not just the deeds and actions of Arthur and his knights. Bradley's Morgan becomes a 'vision of positive female power', re-embracing her original incarnation as a mother

67 L Tobin, 'Why Change the Story? Marion Zimmer Bradley's "The Mists of Avalon"', *Exploration* 34/2 (1993) 147.

68 The beginning of chapter 15 gives an example of this, when Gwenhwyfar's thoughts on Morgan and Beltane rituals are textualised. Bradley, *Mists of Avalon*, 484–85.

goddess within Celtic mythology. She is once again the avatar of the goddess, and as she takes on the mantle of lady of the lake at the end of the book, she not only completes a full metamorphosis back to her earliest origins, but she also understands that her place, the place of the goddess, is alongside that of the male aspect of God found within Christianity.

> But Bridget is not a Christian saint, she thought, even if Patricius thinks so. That is the Goddess as she is worshipped in Ireland. And I know it, and even if they think otherwise, these women know the power of the Immortal. Exile her as they may, she will prevail. The Goddess will never withdraw herself from mankind [...] No we did not fail. What I said to Arthur in his dying, it was all true. I did the Mother's work in Avalon until at last those who may come after us might bring her into the world.[69]

The character of Morgan le Fay is gifted with many faces within the Arthurian tradition and, as evidence has shown, her origins go back into the misty depths of Celtic mythology. She has been famed throughout history as a healer, trained in the magical arts, and while other features of her personality have changed with each subsequent retelling of the tale, she still retains these original features. She has survived the persecution of writers in the thirteenth century, and been adopted as a role-model by feminists and neo-pagans in contemporary society. While Morgan le Fay will never rival Arthur's fame and position within the folklore of the British public, she still enjoys a unique position as a fictional character who continues to be the focus of writers and scholars alike. Her continuously changing presentation within the Arthurian tradition is a reflection of socio-historical location of women within society at the time each version of the tale was composed. Thus, her nature is fluid and never fixed, making her the quintessential shape-shifter that Geoffrey described

69 *Ibid*, 1008–1009.

in his *Vita Merlini.* She is truly a fey figure, deserving of the title Morgan le Fay, Morgan of the Fairies.

Wicca in Eileanan and the problems of history

Lauren Bernauer ⊕

Kate Forsyth's series *The Witches of Eileanan* introduces the reader to a foreign medieval-like world, full of magic, witches and fantastical creatures. However, despite these fantasy components, Eileanan bears relation to our own world. At the beginning of the series, the witches, or magic-users both male and female, of Eileanan are being persecuted and hunted down to be killed, whereas once they were a significant power on this small world. Due to this destruction of the witches, they must now meet in secret to practise their rites, which involve the five elements (earth, air, fire, water and spirit) laid out in a pentagram. It is through their rites that they worship the sacred earth. Although only the persecution of witches correlates with actual human history, if one is aware of and familiar with the beliefs and pseudo-history of the neo-pagan religion, Wicca, often called witchcraft, one will be able to see greater parallels with our own reality. It is obvious from this that Kate Forsyth has been influenced by Wicca, though it is unknown whether or not she is Wiccan herself.

Despite the fantasy setting, Forsyth's work has been influenced by our reality, though imperfectly. Despite the considerable scholarship on the witch-hunts of medieval Europe, Forsyth has chosen to neglect academic findings and adopt the beliefs held by members of the neo-pagan community with regard to the history of witchcraft and the new religion, Wicca. To quote from her website:

> Eileanan is a land far, far away from our own world but it has many echoes with it, except that in Eileanan magic has been celebrated and developed, while we have chosen to follow the path of science

⊕ The University of Sydney.

> and technology. *The Witches of Eileanan* is based on the premise that a group of Scottish witches fled the persecution of witches in the 16th century to discover a new land where they could worship their pagan, pantheistic religion and practice their magic in freedom.[1]

This notion that the witches of late medieval Europe were actually pagan, with their religion being pantheistic, is a view that is advocated by a significant portion of the Wiccan community. However, before the religion of the witches in Forsyth's novels and its relation to Wiccan beliefs are discussed, the persecution issue that is the first major theme in the series *The Witches of Eileanan* will be examined.

As mentioned above, the series begins with the witches living in Eileanan having been driven underground because of the authorities persecuting them. The witch-hunts of Europe are a disputed issue for quite a few Wiccans and witches, as they disagree with the academic scholarship about late medieval and early modern history. They do not acknowledge the heretical sects that the church was trying to remove, nor do they believe that it was Christians who were being killed by the witch-hunters. Instead, Wiccans and pagans maintain that the people tortured and killed by the inquisition and other authorities were actually witches, sometimes alleging that the witches were of the religion of Wicca, and that the church conducted persecutions to destroy the religion and demonise it through association with diabolism. Also, the fact that men were originally persecuted and investigated for magic is generally not acknowledged. For neo-pagans it is women who are always victimised in the witch hunts:

> Persecution began slowly. The twelfth and thirteenth centuries saw a revival of the Old Religion by troubadors, who wrote love poems to the Goddess

1 K Forsyth, *About Me*: available online at http://members.ozemail.com.au/~kforsyth/aboutme2.htm [10 June 2004].

> under the guise of living noble ladies of their times. The magnificent cathedrals were built in honor of Mary, who had taken over many of the aspects of the ancient Goddess. Witchcraft was declared a heretical act, and in 1324 an Irish coven led by Dame Alice Kyteler was tried by the Bishop of Ossory for worshiping a non-Christian god.[2]

This does not accord with historical sources, as Alice Kyteler was subjected to investigation because of her three husbands having died and the children of one of them being upset about her gaining their inheritance. She was also accused of devil worship, not the worship of a non-Christian god.[3] It demonstrates the emphasis on women in these accounts, as Alice Kyteler's trial occurred not long after the trial of the Templars, which was far more brutal than the investigation in Ireland.

> The persecution was most strongly directed against women: Of an estimated nine million Witches executed, eighty percent were women, including children and young girls, who were believed to inherit the 'evil' from their mothers. The ascetism of early Christianity, which turned its back on the world of flesh had degenerated, in some quarters of the Church into hatred of those who brought that flesh into being. Misogyny, the hatred of women, had become a strong element in medieval Christianity.[4]

These figures are not borne out when one consults academic sources on this period of history, which estimate that somewhere between

---

2 Starhawk, *The Spiral Dance: A Rebirth of the Ancient Religion of the Great Goddess* (San Francisco, 1989) 19.

3 R Kieckhefer, *European Witch Trials: Their Foundations in Popular and Learned Culture, 1300–1500* (London, 1976) 14.

4 Starhawk, *Spiral Dance*, 20.

'200,000 and half a million people were executed' for witchcraft.[5] While most who were accused of witchcraft during this period were women, the Wiccan view does not acknowledge places like Iceland, where about 90 per cent of those who were investigated for the use of magic were male. The idea of most witches being female is also found in Forsyth's novels, where the two main witches are female and the majority of the Coven[6] leaders of whom readers are told are females. The notion that the people who were killed in the European witch trials were pagan and perhaps Wiccan is something that is clung to by members of the Wiccan community, regardless of academic research that is available on this topic.

> Although I respect the facts as currently understood, I think drawing this implication from them is not right. To begin with, the fact that the Renaissance witch hunters perceived that their victims were devil worshippers does not, by itself, rule out the possibility that the targets were practicing something akin to modern Wicca. Modern Wiccans are also perceived as devil worshippers by ignorant fundamentalists seeking to exterminate us. In fact, the parallels in perception (however misguided the perception itself is in both cases) should cause us to take seriously the possibility of parallels in reality as well.[7]

While this argument does have some valid elements, it shows the disrespect for scholarship and the lack of real research that are prevalent in the Wiccan community. The fact that Christianity

5 N Ben-Yehuda, 'Problems Inherent in Socio-Historical Approaches to the European Witch Craze', *Journal for the Scientific Study of Religion* 20 (1981) 326–338, at p 328.

6 The Coven being a significant power in Eileanan before and after the persecution of the witches.

7 T T Little, *Why Remember the Burning Times?*, available online at http://paganwiccan.about.com/gi/dynamic/offsite.htm?site=http%3A%2F%2Fwww.telp.com%2Fspirituality%2Fburning.htm [4 May 2004].

had been a major part of society for over 1000 years is disregarded, and the concept of a pagan religion existing underground for all of that time is promoted instead. This raises questions about the pagan religion which the witches practiced, and how it relates to modern Wiccan beliefs, given that Wicca does not reflect the actual religion and practices of pre-Christian Europe, particularly the pre-Christian Celts.

A major part of the pseudo-history of Wicca is the belief that Wicca is the religion of the ancient Celts. This is also a part of Forsyth's world, given that the background premise of the series is that the witches travelled from Scotland. Because of this, the characters use Scottish Gaelic words and speak with Scottish accents. From this, it can be inferred that the beliefs of the people of Eileanan about deities are parallel to those which Forsyth and some Wiccans believe that the ancient Celts held. In the quotation above from Forsyth, she stated that the Scottish witches had taken with them to Eileanan a 'pagan, pantheistic religion'. In the series of novels, this religion has a single central deity known as *Eà*, who is defined as 'the Great Earth-Goddess, mother and father of all'.[8] Although the concept of a single deity is not as common in Wiccan literature as is the duotheism of the goddess and the god, the idea of a single pantheistic deity is still found:

> Before time was, there was The One; The One was all and all was The One.
> And the vast expanse known as the universe was The One, all-wise, all-pervading, all-powerful, eternally changing.[9]

This concept is also expressed on a website about Wicca and witchcraft:

---

8 K Forsyth, *Dragonclaw: Book One of The Witches of Eileanan* (Sydney, 1997) 523.

9 S Cunningham, *Wicca: A Guide for the Solitary Practitioner* (St Paul, 1995) 113.

> There is a single power defined as the One or All, which is comprised of everything it has ever created. This supreme energy force does not rule over the Universe, it IS the Universe.[10]

This notion of The One has influenced Forsyth more than the belief in the Goddess and the God that is found in the majority of Wiccan literature.

> We believe there is a life-force that animates the universe, though we do no' divide it into black or white, good or evil, male or female, night or day. We call this life-force Eà and believe she contains all these opposites within her, or him if ye so prefer. We believe Eà is all gods and goddesses, all devils and angels.[11]

While these sources do not convey the majority belief of Wiccans concerning deity, that being duotheism, it does demonstrate what some Wiccans believe that the pre-Christian Celts and other European peoples believed. While most Wiccans are duotheistic, it is a pantheistic duotheism that pertains to most of what is said about *Eà*. However, despite their claims that the Celts worshipped a single pantheistic deity, or two pantheistic deities, these concepts do not relate to the academic information that is available concerning the pre-Christian Celtic religion, nor is it found in the primary sources on Celtic religion.

Celtic myths were only written down after the conversion of Ireland to Christianity; thus it could be surmised that, athough there are Christian beliefs overlaying the myths, the stories are reflective

---

10 Herne, *Witchcraft, Wicca and Paganism Frequently Asked Questions*: available online at http://www.wicca.com/celtic/wicca/faq.htm [10 June 2004].

11 K Forsyth, *The Forbidden Land, Book Four of The Witches of Eileanan* (Sydney, 2000) 341.

of those told about the gods in pagan times.[12] This is important, for in the myths of the ancient Celts there is no mention of a supreme divine being, but rather many individual deities, as are found in other polytheistic religions.[13] The Celts were not of the religion that neo-pagans and new-agers attribute to them. New-agers and neo-pagans appear to propose a type of belief and religion that from their point of view sits in harmony with Christianity.[14] An all-powerful, all-knowing, all-encompassing deity is far closer to the Christian belief in a single god than the polytheistic religion that the Celts actually followed:

> Christianity: One Divine Source, called 'God', viewed in three different aspects: Father, Son, and Holy Spirit.
> Wicca: One Divine Source, viewed in the Masculine, called 'God', and in the feminine, called 'Goddess'. God seen in the three aspects of Hunter, Father, and Sage, and the Goddess seen in three aspects of Maiden, Mother, and Crone.[15]

Because of this concept of a pantheistic religion, neo-pagans are more easily able to demonise Christianity for being intolerant of the ancient pagan religions, than they could be if they accepted that the ancient Celts performed human sacrifice and worshipped a variety of deities, tenets which go against virtues that Christianity upholds. This idea of pagans and neo-pagans being far more tolerant of other faiths than is Christianity, is another theme which occurs in Kate Forsyth's writings.

---

12 *Early Irish Myths and Sagas*, J Gantz (trans) (London, 1981) 18–25.

13 *Ibid*, 14–15, and T P Cross and C H Slover, *Ancient Irish Tales* (New York, 1969) 28–48.

14 M Bowman, 'Reinventing the Celts', *Religion* 23 (1993) 147–156, at p 148.

15 *Wicca – Christianity & Charges*: available online at http://www.geocities.com/SoHo/Cafe/1614/Celtwicc/Wicca/Wicca07.htm [6 June 2004].

When in discussion with the Christian people of Eileanan, the witches are presented as being far more open-minded about the differences between the faiths, and also as being willing to give up their preconceived notions about what Christians do. However, a number of the Christians refuse to change their ideas about witches, and still believe that they worship the devil, or 'Arch-Fiend', as he is known in the novels:

> 'We shall be made to dance naked around the kirkyard and say our prayers backwards and boil the bones o' murdered children for evil spells …'
> Lachlan interrupted him with a great shout of laughter. 'Is that what ye think the Coven does?' he cried when at last he caught his breath. 'By Eà's green blood! Och, well, happen it be like the stories we always heard about how ye sacrificed babies on your altars.'
> There was an indignant outcry. Lachlan laughed again. 'I can promise ye this, there's no boiling up children, though it is true witches often dance about naked. Never fear! The Coven would never make ye do so if ye did no' want to. We o' the Coven believe all must be free to think and worship as they please. None would be forced to pray in a kirk six times a day if they would rather be ploughing their fields, I assure ye! We believe that living a good and compassionate life and having a care for others is a better way to worship the sacred forces o' life than kneeling in a cold, draughty building, but each to their own!'[16]

This is reflective of neo-pagan ideas about themselves being far more open-minded and tolerant of other faiths:

> 10. Our only animosity toward Christianity, or

16 Forsyth, *Forbidden Land*, 339–40.

> toward any other religion or philosophy-of-life, is to the extent that its institutions have claimed to be 'the one true, right and only way' and have sought to deny freedom to others and to suppress other ways of religious practices and belief.[17]

Yet other elements of the apparently Celtic religion are professed by neo-pagans, Wiccans and witches.

In the modern religion of Wicca, eight major festivals or holidays are celebrated. However, for the ancient Celts there were only four. These four, *Samain*, *Imbolc*, *Beltaine* and *Lugnasad*, are known to have been celebrated by the ancient Celts, through texts in Christian manuscripts, and their incorporation into the new religion, Christianity. The other four holidays that are added to the Wiccan calendar are the solar festivals, namely the equinoxes and solstices. Yet despite the evidence against the Celts celebrating the sun festivals, they are still included in the Wiccan calendar, and many believe that the ancient Celts also celebrated all eight of the Wiccan holidays.[18] Celtic deities, often called facets or aspects of the single or dual divine, are attributed to non-Celtic holidays by neo-pagans. For Yule, an ancient Germanic holiday:

> Deities of Yule are all Newborn Gods, Sun Gods, Mother Goddesses, and Triple Goddesses. The best known would be the Dagda, and Brighid, the daughter of the Dagda.[19]

This idea of the Celts celebrating eight major festivals has also influenced Forsyth, for in the series *The Witches of Eileanan*, they

---

17 S RavenWolf, *Wiccan Principles of Belief*: available online at http://www.silverravenwolf.com/principles_of_belief_adult.htm [8 March 2004].

18 R Hutton, *The Pagan Religions of the Ancient British Isles: Their Nature and Legacy* (Oxford, 1993) 143.

19 Akasha, *Yule*: available online at http://www.wicca.com/celtic/akasha/yule.htm [8 March 2004].

are present. As seen in Wiccan literature, Forsyth also uses the Christian names for some of the holidays, such as *Lammas*[20] instead of *Lugnasad*, and *Candlemas*[21] rather than *Imbolc*.

Another neo-pagan and Wiccan concept that has influenced Forsyth is the issue of good versus evil. This theme does not truly occur in the series, as, for most Wiccans, good and evil are not exactly polarities: things are more shades of grey. However, interfering with another's will through magic is something that is seen as wrong and bad by Wiccan witches. This is clearly a belief Forsyth has incorporated into the beliefs of the witches in the series, as the main body of witches (The Coven) has an oath that initiates must take with regard to this terrible act:

> By the Creed o' the Coven o' Witches, ye must swear to speak only what is true in your heart, for ye must have courage in your beliefs; ye must swear no' to use the Power to ensorcel others, remembering all people must choose their own path.[22]

This idea of not using magic to bend another to one's will is an issue that is raised in most introductory literature on Wicca and witchcraft:

> Under no circumstances is it acceptable to meddle in someone else's life. This is a gross violation of free will and can be called nothing else but manipulation.[23]

It is through disregard for this morality and the attack on people's free will that the reader is able to infer who the 'evil' characters are

---

20 F Horne, *Life's a Witch!: A Handbook for Teen Witches* (Sydney, 2000) 78 and Forsyth, *Dragonclaw*, 525.

21 V Crowley, *Wicca: The Old Religion in the New Millennium* (London, 1996) 158 and Forsyth, *Dragonclaw*, 522.

22 Forsyth, *Dragonclaw*, 73.

23 E McCoy, *Making Magick: What it is and how it works* (St Paul, 1997) 19.

in Forsyth's books. By including Wiccan morality, Forsyth is able to establish the main antagonist to the series through her interfering and manipulating of people using magic. From the first chapter the reader is told that Maya, the *Banrìgh* or queen of Eileanan, uses magic to control people, and the first time she actually appears in the novels, she is working this type of magic:

> For sixteen years her hold on the Rìgh had been without question, so much so that she had let him drift away a little for these past five years. [...]
> Maya sighed gratefully — it was not always so easy to deflect him from some memory of the past, a past that did not include her. So many of his memories were dangerous to her that she tried hard to keep him from remembering at all.[24]

Maya is continually portrayed as evil in the series, for when a group of witches must face a small group of *Fairgean*, or sea-folk, they use the magic of song to bring peace to the conflict rather than either singing them to sleep so the *Fairgean* will drown, or singing a song of death which would kill them. Both of these latter songs are ones Maya uses against the *Fairgean*.[25] Although it would seem that the song of love and peace used by the witches is one that goes against the creed, it is explained that the *Fairgean* would not have fallen sway to the magic of the song if, in their hearts, they did not want peace:

> Ye ken even better than I that the songs o' enchantment can only cast their spell when the listener hears with their heart as well as their ears. These Fairgean, they must have wanted to hear, they must have wanted

24 Forsyth, *Dragonclaw*, 104–107.

25 K Forsyth, *The Skull of the World, Book Five of The Witches of Eileanan* (Sydney, 2001) 349–53 and K Forsyth, *The Fathomless Caves, Book Six of The Witches of Eileanan* (Sydney, 2002) 351–2.

> peace and friendship, for the spell to have worked so powerfully.[26]

Despite the lack of a definite good versus evil theme in the series, the use of the morality of Wiccans with regard to a person's free will is the replacement for it, identifying who the good people are, and those who are to be considered bad and enemies of the good.

After the influence of Wiccan beliefs and pseudo-history on Forsyth have been examined, the impact that these issues have on the scholarly study of religion and history may also be analysed. From the early days of Wicca, there has been promotion of pseudo-history. The founder of this new religion, Gerald Gardner, tried to present his religion to scholars and academics as an ancient pagan religion which he discovered in 1940s England, that had survived through underground groups in Christian Europe. Yet the academics of his time rejected his supposed findings.[27] It is due to Gardner's invented history of Wicca that the belief is held by contemporary Wiccans and witches that an underground pagan religion was persecuted in the witch hunts of late medieval and early modern Europe. This is detrimental to the study of religion and history, for it ingrains in the new members of Wicca that the academic history one has been taught is lies, and that scholars and academics on the subject of history cannot be trusted. The introductory literature on Wicca and witchcraft tells the reader that Christianity and its adherents have distorted history to their own ends, and thus accepted history of the middle ages and witches is simply covering up the truth about a peaceful goddess-worshipping religion that existed during this period in history. This is unfortunate, both for academia and for the members of Wicca who believe this false information. The pseudo-history promotes anti-intellectualism and distrust in what one has been taught and in those who are authorities on history. In an interview with a Wiccan author, an article relates:

---

26 Forsyth, *Forbidden Land*, 294.

27 R Hutton, *The Triumph of the Moon: A History of Modern Pagan Witchcraft* (Oxford, 1999) 206.

> She seemed proud of her self-admitted anti-scholastic status and could offer me no source material or justification for any of her more outrageous claims. When pressed for answers, she would simply complain of my 'negativity' and of how 'mean, cruel and academic' I was.[28]

The authors of Wiccan introductory literature spread misinformation about the history of Wicca and witchcraft, and tell the reader not to trust scholarly books and information they read with regard to pre-Christian paganism and the European witch hunts. Pseudo-history, especially this kind, which tells the reader that the history they have been told before is based on lies, is extremely harmful to academia and intellectualism, but also to the more open members of the religion and community, who know the truth about their religion, yet are silenced and shunned when they try to inform newer members about the real history of their religion.

This is not the only problem caused by the pseudo-history of Wicca and witchcraft. The spreading of the beliefs that neo-pagans hold about their religion being Celtic is not only detrimental to the study of the history of the Celts and the Celtic lands; it also trivialises the Celts of today and their culture. While this issue is connected to the previous one, this problem should be dealt with separately, as it affects not only academia but also a people and their culture. Neo-pagan pseudo-history is leading members of the younger generations of Ireland, Scotland and Wales to believe that the history they were taught about their pagan ancestors is false. Wiccans in Ireland are forgetting the truth about their ancestors and embracing the belief that Wicca or witchcraft, a nature-worshipping, peaceful religion, was what their ancestors followed and practised. This is detrimental to the culture itself, for while outsiders believing

28 J Hautin-Mayer, *When is a Celt not a Celt: An irreverent peek into Neopagan views of history*: available online at http://www.cyberwitch.com/wychwood/Library/whenIsACeltNotACelt.htm [10 June 2004].

misinformation about Celtic cultures and history is irksome, the fact that members of those cultures are duped by it could cause major problems for the future of already fragile Celtic cultures.

Although Wicca is a legitimate religious belief, with its own history, the false history distributed by some of its members has grave implications. Although it is fine for these beliefs to influence a writer when they are creating a new story, the effect this false history has can be dire. While some may read Forsyth's series without even realising the ideas behind the beliefs of the witches, for those who know the pseudo-history and embrace it, this series reinforces those beliefs. The false history that is propagated by neo-pagan and Wiccan authors is detrimental to academia and to Celtic cultures. Kate Forsyth's series fuels this pseudo-history and thus perpetuates the problems started by beliefs that actual witches were persecuted, underground pagan cults existed in Christian Europe and Celts were Wiccan witches and believed in a single divinity that permeated all creation. The themes found in this series reinforce these problems in an easy-to-read fashion, while at the same time helping to promote the anti-intellectualism found in Wiccan and neo-pagan literature.

Celts in the Diaspora

Irish and Scottish child migrants at Pinjarra: maintaining a Celtic identity

Paula-Lee M Magee ⊕

Child migration from Britain had its inception in 1618, when the first group of 100 children emigrated from England to Richmond, Virginia to work on tobacco plantations. The demand for the child migrants' labour became so great that in 1698, the *Flying Post* [London] alleged that 500 boys from Aberdeen, Scotland had been kidnapped and transported to Virginia against their will.[1] The practice of spiriting ended in 1757 after a number of Aberdeen businessmen and magistrates were exposed for their involvement in the trade.[2] In the early part of the nineteenth century, about 440 children were sent to South Africa as a substitute for slave labour, which had recently been abolished.[3] It was after 1850, however, and amendments to the poor laws of the United Kingdom, that the practice became an institution.[4] Between 1922 and 1967, about

---

⊕ Murdoch University.

This working paper is based upon my PhD research, *Child Migration to Western Australia in the Twentieth Century: The Kingsley Fairbridge Farm School at Pinjarra.* I wish to thank my Supervisor Professor Bob Reece at Murdoch University, Western Australia, for his advice on the preparation of this paper.

1 *Flying Post* (1 September 1698), cited in D P Nicholson, 'The genealogical value of early English newspapers', *Genealogical Magazine*, 17/3 (August 1983) 71.

2 *The Children's Friend Society:* Available online at http://ist.uwaterloo.ca/~marj/genealogy/children/Organizations/cfriend.html [cited 20 February 2006].

3 *The Children's Friend Society.*

4 A Buti, 'British Child Migration to Australia: History, Senate Inquiry and Responsibilities', e*LAW Journal: Murdoch University Electronic*

150,000 children, with an average age of eight years and nine months, were transported from England, Scotland and Ireland 'to help populate the British Dominions of Canada, Rhodesia, New Zealand and Australia with good white stock'.[5] Estimates of the number of children sent to Australia vary from 5000 to 30,000. Most of them were sent to charitable and religious institutions.[6] The majority of these children were employed in rural areas, the boys as farm hands and the girls as domestic servants.

Journal of Law 9/4 (December 2002). Available online at http://www.murdoch.edu.au/elaw/indices/issue/v9n4.html [cited 8 March 2006].

5 Parliament of Australia Parliamentary Library, *Child Migrants from the United Kingdom:* Available online at http://www.aph.gov.au/library/intguide/sp/childmigrantuk.htm [cited 20 February 2006].

6 For example, see G Sherington and C Jeffery, *Fairbridge: Empire and Child Migration* (Perth, 1993) 265; House of Commons Health Committee *Inquiry into The Welfare of Former British Child Migrants*, 'Minutes of Evidence', HC 755 (London, 1997–98); Commons *Inquiry*, Memorandum by Barnardo's, 'Welfare of Former British Child Migrants', CM 110 Section 2.3 (1998); A Gill, 'Britain's stolen children', *For A Change* 12/5 (Oct–Nov 1999), 24–36 and his work *Orphans of the Empire* (Milsons Point, 1998); B Coldrey, National Archives of Australia: K1184, 240; PP168/1, W57/2603, *Good British Stock, Child and Youth Migration to Australia*, Research Guide (1999) and *The Scheme: The Christian Brothers and Childcare in Western Australia* (Perth, 1993); Department of Community Development WA, *Signposts – A guide for Children and Young People in Care in WA from 1920*, available online at http:/www.signposts.comunitydevelopment.wa.gov.au [cited 8 November 2004]; Senate Community Affairs References Committee, 'Lost Innocence: Righting the Record', *Report on Child Migration*, August 2001; P Bean and J Melville, *Lost Children of the Empire* (London, 1989); S Constantine, 'British Emigration to the Empire-Commonwealth since 1880: From Overseas Settlement to Diaspora?', *Journal of Imperial and Commonwealth History* 1, 32/2 (May 2003) 16–36 and his works 'The British Government, child welfare, and child migration to Australia after 1945'; *Journal of Imperial and Commonwealth History*, 1, 30/1, (Jan 2002) 99–132; 'Waving goodbye? Australia, assisted passages, and the Empire and Commonwealth Settlement Acts, 1945–72', *Journal of Imperial and Commonwealth History* 2, 26/1 (May 1998) 176–195; J Eekelaar, 'The Chief Glory – The Export of Children from The United Kingdom', *Law and Society* 21/4 (Dec 1994) 44–63.

The Fairbridge Society and the establishment of its farm schools represent an example of the belief that social utility would be served if the 'deprived' child was taught farm and domestic skills and that such children would be more productive in society, whilst their British identity in Australia would be preserved. This paper aims to broaden the historiography of Irish and Scottish child migrants placed at the Kingsley Fairbridge Farm School at Pinjarra, Western Australia. The school was initially used to settle English children, and then later in the 1960s the children of large Irish and Scottish families. The paper seeks to provide an insight into the child migrants' personal lives at Pinjarra, where for one reason or another they felt they were denied their rights to a Celtic identity and a sense of belonging in the Australian community. This paper acknowledges that child migration is a very emotive issue and that there is a diversity of strongly held views by individuals, groups and academics.

It is important to note that, although classified as British, the former child migrants I interviewed were such a distinct sub-group that their geographic origins should not be used to classify their ethnicity. Most of them considered themselves to be 'Celtic'. They felt no great allegiance to 'Britishness', let alone to the Fairbridge Society's custom of following its founder's 'Rules of British Life', and were committed to their own sense of identity and cultural heritage.

Kingsley Fairbridge, a Rhodes Scholar and the founder of the Fairbridge Society, was born at Grahamstown, South Africa, in 1885. On 19 October 1909, he addressed a meeting of the Colonial Club at Oxford University to gain support for his child migration scheme. At the meeting, he proposed:

> to immigrate destitute orphans and neglected children between the ages of eight and ten before they have acquired the vices of professional pauperism and before their physique had become lowered by adverse [social and environmental] conditions.[7]

7 K Fairbridge, *The Autobiography of Kingsley Fairbridge* (London, 1928)

Kingsley recommended establishing self-contained cottages under the care of a 'cottage mother'. The children would be educated under the curriculum set by the Education Department and would receive farm training until the age of 16.[8] At this point, the boys would be employed as farm labourers and girls as governesses, housekeepers, cooks, domestic servants and farmers' wives.[9] However, Kingsley's farm school scheme and his suggestion of the use of cottage mothers were not unique. It is highly likely that he was influenced by the work of Samuel Gurney, who in 1846 established a farm school on 350 acres at Redhill, Surrey, where Kingsley's future father-in-law, Tom Harry Whitmore, owned a tannery. At the Redhill farm school the children resided in cottages and cottage mothers looked after them. Moreover, the boys were taught farming skills and girls domestic service before being sent to the colonies, including Western Australia.[10] More recently, however, it has been suggested that Kingsley based his 'cottage community' on Barnardo's United Kingdom Girls Village Home in London.[11]

Forty-nine of his fellow Rhodes Scholars attended the meeting and each of them present gave Kingsley five shillings and pledged his support, enabling him to establish the Society for the Furtherance of Child Emigration to the Colonies (later incorporated as the Child Emigration Society).[12] The aim was to educate orphaned and neglected children at farm schools located throughout the British dominions of Canada, New Zealand and Australia. To achieve

---

234.

8 In 1919, the farm school's training age was changed to 14 years. See University of Liverpool Library, Special Collections and Archives: Fairbridge Archives, *Child Emigration Society Oxford Executive Committee minutes September 1912 to June 1920, D296* B1/1/2.

9 *Ibid.*

10 C Neff, 'Youth in Canada West: A Case Study of Red Hill Farm School Emigrants, 1854–1868', *Journal of Family History* 25/4, 432–490 (2000), at p 432.

11 'Memorandum by Barnardo's', CM110.

12 Now referred to as the CES.

this aim, Kingsley believed the most important step in 'preventing pauperism was the permanent removal of children from the contaminating influences of family, friends and neighbours'.[13]

In his autobiography, Kingsley described the expectations and anxieties he experienced in appealing to his peers about his child migration scheme:

> Now there are in England over sixty thousand 'dependent' children — children, orphans or homeless — who are being brought up in institutions, who will be put into small jobs at the age of twelve or fourteen, jobs for which they become too old at eighteen. They have no parents, and no one standing in any such relation to them. What have they before them that can be called a future?
>
> Here and now, I said, let us found a society to take as many as we can of these children overseas, to train them in our own colonies for colonial farm-life. We want 'schools of agriculture' in every part of the Empire where good land is lying empty for lack of men. This will not be charity, it will be imperial investment. There will be no pauper strain attached to our farm-schools; every child will be worth far more than the price of his training to the colony he will eventually help to build.[14]

Kingsley's recollections of the evening reveal in many ways his personality and his enthusiasms:

> Together in a tobacco smoke filled restaurant on High Street in Oxford clinking glasses and laughter were men from all parts of the Empire [...] Gazing around the room, [I saw] the powerful thoughtful

---

13 Fairbridge, *Autobiography*, 131.

14 *Ibid*, 171–178.

> face of an Alberta scholar. The 'iron jaw' of a Prince Edward Island man, the strong, sun-tanned face of a Queenslander, the bull-necked sturdiness of a New Zealander, the ingenious gaze of a South African and the wide open, untroubled eyes of a Newfoundlander. Fate has willed it that the first farm-school has been started in Western Australia. But if God pleases we shall one day take up Sir Edward's offer. My heart has always turned towards that dim island and ancient colony. 'The Way', I thought, 'that is it. I am still to find the Way. But we are on it. We — that is it — fifty of us now [...] My Child Emigration thought has spoken — it is become part of the world.[15]

He noted that these 50 men 'were animated by no common shibboleth, no single interest that would tend to make them all think alike'.[16] Clearly, however, they did have a great deal in common. The majority were beneficiaries of Cecil Rhodes and therefore met the stipulations laid out by the Rhodes trust. Thus, they must have been unmarried and between 18 and 25 years of age, held a 'fondness of success in manly sports' and demonstrated qualities of 'manhood', such as truth, courage, devotion to duty and sympathy for the protection of the weak. Kingsley indicated in his speech that the audience constituted an 'imperial Parliament' representing the Empire.[17] However, as Patrick Dunne has pointed out:

> Kingsley and his peers' intentions may have been well intended. But in reality what did these young men from affluent colonial families know about underprivileged children and childcare?[18]

---

15 *Ibid.*

16 *Ibid*, 178.

17 *Cecil Rhodes' Will*, available online at http://users.cyberone.com.au/myers/rhodes-will.html [cited 30 September 2006].

18 P Dunne, 'Gender, Generations and Social Class: The Fairbridge Society

Essentially, his proposal reveals a scheme to make available for exploitation the lower echelons of the British labouring working class for the benefit of the British empire. Moreover, it seems to have been taken for granted that farm and domestic work was the only choice for pauper children. Significantly, that farm and domestic work was one of only two occupations available; the other was juvenile delinquency.

In 1912, with assistance from the Western Australian state government in the form of a land grant, Kingsley and his wife Ruby née Whitmore established a farm school at Coolup near Pinjarra,[19] to accommodate and train underprivileged British children in farming practice and domestic service. On 21 January 1913, the first group of 13 child migrants,[20] aged between seven and 12, arrived at Fremantle.[21] This first party travelled 'under the charge' of Mrs Wickham, a widow who was employed by the Child Emigration Scheme (CES) to work as a matron at the farm school and brought

---

and British child migration to Canada, 1930–1960' 53–82 in J Lawrence and P Stakey (eds), *Child Welfare and Social Action in the Nineteenth and Twentieth Centuries* (Liverpool, 2001).

19 Pinjarra is 88 kilometres south of Perth, Western Australia. A rural area which consisted of farms, dairy, beef cattle, fishing, oats, orchards, sawmilling and a large aluminium refinery, Pinjarra was one of the first districts settled in Western Australia. The Fairbridge farm school was built 8 kilometres north-east of the town of Pinjarra.

20 There was little organised child migration to Australia before World War I except for the Dreadnought Trust in New South Wales from 1911 and the Fairbridge Society in Western Australia from 1913. However, Fairbridge Farm School was the first government-assisted body of migrants to consist exclusively of minors: 'Lost Innocents: Righting the Record', Senate Committee Affairs References Committee, *Report on Child Migration* (2001) 32. Also see National Archives of Australia (NAA), *Good British Stock: Child and Youth Migration to Australia, 1901–83,* Research Guide No 11, 1999, Chapter 3. Writer Alan Gill argues that young migrants were sent to the colonies of Canada and Australia as early as 1908. However, the precise arrangements and ages of the migrants are disputed: see A Gill, *Orphans of the Empire* (Milsons Point, 1998) 55.

21 'Lost Innocents', 29–31.

her own four sons with her.[22] Most of the boys were nine or ten years old; almost a third had come from Scotland and one from Wales. In May of that year, another party of 22 children was sent to Coolup.[23]

Rules of British Life at the farm school

Within a few weeks of the arrival of the second party of child migrants at Coolup, they had adjusted to their daily routine of work and leisure, and Kingsley felt it was now necessary to introduce a 'Code of the Fairbridge Farm School'. The first part of the code outlined the 'General Ethics, of the Rules of British Life', emphasising the values of thrift, thoroughness, unselfishness and obedience. The second part outlined the rules for daily chores and duties which Kingsley had implemented earlier. The third part of the code was 'Standing Orders', which addressed how the boys' duties were to be performed, for instance washing up the dishes. Lastly, he introduced codes on 'Manners' and 'Speaking'. In terms of manners, Kingsley paid particular attention to table manners. The boys were told to avoid speaking with a full mouth, to sit upright, to eat in moderation, to keep their mouths closed when chewing, to stand to attention during Grace, and to avoid spitting, 'which caused thousands of cases of disease and death'.[24]

The Fairbridges had a loathing not only of English working-class accents but also of the Australian way of speaking. They considered the working class accent 'lazy and uncouth'. The 'Speaking Code', which the boys had to follow, reminded them that 'every word' has a meaning and had to be chosen carefully. The Fairbridges reminded the children that they were English (although some of the boys came from Scotland and Wales) and they were informed that it was 'always best to speak pure English'.[25]

---

22 *The West Australian* (22 Jan 1913).

23 *Ibid.*

24 J S Battye Library of Western Australian, Fairbridge Society Records, *General Ethics, of the Rules of British Life*, 934A/2b, (1913).

25 *Ibid.*

As part of their lessons to speak pure English, they had to master the letter 'h' and the suffix 'ing'. Swearing was to be avoided, particularly 'dirty and unpleasant words' which 'clean people, especially women, disliked'. They also learnt to stand at attention when speaking to the headmaster, so that 'their mind kept on business at hand'. The boys were advised to use a soft and gentle voice when speaking, choosing pleasant and interesting subjects for conversation, avoiding scandal and loose tongues.[26]

Mary Bond[27] remembered the Fairbridges' instructions on duty, conduct, manners and speech:

> They [the children] starched their [the Fairbridges'] tablecloths and they polished the silver. They encouraged the children too. They were trained in manners and courtesies and to live.[28]

The Fairbridges' daughter Barbara revealed that her mother's prejudice against working class accents was so strong that she sent her children to a private school in Cottesloe, an affluent suburb of Perth. Later, she employed a governess to teach her children so that the child migrants would not influence them:

> I was in Cottesloe and then we moved to the new farm school. I think there was a period when I didn't go to school at all. Mother did not like the Australian accent and nor did she much like Cockney

26 Battye, Fairbridge Society Records, *Code of the Fairbridge Farm School*, 934A/9, (1913).

27 Mary Bond, née Cox, the daughter of James Norman Cox (J N Cox) and Mary Agnes, née Fawcett, who were a very wealthy and influential family in the Coolup and Pinjarra districts. She married Alec Bond who worked as a teacher and labourer at the farm in 1913.

28 J S Battye Library of West Australia History, 'Oral History Programme and Fairbridge Farm Scheme 'Transcript of interview with Mary Bond née Cox, OH1877 18 July 1985: Dr C Jeffery and Dr G E Sherington, University of Sydney and Library Board of Western Australian.

> and Scottish accents and Midlands accents that the children spoke with, so she didn't want us to go to primary school, which was on the farm, which the children went to [...] we had a governess. She was determined that her four children were going to have a really good education and tertiary education as well.[29]

The rules of British life and the speaking code that Kingsley had established governed the farm school curriculum until the late 1960s, as this paper will illustrate.

By the end of the war, Kingsley had decided that the property at Coolup was too small and unsuitable for his plans to accommodate the number of children he wanted to migrate. He was then offered 3200 acres of private land on the William Paterson estate, located north-west of Pinjarra on the South Dandalup River. On the new farm school's premises, the buildings were intentionally erected all over the property so that the children would not become dependant on neighbours nor attempt to assimilate with their children. In the middle of the cottages, there was a large square of 40 acres, which was kept in its natural state so the children would become used to making their way in the thick virgin bush after dark, when walking from their cottages to other buildings. Kingsley had designed the cottages to be comfortable but without conveniences so that the children would learn about conditions they might experience when they were sent to work on isolated farms.[30]

Kingsley Fairbridge died in July 1924, but under his successors, the Fairbridge Society prospered. The philosophy of 'rescuing' children had gained support at the highest levels of governments in Britain and Australia and with various humanitarian organisations.[31]

---

29 Battye, Oral History, Transcript of interview with Barbara Rowley, May, June and July, 1985, OH1873.

30 R Fairbridge, *Fairbridge Farm* (Perth, 1948) 142.

31 The Fairbridge Farm School at Pinjarra was the first of the seven Fairbridge Farm Schools to be built in various parts of the dominions.

However, within a week after Kingsley's death, the CES and the local Perth societies began to argue over the administration of the farm school, and specifically the appointment of a headmaster.[32] Despite its previous agreement that the Perth branch would have control over the administration of the farm school, the CES sent a telegram to the Perth committee to inform them that, in view of the large number of Barnardo's children at Pinjarra, it had accepted the offer of Herbert Armitage, one of Dr Barnardo's welfare workers who was returning to Australia for two months, to fill the temporary position of acting headmaster. The Perth committee replied that it wanted the freedom to consider this but would welcome Armitage as a visitor.[33]

Although Armitage's appointment at the farm school was for a short period, he immediately began applying his personal beliefs and views in the school's curriculum, for instance providing the children with protestant religious instruction.[34] As a welfare worker, he also paid particular attention to the farm school's daily operations and its social welfare practices towards the children. When Armitage returned to England, he submitted a report to the CES and made it clear that, while he considered the training of children at the farm school met with his approval, the social welfare of the children and the school's child care practices raised some concern. He noted that children were forbidden to enter their cottages after school in order to keep them clean and tidy. He considered that this practice deprived the children of a normal 'home-life' atmosphere. Armitage was also concerned about the lice in the children's hair and the practice of children not wearing shoes. His main criticism, however, was the large number of Roman Catholics employed at the farm school

It was the only one established and personally managed by Kingsley and the only one still surviving largely intact today.

32 The title of principal was not used at the farm school until 1936.

33 Fairbridge, *Fairbridge Farm*, 120. Also see J S Battye Library of Western Australia, B T Fairbridge, *Fairbridge Family,* ACC526A. (1924), 21.

34 Battye, 'Fairbridge Society Records', H Armitage, *Report Aug–Sept 1924.* 3026A/28, (29 Oct 1924).

who were in a position of authority over the children's daily lives, such as Mary Dennehy, Cedric Giles and some cottage mothers. He recommended that they, as Roman Catholic workers, needed 'overhauling'. While he did not think that the protestant children were being influenced by the Roman Catholic staff to convert, he was anxious about the lack of Christian prayers at meals, and had observed that no scriptures were being read to the children. Armitage's evaluation of the existing child care practices at the farm school brought a strong rebuttal from Mary Dennehy, who refuted all the claims made in the report.[35] Nevertheless, Armitage's report fuelled the existing friction between the CES and Pinjarra, and for the next 18 months they fought over how and when to appoint a new headmaster at the farm school.

By 1930, child migrants were in great demand for their labour and many were sent to remote farms and stations in Western Australia's north-west. With more than 600 Fairbridge boys and girls to visit and report on, the 'after-care' method became impossible for staff to manage. That same year, the Old Fairbridgians Association was formed to deliver 'out care' for boys and girls who had left the farm to undertake employment. The association received a great deal of monetary and other gifts, which shaped the start of the Benevolent Fund. One of the association's first tasks was to build a clubhouse for the boys and girls to use when they returned to the farm for various reasons, such as illness or if they were between jobs. By then the farm school was receiving government subsidies from the Australian, state and British governments. The Australian government and state government contributed three shillings and five shillings per child each week, respectively, and the British government was providing five shillings per week for each child.[36]

In 1935, the improved financial position of the Fairbridge Society ensured that the establishment prospered, and there were

35 Battye, 'Fairbridge Society Records', H Armitage, *Report Aug–Sept 1924* and *M Dennehy letter to A F Stowe*, 3026A/28 (29 Oct 1924).

36 Western Australia Legislative Assembly, Select Committee into Child Migration, *Interim Report* (1996) 29–31.

370 children at Pinjarra. Such was the demand for the children's labour that 1000 employers applied for the 100 children ready to be sent out to work in remote areas of Western Australia. However, the conflict between the CES and Pinjarra's refusal to offer children the opportunity to seek work outside farm labour and domestic service reached crisis point.[37] The CES, as a result, reduced the number of child migrants to be placed in Pinjarra's care; this tension was unresolved until well after the war. Furthermore, in 1944 the London Society approached the British High Commissioner in Australia, Mr W Garnett, to investigate the practices and situation at Pinjarra. Garnett was surprised that despite the fact that nearly 100 girls had been sent to the farm school in Pinjarra, no women had ever sat on the local Perth committee.

By the early 1950s, Pinjarra could see the 'writing on the wall' for the farm school project, because fewer children were available every year. Furthermore, child migration from the United Kingdom had almost come to a standstill, because the British government believed that children from its empire were neglected and abused in Australia's private and state child institutions.[38] Consequently, it was crucial for the Fairbridge Society to find an alternative method to recruit British child migrants to preserve its Fairbridge farm school.

At the same time, the Australian government faced a dilemma. The annual flow of British migrants had slowed down, because the British economy was recovering and Britain was concerned that it was losing its skilful workers to Australia.[39] In late 1958, the Australian government and the Fairbridge Society negotiated an agreement to privately sponsor the migration of large families to Australia under the proposed *Fairbridge Society Family Migration Scheme*,

---

37 NAA, Chapter 3, Part 10, Research Guide – Child and Youth Migration to Australia, Chapter 3: Guide to the records – Fairbridge Farm Schools.

38 'Lost Innocents: Righting the Record', *Senate Committee Affairs References Committee, Report on Child Migration* (2001) 29–31.

39 D Midalia, 'Collections in Perth: A guide to Commonwealth Government Records', *Research Guide National Archives Guide* (2002) 11.

on the condition that the children were placed into the Society's legal custody. Sponsorship for those large families was needed, because they were not acceptable as commonwealth nominees as they had too many children.[40] Traditionally, the Commonwealth Immigration Department's philosophy for the 'ideal family' to settle in Australia was based on a 'British' married couple with two, or no more than three, children.[41]

Consequently, because large families were not considered suitable as commonwealth nominees, the Society sponsored those families to Western Australia. The Society received funds from the federal and state governments, as well as funding from the British government for assuming responsibility for the children, in the form of child maintenance, child support and building grants. These, together with the children's labour power, effectively prevented the closure of the farm school. It was a brilliant business arrangement. Writer Alan Gill[42] summed it up perfectly when he stated:

> The placement of children under Fairbridge guardianship may have been motivated by a desire to swell the numbers and possibly gain building grants rather than by a wish to help the underprivileged.[43]

Ruby Fairbridge, the widow of Kingsley, personally promoted the society's intention to sponsor large families to Australia under its family scheme. Her support was reported in the *West Australian* newspaper. She said:

> The need and purpose for which the Fairbridge

40 B Coldrey, *Good British Stock, Child and Youth Migration to Australia,* (1999) Chapter 3, Part 10.

41 NAA, PP396/1/6; *Bring Out a Briton Scheme* (Perth, 16 May 1957).

42 Alan Gill researched the abuse of children at the Fairbridge farm school, from the 1930s to the late 1960s. His research was later published as a book: A Gill, *Orphans of the Empire* (Milson Point, 1998).

43 *Ibid*, 808.

> farm schools were founded no longer exists. We have to look for child migration in other terms [...] Children are now coming into our farm school that have parents. When the parents are able to afford a home the children can rejoin them.[44]

This begs the question of whether Fairbridge existed for the good of the children, or as a child-migration business. Many people believe the latter.

The Australian Department of Immigration established information branches in the major cities of the United Kingdom to recruit potential migrants to Australia. Australian advertising and migration officers were employed in the Liverpool region of England to persuade some Irish working-class families living there to 'take the chance provided by the assisted passage schemes'.[45] The Australian recruitment propaganda targeted nuclear families made up of skilled tradesmen and promising young children, all vital elements for the rapid socio-economic development and homogeneity of Australia.[46]

However, in 1966, when the farm school was once again in danger of being shut down, Ruby, as a member of the council and executive of the Fairbridge Society, travelled to Perth and gave another interview with *The West Australian* newspaper. She stated that:

> The school was not doing what had been envisaged originally [...] it was originally founded to bring deprived English children from a country where

---

44 'Child Migration Needs Different System', *The West Australian* (8 January 1959) 26.

45 C Price, 'Migration to and From Australia', in *Commonwealth Migration: Flaws and Policies* (1981) 50.

46 See K Paul, *Whitewashing Britain, Race and Citizenship in the Post-War Era* (Ithaca NY, 1997) 50; R T Appleyard, *British Emigration to Australia* (Canberra, 1964) 88 and R T Appleyard, *The Ten Pound Immigrants* (London, 1988) 14.

> they were not wanted to a country where they were [...] it has been difficult to find children to bring out, because they were not allowed to travel without parents. The Scheme brought out families who could not migrate [...] especially big families [...] Taking these very young children away from their parents was not a hardship [...] Really what parents are getting here is a first-class boarding school for nothing.[47]

On the contrary, the reality of the child migrant's experiences for many at the farm school was very different from the rosy picture Ruby Fairbridge painted. For instance, in 2000, the Federal Senate, led by Senator Andrew Murray, a former Fairbridge ward, held an enquiry into the alleged abuse of former child migrants in various institutions including the Fairbridge Society farm school at Pinjarra from the 1920s to 1970.[48] The select committee found that documents had been altered, including birth names, ages and details of family status having been sometimes forged.[49] For example, a former child migrant who arrived in 1935 believed he was born in England. He was told:

> You are an orphan, your parents have died. And you have no family: you may as well go there [to Australia] [there is] nothing left for you here.[50]

To his surprise, he found out that his surname had been changed and he had been born in Dublin. Another child migrant says:

---

47 'Mrs Fairbridge Talks of Farm Changes', *The West Australian* (1 October, 1966) 7.

48 The evidence of the abuse suffered by children at the Fairbridge farm schools is found in 'Lost Innocents'.

49 *Ibid.*

50 G Parsons, *Interview* (10 April 2006).

> Seven years ago, Margaret Humphries found my original birth certificate. Until then I did not know who I was, I had no identity. My place of birth and my name had been changed. They always told me I was born in England. So I was looking for relatives in England but hit a brick wall. I found out through the certificate I was born in Ayrshire, Scotland. I since then found my mother [...] in Scotland.

Many child migrants, like Norm, are angry and frustrated at being denied their cultural heritage. Norm was born in Aberdeen, Scotland, and sent to Fairbridge in 1950 when he was five years old. He spent his remaining childhood years at the farm school. He was also told that he was an English orphan, though, like many others, he found out later through the Child Migrants' Trust that his name, date of birth and country of origin had been deliberately altered. Looking back, Norm describes his anger at being denied his Celtic identity:

> When I left Fairbridge I was not given my birth certificate. I was told that I was English, British if you will, but it never sat right with me. After much mucking about I got my birth certificate and I was not born in England but Scotland. When I discovered this I was furious because I always did have a fascination with Scotland. When I left Fairbridge I read everything I could on the history of Scotland and the Celts. The first thing I bought was a Scottish flag! I am angry; I often got 'six of the best' for my obsession with Scotland and reminded I was an English orphan. Bastards, they couldn't even let a child have their own Celtic identity. Instead invent some English moral which represented and justified their purpose of exporting kids to Australia.[51]

51 Norm (pseudonym), *Interview* (22 March 2006).

Likewise, the children sponsored under the Fairbridge Family Migration Scheme were confused and extremely upset that they were not given the opportunity to maintain their religious traditions and cultural identity. For example, Sophia remembers:

> My family emigrated from Ireland, I was about seven, and I remember when we got there my brother John and my sister Marie-Therese laughing about the principal's accent. John said he sounded like a motor that needed oiled. I had never heard that accent before, even on the boat no-one sounded like him [...] I remember we weren't allowed to wear shoes, only on Sunday when they took us to church. I knew that it wasn't what my Mum would like because we called it Mass. When we said prayers we always blessed ourselves. It didn't matter how many times the cottage mother would tell us off and remind us we were English, we kept doing it. John would whisper to us, 'It's for our Mammy and we are Irish'.[52]

A common factor which emerged in my interviews with the child migrants placed at Pinjarra was that they found it difficult to assimilate into the Australian community. This was due to the numerous issues they faced, such as disorientation, alienation and isolation. Bernadette shares her memories of the farm school, and how her older siblings were discouraged from mixing with 'outsiders'. She also reveals her family's determination to maintain their cultural identity:

> My parents emigrated from Scotland in November 1967, under the Family Migration Scheme. We were a big family. I am one of 17 children [...] Our treatment at Fairbridge was not pleasant [...] On the 11 January 1968 two months after our arrival at the

52 S Morrison, *Interview* (11 May 2002).

> farm school, my younger sister Kathleen, who was only nine years old, was electrocuted and died at Fairbridge whilst drinking from the water tap near the staff's tennis courts. The electrical cables had come in contact with the water, conducting electricity through to the drinking tap […] Our parents took Fairbridge to court for negligence but lost the case. Her death was ruled as an Act of God. Fairbridge paid for a cheap funeral for Kathleen to be buried at Karrakatta. We are Scottish and my parents were determined that Kathleen's Scottishness would be honoured at her funeral. I remember I was always reminded to concentrate on losing my accent and to speak English. It only made me more determined to keep it! I think my older siblings had it harder because us younger ones never left the farm, but they had to attend high school and were told often not to mix with kids outside the farm.[53]

The *West Australian* newspaper reported that, when told of Kathleen's death, her father, George Donaldson, suffered a heart attack and was taken to the Royal Perth Hospital.[54] His eldest daughter, Anne, believes that both her parents

> never recovered from the shock of our Kathleen's death, my mother suffered deep depression and my parents were left with painful regrets of leaving Scotland and us kids going to Fairbridge. With so many kids they could not afford to take us back home to Scotland. Mum died at 51 years old.[55]

---

53 B Donaldson, *Interview* (15 May 2007).

54 'S.E.C. Inquiry On Girl's Electrocution', *The West Australian* (12 January 1968).

55 A Donaldson, *Interview* (22 August 2007).

Similarly, Andrew, who emigrated from Scotland to Western Australia with his four brothers in 1967, describes his painful memories of his friend's death at the Fairbridge farm school. In so doing, he supports Bernadette's testimony that children were given instructions not to mix with 'outsiders'. He also reveals his confusion about the lack of English children at the farm school.

> Shortly after our arrival a young girl was killed, she was electrocuted. We received no counselling. A few weeks later, a friend I had made there was also killed, electrocuted. I remember knocking on the principal's door and yelling 'I think Steven is dead'. The next day I got six of the best for upsetting the younger children. I don't recall any English kids there, I am sure there must have been a few, but I can only recall that there were lots of Irish and Scottish kids. No, I can't say I remember any English kids at Pinjarra. It's rather confusing since we are portrayed as English orphans. I recall we were not allowed to associate with kids outside the farm. I went to Pinjarra High School and we were given horrible vegemite and cheese sandwiches for lunch every day. We caught the Fairbridge bus to school and back. Bringing other kids home was forbidden and we were not allowed to go to their place. We copped a real slagging at school for being the scum of the earth – Fairbridge kids. But it didn't make things easier knowing we couldn't really make friends. People would now compare it to a cult.[56]

In conclusion, this paper has described Kingsley Fairbridge's belief that removing destitute children from Britain and sending them to the colonies to train as farm hands and domestic servants would be a form of child rescue. It has revealed that Kingsley's

56 A Fyfe, *Interview* (21 May 2007).

Kathleen Donaldson, aged 9: photograph taken in Glasgow, Scotland, September 1967. Courtesy of Donaldson family.

account of the importance of following his 'Rules of British Life' displayed a distinct class attitude with regard to the future 'English' characteristics and lives of the child migrants. Indeed, while encouraging an English morality among the children, he opposed any attempts by the children to assimilate into the Australian community. This policy and practice of segregation remained on the farm school agenda for over 50 years following his death. Most importantly, the former child migrants have provided us with an account of what life must have been like at the farm school. They have told us that despite the Fairbridge farm school's tradition of upholding Kingsley's codes of conduct they have maintained their Celtic identity. Certainly, as my paper has indicated, there is an enormous scope for future research which engages theoretical debates concerned with Irish and Scottish child migrants who were sent to Australia during the twentieth century.

The Irish language in Australia: survey of a community language

Dymphna Lonergan ⊕

The history of the Irish language in Australia begins in 1788 with the First Fleet, and it has had an unbroken tradition in the country for the past 215 years. Although we may not have primary evidence for it, we can safely speculate that the First Fleet carried convicts and soldiers who had some level of Irish. The first written account we have of the language coming to the country is from 1800, in a diary kept by the wife of the captain aboard the *Friendship*, who recorded that there were at least 30 monoglot Irish rebels on board the ship, rounded up as part of the crack-down after the 1798 rebellion.[1] In a later trial at Toongabbie, New South Wales, Irish-speaking prisoners were reported as speaking the language for the sole purpose of plotting rebellion in the penal colony. Among those was Paddy Galvin from Kerry, whose strange and poetic words were recorded and have been commented on since: 'You can hang me if you like, but you will not get my music from me so'.[2]

Our next written records relate to the Catholic ministry in Australia and the need to send for Irish-speaking priests in order to hear confession.[3] The language moved into the surrounding bush, and we have scattered references to Irish-Aboriginal language contact, including the Mitchell expedition in 1839, that met a group

---

⊕ Flinders University.

1 *Canberra Sunday Times*, 23 January 2000, p 19; D Lonergan, *Sounds Irish: The History of the Irish Language in Australia* (Adelaide, 2004) 6.

2 J Holt, *Life of General Joseph Holt* (Sydney: Mitchell Library CY 17.A2024, 1827); Lonergan, *Sounds Irish*, 7.

3 C Costello, *Botany Bay* (Cork, 1987) 87; Lonergan, *Sounds Irish*, 6.

of Irish-speaking indigenous people.[4] Other primary references include notes in official records of the inability to speak English and first- and second-hand family anecdotes of Irish-speakers.[5] One would imagine that all of this would be enough to promote research into the history of this Celtic language in Australia, but there has been surprisingly little, given the legacy left by Irish-speaking convicts and settlers.

The legacy of the Irish language in Australia has been one of significant influence on Australian English language and literature and on Catholic community life. Iconic Australian words such as *didgeridoo, sheila*, and *brumby* are of Irish origin.[6] The latest *Macquarie* (2004) dictionary includes the Irish connection with the word *brumby*. The language has influenced Australian slang in phrases such as 'crack-on', and 'humping the bluey', and can be seen in some regional markers (the use of 'youse' as a plural for *you* and the use of 'but' at the end of a sentence have their origin in the Irish language).[7] Sometimes Irish words in Australia change their meaning over time, such as the word *spalpeen*, recorded in Tasmania as meaning a mischievous child, whereas traditionally it has been a pejorative word for an adult.[8] The Irish language is becoming a useful alternative for the Australian writer who wishes to use an Irish marker to depict a major Irish character.[9] The language appears occasionally now in Hollywood movies,[10] and Australian movies may, in time, follow suit. Sean Byrne, a Sydney

---

4 D W A Baker, 'John Piper, Conquerer of the Interior', *Aboriginal History* 1.17 (1993) 21; Lonergan, *Sounds Irish*, 9.

5 Destitute asylum records (Adelaide) and various family histories and personal letters.

6 Lonergan, *Sounds Irish*, 14–33.

7 D Bradley, 'Mixed Sources of Australian English', *Australian Journal of Linguistics*, Vol 23, No 2 (2003) 143–150.

8 Australian Broadcasting Corporation (2005), http://www.abc.net.au/wordmap/. Available June 9, 2010.

9 Lonergan, *Sounds Irish*, 45.

10 For example, Martin Scorcese's 2002 movie, *The Gangs of New York*.

PhD film student, showed his short film, *An Dúslán* at the Irish language winter school in Sydney in June 2007. The film's subject is the famous Australian boxer, Les Darcy, who in the film is depicted as an Irish-speaker, not as a point of fact, but as a stylistic device to make a point of difference.

The Irish language in Australia occupies both ends of the language continuum: as a primary language for many eighteenth- and nineteenth-century inhabitants, and as a linguistic marker in the Arts that significantly transcends the stereotype. Irish is also at play in the middle spaces of the language continuum as a community language.

Irish as a community language

The recorded history of Catholic community life in Australia as depicted in newspapers, in particular, shows the language as playing a distinctive role as a link to the past and as a cultural and community enhancer.[11] Through cultural, historical, linguistic and community items occurring in Catholic newspapers, interest in the Irish language in Australia has kept pace with Ireland's troubled history up to the middle of the twentieth century. The Catholic church in Australia moved away from Irish matters in the mid-1940s,[12] a time when Ireland's struggle for independence was fulfilled to a great extent in the declaration of the Republic in 1948. The resurgence of conflict in Ireland in the 1970s and 1980s led to prominence for the language once again, this time through Irish-Australian lay community newsletters,[13] and in a resurgence of language classes in local halls and community centres.

Technology today affords even greater access to the Irish language through internet support for learners. Cheap air travel allows the influx of Irish-speaking backpackers who are welcomed in a local Irish language group for their language expertise and

---

11 D Lonergan, *The Irish Language in Australia* (unpublished PhD thesis, Flinders University Adelaide, 2002) 33–85.

12 *Ibid.*

13 *Ibid.*

especially for their use of current Irish. Irish migrants to Australia today, who have gained a passive competence in the language through school, can reactivate that skill by interacting with other speakers, both here and at home through technology. The development of language schools in Australia over the past 20 years has demonstrated resurgence in the language for its linguistic, cultural, communal, and personal value. This new phase in the language's history in Australia is significant, and is the focus of the rest of this paper.

Scoil Gheimhridh Sydney 2007 language survey

While Irish language learning activities have been part of Australian culture for hundreds of years, the language movement manifested in the annual *daonscoileanna* is only around 15 years old, and for the past ten years has developed a distinctively strong, national focus. The annual *daonscoileanna* in Sydney during the winter, and in Bacchus Marsh, Victoria, during the summer, have grown in numbers, attracting, as they do, not only members of Irish language classes in the various organisations around the country, but also people who are not necessarily involved in class learning. Some of these are native speakers who take the opportunity to engage or re-engage with their native language in the setting of a *daonscoil*. The fifth *Scoil Gheimhridh* was held in Sydney in 2007, and 100 participants from Sydney, Melbourne, Brisbane, Adelaide and Canberra filled the Chevalier Centre in Kensington, Sydney, and surrounding motels. Classes ranged from the *bun rang*, beginners, to *an ard rang*, the highest level. Of note that year, too, was the inclusion of Scottish Gaelic learners in the weekend activities. The large attendance at the Old Irish class delivered by Scottish Gaelic teacher and Old Irish scholar Dr Pamela O'Neill points to a fruitful future for a shared approach to the study of these two language cultures. For the first time, too, the Irish ambassador to Australia came from Canberra to open the proceedings.. This fluent Irish-speaker also took part in the activities for some of the weekend.

Survey background

In 2006, Michael Newton of the University of Richmond published

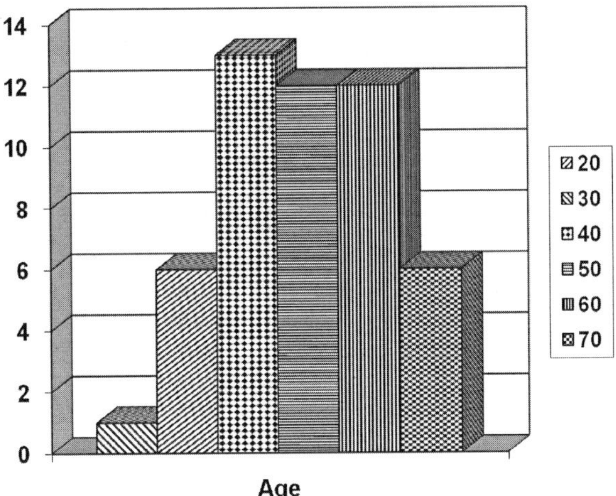

Figure 1: *Sydney survey 2007 participants' age*

an essay in the *e-Keltoi* journal on his survey of Scottish Gaelic learners in North America and Canada.[14] Using the same survey form, and substituting 'Irish' for 'Gaelic', I conducted a similar survey of Irish language learners in June 2007 at the Sydney *Scoil Gheimhridh*. A comparison of the US survey results and my own shows similarities and differences that point to opportunities for further research, especially into the personal benefits to an educated aging group in Australia of learning a Celtic language.

A Profile of Irish language learners

While there are some differences in the survey methods used and the number of respondents,[15] both Newton's and my own survey results show that the average learner of a Celtic language is middle-aged,

14 M Newton, 'This Could Have Been Mine: Scottish Gaelic Learners in North America', *e-Keltoi: Journal of Interdisciplinary Celtic Studies*, July 2006, http://www.uwm.edu/Dept/celtic/ekeltoi/volumes/vol1/index.html [accessed 9 March 2007].

15 Newton distributed his questionnaire over a number of years from 2002 via the internet and also at a couple of events using hard copies. His survey results are of 65 respondents while mine are of 47.

close to or past retirement age, is tertiary-educated, has learnt one or two languages previously, and has made a long-term commitment to the study of the language. Fewer learners are motivated by ancestral connection with the language than might have been anticipated, and neither is religious affiliation an indicator of interest in learning a Celtic language. The first point of comparison between Newton's and my study is age.

Newton's survey shows an average age of 45, with those in their 50s being the greatest number of respondents. Those in their 60s and over represent less than five per cent. My 2007 survey shows almost equal distribution of majority responses between the 40s, 50s, and 60s age groups and significantly more in the 70s and older.

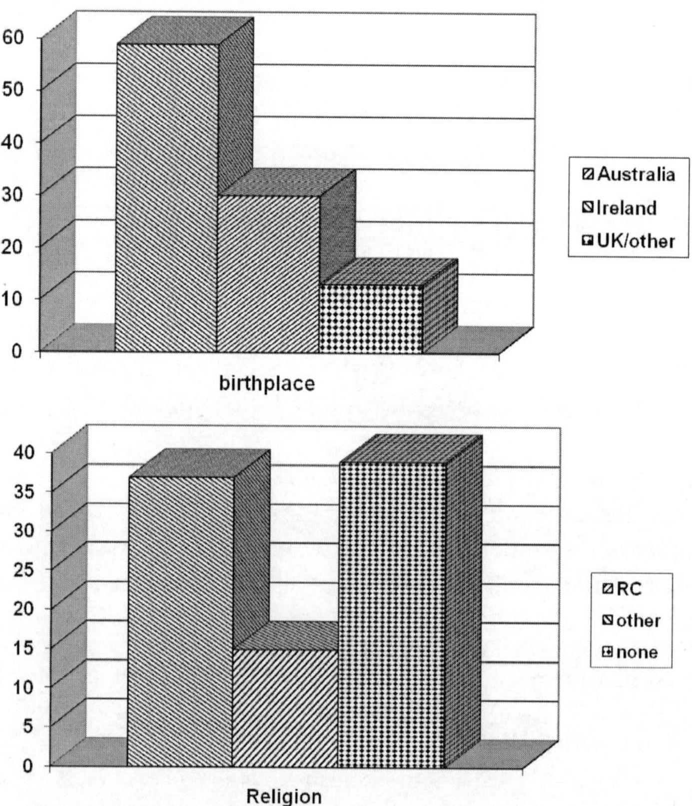

Figure 2: *Sydney survey 2007 birthplace and religion*

We can expect that fewer young people (under 20s) attend the *daonscoileanna*. Some of the young people who attended the Sydney weekend *daonscoil* were children of participants. It is not certain, however, whether those who filled in the survey also had parents who knew or were studying Irish.

Newton found that Scottish heritage in America is usually linked with the Presbyterian church, but that this is not the case with those studying Gaelic. By far the majority of Newton's respondents claimed not to have any religious affiliation, and there was a scattered representation of smaller religions such as Quakers, Buddhists, Mormons and so on. The Sydney 2007 survey result shows an almost equal number claiming to have no religion as those who claimed to be Roman Catholic (the majority). Around 15% of the Irish language respondents claimed smaller religious group affiliation. In both surveys, most respondents claimed that religious affiliation was not relevant to Irish-Australian or Scottish-American identity.

Irish and Gaelic learning: motivation and goals

Four questions on the survey form were designed to obtain information about the motivation that drives those who choose to learn a Celtic language as adults. Question 8 asked respondents to rank, in order of importance, a range of motivating factors. The comparative table below show many similarities and some significant differences.

Motivation in order of importance	
Scottish Gaelic	**Irish**
I would be keeping Gaelic alive	Irish is a rich language
I would be able to speak to native speakers in their own language	I would be able to read Irish literature
Gaelic is a rich language	I would be keeping Irish alive
I would be able to read Gaelic literature	Language broadens one's knowledge

Language broadens one's knowledge	I would be able to speak to native speakers in their own language
Gaelic music	Gaelic music
Some of my ancestors spoke Gaelic	You can't understand Ireland without Irish
You can't understand the Highlands without Gaelic	Some of my ancestors spoke Irish

The idea of keeping the language alive ranked highest for the American and Canadian respondents, but was third on the list in the Australian response. This difference may be accounted for by government support in Ireland for the language in education and politics. Almost half of the Sydney respondents were born and schooled in Ireland and their knowledge of the Irish language began in primary school there.[16] For them, the language may be perceived as stable because it plays a crucial role in the education curriculum. One Irish-born respondent claimed to be 'proud that [Irish] is not a dying language any more'. Another key difference in the comparative motivation table is how learners of Scottish Gaelic appear to be more optimistic than their Australian-based counterparts that one day they may be able to speak comfortably in Irish with a native speaker. The Australian survey respondents filled in their survey forms on site and were surrounded by native and fluent speakers (the *ard rang* at the Sydney *daonscoil* is the largest class), while the Americans and Canadians were answering the survey questions presumably alone at home. As a result, the Australian respondents may have been more aware of the gap between their own language ability and the native speakers who surrounded them.

Survey 2007 participants' oral tradition preferences

Question 23 in the survey asked to what extent respondents were 'engaged in tradition'. Respondents nominated up to two aspects of oral tradition that interested them. These results may be of use to

16 The Irish language is taught in Irish primary schools from the beginning of schooling.

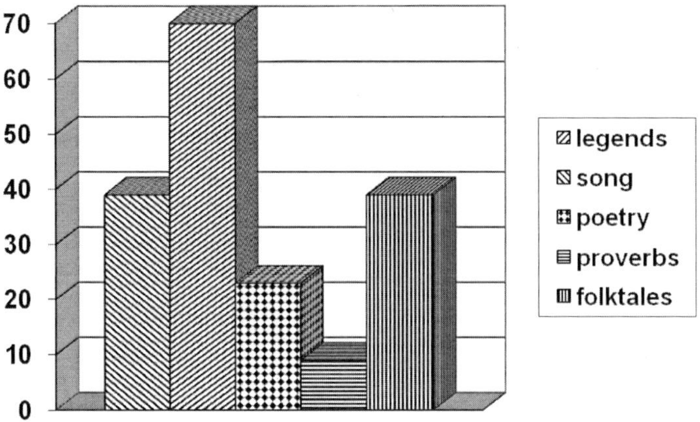

Figure 3: *interests*

language teachers in particular.

Many come to learn Celtic languages by way of music, so it is not surprising to see a majority of respondents offering 'song' as a favourite way of engaging with Irish oral tradition. A high response nominating legend and folktales may be surprising in a survey on language, as it is likely that most respondents would know Irish and Scottish folktale and legend in English only. It may be that for the Irish-born respondents, in particular, the intriguing and romantic folktales and legends of Ireland were met with for the first time in their formative years, and so remained potent throughout their lives. Australian-born respondents of Irish parentage may also have been introduced to Ireland through English-language folktales and legends.

Survey 2007 participants' education and other language learning

Both the Newton and my own survey results reveal that a high number of Irish and Gaelic students in Australia, America and Canada are tertiary-educated and have experience in learning another language or two. Many of the Australian respondents were retired teachers.

A high percentage of respondents in both surveys had learned

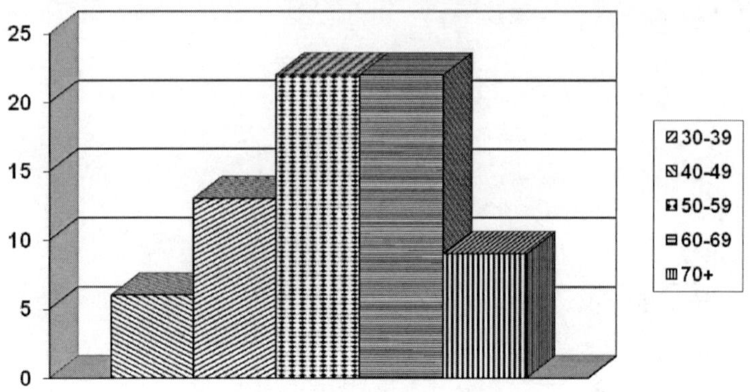

Figure 4: *tertiary education*

a second language previously, and almost half had learned more than one other language. As Michael Newton stated, 'Learning a language can be a serious challenge to an adult, and it should be no surprise that most active learners are well educated and multilingual'. When the Australian respondents put 'Irish is a rich language' as their top motivating factor, they may have had in mind the linguistic challenge involved in engaging with a non-Romance or -Germanic language that has a complicated spelling system.

Survey 2007 ethnic and group identity

Irish-Australian identity is a little over 200 years old. Engagement with the Irish language is one of a number of ways for Australians with Irish ancestry to engage with their own heritage. While it may be difficult to prove, there is some statistical chance that Australians with a west-of-Ireland background had an ancestor who was an Irish-speaker.[17] The comparative table on motivation, however, shows that Irish-speaking ancestry was the least motivating factor in the Australian study. While we could expect that Irish-born people might feel a greater Irish identity in Australia, not all identified solely as 'Irish' in the survey. The Irish-born respondent

17 G FitzGerald, 'Estimates for Baronies of Minimum Level of Irish-Speaking amongst Successive Decennial Cohorts', *Proceedings of the Royal Irish Academy* 84 C (1984) 117–155.

who was proud that Irish was not a dying language any more offered 'Australian/Irish/European' as their 'specific identity or identities'. Another offered 'Australian' first — 'I've spent most of my life here' — and then 'Irish'. Yet another chose to answer this question in Irish: '*rud meascán é*' (it is a mixed thing). A rather sanguine view was held by another: 'Irish and Australian — but I wouldn't fight for either'. Below is a table of personal comments made by respondents in response to the questions on ethnic identity and a sense of belonging.

Ethnic identity and belonging

Part of a community	Specific identity
A small part of the diaspora	Australian of Irish descent (2)
Extended family	Irish and Australian
Good friends in the Irish language community/Circle of friends	Irish-Australian
Friends with wide background of life experiences and with Irish as mutual interest/Family of learners supportive of each other	Australian, Irish, European
Member of the Irish, Irish-Australian community and like-minded people	Born there (in Ireland)
Comfortable/mutual respect/ help one another/Belonging and recognition and acceptance of my ancestors' history	I feel Australian
Irish community/Part of a community that shares a similar passion and one that shares much of the same ancestry	Australian – I've spent most of my life here – Irish (3)
As an Australian I felt disconnected from my roots before/Group is community; feeling of belonging	My ethnic identity is Irish
I grew up ethnic Irish: I feel that learning Irish validates my feeling of relationship to Ireland/Canberra	Rud meascán é (it's a mixed thing)
Cairde na hEireann (2)	Feel more Irish than before
	Being a (family name given) and linked to both Ireland and Australia
	Identify closely with my Irish heritage
	I identify more with Irish, although I also have Lebanese ancestry
	Welsh
	Irish,Welsh,Australian
	Irish, Scottish, Welsh
	Australian, Irish
	Irish, more so now than when I grew up (in Australia)
	I'm a mix
	Australian (mixed Irish English)
	My husband and great-grandmother were Irish

Great friends with common interests Part of a very interested group/ Keeping the language alive Something in common/Friends Language learning movement/Big family away from home/Interest and learning Small beginnings of greater/ Dynamic Loosely knit	My husband and great-grandmother were Irish Irish heritage – connection with Irish people Irish colonial Frankish, Austrian Irish Scottish Australian, Irish, English Celtic Australian Irish, Scots, Chinese

Hobbies, leisure pursuits and community involvement often provide a salutary sense of belonging, so it is not surprising that respondents felt part of a learning community that was supportive. The question on ethnic identity produced unexpected results: only three of the 14 respondents who were Irish-born named 'Irish' as their ethnic identity. Three circled 'N' for none and one did not respond to that question. Two referred to an identity that was mixed, and others included Australian. The word 'ethnic' may have been misleading, if respondents who circled 'N' interpreted the word as meaning of non-English speaking background. Another question asked whether the respondent's sense of identity had changed since taking up the Irish language. In this case, 12 of the Irish-born said 'no', while the remaining two said that their identity had become more positive. Of the Australian-, UK- and European-born respondents, 15 said that their sense of Irish identity had deepened, but for 18 there was no change. One respondent commented that they had realised they were not really 'Irish'.

Personal comments

Newton's Gaelic survey yielded 'articulate and insightful' comments about the learning experience of the respondents. The respondents to the Irish survey also included personal comments. Some inserted Irish words or used whole Irish phrases in their responses, and some even printed answers using the Gaelic script they had learnt in school. Great feeling was often expressed in answering the final question: How long more do you think you will be involved with the Irish language? This question was sometimes answered in Irish in phrases that mean a long time, such as *go bráth*; *go deo*; *i gcónaí*. All but three respondents indicated a commitment to the end of their life or as long as they retained the mental and physical capacity. This may reflect the age of the respondents, but is probably more reflective of the commitment to the language and the ongoing satisfaction with the rewards for that commitment. Certainly, if the linguistic value of the language is a primary motivator for the average learner of the Irish language in Australia, then the more that is studied the greater the yield, not least the prospect of moving up through the ranks of speakers to the *ard rang*. The *ard rang* at the Sydney *daonscoil* was the largest class, with around 20 participants.

The history of the Irish language in Australia has been one of great significance in that the language has influenced Australian expression, culture, and community life. More than that, however, the study of the language brings personal rewards to those who engage with it, not only in the salutary effects of the mental stimulation involved in struggling with grammar and a challenging spelling system, but in the community support afforded by the local classes and annual *daonscoileanna*. There are new friends to make, maybe even a *cara cléibh*, a friend of the heart, and a sense of belonging. For those who learned the language as a child in Ireland, there is the added reward of revisiting the *rann*, rhyme and song, learned through Irish, that still lives in 'the deep heart's core'.

'A class equal to any for making prosperous colonists ...': Ulster Protestant migrants in the Antipodes

Brad Patterson ⊕

For Sydneysiders, and citizens of New South Wales, Jindabyne is probably best known as a year-round holiday resort. It is a modern place in appearance, the original town having been drowned as a result of the Snowy Mountains Scheme. For international audiences it brings to mind the somewhat haunting film of the same name released in 2006.

But old Jindabyne has another claim to fame. Over a century ago it was celebrated by *Bulletin* poet Victor Daley as the site of a famous clash, recorded in the mock epic 'The Glorious Twelfth at Jindabyne'. This poem has everything: violence, romance, bravery — and, with echoes of more recent developments in Northern Ireland, ultimately reconciliation.

A selection from the 32 verses that appeared in Bulletin on 9 July 1898[1] will demonstrate the range:

> Came a horseman to O'Brien's, and his voice was stern and high;
> "Mick, the Orangemen are mustherin' by scores at Jindabye,
> And, unless the boys are gathered quick, 'twill be a woeful sight,
> For there'll be a big procession and there won't be any fight."
>
> Mick O'Brien heard the summons as he stood beside his gate.
> He was six-foot-two in stockings, sixteen stone his fighting-weight.

⊕ Director, Irish-Scottish Studies Programme, Victoria University of Wellington.

1 I am grateful to Dr Frank Molloy, Charles Sturt University, for providing a photocopy.

"Pat O'Connor," he said softly, "take a drink before you go,
And thin ride and rouse the Callaghans — we'll all be at the show."

O'Brien's mates then proceed to raise the neighbourhood, or at least the Catholic part of it, but the hardest to raise, are some of his own family.

He called unto his stalwart sons: "Get up! Get up!" cried he.
"Now, I wonder," said Cornelius, "what the old man's game can be?"
But the old man's voice in thunder rose, "Remimber, boys, Athlone!
And remimber Boyne and Aughrim,
and the Broken Threaty Shtone!"

Then Cornelius said to Denis, "What in thunder does he mean?
We have heard of Boyne and Aughrim; we have heard of Skibbereen;
And we knew that dear old Ireland of the ocean is the gem —
But why, why, should we go breaking heads because of it or them?"

Maybe one reason for their reluctance is that their sister is going out on the sly with a Protestant lad, one of the Leamans. Mrs O'Brien, however, soon puts them right:

"Holy Pathrick, are ye traitors? Rise up quickly Con and Din!
We were only lowly wimmin, but we had the hearts of min;
In ould Ireland, whin the Twelfth came round,
oh faix, 'twas our delight,
For to bandage up the wounded whin they tottered home at night."

Finally the posse is assembled.

At the township's end they saw a sight right madd'ning to behold,
All the Orangemen in trappings fine of purple and of gold:
There were Lyonses and Leamans there, and Nugents and McCalls,
And they marched along so boldly to the tune of "Derry Walls".

All might yet have passed peacefully, we are told, had it not been for Doolan's educated cockatoo, which perched on the roof of the pub screeching 'To Hell with King Billy'. It was all on when there was a rush by the Orangemen to despatch the offending bird. The battle then raged for quite some time, and might have continued for longer, but for a realisation of the thirst-inducing effects of fighting.

Big McCormack looked at Hamilton, and whispered with a wink,
"If you've had enough of bloodshed, Bill, we'll go and have a drink."
When the fight was o'er the battlefield a man might proudly scan
Who was Irish — whether Papist fierce or furious Orangeman.

O the night they had at Doolans! — sure its like was never seen
For the Lyonses and Leamans roared 'The Wearin' of the Green',
And the Finns, and Quinns, and Fagans,
sang 'Boyne Water' without check,
And they called each other "brother", and fell on each others' neck.

Now the moral of this yarn is — if to Jindabye you go,
Never aggravate a Lyons, or you'll make a Quinn a foe!
Never strike at an O'Brien in your very angriest spasm,
Or a Leaman will reduce you to organic protoplasm!

There are bonds of blood and marriage now
these ancient foes between,
And the Orange is inextricably mingled with the Green:
And that this broad, kindly feeling should increase in coming time
Is the wish for Green and Orange of the writer of this rhyme.

Beyond its entertainment value, this piece of verse embodies several messages. Victor Daley, Armagh-born in 1858 of a mixed marriage, clearly looked to the day when quarrels from the old country were put behind.[2] He suggests such a day is at hand: there is the reluctance of the O'Brien boys to fight; their sister's cross-religion liaison. The street scrap, though symbolic, is more redolent

2 F Molloy, *Victor J Daley: A Life* (Sydney, 2004).

of local football rivalry, including the after-match function. Daley also makes clear that in 1898, at least in his Jindabyne, there was no question but that the Protestants were part of the Irish family.

If Daley had lived longer (he died in 1905) he would have been disappointed. His vision of Antipodean Irish communities in which the constituent parts maintained their sectional traditions but shared a common Irish identity quickly faded, with the sectarian divide becoming even more entrenched in the early twentieth century. In the process, Irish and Catholic came to be regarded as synonymous, with the Protestants disappearing virtually without trace and largely fading from public consciousness. So much so that they have come to be described variously by recent researchers as 'the hidden Irish', 'the invisible Irish' and 'the forgotten Irish'.

Patrick O'Farrell and Donald Akenson were among the first modern historians to note the historiographical void,[3] and a quick survey of writings on the Irish in Australia and New Zealand bears this out. For example, contributing to *Australia and Ireland: Bicentenary Essays* in 1988, Geoffrey Bolton offers a survey of 'The Irish in Australian Historiography' with no mention of the Ulster Protestants whatsoever.[4] Three years later, in 1991, in an essay entitled 'Writing about Irish in Australia', Bob Reece is only a little more forthcoming about the Ulster Protestants, but he nevertheless makes several perceptive comments: "One of the problems with the great burst of interest in the Ireland-Australia connection in recent years," he suggests, "is its celebratory and somewhat indiscriminate nature."[5]

In many instances writing about the Irish in Australia has been 'an act of filial piety or nationalist and religious affirmation

3 P O'Farrell, *The Irish in Australia: 1788 to the present*, 3rd ed (Sydney, 2000) 93–4; D H Akenson, *Half the World From Home: Perspectives on the Irish in New Zealand 1860–1950* (Wellington, 1990) 198–9.

4 G Bolton, 'The Irish in Australian Historiography', 4–19 in Colm Kiernan (ed), *Australia and Ireland: Bicentenary Essays* (Dublin, 1986).

5 B Reece, 'Writing about the Irish in Australia', in J O'Brien and P Travers (eds), *Irish Emigrant Experience in Australia* (Swords, 1991) 226.

on the part of Irish-born Australians'.[6] In no way should this be construed as an attack on Professors Bolton or Reece, who, in their historiographical reviews, simply reflect what have been scholarly trends. A recent unpublished paper by Elizabeth Malcolm suggests the Ulster Protestants are missing even from major reference works.[7] She cites two recent publications.

First is James Jupp's monumental volume on Australia's immigrant communities, *The Australian People*, published in 1988 and reissued in 2001.[8] Over 124 immigrant groups are covered in the near 1000 pages. The entry on the Irish is substantial, running to 43 large format pages, and incorporates sub-sections by 13 separate authors. Most of the authors follow the convention that 'Irish' is synonymous with Catholic, although there is a subsection on the Anglo-Irish, termed by the author 'the privileged Irish minority', the few thousand whose migration to Australia had all but ceased by the late nineteenth century. The short section on 'Protestant Irish Settlement' opens with: 'the history of the Protestant Irish is still a much neglected area of research'.[9] As much concerned with the Anglo-Irish as Ulster Protestants, it suggests the term Ulster-Protestant is hard to define; 'it covers not only a variety of theological beliefs, but a cross-section of social classes and political views as well'. The author concedes that they are generally viewed in terms of stereotypes. Summarising, Malcolm notes: 'Jupp's huge volume … is, at least in terms of its entry on the Irish, riddled with old-fashioned and inaccurate assumptions, not to say prejudices and politically inspired value judgements'.[10] Malcolm then turns to

---

6 *Ibid.*

7 E Malcolm, 'Searching for a Forgotten People: The Ulster Scots in Australia', unpublished paper. I am grateful to Professor Malcolm for making this available.

8 J Jupp, *The Australian People: An Encyclopaedia of the Nation, its People and their Origins* (Cambridge, 2001).

9 T McClaughlin, in Jupp, *The Australian People,* 463.

10 Malcolm, 'Searching for a Forgotten People', 4.

the much praised *Oxford Companion to Australian History.*[11] First published in 1998, the article on the 'Irish in Australia' at no point discusses the composition of the Australian Irish in religious or ethnic terms. Protestants are not mentioned, nor indeed are the Anglo-Irish.[12] The impression, once more, is that all Irish migrants to Australia were Catholic. In the light of such silences, it should be no surprise that general historians tend to be equally silent.

Twenty years ago, a similar report for New Zealand would have been wholly appropriate. In fact, it is difficult to speak of a historiography of the New Zealand Irish at all before 1990. Attracted to New Zealand by the discovery that available raw data promised unique insights, Canadian historian Donald Harman Akenson found that there was little in the way of supporting historical literature documenting the New Zealand Irish experience. The sum total as best he could establish, as he records in the preface to his ground-breaking *Half the World from Home: Perspectives on the Irish in New Zealand, 1860–1950*, was 'one significant monograph' and 'a few fugitive articles'.[13] To be fair, there was more than that, but not a significant amount.

Ironically, the one Irish settlement to have attracted any scholarly attention, Katikati, was an Ulster Protestant settlement.[14] Yet there is no reference to Katikati, to the Irish at all, in Keith Sinclair's classic *Penguin History of New Zealand*, published 1959, and W H Oliver's *Story of New Zealand*, published a year later, merely records that there were Irish Catholic miners in the 1860s gold rushes.[15] The index to the first edition of the *Oxford History of*

---

11 G Davison et al, *The Oxford Companion to Australian History* (Melbourne, 1998).

12 E Richards, 'Irish in Australia', in Davison et al, 350–1.

13 Akenson, *Half the World from Home,* 38.

14 B Patterson, 'New Zealand's "Ulster Plantation": Katikati Revisited', in B Patterson (ed), *Ulster-New Zealand Migration and Cultural Transfers* (Dublin, 2006) 85–102.

15 K Sinclair, *A History of New Zealand* (Harmondsworth, 1959); W H Oliver, *The Story of New Zealand* (London, 1960).

New Zealand, edited by Oliver and Bridget Williams and appearing in 1981, contains a few isolated references and there is little more in the revised 1992 edition.[16]

Akenson's 1990 monograph should therefore be recognised as a benchmark. He outlined what he believed to be the important issues in studying New Zealand Irish history. He also presented an agenda for future research, and amongst his strongest enjoinders was that it should always be remembered that the Irish were both Catholic and Protestant.[17] In many respects Akenson's challenges have been taken up, a number of important monographs emerging over the past 17 years, while in the universities research students have exhibited increasing interest in the New Zealand Irish. A collection of essays published in 2002, *The Irish in New Zealand: Historical Contexts & Perspectives*,[18] was conceived as a stock-take on the extent of progress. The 12 essays published demonstrate diverse interests, ranging from demography and migrant letters to politics and religious leadership. Significantly, two of the essays, Alasdair Galbraith on the Pukekohe settlement and Vincent O'Sullivan on writer John Mulgan's experiences in Ulster, are primarily concerned with Ulster topics.

There are hopeful signs the new research is starting to percolate into general works. In many respects James Belich's 1996 general history, *Making Peoples*,[19] was the first to write with any sophistication of the contributions of Irish migrants, of several persuasions, to New Zealand life and identity. It is nevertheless puzzling that Michael King, author of the latest *Penguin History of*

---

16 W H Oliver and B Williams (eds), *The Oxford History of New Zealand* (Oxford and Wellington, 1981); G W Rice (ed), *The Oxford History of New Zealand*, 2nd edn (Auckland, 1992).

17 Akenson, *Half the World from Home*, 193–203.

18 B Patterson (ed), *The Irish in New Zealand: Historical Contexts & Perspectives* (Wellington, 2002).

19 J Belich, *Making Peoples: A History of the New Zealanders* (London and Auckland, 1996) 315–21.

New Zealand,[20] maintains the reticence of his predecessor. While New Zealand has, as yet, no equivalent to Jupp, a volume produced last year by the Ministry of Culture and Heritage is by far the most comprehensive book on New Zealand's migrant communities yet produced. *Settler and Migrant Peoples of New Zealand*[21] is a spin-off from *Te Ara*, the online encyclopaedia of New Zealand. The section on the New Zealand Irish totals 14 pages, with Ulster Protestants fully integrated into the discussion. A more extended study from the same source of settlers from the United Kingdom and Ireland is currently in press.[22]

In sum, while Australian and New Zealand historians paralleled each other in their lack of interest in the Ulster Protestants to at least the 1980s, there have been recent flickerings of curiosity on both sides of the Tasman, but systematic research is probably further advanced in New Zealand.

So why were the Ulster Protestants lost from sight, why did they become a forgotten people? It is arguable that with the steady drift towards an independent Irish state in the late decades of the nineteenth century and the first two of the twentieth century, both in Ireland and in the Antipodean Diaspora, the existing divisions between constituent elements widened and deepened alarmingly.[23] Linked to this, the latent sectarianism the settlers had brought with them was enflamed, even stoked up. Obvious manifestations were rather unpleasant organisations such as the Australian Protestant Defence Association, or the Protestant Political Association in New Zealand, but it would be fatuous to deny that there were willing incendiarists on both sides of the religious divide. A case might be made that the 1921 partition of Ireland came to overshadow understandings of all things Irish, on both sides. It arguably created

20 M King, *The Penguin History of New Zealand* (Auckland, 2003).

21 Ministry of Culture and Heritage, *Settler and Migrant Peoples of New Zealand* (Auckland and Wellington, 2006).

22 J Phillips and T Hearn, *Settlers, New Zealand Immigrants from England, Ireland and Scotland, 1800–1945* (Auckland) 93.

23 O'Farrell, *Irish in Australia*, 93.

mind sets that had not previously existed.

Can it be assumed, then, that the failure by twentieth-century historians in this part of the world to identify Ulster Protestants as part of the wider Irish immigrant community is an outcome of deep convictions that they cannot be truly regarded as Irish? Several writers have suggested that when the 'Irish' and 'Ireland' were spoken of by nineteenth-century and later commentators, it was implicitly understood that the Protestant Irish were not included.[24] I am not convinced that this was wholly so, or not everywhere, and I am quite certain this was not the case in New Zealand. It is possible, however, that reluctance to accept the Ulster Protestants and their descendants as Irish intensified in some quarters in the twentieth century, and has been retained with feeling until very recently.

A telling demonstration was the mid-1980s reaction to Patrick O'Farrell's *Letters from Irish Australia 1825–1929*, published in 1984.[25] O'Farrell's credentials as an Irish Catholic historian were impeccable. His sin was to select most of his letters from the Public Record Office of Northern Ireland (PRONI), the majority of the correspondents, predictably, being Ulster Protestants. In the introduction, he freely conceded that Protestants and Ulster migrants were over-represented, but also commented that, despite their 'non-Gaelic names' and 'non-Catholic cultural roots', all 'in their different ways were firmly and intensely Irish and proud of it'. Some reviewers disagreed. The resulting invective clearly startled O'Farrell. In a 1985 conference paper he outlined a number of the criticisms.[26] These people were not 'true Irish'; they were 'expatriate planter stock from Scotland ... mere squatters in Ireland'; their representatives in Australia were 'shiftless', 'unstable', not self-reliant, not at all suited to pioneering; they wrote 'mawkish — high

24 This is apparent in the contributions to Jupp, *The Australian People*, 443–85.

25 P O'Farrell, *Letters from Irish Australia 1825-1929* (Sydney, 1984).

26 P O'Farrell, 'Writing the History of Irish-Australia', 217–228 in O MacDonagh and W F Mandle, *Ireland and Irish-Australia: Studies in Cultural and Political History* (London, 1986).

falutin' epistles' and they were affected by 'basic pessimism'. It was observed that the Ulster Protestants came from 'established homes, whereas the real native Irish were mainly the dispossessed of the earth'. Some critics considered that such people were no part of Irish Australia, labelled them 'the men of the north' and more disparagingly, dismissed them as 'the O'Farrell writers'.

O'Farrell's rejoinder, not uncharacteristically, was terse. He condemned what he termed 'the takeover bid for sole possession of the identity of being Irish by Catholic and lapsed Catholic forces'.[27] If this was accepted, he continued, 'for the job of being Irish in Australia … no other but Catholics need apply'. Looking towards his projected *Irish in Australia*, he made it clear his overview would be about the 'kinds, ways and degrees of being Irish in Australia: all are welcome, and if they do not like each other they must settle it amongst themselves'. There may well have been similar examples of academic bile — one is tempted to say reverse bigotry — in New Zealand, but I have not encountered them. Several years ago, when I organised a conference on Ulster-New Zealand migration, the first registrant was Fr Shannahan of the Catholic Enquiry Centre.[28] It is likely that over half the paper deliverers were of Irish Catholic background and Ireland's Consul-General in New Zealand participated in the opening. My sense is that such divisions have been, and remain, much stronger in Australia.

The grounds advanced by O'Farrell's reviewers for excluding Ulster Protestants from the goodly and godly company of the Irish 'other' merit some brief consideration. That as a group they were feckless, poor settlers, pessimistic, without drive, is patently nonsensical. There are too many independent testimonies to their industry and initiative.[29] That many were descended from 'expatriate planter stock from Scotland' is undoubtedly true. But this ignores the consistent flow of people backwards and forwards across the

27 *Ibid*, 226.

28 'The Hidden Irish: Ulster/New Zealand Migration and Cultural Transfers', Victoria University of Wellington (29–31 July 2004).

29 Malcolm, 'Searching for a Forgotten People', 5.

North Channel for millennia.[30] Moreover, if Ulster Protestants remained 'mere squatters' after up to 300 years, how must we classify the Gaelic Irish who colonised the Scottish Highlands? How many generations must individuals or families live in a location before they become part of place?

Notwithstanding assertions to the contrary, some from reputable scholars, it is arguable that up until the 1900s, conceivably for even longer, a good number of Ulster Protestants were seen, and just as importantly saw themselves, as Irish. Evidence from extant settler correspondence points to this. In a 1991 paper David Fitzpatrick explored the connotations of Irishness in Irish-Australasian letters from the 1840s to World War One.[31] He concluded that little divided the Protestants and Catholics in the colonies. These findings are corroborated by Angela McCarthy in her recent *Irish Migrants in New Zealand, 1840–1937: 'The Desired Haven'*.[32] 'Ulster Protestant migrants', she observes, 'maintained their sense of being Irish'. They were explicit in the articulation of their Irish identities.

If I may interpose a personal note here, my own father was born in Armagh in 1893, and into a Protestant family. He migrated to New Zealand in 1921. Until the end of his life he regarded himself as Irish — nothing more, and certainly nothing less. He didn't recognise other labels. It is possibly symbolic that when seeking a copy of his birth certificate, applying for my own Irish passport, it was to Dublin, rather than Belfast or Somerset House, that application had to be made. There is, however, another consideration. The twentieth century events that I have suggested accentuated the traditional divisions amongst the Antipodean Irish almost certainly

30 J R Young, 'Scotland and Ulster in the Seventeenth Century: The Movement of Peoples across the North Channel', 11–32 in W Kelly and J R Young (eds), *Ulster and Scotland, 1600–2000: History Language and Identity* (Dublin, 2004).

31 D Fitzpatrick, '"That beloved country that no place else resembles": Connotations of Irishness in Irish-Australasian Letters, 1841-1915', *Irish Historical Studies* xxvii (108), (1991) 324–51.

32 A McCarthy, *Irish Migrants in New Zealand, 1840–1937: 'The Desired Haven'* (Woodbridge, 2005) 263.

impelled some Ulster Protestants to retreat from their Irishness, to seek shelter with the British majorities.[33] In truth, assimilation was a process that started a great deal earlier for a significant number of Ulster Protestants, sometimes within a decade of their arrival in the colonies. In New Zealand's case, assimilation may well have been the single greatest influence on the group's disappearance. Evidence from New Zealand's several planned Ulster settlements suggests they were transformed within at most two generations. Alan Mulgan, grandson of one of the founders of Katikati, writes in his autobiography: 'to a boy who had been born in New Zealand … Ulster was a shadowy place. England and English things were always before our eyes'.[34]

Akenson has proposed that New Zealand's Ulster Protestants had a predisposition to assimilate. More than in Australia, there was a natural fissure between Church of Ireland adherents and the various strands of Presbyterianism. There were also sharper class divides within the Ulster Protestant migrant body, with greater numbers of middle and upper class settlers. The corollary is that they sought association with status and religious likes, rather than with other members of the migrant group. The Ulster Protestants, Akenson concluded in 1990, 'were the perfect colonists of the nineteenth and early twentieth century: Protestant in religion, imperial enthusiasts by conviction. And, because of this, their culture was almost perfectly designed to disappear into that of the rest of the New Zealand British population.'[35] These propositions are in the process of being tested.

Australia's Ulster Protestants

What, then, do we know about Australia's Ulster Protestants? With no specialist study of the group, and even relevant book chapters hard to find, impressions can only be drawn from fragments. Well-known international writers on the Irish — for instance, Akenson

33 O'Farrell, *Irish in Australia*, 93.

34 A Mulgan, *Home: A Colonial's Adventure* (London, 1929) 6.

35 Akenson, *Half the World from Home*, 158.

and Fitzpatrick — have afforded the Ulster Protestants at least passing attention in wider studies, as has Eric Richards.[36] Other Australian-based scholars have made occasional contributions. There are scattered references throughout Patrick O'Farrell's *The Irish in Australia*, and a 1992 Australian National University thesis by Richard Reid, on Irish assisted immigration to NSW between 1848 and 1870,[37] is invaluable. Also helpful are several papers by Ulster historian Trevor Parkhill,[38] but the most promising current project is Lindsay Proudfoot and Dianne Hall's Leverhulme Trust-funded study of Irish identities and landscape in colonial Australia.[39]

There is general agreement that between 1788 and 1914 the Irish made up the second-largest component of Australia's immigrant flows. Fitzpatrick estimates that between 1840 and 1914 over 300,000 Irish men and women landed in Australia.[40] In 1846 the Irish-born numbered 46,000. By 1861 this had climbed to 177,405. The all-time peak was reached in 1891 with 229,156. What percentage of the inflow was of Ulster Protestant origin, however, remains a matter

36 D H Akenson, *The Irish Diaspora: A Primer* (Toronto and Belfast, 1996); D Fitzpatrick, *Oceans of Consolation: Personal Accounts of Irish Migration to Australia* (Ithaca, 1994); E Richards, *Britannia's Children: Emigration from England, Scotland, Wales and Ireland* (London and New York, 2001).

37 R Reid, 'Aspects of Irish Assisted Immigration to New South Wales, 1848–1870', unpublished PhD thesis, Australian National University, 1992.

38 T Parkhill, 'Convicts, Orphans, Settlers: Patterns of Emigration from Ulster to Australia 1790–1860' in J O'Brien and P Travers (eds), *The Irish Emigrant Experience in Australia* (Swords, 1991) 6–28; T Parkhill, 'That Infant Colony: Ulster Emigration to Australia 1790–1860', *Familia* 2 (3), (1987).

39 See for example, L Proudfoot and D Hall, 'Points of Departure: Remittance Emigration from South-West Ulster to New South Wales in the later Nineteenth Century', *International Review of Social History* 50 (2005) 241–277.

40 The statistics in following paragraphs draw heavily from Fitzpatrick, *Oceans of Consolation*, and D Fitzpatrick, *Irish Emigration 1801–1921* (Dublin, 1984).

of conjecture. O'Farrell has suggested it fluctuated between 10%–20%.[41] But Irish, and for that matter Ulster, migration to Australia obviously didn't just commence in 1840. With up to 40,000 Irish transportees in the convict years, O'Farrell posits that around 10% of them were of Ulster Protestant origin, but there are indications this could be a significant underestimate. A G L Shaw notes that between 1817 and 1829 nearly 25% of all Irish convicts (around 2,300 individuals) were shipped from Ulster, many being subsequently joined in the penal colonies by family members.[42] Shaw, however, does not distinguish between Protestant and Catholic convicts from Ulster. Parkhill, from analysis of newspaper reports, suggests that between 1830 and 1845 perhaps another 2,500 Ulster convicts arrived. It is assumed, on place of conviction, that a majority were Protestants.[43]

From the early 1800s, a small number of free settlers relocated to the penal colonies, many of them men of substance in search of free land grants. A sprinkling of prominent Ulster Protestants can be found amongst them, examples including Henry Osborne in New South Wales and Samuel Dawson in Van Diemen's Land.[44] From the 1820s the number of free settlers of more humble origin increased. With many taking advantage of a bounty scheme, over 12,000 free Irish were recruited in the decade prior to the Famine. Although it has been generally assumed that the Ulster Protestant proportion was in the vicinity of 25%, it could have been more, as Proudfoot has recently argued that by the mid-1840s Ulster Protestants made up 45% of the total Irish population of the colony of New South Wales.[45] The share was, however, far less in Victoria, Van Diemen's

---

41 O'Farrell, *Irish in Australia*, 13.

42 A G L Shaw, *Convicts and the Colonies* (London, 1966) 179.

43 Parkhill, *Convicts, Orphans, Settlers*, 11–12.

44 McClaughlin, 'Protestant-Irish Settlement' in Jupp, *The Australian People*, 464.

45 L Proudfoot, 'Landscape, Place and Memory, Towards a Geography of Irish Identities in Colonial Australia', in O Walsh (ed), *Ireland Abroad: Politics and Professions in the Nineteenth Century* (Dublin, 2003) 176.

Land, or for that matter South Australia.

As far as can now be established, the main source areas for the pre-Famine free Ulster migrants were the northwest counties. Part of the reason was that Londonderry, Donegal and Tyrone had been badly affected by the accumulating difficulties facing arable agriculture after the Napoleonic wars. At the same time a downturn in the viability of the domestic linen industry meant many smallholders who had augmented their income from yarn spinning were badly hit. Faced with reduced incomes, increased rents, and sizeable families to feed, these primarily farming folk found prospects in the colonies attractive.

Although Australia was not a primary destination for Famine refugees, from the 1850s Irish migration, and by extension Ulster Protestant migration, increased from a trickle to a steady stream. The flows continued through to the 1880s, then sharply dried up. O'Farrell observes that, as a whole, the post-1850 migrants were a 'much more accomplished, venturesome and happy lot than those the Famine had dropped on America'.[46] It is this Ulster Protestant group which, thanks to Richard Reid, we know most about.[47] From his thesis it is possible to generalise that New South Wales was the most popular first Australian destination for Ulster Protestants; that assistance was readily available from the colonial governments; that the most common vehicles were nomination and remittance schemes, both of which facilitated chain migration (the corollary to this is that recruitment focussed on the same areas for quite lengthy periods); and that over half of the new arrivals disembarked in kinship groups. Reid estimates that around 19% of the assisted Irish migrants in the mid-nineteenth-century decades were Ulster Protestants.

46 O'Farrell, *Irish in Australia*, 63.

47 Reid, 'Aspects of Assisted Immigration'; 'From Ballyduff to Boorowa: Irish Assisted Emigration to NSW 1830–1896', in *The Irish Australians* (Belfast, 1984); 'Emigration from Ireland to New South Wales in the Mid Nineteenth Century', 304–17 in O MacDonagh and W F Mandle, *Irish-Australian Studies: Papers Delivered at the 5th Irish-Australian Conference* (Canberra, 1988).

Between the 1850s and the 1880s the principal source areas for Australia's Ulster Protestant migrants also changed, from the northwest to the southwest counties of the Province, the focus now switching to the counties of Fermanagh and Cavan. Several other points about the mid-century assisted migrants emerge: they tended to be young, literate, Church of Ireland males.

If little is known about the mid-century Ulster Protestant migrants, then next to nothing is known about those arriving in the later decades and the years leading up to World War One. There are strong suggestions that, while total Irish immigration may have dropped away, the Ulster Protestant component increased. By 1911, the first census in which birthplace was cross-tabulated with religion, the non-Catholic component of Australia's Irish-born stood at 29%.

As a ball-park estimate, in the vicinity of 80,000 Ulster Protestants may have relocated to Australia between 1788 and 1914. As to where they located, it is assumed, despite their tendency to migrate in kin groups, that they dispersed widely. Sadly, early attempts to map Irish settlement in Australia are of little assistance in respect of Ulster Protestants. In the absence of apposite census data, several researchers have employed religious data as a substitute, but with Irish and Catholic being equated, Protestants are automatically excluded. More recently the American academics Jordan and Greiner have sought to identify distinct Irish settlement clusters through analysis of tombstone epitaphs.[48] From the 1901 Census they detect five main clusters in Australia's eastern seaboard states. None is Ulster Protestant-dominated, not even Kiama on the Illawarra, often dubbed 'the little Ulster of New South Wales'.

Kiama, of course, is the Australian settlement most frequently advocated as classic Ulster. In the 1820s and 1830s Henry Osborne of Tyrone and James McKay Grey of Armagh, both men of means, successfully sought large land grants in the district.[49] As they

---

48 T G Jordan and A L Greiner, 'Irish Migration to Rural Eastern Australia: A Preliminary Investigation', *Irish Geography*, 2 (2), (1994) 135–42.

49 McClaughlin, 'Irish-Protestant Settlement', 464.

expanded their holdings in the 1840s they were instrumental in bringing out family groups, tenant farmers and labourers from their home counties and Fermanagh. Through the 1850s and 1860s the privately-introduced Ulster Protestants used the New South Wales government's assisted immigrant schemes to sponsor the migration of further friends and relatives. Late nineteenth-century visitors to Kiama proclaimed it to be almost a replication of West Ulster society. Yet, although Kiama clings to its heritage, with its Family History Centre at the core, there is no evidence of any rigorous scholarly scrutiny, although there is a clear need for such studies. Other significant Ulster Protestant clusterings may yet be discovered; there were loose groupings in Gippsland and parts of Queensland.

It has been suggested that the 'siege mentality' that was believed to be part and parcel of the cultural baggage brought by Ulster Protestants to Australia was reflected in Kiama politics, as were the religious and political conflicts of the old country.[50] Even the usually judicious O'Farrell records 'the area sprouted Orange Lodges, there were nine in the 1880s'.[51] But more needs to be known about the dynamics of the settlement. While unquestionably Ulster settlers brought the Loyal Order with them, to Kiama as well as many other places, there is evidence of a takeover by English and Australian-born anti-Catholic factions as early as the 1860s. David Fitzpatrick's in-progress study of the Orange Order in Australia will hopefully offer desperately needed new insights.[52] Until more research work is initiated, Australia's Ulster Protestants will remain shadowy, insubstantial, a group historically out of focus.

New Zealand's Ulster Protestants

What, then, of New Zealand's Ulster Protestants? As little as 20, even ten, years ago, very similar comments to those about Australia

50 *Ibid.*

51 O'Farrell, *Irish in Australia,* 101.

52 D Fitzpatrick, 'Exporting Brotherhood: Orangeism in South Australia', *Immigrants and Minorities* 23 (2-3), (2005) 277–310.

would have applied. When presenting his 1990 research agenda Akenson highlighted the lacuna in respect of the Protestants. What was required as a foundation for future studies, he stated, was accurate definition of the scale and nature of Irish, including Ulster Protestant, migration to New Zealand; then scores of case-studies of settler groups and clusters.

Since the challenge was issued, there has been steadily-growing scholarly interest in New Zealand's Ulster Protestants.[53] As but one example, Ulster Protestant migration to New Zealand has been one (but only one) of the research thrusts of the Irish-Scottish Studies Programme at Victoria University. Since 2003, the programme has worked closely with researchers in Northern Ireland, from the University of Ulster, Queen's University Belfast and the Ulster Historical Foundation. Products of this collaboration have included a joint conference, held in Wellington in July 2004, publication of the first substantial book devoted exclusively to the cultural links between New Zealand and Ulster,[54] and a 2007 seminar/colloquium.

How far, then, has the defining of the scale and nature of Ulster Protestant migration to New Zealand proceeded? The deficiencies of the Irish official statistics are generally recognised, and in New Zealand there are few tidy time series providing answers to even the most basic questions about migration. It has therefore been necessary to resort to estimates. It was Akenson himself who proffered the first partial estimates.[55] Employing a variety of sources, his estimate for the half-century 1870 to 1921 was around 140,000 Irish migrants in total, with perhaps up to 25% (35,000) from Ulster. There were two challenges to these estimates in the course of the 1990s, although in both instances the time-frames were extended. The first came in 1995 from New Zealand genealogist Heather Webber, who in a post-graduate research paper suggested the Protestant component

53 B Patterson, 'Celtic Roots Amidst the Fern: Irish-Scottish Studies in New Zealand', *Journal of New Zealand Studies* 2 (2003–04) 197–217.

54 B Patterson (ed), *Ulster-New Zealand Migration and Cultural Transfers* (Dublin, 2006).

55 D H Akenson, 'The Irish in New Zealand', *Familia* 2 (5) (1989) 7–12.

of Irish migration between 1840 and 1950 should be raised to around 40%.[56] These findings were based on a sampling of 1,000 death certificates. Three years later Alasdair Galbraith presented an outstanding thesis on the North Island's Irish Protestants to 1900.[57] Drawing from the admission records of the Auckland provincial hospital, he also posited a Protestant component of around 40%. By this point the most ambitious estimation of migrant flows to New Zealand yet attempted, what was termed the 'Peopling of New Zealand' project, had been initiated by then government Chief Historian, Jock Phillips.[58] The core of the research was a scientific sampling of over 11,000 New Zealand death certificates. The results from the study provide the best available statistical profiles of New Zealand's British and Irish migrant groups, including Ulster Protestant migrants.

Raw data from this study indicates that until the post World War Two years, more than 90% of all immigration to New Zealand was from the United Kingdom and Ireland.[59] How then did the Irish compare with other ethnic groups from the Atlantic archipelago? Several trends stand out. As in Australia, English migrants always dominated, making up over 50% of all migrants in all periods. However, in New Zealand the Scots, not the Irish, comprised the second-largest ethnic group. The analysis also shows that Irish migration to New Zealand tended to be heavily concentrated between the 1850s and the 1870s. In fact, the number of Irish-born in New Zealand peaked at an all-time high of 51,408 in 1886. This is a much smaller number than the peak in Australia, but the total New Zealand population in 1886 was only 620,000.

---

56 H J Webber, 'Emigration: Ireland to New Zealand 1850–1900', *Genealogical Research Institute of New Zealand Yearbook* (1995) 17–28.

57 A Galbraith, 'New Zealand's "Invisible" Irish: Irish Protestants in the North Island of New Zealand, 1840–1900', unpublished MA thesis, University of Auckland, 1998.

58 Phillips and Hearn, *Settlers*, v–vii.

59 I am grateful to Dr Phillips for making available to me the raw data derived from the 'Peopling of New Zealand' research. It provides the statistical basis for much of the commentary in following paragraphs.

The particular concern of this paper is the Ulster Protestant component. Two points have to be made: firstly, in New Zealand the convict system never operated; hence there was no forced migration; secondly, migration to New Zealand commenced a good half-century after transfers to Australia began.[60] In the 12 years after 1840, while New Zealand was a Crown colony, both the Irish and Ulster migration flows were moderate. Few Irish came directly to New Zealand before or during the Famine years. While the New Zealand Company, the principal colonising agency in the 1840s, certainly offered assisted passages to their settlements, fewer than 2% of those sent were of Irish birth. This was deliberate policy. The Company simply did not consider 'illiterate Irish peasants' to be desirable immigrants. By 1848 there were still no more than 275 Irish in the Company's settlements.[61] In contrast, by 1851 there were already over 2,800 Irish settlers (32% of the population) at Auckland, the principal non-New Zealand Company settlement, then the colonial capital.[62] Few had arrived directly from their homeland: some had drifted across from the Australian colonies, but the majority were part of a contingent of 700 former Imperial soldiers and their families (the Royal NZ Fencibles) brought to Auckland to man pensioner settlements formed to protect the waterway approaches to Auckland. Roughly one third of the pensioner migrants were from Ulster, but by no means all were of Protestant persuasion.

Between 1853 and 1870, numbers built slowly initially, then more spectacularly in the 1860s. Both the Irish and Ulster inflows climbed, the latter nudging towards 40% of all Irish migration to New Zealand. The single greatest impetus was the discovery of gold in the South Island, this attracting many Irish who had migrated to

60 B Patterson, 'Half the World from Home? Nineteenth Century Irish Migration to New Zealand Reviewed', unpublished paper (2005) 3.

61 C G F Simkin (ed), *Statistics of New Zealand for the Crown Colony Period, 1840–1852* (Auckland, 1954) Table 5.

62 Ministry of Culture and Heritage, *Settler and Migrant Peoples*, 173-4.

Australia in the previous decade.[63]

Yet, if gold was the greatest magnet, there were catalysts not present in the Australian colonies. In the course of the Land (or New Zealand) Wars, military settlers were again introduced to the upper North Island districts.[64] Contemporaneously, several of the New Zealand provincial governments actively sought to recruit migrants, utilising nomination and remittance schemes similar to those across the Tasman, Auckland and Canterbury being in the forefront of these initiatives.[65] The available evidence suggests that there were appreciable differences between the various 1860s Irish migrant flows. The goldfield migrants predominantly came via Australia and were twice as likely to be Catholic single men from Ireland's south-west, both men and women being in the prime working age group. In contrast, the northern military settlers again came in family groups, and tended to be older, with a far stronger bias towards Ulster Protestants. The assisted migrants brought out by the provincial governments had mixed religious backgrounds, but there had been determined efforts to recruit single women, and the Ulster component was again strong.

The 1870s are generally recognised as New Zealand's great nineteenth-century migration decade, the era of Sir Julius Vogel's grandiose assisted immigration and public works schemes.[66] This was a time when opening up lands and closer settlement became the driving objectives. More than a quarter of all assisted passages to New Zealand in the decade were allotted to Irish-born. That the number of Ulster migrants should also continue to climb, comfortably exceeding 40% of all Irish migrants, should be no

---

63 L Fraser, 'Irish Migration to the West Coast, 1864–1900', *New Zealand Journal of History* 34 (2) (2000) 197–225.

64 As an example, see A Galbraith, 'A Forgotten Plantation: The Irish in Pukekohe, 1865–1900', 117–130 in Patterson, *The Irish in New Zealand.*

65 L Fraser, *To Tara via Holyhead: Irish Catholic Immigrants in Nineteenth Century Christchurch*, (Auckland, 1997).

66 J Morris, 'The assisted migrants to New Zealand, 1871–79', unpublished MA thesis (University of Auckland, 1973).

surprise. Active Government recruiting in Ireland in the 1870s was heavily concentrated in and around Belfast and Derry. Ulster husbandmen, spinners and weavers, it was stated in the colonial parliament, were migrants of the best stock.[67] Perhaps the most celebrated manifestation of this zeal for Ulster folk was the New Zealand Government's enthusiastic support for 'special settlements' in the Bay of Plenty, the best known of them being Katikati.

On reflection, it was probably only the relative reluctance of other British ethnic groups to take ship that ensured more than 50% of the Irish immigrants in the decade continued to hail from the other provinces.

Over the last two decades of the nineteenth century, and the first 15 years of the twentieth, the flow of Irish migrants to New Zealand started to drop.[68] In the depression of the late 1880s assisted migration was curtailed, only to be revived, modestly, in the early 1900s. Moreover, while temporary movements from Australia continued, permanent transfers attenuated. The counter-trend to all this was the increasing dominance of Ulster as a source of Irish migrants. Between 1881 and 1910 the share was around 50%, and in the four years immediately prior to World War One it exceeded 60%, a trend which continued in the post-war years.

To this point the focus has been primarily the relative importance of Irish migrants as a percentage of all migrants to New Zealand, and most particularly with Ulster as a source of Irish migrants. What did this mean in real numbers? There are now some reasonable estimates.[69] In New Zealand's founding decade there were probably not many more than 1,000 Ulster migrants, a figure which doubled between 1853 and 1860, then doubled again in the 1860s. By the 1870s, the influx is estimated at over 11,000, but

---

67 E Bohan, '"A recollection of the unfortunate failings of my own countrymen": the Irish in New Zealand Politics', in Patterson, *The Irish in New Zealand*, 59.

68 Akenson, *Half the World from Home*, 16–17.

69 J Phillips, 'Who were New Zealand's Ulster immigrants?', 55–70 in Patterson, *Ulster-New Zealand Migration*.

in the 1880s and 1890s the numbers dropped by around one third. In the early twentieth century the Ulster numbers surged again, the total between 1901 and 1915 substantially exceeding that for the 1870s. Thereafter, with the exception of a minor surge in the early 1920s, migration from Ulster tended to dry up. Assuming these estimates are at least roughly accurate, up to World War Two there were over 52,000 Ulster migrants, most of whom arrived between 1870 and 1920. Such numbers leave little room for doubting that New Zealand was one of the last Ulster frontiers.

Additional useful information has been extracted from the death certificates, mostly obviously data on the age and sex of individuals, but also, more relevantly for this study, information on religious allegiances.[70] It has been traditionally assumed that New Zealand's Ulster influxes were almost exclusively Protestant, but how true is this? Comparing the information gleaned with the distribution of religions in Ulster itself in 1861, the sample suggests that, with the exception of the 1840s (when Catholics made up nearly 37% of migrants from Ulster), Protestants accounted for more than 75% of the Ulster influx throughout, increasing to around 85% in the twentieth century. In terms of the Protestant denominations, the Church of Ireland made a solid showing in the early decades, but thereafter Presbyterianism had the strongest following. Although these figures may bear out Akenson's proposition regarding the religious divisions amongst Ulster's Protestants, it is harder to be sure about his suggestion that there were major class differences amongst the Ulster settlers. The certificates also record what were believed to be the occupations of migrants' fathers, possibly providing some suggestions. Closer scrutiny shows that the founding decade is the odd one out. In the 1840s, those from farming backgrounds were almost matched by those from traditional trades. Thereafter the migrants were predominantly from farming backgrounds. And here is the conundrum: how does one differentiate between landowners, more impecunious tenant farmers, and farm workers?

---

70 *Ibid*; T Hearn, 'The Origins of New Zealand's Irish Settlers, 1840–1945', 15–34 in Patterson, *Irish in New Zealand*, at pp 26–28.

Where, then, in Ulster, did the migrants come from?[71] In the founding decade the Ulster recruits were drawn almost totally from the counties of East Ulster, but lightly compared with the later years. During the gold rushes and second military settlement era, between 1853 and 1870, as the Ulster flow grew in strength, strongly Protestant Antrim and Down became the major supply areas. In the 1870s and 1880s, with migration from Ulster peaking, substantial numbers were drawn from all the northern counties save Fermanagh and, significantly, Cavan. Antrim continued to stand head and shoulders above the others, but Donegal, and especially Tyrone, became important for the first time. When Ulster migration to New Zealand surged again, at the beginning of the twentieth century, Antrim, Londonderry and Down were the main suppliers.

Without more research, it is far more difficult to establish precisely where in New Zealand the Ulster migrants settled. The only information death certificates convey is where migrants died, which, although suggestive, may have been far different from where they landed, or indeed where they lived out most of their colonial lives. From the 1878 Census, however, totals of Irish-born were recorded by counties and boroughs. Maps prepared for that year are again suggestive, although there is no firm information as to where, or indeed if, the Ulster Protestants clustered.[72] In the North Island it is possible to guess with reasonable certainty: Manakau and Waikato Counties, in the north, incorporate the Ulster military settlers of the 1840s and 1860s. Tauranga County is the locus for George Vesey Stewart's Katikati settlement of the mid-1870s. In the South Island the likely clusters are in Canterbury, especially in Selwyn and Ashburton counties.

So much for defining the pulses and scale of Ulster Protestant migration to New Zealand. It is also possible, of course, to extract from the statistics valuable information about the age and sex of

---

71 Hearn, 'The Origins of New Zealand's Irish Settlers', 21–25.

72 Maps prepared by Gerard Horn, a PhD candidate in the Irish-Scottish Studies Programme, Victoria University of Wellington.

the Ulster migrants.[73] In the 1840s, then again in the 1870s, there appear to be more Ulster women than men coming to New Zealand, but in all other periods there was an appreciable surplus of males. Unsurprisingly perhaps, throughout the nineteenth century there was a preference for young adults, those under the age of 30 years.

There has clearly been a positive response to Akenson's first 1990 call. But to develop a deeper understanding of New Zealand's Ulster migrants, their aspirations and expectations, their motivations for leaving, how they adapted, and how they lived their new lives, it is necessary to put the aggregates to one side and look closely at identifiable communities and individual cases. There will be a continuing need for detailed searches into traditional sources, the official archives at both ends of the migration process, newspapers, the personal records left by the migrants themselves — diaries, letters, reminiscences, what are now termed personal testimonies.

Historians such as O'Farrell and, more recently, Fitzpatrick, have, of course, demonstrated the utility of personal letters in the Australian context.[74] Donald Akenson and Trevor Parkhill have previously highlighted the potential of Ulster–New Zealand correspondence,[75] but the most comprehensive study of New Zealand migrant letters is Angela McCarthy's *Irish Migrants in New Zealand, 1840–1937: The Desired Haven*, published in 2005.[76] Based on a Trinity College PhD, the study examines 36 migrants who wrote to or received letters from their connections in Ireland. Interestingly, over half of the correspondents (20) were Ulster natives, with 13 from the north-eastern counties of Antrim, Down and Londonderry. This over-representation mirrors what O'Farrell found in Australia, and may well reflect the fact that on the whole Ulster migrants appear to have been better educated. The topics

---

73 Phillips, 'Who were New Zealand's Ulster immigrants?', 66–68.

74 O'Farrell, *Letters from Irish Australia*; Fitzpatrick, *Oceans of Consolation*.

75 D H Akenson, 'Letters from the Irish Emigrant: Texts from Real Life', 1–17 in Stout Research Centre, *Migration and New Zealand Society* (Wellington, 1990).

76 McCarthy, *Irish Migrants in New Zealand*.

covered range over such matters as the voyage out, differences between Ireland and New Zealand, the nature of work, family relationships and social networks, politics and identity.

The second of Akenson's 1990 calls is also being heeded, even if case-studies of settler clusters and communities have not yet reached double figures, much less scores. In the north of the North Island, Alasdair Galbraith has probed the South Auckland settlement of Pukekohe, a township surveyed for Ulster military settlers in the mid 1860s.[77] This, he found, was not only a settlement that was overlooked by historians, but one which had largely forgotten its own heritage. From Christchurch, Lyndon Fraser and Sarah Dwyer are working on Ulster settlements on the Canterbury Plains, especially the small farmers of Ellesmere County[78], and in Wellington, Gerard Horn is investigating the Irish Protestant community in an urban setting. Then there is another project currently in the planning stages. Bruce Elliott's new almost-classic study *Irish Migrants in the Canadas: A New Approach* has convincingly shown the utility of genealogical methodologies in the study of migrant flows.[79] Elliott meticulously traced the life histories of 775 Tipperary Protestant families from their home county to their first Canadian destination and beyond. His generalisations were drawn not from aggregate statistics but from close observation of the lives of specific individuals. Following this model, a longitudinal study of New Zealand's most celebrated Ulster settlement, Katikati, on the North Island's Bay of Plenty coast is proposed.

Katikati is unique in New Zealand, some argue in the world.[80]

---

77 Galbraith, 'A Forgotten Plantation'.

78 L Fraser and S Dwyer, '"We are all here together like so many on the cockle beds"; Towards a History of Ulster Migrants in Nineteenth-century Canterbury', 115–130 in Patterson, *Ulster-New Zealand Migration.*

79 B Elliott, *Irish Migrants in the Canadas: A New Approach* (Kingston and Belfast, 1988).

80 B Patterson, '"Be you an Orangeman, you shall meet Orangemen": New Zealand's Ulster Plantation Revisited', 46–58 in L M Geery and A J McCarthy, *Ireland, Australia and New Zealand: History, Politics and Culture* (Dublin, 1988).

It was the only known settlement conceived as a transplanted slice of Ireland, or rather one particular part of Ireland. It was created with the support of the Loyal Orange Lodge. Led by Tyrone entrepreneur George Vesey Stewart, 238 settlers travelled to the site in 1875; three years later a further 378 settlers followed. There is thus a finite population of 616, organised into 77 families, for study.

Curiously, Katikati has been the most written-about of all New Zealand's Irish settlements.[81] So much so that some writers, claiming it is atypical, have counselled that it be put to one side, with attention shifting to other aspects of the Protestant Irish experience. However, there are many key issues relating to the settlement still to be addressed. The emphases in most past accounts have been on romantic tales of the brave pioneers. Little attention has been given to the fact that within 15 years of the settlement's founding nearly half the original settlers had drifted away. Few have asked why, by the early 1890s, the Orange ethos so evident in the 1870s had all but evaporated. In considering this settlement, a number of obvious questions occur. How spatially mobile were the Katikati settlers? Did the early defectors shift elsewhere in New Zealand, to other colonies, or did some return home? What was the extent of occupational and social mobility? Were there switches between religious denominations? Did the Ulster settlers 'marry in'? What were the sizes of their families? Was chain migration significant in this settlement?

In a quest for even partial answers to these questions, it is now proposed, with the assistance of New Zealand genealogists, to reconstitute the life histories, the genealogies, of the 77 founding families and to trace descendants for three, possibly four, generations.[82] But this is only one part of the project as envisaged. Just as it is possible to take the 77 foundation families as a base for projecting the generations forward in New Zealand, it is equally possible to use it as a foundation for extending the research

81 Patterson, 'New Zealand's "Ulster Plantation"'.

82 A funding proposal is in preparation, involving researchers from both New Zealand and Ulster.

backwards for several generations in Ulster. This should enable a much better understanding of just who the Katikati settlers were (to date, all studies of the settlement have been essentially from the New Zealand perspective).

That studies of the Ulster Irish, and in particular Ulster Protestants, are alive and well in New Zealand has, I hope, emerged from these partial and very quick sketches. It is perhaps an index of recent progress that in mid-September 2007 Victoria University will host a gathering that aims to establish an agenda for Ulster-New Zealand research over the next 5–10 years. There will be contributions from around 20 scholars with known interests in the area. With the colloquium being co-hosted by the University of Ulster's Institute of Ulster-Scots Studies, senior historians from that part of the world will also be attending.

There can be little doubt there has been an upsurge in interest in the Ulster Protestant diaspora in recent years.[83] In conclusion, I would like to suggest some explanations. One reason, in countries like New Zealand, Canada, and I suspect also Australia, is the greater consciousness of personal identity, the growing interest in family and group roots. The genealogical industry is just one manifestation. But there has also been a widening of scholarly horizons in the past decade. Whereas Institutes of Irish Studies have long fostered research, and Centres for Scottish Studies have emerged beyond Scotland, the founding of the Research Institute for Irish and Scottish Studies at the University of Aberdeen in 2000 signalled a drive for greater inclusivity, for recognition of the close historical ties binding the sometimes fractious peoples of Ireland and Scotland. Establishment of the University of Ulster's Institute of Ulster-Scots Studies has also played a part. Although dismissed by some critics as a ploy by Northern Ireland's Protestants to appropriate cultural legitimacy, the Institute's positive support for wide-ranging research, at home and abroad, cannot be questioned. My unit has worked closely with the Institute since 2003, as it does

83 See the bibliography on the website of the University of Ulster's Institute of Ulster Scots Studies: http://www.arts.ulster.ac.uk/ulsterscots.

with Aberdeen, Trinity College, University College Cork and, for that matter, Melbourne. This has been a productive relationship, with no strings attached. Two of the Institute's stated aims bear quotation; firstly: 'to provide a forum for debate within the diverse heritages of the island of Ireland'; secondly: 'to unify national and regional histories of the peoples of the Atlantic Archipelago and beyond'. In explanation, the Institute's Director has stressed that no special place for Ulster Scots, for Ulster Protestants generally, is sought, only acknowledgement that they have a place among the historical family groups of Ireland and Scotland.[84] In short, that the Ulster Protestants should not be invisible or hidden, much less forgotten. To my mind, such recognition would be fully in keeping with the 1898 sentiments of Victor Daley, writer of 'The Glorious Twelfth at Jindabyne'.

84 *Ibid.*

'Migrant fairies': an anthropological investigation of contemporary Celtic identity in the Australian setting as endorsed by mythical symbolism

Jeffrey Parker ⊕

Upon that night, when fairies light
On Cassilis Downans dance,
Or owre the lays, in splendid blaze,
On sprightly coursers prance;
Or for Colean the route is ta'en,
Beneath the moon's pale beams;
There, up the cove, to stray and rove,
Among the rocks and streams
To sport that night.

(extract from the 1785 poem Halloween *by Robert Burns)*[1]

This paper emerges from an anthropological analysis of change and continuity of cultural practice in migrant and post-migrant contexts in the contemporary Australian setting. In fieldwork conducted on this topic, the centrality of faerie motifs as a prolific and ubiquitous icon of 'Celticness' has become increasingly apparent. Used in the promotion of a distinctive descent-based ethnicity, representations of 'the little people' abound in popular imagery, visual media, performance contexts, and as a significant feature of many migrant family narratives. Evoked in this manner as emblematic motifs of 'Celticity', faerie imagery also acts to produce metaphors of cultural and community connection. It is thus argued that faerie motifs can

---

⊕ University of Queensland.

1 *Halloween*: available online at The Literature Network http://www.online-literature.com/robert-burns/2365/ [accessed 2 October 2007].

operate as representations or symbols of the relationship between contemporary 'Celts' and what they identify as their continuous traditional practices. The combination of such 'cultural' metaphors is further argued to be present in the mythic narratives which are frequently referred to in performance, community and family settings, producing whole allegories of worldview, spirituality, attitudes to nature, family and a connection to homeland. The allegoric use of the faerie faith as a 'figurative treatment of one subject under the guise of another'[2] allows this mystical imagery to act as a conduit of cultural currency and congruency, and gives agency to the projection of a Celtic identity as a liminal other on the global stage.

Doing fieldwork on this subject has been an absorbing yet often perplexing task, as many people seem to find being asked about their beliefs on the topic rather confronting at first, often finding it difficult to express their somewhat intangible beliefs in a clear response. However, more often than not, after this initial awkwardness a wealth of information seems to pour out, especially from the older participants. It has indeed been exciting to discover a flourishing sense of cultural association with the subject being practiced, or at very least remembered, in the Australian setting. Although various transformations have occurred in how people view the faerie, there is a degree of consistency in the cultural significance of the phenomenon through time and space. A multitude of folkloric sources attest to how such belief systems were firmly embedded in the classical world view of the Irish, Welsh and Scottish peasantry; however, notions of the faerie also generate emotive meaning for many of those who identify as contemporary Celts.

The search for origins is a search for meaning

Definitions of faerie are elusive by nature. Due to the amorphous quality of the subject matter and the discursive range of sources from which it is assembled, there exists an inherent impenetrability

2 *Dictionary.com*: available online at http://dictionary.reference.com/browse/allegory [accessed 16 July 2007].

to forming any single definition; alternatively, the topic does offer itself more willingly to an exploration of a range of diverse meanings and associations. Note JRR Tolkien's cautionary observation that 'Faerie cannot be caught in a net of words; for it is one of its qualities to be indescribable though not imperceptible'.[3] Any single definition is also inadequate, due to the many distinct regional variations and local speciations of the faerie clans as recorded by folklorists, whilst other affiliates of the sylvan folk seem to meld between these classifications. It has been suggested that they are more easily known by their behaviour than by their pedigree. In 1888, William Butler Yeats, in the introduction to his collected *Fairy and Folk Tales of the Irish Peasantry*, urges the observer to

> witness the nature of the creatures, their caprice, their way of being good to the good and evil to the evil, having every charm but conscience — consistency. Beings so quickly offended that you must not speak about them much at all, and never call them anything but the 'gentry', or else *daoine maithe*, which in English means good people, yet so easily pleased they will do their best to keep misfortune away from you, if you leave a little milk for them on the window-sill overnight'. [4]

Although many facets of faerie folklore have a literary basis from as early as dark-age classical manuscripts such as *The Book of the Dun Cow* and *The Book of the Conquests of Ireland*, the great wealth of this tradition was passed on in an oral form which was simultaneously embedded in cultural practice and ritual, and often syncretised with more mainstream religious and secular concepts. With the inception of the age of reason around the seventeenth century, and

---

3 E J Cowan and L Henderson, *Scottish Fairy Belief: A History* (Scotland, 2004) 1.

4 W B Yeats (ed), *Fairy and Folktales of the Irish Peasantry* (New York, 1991 [1888]) 1–2.

the resulting compulsion to document and catalogue the world in all its facets, there was a burgeoning academic interest in the subject, resulting in a profusion of texts about faerie matters, transforming much of the oral form to the written one. These differing modes of transmission also emphasised, and symbolised, the social and economic gulf between peasants and gentry; educated and rustic; elite and folk, and efforts were made by those early ethnographers to distance themselves from the creative mystique of the faerie faith and to justify their methodologies and approach to the subject as rational and scientific endeavours. The separation of these cultural modes of, on the one hand, an everyday, phenomenological engagement with the faerie world as a lived experience, and on the other, a shift to perceiving the mystical 'little people' as imaginative 'fantasy', whose value is situated in recreation and celebration, has continued to characterise human relations with the fay from that time to the present.

The academic fascination with the faerie faith continued fervently through the nineteenth and early twentieth centuries, with the folklorists of this era divided in their approach to the ethnographic data they collected. This divide in methodology manifested itself between those who aimed to provide a structure and social function to the plethora of faerie phenomena, such as Lewis Spence, and others, like Yeats and Evans Wentz, who also sought artistic inspiration and insight into the metaphysical aspects of the fay. Those on the latter side of the divide, who were often believers in the faerie realms themselves, were able to establish an immediate rapport with their — in most cases, rural — informants and 'encountered believers without a trace of scepticism or condescension, and [were] therefore given access to experiences and beliefs that would have been withheld from [the] more sophisticated investigator'.[5] An additional impetus for scholars assembling the wealth of ethnographic data on the subject was also motivated by the concern that, in a rapidly industrialising world, the rich oral

5 K Briggs, *The Vanishing People: Fairy Lore and Legends* (New York, 1978) 31.

mythos of the 'folk' would soon vanish into the mist like the faerie themselves.

A clearly positivistic approach was, however, attached to most of the conventional academic investigations of the subject, which reached their culmination in the well known volume *British Fairy Origins* written by Lewis Spence in 1946. In an attempt to provide a historical survey of the various theories that had been advanced concerning the genesis of the faerie phenomenon, Spence believed that the 'ideas associated with it strike at the very roots of human belief and primitive methods of reasoning'.[6] The

> main theories have been advanced to explain the origin of the belief in fairy spirits: (1) that they are the spirits of the human dead; (2) that they are elementary spirits — that is spirits of nature, the genii of the mountain, flood and forest; (3) that belief in them is due to reminiscences of former peoples or aboriginal races [and] (4) the possible derivation of the idea of fairy spirits from classical forms, such as pagan gods [and] totemic forms.[7]

This approach, while considered overly simplistic in its analysis of the myriad complexities of the relationships between these beliefs and the communities in which they arose, does have some relevancy to the current study in terms of the themes generated by this research. In the post-structuralist analysis, however, the search for origins of the faerie via structural classifications is replaced by a quest for the phenomenological 'meaning' of the mythic symbolism, with the aim of determining what the faerie faith can tell us about the relationships between people, their sense of connection to the past and the present, and the landscapes they inhabit and imbue with meaning.

6 L Spence, *British Fairy Origins* (Northamptonshire, 1981 [1946]) vii.

7 Spence, *British*, 53.

Ancestral voices

The connection between the faerie world and a wider sense of continuous community is apparent in neo-Celtic constructions of self and of kinship. Spence's observation of the connection between the 'good people' and a community's ancestral roots is observably relevant to how members of the Australian Celtic community employ the faerie metaphor. When interviewed about the faerie tradition, most people of migrant Celtic heritage immediately associate these concepts with their grandparents (especially grandmothers), and there is a definite theme of transmission through the female line, which is often centred around domestic activities. This association between the faerie and the past is used by people to evoke a connection with what they perceive as their ancestral customs, and as such, family narratives which feature ancestors' otherworldly beliefs and practices provide an allegoric link to a notion of traditional and ethnic continuity. Many of those interviewed, especially those of Scottish descent, referred to the concept of 'second sight' as a gift or talent that was connected both to the faerie and to the family unit itself. Some even noted how this extra-sensory ability, relating to premonitions, dreams and an uncanny awareness of the natural surroundings, was believed to have been 'passed down' to them from ancestral family members, who in some cases were renowned and even respected for this skill. There exists a similar tradition in the Australian Cornish community, where the 'gift' is associated with people believed to have the abilities of a *pella*, or white witch, by inheriting such talents 'by blood' from a faerie ancestor. One Australian-Cornish informant, a male in his forties, told me that his mother and sisters were renowned in the family for their clairvoyant skills, however he had 'only' inherited the ability to divine water.

Certain specific faerie entities seem to encapsulate this ancestral connection in a very direct way. The Irish banshee (*bean sidhe*, literally 'woman of the faerie') is recorded as being attached to specific established families, and by her appearance on the ancestral estate 'dressed in green, perhaps wearing a grey cloak over her wizened body, with long streaming hair and eyes red from weeping',[8] the family is warned of an impending death. The nurturing 'fairy godmother' figure, as a frequent motif of popular cultural iconography, would also seem to have a direct connection with the relationship between the faerie world and that of the protective ancestors. Numerous informants related how fairy-tale books, often handed down to them by grandparents or great-aunts, were regarded as significant items of material culture, which were imbued with a sense of mystical agency and regarded as a conduit of belief between one generation and the next.

Many of the earlier rural ethnographies collected in the nations of the Celtic fringe also stress this relationship between the ancestral spirits of the dead and the eldritch realms. Lewis Spence noted of the faerie that '[t]hey are almost universally believed to have their dwellings underground — like the dead — and they are fond of snatching the living down to their dark abode, in this resembling all chthonic powers. They are credited with superhuman wisdom, as are ancestors generally'.[9]

Manx and the 'quaer fellas'

During fieldwork with members of the Queensland Manx Society, the oldest of the Queensland Celtic organisations, the notion that concepts of faerie are used as a metaphor of community, heritage and landscape became very apparent. The Queensland Manx are a small but close-knit society, who readily use mythic symbolism as an expression of their identity and cultural legacy. The Manx faerie, often termed the 'quaer' or 'lil' fellas' or 'themselves', out of respect and in an effort not to offend these oft-mischievous beings, are perceived by many members of the group as a quintessential factor of the Manx culture and landscape. The notion that the topography of the Isle of Man inherently contains faerie abodes is an old one.

One visitor maintained in 1794 that the Isle of Man

8 *The Banshee*: available online at *Mysterious Britain* http://www.mysteriousbritain.co.uk/folklore/banshee.html [accessed 3 July 2007].

9 A Krappe, cited in Spence, *British*, 54.

> was the only place where there was any probability of seeing a fairy […] His informant — 'an aged peasant of pensive and melancholy aspect' — had told the visiting investigator that the elves were most likely to be seen sitting beside brooks and waterfalls, half concealed among bushes, or dancing on mountain tops […] The visitor considered that Manx people were more susceptible to fairy sightings because of [the] scenery and 'a sombrous imagination heightened by traditionary terrors'.[10]

This reputation has continued in the migrant setting, where other Australian Celtic groups consider the Manx community to be strongly superstitious and particularly attentive to the influences of the 'other' world as described in their folklore. An instance of this was reported to me by participants at the Australian Celtic Festival, at Glen Innes, who noted that on a recent trip returning from Britain, members of the Manx Society were heard thanking the 'fairies' for their safe journey, and when asked about it said that this was a common practice. Some of the older members of the society have also told me about the significance of a local landmark known as the *Ballalona* or 'Fairy Bridge' and how when returning to the Isle of Man on vacation it is considered important to call out a greeting to the lil' fellas when crossing it. One Brisbane woman, who was born on the Isle, relates how her grandfather's fireplace storytelling would often include the tale of how he was returning from an overnight horse-buying trip to Dublin and how, after a rough sea passage, he tried crossing the bridge around midnight. The horses, rearing up with rolling eyes, refused to cross and he was forced to continue his journey by a much longer route.[11] This dark side of the faerie tradition is also expressed in the legends of

10 Cowan and Henderson, *Scottish*, 18.

11 E Dolejsi, 'A Manx Childhood', 72–75 in L Witherington (ed), *Gems of God's Earth: The Queensland Manx Society Inc. 1914 to 2004* (Brisbane, 2004) at p 72.

the terrifying *Moddey Dhoo* (or 'ghost dog'), believed to haunt the ruins of Peel Castle. Although various historical folklore accounts tell of the dangers of being in this place alone at night and of the fate of those who have scorned this warning, I have also been told of a more recent account, albeit in classic urban legend genre of a 'friend of a friend', by a gentleman at a Manx Society dinner. A few years ago, so the story goes, a young man, full of bravado, who wished to test the accuracy of the *Moddey Dhoo* ghost stories, spent the night alone in the haunted castle. Evidently he was found in a state of shock the next morning, sporting a nasty scratch, and refused to talk about his frightful experience.

Although these narratives are usually recounted in a jovial manner, there is usually a sense of seriousness in the tone in which such remarks are made: an almost maternal concern about the significance of this faerie knowledge as a fundamental tool that one needs to protect one's self from the elements of the natural world. The embedded quality of these beliefs seems directly related to both the active and the tacit maintenance of a distinctive cultural community and a longing to remember 'home'.

Domestic spheres

The ethnographic evidence also attests to the significance of the domestic spheres of the home and farmyard as a primary setting for mortal interaction with the faerie folk 'that doth haunt hearth and dairy'.[12] Spence records the belief that entities such as the brownies (or *broonies*) and the *glaistigs* (female nature spirits) would 'keep things ship-shape in houses, wash the dishes, and polish the furniture, and […] pelt untidy cottages with turfs and stones'.[13] The *broonies*, originally identified as dwarf-sized hairy people who would complete miscellaneous untended farm chores for a place at the fire and some oat cakes, are particularly interesting in terms of migration patterns, because they were believed to attach themselves to certain families and even move abroad with them.

12 Jonson, cited in Spence, *British*, 88.

13 Spence, *British*, 27.

This relationship between domesticity and the 'good people' is apparent in the faerie narratives that continue to be relevant to an experiential Celtic identity in the Australian setting.

When asked about the existence of family faerie traditions, a female informant in her early twenties, originally from a rural town in south-east Queensland, recounted a story about how as a child she and her sisters would participate in the weekly scone-baking with their grandmother, who was of Irish descent. After the scones were taken from the oven, she remembers that her grandmother would always take one into the garden, break it open and leave it there. She remarked how, 'although nothing was really spoken about it, we all knew it was for the fairies – to keep them happy'. The offering of a small portion of food or drink in this manner has been documented as an ancient Gaelic practice where, 'in Ireland "you must never drain your wine-glass at a feast, nor the poteen flask nor the milk-pail" if you wish to "keep in with" the fairies'.[14]

Another example of the link between the kitchen and the other realms came from a woman in her fifties, a migrant from the Scottish Highlands who works as a medical specialist. This informant laughed about how her 'Aussie' grandkids tease her about her compulsion to smash up all the egg shells after baking, so that the witches, in this case little ugly sprite-like creatures, can't use the shells as boats to sail to the Isle of Skye and cause havoc. Another participant, who emigrated from Belfast as a child in the 1960s, recalls how her mother would place sewing needles under the front door mat, out of respect for the 'little people' to aid them with anything they needed to fix. She also remembers how, on Saint Patrick's Day, her father would muster the children to search the backyard bush for a glimpse of Brian Boru, in the guise of king of the leprechauns. The relationship between faerie faith and celebrating important annual events as a family unit seems to be a recurrent theme.

When asked about mystical family traditions, many people of Scottish heritage talked about how they remembered participating in New Year's Eve, or *Hogmanay*, rituals with their kith and kin in

14 Lady Wilde, cited in Spence, *British*, 89.

Australia earlier in the century. Although certain aspects of the rite varied with each family that practised it, some central themes were involved that included protecting the household from mischievous and even malicious spirits for the year ahead. One version, recounted by a woman in her nineties, emphasised the importance of participating as a family unit on this occasion, to ensure good luck and prosperity. She explained how just before midnight on New Year's Eve the whole family would sweep the dust through the house out the back door, symbolising the brushing away of all the bad luck, and then run around the outside of the dwelling together to the front door. At the stroke of midnight they would re-enter, led by a dark-haired male, performing the 'first footing' and carrying a loaf of bread, whisky and a bucket of coal (which was a ward against malevolent pixies). Ross's *The Folk Lore of the Scottish Highlands* notes how the *Hogmanay* 'ritual was believed to have an apotropaic effect and to keep at bay fairies and evil spirits and hostile forces of every kind'.[15] The presence of the celebration as a migrant narrative is of interest to folklorists because although the ritual of 'First Footing is still carried out, as in other parts of the Highlands [...] elsewhere, it is a dying custom'.[16]

Faeries in the garden

In the interviews that were conducted for this research, the association between the faerie and the natural environment was another central theme that emerged. One family of Irish descent who participated in the study talked about their grandmother's intrinsic belief in the faerie and how they inhabited her verdant and overgrown garden on a large block of land in Brisbane's southern suburbs. The grandmother had moved to this house as a young child, with her large family, from Brisbane's Fortitude Valley district, which was known in the late nineteenth and early twentieth centuries for its predominantly Irish community. Her son recalls how the faerie world was presented to him as an ordinary part of life by his mother

15 A Ross, *The Folklore of the Scottish Highlands* (Totowa, 1976) 120.

16 *Ibid*, 120.

and other neighbours of Irish stock, and how this belief was in turn passed on to his children by his mother's influence. Although this community's faerie faith was described as amorphously mixed up in everyday life, with no definite distinction made between real and unreal, it also contained many precepts concerning protective moral action. For children, being naughty was to risk the wrathful appearance of a grumpy leprechaun or an enraged banshee. The faerie metaphor was also a vehicle for didactic principles, often in reference to the beneficial and harmful properties of plants and wider attitudes toward nature. The grandmother, who often talked of her own mother's renown as a mystic who used local herbs to cure all sorts of ailments, was very concerned with the possibility that certain plants, such as wattle or mayflowers, might be brought into the house, thus offending the faerie folk. She also warned of the hazards of watering the garden too late in the afternoon and provoking the anger of 'the little people' if they got wet. The children were made acutely aware of how certain plants were not to be disturbed, as they were sacred to the faerie, such as the orange 'snake bread' fungi, ferns and clover, and to be mindful of toadstools because 'that's where the little ones lived'. This ethnobotanical link, with the faerie acting as a medium between human culture and the pharmaceutical qualities of nature, has also been noted by folklorists, such as Spence, who records how 'most of the "Folk" are knowledgeable in the lore of medicinal plants. At times they communicate their knowledge of these matters to human beings'.[17]

Identity and the liminal other

The faerie motif, with its suggestion of an intrinsic difference and liminality – betwixt this world and the next – is also apparent as a statement of 'otherness', and is used in the migrant setting to project and negotiate a distinct cultural and ethnic identity. The stimulus to migrate to Australia was in many cases attributed to the hegemonic pressures experienced in the Celtic homelands and the resulting discrimination of ethnic stereotyping. The use of this symbolism

17 Spence, *British*, 28.

as a type of cultural critique signifying 'otherness' is a theme that occurs elsewhere in the anthropological literature. For instance, Gilad Pavada, in analysing contemporary queer cinema, has identified the use of the faerie metaphor as symbolising the struggle between the hegemonic negotiation of positive and negative identity representations of gay subculture. Pavada draws attention to the use of the 'fairy' label as an assigned derogative, originally intended to reject, humiliate and marginalise gay people, by implying that they existed in the liminal space between standard gender expectations.[18] There is folkloric evidence to support this link between a liminal gender and the faerie world at least as far back as the early middle ages, when in Germany, England, Bavaria and Italy, 'men played the role of female fairies in European rites and festivals for many centuries'.[19] In winter solstice celebrations relating to the snow queen *Holda* and the old fairy godmother *la Befana*, 'men dressed in female [fairy] attire, and carrying brooms, travelled from house to house, blessing families and distributing presents'.[20] Although this association became a derogative label around the 1920s, the term 'fairy' was 'reclaimed' by gay activists in the 1970s to become part of the counterculture's popular iconography, 'to describe a radical gay [person] with a sense of spirituality [...] and the motif of white, golden or transparent wings has been reproduced in recent films and videos to signify power, pride and liberation'.[21]

This reclamation of a derogative stereotype, associated with a liminal and somewhat fanciful 'other', seems to be relevant to negotiations of neo-Celtic identity, especially in migrant contexts. The continuing ethnic stereotype of the Celt as wild, rural and quaint 'folk', paralleling the distinctions between mortals and faerie, has to some extent been reclaimed by those it was intended to constrain.

---

18 G Pavada, 'Radical fairies and Stereotyped Fairies in Laurie Lind's "The Fairy Who Didn't Want to be a Fairy Anymore"', *Cinema Journal* 5(1) (2005) 66–78, at p 67.

19 *Ibid*, 69.

20 *Ibid*, 69.

21 *Ibid*, 70.

Letcher's study of how eco-protesters have used a symbolic identification with the faerie as a significant belief narrative in their efforts to 'position themselves outside, or opposed to, mainstream society',[22] and to promote a form of 'green radicalism', is also indicative of the value of mystic imagery in endorsing and sustaining a sense of otherness. In this context, faerie motifs are used: in the production and performance of music, song and poetry as a regular activity in the protest camps; in the adoption by the protesters of faerie nicknames, to identify more readily as a group and distance themselves from their former mainstream identities; and in the coining of such terms as 'pixieing' to refer to an 'act of cheeky defiance of authority, such as the snatching and wearing of a security guard's hat',[23] or even more serious 'eco-sabotage' of heavy machinery. In this way, in a similar fashion to features of migrant Celtic identity promotion, the protesters 'see themselves as the "little people" standing up to the power of the state [...] and the adoption of fairy mythology helps to justify their counter-cultural morality'.[24]

This metaphorical association between the faerie and the struggle for social, political and economic equality for the peoples of the Celtic 'fringe' was particularly apparent in the close association between Irish nationalism and the faerie motif in art and literature in the late nineteenth and early twentieth centuries, as is evidenced by the works of poets such as Yeats. The notion that a distinctive Celtic personality and world view could be gleaned from the study of the culturally idiosyncratic features of folklore from this part of the world — in particular an association with the *Sidhe* (faerie people) — is located even earlier in time. The brothers Grimm, renowned for their extensive ethnographic work in collecting German folk tales, noted, in their translation of Thomas Crofton Croker's 1825 volume *Fairy Legends and Traditions of the South of Ireland*, how Irish folklore was the best medium to offer

22 A Letcher, 'The scouring of the Shire: fairies, trolls and pixies in eco-protest culture', *Folklore* 112(2) (2001) 147–161, at p 154.

23 *Ibid*, 154.

24 *Ibid*, 153.

> a picture of the Irishman's nature, always excitable, tinged with a certain wildness, and yet endowed with spiritual powers. Only such an agile imagination was capable of giving to the fundamental thought of the saga a narrative expression which constantly surprises us with new and unexpected turns. Nearly always the events become entangled or are unravelled by the intervention of one of the spirit beings who in countless numbers inhabit water and land, wood and mountain, rock and wilderness, and who take on both the most charming and the ugliest forms.[25]

This association, where a Celtic identity is promoted through, among other things, an intimate and numinous affiliation with all things faerie, has clearly endured into the twenty-first century. It is a relationship that is actively maintained in both etic and emic modes, where on the one hand the faerie icons in mass media are often portrayed as quintessentially 'Celtic' — like the Welsh-speaking elves in fantasy epics like *The Lord of the Rings* — while on the other, such associations are simultaneously sustained and workshopped by contemporary Celts themselves. The result is an internal and external perception that Celtic tradition acts as a custodian of ancient faerie lore and as a conduit of accessibility to a mystical spiritualism, in a world where facts are privileged over fantasy.

The predominance of the way in which Celtic identity continues to be articulated, in part, through the medium of faerie metaphors, generates questions as to why such associations have continuing relevance in the postmodern world. How do we account for this relevance, when many of those who assert a contemporary Celticity reside in an industrialised urban setting, far removed from the ancestral and rural 'folk' whose everyday lifeways were embedded with mystical belief systems? It is argued here that in a similar fashion

---

25 Grimms, cited in R Meyer, *Wisdom of Fairytales* (Edinburgh, 1995) 249–250.

to Levi-Strauss's classical observation via structural anthropological analysis 'that animals are good to think with',[26] it would seem that the Faerie are important to people and their cultural identity for what they allegorically represent. The continuing significance of the fay seems to emerge from, in part, a search for personal agency, ontological meaning and the pursuit of a sense of belonging to a wider cultural community. Although the faerie metaphors are obviously complex and somewhat discursive in what they represent for contemporary people, there is also an apparent emphasis on the manner in which they restore 'play and fancy and theatricality to a central position'[27] in people's lives. As such, an engagement with the faerie faith by those living in an industrialised community actively and tacitly furnishes people with a sensation of enchantment and excitement, which might otherwise be lacking in their everyday lives, and connects them to a cultural yearning for what they believe has been left behind.

The faerie would also seem, then, to have a place in the present-day world, not only as an articulation of contemporary Celtic identity, but, according to Peter Rojcewicz's research, in how they reflect 'problems of relativity of knowledge and human estrangement from the world'.[28] Rojcewicz explores the idea that modern UFO phenomena are in actuality a resurgence in fairy faith, and thus represent an 'unbroken continuum of folk imagination and reality'.[29] In constructing the socio-cultural worlds in which we live, we inadvertently create gaps between what is perceived and what exists. As a result, the faerie, in all their many guises and in both metaphorical and experiential forms, are argued to be

---

26 O Lofgren, 'Our friends in nature: class and animal symbolism', *Ethnos* 50 (3–4) (1985) 184–213, at p 184.

27 D Purkiss, *Troublesome Things: A History of Fairies and Fairy Stories* (London, 2000) 195.

28 P Rojcewicz, 'Between one eye blink and the next: fairies, UFOs, and problems of knowledge', 479–514 in P Narvaez (ed), *The Good People: New Fairylore Essays* (Kentucky, 1991) at p 481.

29 Rojcewicz, 481.

what remains after a too-orderly construction of human knowledge and social reality is interpretively applied. As representative of a dialogue between bounded concepts, 'neither purely physical nor mental, existing at the momentary interface between mind and matter',[30] it is no wonder that present-day expressions of Celticity, unbounded itself by heterogeneity, migration and its 'fringe' status, have such an intimate reliance on the faerie in their promotion of a distinctive ethnic identity narrative on the global stage.

A similar analysis has been made by Diane Purkiss, who, in an investigation of faerie themes as they have appeared throughout western literature, raises the question of why humans need the faerie so badly. Evidencing the 'sheer variety of human interactions with fairy from commercial to terrific',[31] Purkiss is enthralled by the endurance of this relationship between people and the fay throughout time and space. Her research emphasises the metaphorical quality of this long-lived association, in which the 'little people' are seen to embody a dialogue between those forces which simultaneously evoke both fear and fascination in the human condition: life and death, imagination and aspiration, emotion, and the inexplicable dimensions of the environment. In this analysis, people also need the faerie as an interface between the subjective and the objective worlds in which they live.

> Human nature seems to abhor blank spaces on the map. Where there are no human habitations, no towns, where villages dwindle into farms and farms into woods, mapping stops. Then the imagination rushes to fill the woods with something other than blank darkness: nymphs, satyrs, elves, gnomes, pixies, fairies.[32]

The faerie are thus, among other things, an organic outcome of the

30 Rojcewicz, 483.

31 Purkiss, *Troublesome Things*, 3.

32 *Ibid*, 4.

processes involved in the social construction of reality. Springing out of the disparity generated by strict human classifications of 'nature' and 'culture', they are to be found where the edges become blurry: at the bottom of the garden; at twilight; and in dreams, poems and stories. Ironically, the faerie are given power by the very boundaries that deny their existence, and must remain hidden, indescribable and amorphous so as to not disturb or reveal the imposed artificiality of the social and perceptive artifices which conceal them. As such, the faerie 'are not part of a dead and gone past. We need them in order to understand ourselves'.[33]

Conclusion

The ancient and otherworldly connections to the faerie envisaged by people of Celtic descent in Australia can be seen to act as a prolific metaphor for cultural revival and survival in the contemporary setting. Allegorical narratives, which have been relocated to a new landscape yet embrace a direct reference to the old-world context from which they arose, play a vital role in re-imagining and sustaining a sense of community and traditional cohesion. Due to its liminal quality, the repositioning of this mythic imagery to the antipodes has resulted in a profuse and multifaceted cultural expression. Cloaked in mystique and humour, the Celtic faerie faith has withstood many of the ravages of hegemony and assimilation and has been fluently reshaped into a contemporary mode. By bringing the fairies to Australia with them, migrants also conveyed the comfort, familiarity and protection of the homeland to their new beginnings.

---

33 Purkiss, *Troublesome Things*, 3.

Competing Celticities: Cornish and Irish constructions of Australia

Philip Payton ⊕

'Reflexivity', the willingness and ability to reflect upon the formative influences of one's life's experiences, is a quality increasingly demanded of historians. A full biographical explanation of my personal entwinement with Cornwall, Ireland and Australia would be self-indulgent (as well as tedious) but one 'reflexive' anecdote is relevant here, a penetrating insight — or so it seemed to me at the time — into the complexity of competing constructions of Celticity in Australia. In 2001, I revisited South Australia, a state with which I have been familiar for some 30 years, where I had lived and worked in the past, and which I had subsequently visited on numerous occasions. In 2001, I had been invited to address the biennial Cornish festival — the 'Kernewek Lowender' — held at Moonta, Wallaroo and Kadina, the 'Australia's Little Cornwall' former copper-mining district on the northern Yorke Peninsula. I had already written extensively on the district's Cornish community, and would do so again in the future, and by then knew the locality intimately.[1] I also knew Burra, Kapunda, Callington and a host of other smaller South Australian places where once there had been recognisable 'Cornish communities', and where today there were often traces of that influence. South Australia was, as Geoffrey Blainey had reminded his readers in 1994 in his *A Shorter History*

⊕ Institute of Cornish Studies, University of Exeter (Cornwall Campus).

1 P Payton, *Pictorial History of Australia's Little Cornwall* (Adelaide, 1978); P Payton, *The Cornish Miner in Australia: Cousin Jack 'Down Under'* (Redruth, 1984); P Payton, *The Cornish Overseas: A History of Cornwall's Great Emigration* (Fowey, 2005); P Payton, *Making Moonta: The Invention of Australia's Little Cornwall* (Exeter, 2007).

of Australia, the 'Cornish corner' of the continent.[2]

However, alongside this periodic renewal of my immersion in South Australia's Cornish heritage, I was in 2001 also invited to address the State Historical Trust's annual conference, held that year at the tiny settlement of Pekina on the edge of the southern Flinders Ranges. Once again, my theme was 'the Cornish' — and I knew that during the nineteenth century the Cornish had been briefly at Pekina searching for copper[3] — but this was new territory for me. Well off the beaten — or at least bitumen — track, Pekina, even today, has more than a hint of the frontier, of being on the margins of South Australia's wheat belt and gateway to the outback. Initially familiar in appearance — modest stone-built buildings in the South Australian style — it was soon obvious that Pekina was unexpectedly 'different'. One of those modest buildings, despite its Nonconformist appearance, turned out to be a Roman Catholic church — a comparative rarity in rural South Australia — and from the civic flagpoles in the village centre flew the national flags of Australia, the United States of America, and the Republic of Ireland. The juxtaposition spoke volumes: here was an overt expression of Irish nationalism, one which claimed kinship with Irish-America but also constructed Australian nationality through the prism of Irishness.

One might have expected it elsewhere in the continent, perhaps, but in South Australia it came as a surprise. As Eric Richards had observed in 1991, in a corollary that anticipated Blainey's later remark, 'South Australia was the least Irish part of nineteenth century Australia [...] South Australia seemed in Irish eyes the most alien quarter of the continent'.[4] In the twentieth century, the Irish had appeared no more visible. Yet here in Pekina, in the early twenty-first century, was an enduring, even aggressive, Irishness: in

---

2 G Blainey, *A Shorter History of Australia* (Melbourne, 1994) 50.

3 *Yorke's Peninsula Advertiser* (20 September 1878).

4 E Richards, 'The importance of being Irish in colonial South Australia', 62–102 in J O'Brien and P Travers (eds), *The Irish Experience in Australia* (Dublin, 1991) 62.

the Catholic church hall, where some of the conference proceedings were to be held, a framed picture of her majesty the queen had intentionally been hung upside-down.

For me, the Pekina experience was salutary. Almost complacent in my assumption of the salience of 'Cornishness' in constructing the distinctive and largely protestant identity of rural South Australia, I had not been prepared for the assertion of what was in many ways an oppositional — even dissenting — construction, one which had been established by Irish immigrants in the nineteenth century and remained very much alive today. Part of my surprise, perhaps, was that I had become used to the rhetoric of contemporary pan-Celticism — in the UK but most especially in Australia — where it was the similarities between the several Celtic peoples that were stressed routinely, and where differences were glossed over. According to the ideology of pan-Celticism, the shared historical experiences and cultural identities of the Celtic peoples were more important than divisions between them.[5] The Celts had much in common, it was argued. In Australia, in particular, the distinctions that had been noticeable in the nineteenth century — the rivalry between Cornish and Irish, for example, or differences between Scottish Highlanders and Lowlanders, or tensions between 'Celts' of varying protestant and Catholic hues — could be conveniently smoothed over. Australia, indeed, was the perfect multicultural stage on which pan-Celticism might be performed. A 'Celtic' stone circle was erected at Glen Innes in New South Wales, a mecca to which 'Celts' from across Australia would return periodically for affirmations of inter-Celtic solidarity, and an 'Australian tartan' was devised as a sartorial expression of such solidarity, to be displayed proudly on Scottish or Cornish or Manx kilts and a variety of other culturally appropriate clothing. As Peter Alexander explained in 1989, 'The recently-created Australian tartan is a move [...] to achieve Celtic unison. Based on the colours of Central Australia [...] this "tartan for a Sunburnt Country" is intended to cater for

5 See P Berresford Ellis, *Celtic Dawn: A History of Pan-Celticism* (London, 1993).

those proud of being both Celtic and Australian. It is intended for all Celts'.[6]

Against the prevailing sentiment of pan-Celticism, the alternative Irish construction of South Australia, so apparent at Pekina in 2001, had come as a surprise. And yet it ought not to have done. Despite the relative invisibility of both Irish immigrants and Roman Catholics in nineteenth-century South Australia, the state had never been homogenous in its make-up. Alongside the Cornish and English, there had been large German communities, as well as distinctive groups of Welsh-speaking immigrants from Wales and Gaelic-speaking Highlanders. In this, South Australia had been a microcosm of the Australian experience as a whole. As Patrick O'Farrell has argued in his *The Irish in Australia*, Australia was, from the earliest days of European settlement, a decidedly pluralistic society, with the potential for religious and ideological conflict between groups from different backgrounds with different experiences, beliefs, values and aspirations.[7] Among these different groups, of course, were the several Celtic peoples. And if their potential for conflict had been conveniently forgotten by today's pan-Celticists, then until comparatively recently it had also been hidden by the prevailing conventional wisdom of Australian historiography. This insisted that Australian society in the colonial period, and indeed up until the 1950s, was remarkably homogeneous, the vast majority of the European population the descendents of immigrants from Britain and Ireland, any differences between individuals and groups largely ironed out by the shared experiences of migration and settlement.

And yet, even as the academic proponents of 'Anglo-Celtic' homogeneity expounded their position, some of their more imaginative and individualistic colleagues were prepared to embrace — indeed, demand — new perspectives. As early as 1954, for

6 P Alexander, 'The survival of the Celts in Australia', *Australian Celtic Journal* 2 (1989) 11–20, at p 19; see also P Payton, 'Re-inventing Celtic Australia' 108–125 in P Payton and A Hale (eds), *New Directions in Celtic Studies* (Exeter, 2000).

7 P O'Farrell, *The Irish in Australia* (Sydney, rev ed 1993) 10.

example, Manning Clark had criticised the 'middling' assumptions of Australian historiography. Australian historians were in danger of drawing a picture of their country's history as culturally drab, uninspiring and essentially uniform, he complained, while much of the evidence was to the contrary, pointing to a vibrant and sometimes pugnacious diversity, not least the divide between Catholic and protestant: 'So let us drop the talk about middling standards, mediocrity, and sameness, and have a look at these differences'.[8] Later, in 1985, Geoffrey Blainey added his voice to this criticism. The current debate about multiculturalism, he observed, assumed that between 1788 and 1950 — because Australia 'was populated largely by people from the British Isles' — the country had exhibited 'a cultural unity, a homogeneity which is the very antithesis of multiculturalism'. However, Blainey argued, '[i]n the true cultural sense [...] Australia before 1950 was a multicultural society because the cultural difference between Irish Catholics and Scottish Presbyterians and Cornish Methodists and many other groupings was intensely felt, at times too intensely'. Moreover, '[t]hese differences permeated politics, culture, education, sport, business, the public service and every branch of national life'.[9] A year later, Patrick O'Farrell offered a very similar analysis in *The Irish in Australia*, criticising the 'lazy history' that assumed homogeneity, and pointing instead to the pluralist diversity of colonial Australia.[10] In 2003, Blainey returned to his theme, explaining that in nineteenth-century Australia there had been different 'social rules for each section of society [...] a Cornish funeral in South Australia was not like a Scottish funeral in Brisbane'.[11]

In early twenty-first-century Australia, there is now — notwithstanding the continuing vibrancy of pan-Celticism — a

8 M Clarke, *Occasional Writings and Speeches* (Melbourne, 1980) 9.

9 G Blainey, *Blainey – Eye on Australia: Speeches and Essays of Geoffrey Blainey* (Melbourne, 1991) 47.

10 O'Farrell, *Irish in Australia*, 10.

11 G Blainey, *Black Kettle and Full Moon: Daily Life in Vanished Australia* (Camberwell, 2003) 149.

greater willingness to accept the diversity of pre-1950s Australia, and Australian historiography has shifted accordingly. The Pekina experience, then, though upsetting preconceived notions of pan-Celticism, has not only alerted us to a hitherto under-recognised diversity within South Australia itself, but has mirrored current pre-occupations and imperatives in the writing of Australian history. It is in this context that we can begin to look beyond the rhetoric of pan-Celticism to lay bare and track competing Celticities — in this case, the Cornish and Irish — in the cultural construction of Australia.

As Blainey recognised, religious affiliation was often a proxy for ethnic identification. At its simplest level, Irish tended to be Catholic and Cornish Methodist, and this distinction in itself was more than enough encouragement for rivalry and conflict. Likewise, ecclesiastical institutions — not least the churches and chapels themselves — were as much vehicles for cultural and political expression as they were for religious observance. As Blainey wrote of nineteenth-century Victoria, 'Catholic churches were the societies for Irish settlers and custodians of Irish nationalism. Many Methodist congregations in mining regions were virtually Cornish societies'.[12] In South Australia, where the Cornish were dominant in the mining communities, they outnumbered the tiny pockets of Irish with whom they co-existed. In the copper-mining town of Moonta on the northern Yorke Peninsula — the 'Australia's Little Cornwall' of popular fancy — it was reported that in 1870 '[t]he Cornish men [...] declared there would be no Catholic church in their town'. Although ultimately unsuccessful, this was a move designed to frustrate Irish aspirations locally.[13] Later, in 1904, the Methodist minister at Moonta Mines told his largely Cornish congregation that '[t]he work of Protestantism would not be finished and the Orange Institution would not survive the need of its existence until the Church of Rome came back to the New Testament and the sway of

12 G Blainey, *A History of Victoria* (Melbourne, 2006) 116–117.

13 Anon, *St Lawrence's Friary, 1898–1973, North Adelaide, South Australia* (Camberwell, nd) 11.

the Papacy was at an end'.[14] The reference to the Orange Institution was not hypothetical: in 1905, there were no fewer than five Orange Lodges in Moonta and its immediate hinterland.

Religious tension slipped easily into other expressions of ethnic hostility. In 1884, at Wallaroo Mines, near Moonta, the small collection of cottages known colloquially as 'Irish Town' was singled out for stinging criticism. In contrast to the surrounding Cornish cottages, it was alleged, the 'houses [in Irish Town] are smaller and dirtier, with filthy pigsties and cesspits close to water tanks. On top of several tanks in the place [were] thick layers of goats' and fowls' dung, all of which is likely to be washed into the tanks at the first rains'.[15] Here was an unequal power relationship and a sense of ethno-territorial exclusivity, for the Cornish vastly outnumbered the Irish, claiming this particular corner of South Australia as their own, and had no hesitation in exercising their regional hegemony. This was a tension specific to this place in Australia. But it was also evidence of a characteristic disdain which followed the Irish wherever they ventured — from as near as Liverpool to as far as New Zealand — and which saw old antipathies from the British Isles re-enacted anew in the lands of the British and Irish diaspora. Amongst these antipathies was the Cornish-Irish rivalry, exhibited wherever the two groups found themselves in close proximity: usually on the mining frontiers of the New World, where religious hostility was complemented by competition for employment in the mines.

Yet in Australia this was more than re-enactment, for Australia proved the backdrop for two competing ideologies of place *and* for two competing ideologies of Celticity: Cornish and Irish. Both groups often congregated in their own distinct precincts, usually for socio-economic reasons. In this way, for example, some Melbourne suburbs, such as Richmond and North Melbourne, were in the nineteenth century regarded as overwhelmingly 'Irish' areas. In 1861, there were Melbourne suburbs that could sport greater

14 *Australian Christian Commonwealth* (17 June 1904).

15 *Yorke's Peninsula Advertiser* (15 April 1884).

numbers of Irish females than English, and there were Victorian country towns, too, that acquired reputations as concentrations of Irish: notably Kilmore, Kyneton and Bungaree.[16] For some, indeed, these were 'Irish towns'. Initially, there were Irish immigrants who saw Australia as simply a new launching pad for Irish nationalism, another place for organising themselves politically and mobilising at a distance to oppose British rule in Ireland. To its detractors, this activity was merely Fenianism in the antipodes, an unfortunate attempt to recreate in Australia the political antagonisms of home. But for its supporters, this agitation was a legitimate antipodean expression of Irish aspirations, one that could be articulated in a democratic arena more conducive to sympathetic debate, without the 'old country' connotations of subversion and conspiracy.

At the cultural level, Irish nationalism also found fertile ground in nineteenth-century Australia, although — as both Patrick O'Farrell and Jonathan M Wooding remind us — the 'Gaelic revival' of the late nineteenth and early twentieth centuries had less impact in Australia than it did in the United States.[17] There was, nonetheless, some enthusiasm for learning and propagating the Irish language and for 'Gaelic sports', and 'Celtic Crosses became the ubiquitous funerary monument for the secular Irish-Australian community' as well as iconographic devices to be deployed for religious purposes by the Catholic church. Gaelic revivalism had a particular appeal for Irish-Catholic clergy, many of whom had trained at Maynooth and had learned Irish as part of their studies. Those clergy arriving in Australia in the late nineteenth century brought their enthusiasms with them. Inevitably, therefore, as the causes of Irish nationalism and Roman Catholicism became ever more closely entwined in Australia in the years after 1890, so the clergy, with their increasing leadership of the nationalist movement, brought their Gaelic enthusiasms to bear. Nonetheless, Australia

---

16 Blainey, *History of Victoria*, 118.

17 J M Wooding, 'Priests, the Gaelic revival and Irish-Australian identity, 1880–1920', 119–136 in J M Wooding and D Day (eds), *Celtic Australian Identities* (Sydney, 2001).

was not Ireland, and the overt expression of the Gaelic vision of Irish nationalism observable in the commemorative events in Australia of the centenary of the 'Rising of 1798' caused some discomfort in Irish-Australian circles. By now, Irish nationalism in Australia had taken its own trajectory. As Wooding has explained, 'In Australia [...] interest in rebellion was limited by demographics, distance and the belief — inspired by the success of the campaign for Australian home rule — that home rule [for Ireland] was achievable by parliamentary means'.[18] Opposition to the potential for rebellion in contemporary Ireland meant discomfort in honouring the events of 1798, while the triumph of Australian self-government — first in responsible government for each of the colonies, and now in the impending federation of the Commonwealth of Australia — provided a credible, indeed inspirational model for Irish nationalists to follow at home. As John Hirst has put it, '[t]he Irish had done well in Australia and saw the adoption of self-government within the empire as the solution to the Irish problem at home, the system which had worked so well in the colonies'.[19]

'Doing well' in Australia was not just a question of economic success. For the Irish, a large measure of their success in Australia was the achievement of a 'level playing field', one which was able to accommodate — even assimilate — the politics of Irish nationalism as well as smoothing the antagonisms between protestant and Catholic. As Hirst has noted, the latter was in large measure the result of the equality between denominations achieved in Australia. South Australia, the 'Paradise of Dissent', became the first British territory to eschew entirely a link between church and state, but before that in 1836, Governor Burke of New South Wales — a protestant Irishman — had come up with an ingenious solution. Turning the notion of 'establishment' on its head, he decided that each of the principal churches active in the British Isles — the Anglicans, the Presbyterians and the Roman Catholics — should be

18 Wooding, 'Priests, The Gaelic Revival and Irish-Australian Identity', 132.

19 J Hirst, *Sense and Nonsense in Australian History* (Melbourne, 2006) 12.

allocated support from public funds. As Hirst has remarked, '[t]his truly amazing measure was the clearest signal to the Irish that life in Australia was to be truly a new dispensation. A British government was financing the Roman heresy'.[20] The scheme was later expanded to include other denominations and faiths — including the Jews — and lasted until 1862. In neighbouring Victoria, a similar policy lasted until 1870, both colonies then following the example of complete separation already set by South Australia.

Australian identity was, by the late nineteenth century, emerging as something like a composite 'British' identity, of which the Irish were an integral component: partly as a result of numerical strength, and partly because of their social and religious accommodation within Australia. Yet this 'Britishness' did not lead to a lessening of its component parts, with the Scots, Welsh and Cornish continuing to foster separate identities. And most of all, as Hirst has observed, '[t]he Irish of course could still bridle at a British identity even when it included them as equals'.[21] Here, for all the willingness to seek Irish self-government within the British empire, there could still be firm insistence that the Irish were emphatically *not* British. This insistence, brought to Australia by immigrants from Ireland, was further reinforced by the Gaelic revival of the late nineteenth century. In the Gaelic vision of Australia, the Irish were fundamentally 'Celtic'; and to be Celtic was to be both non-British *and* anti-British.

Here was a construction of Celticity with which, inevitably, the Cornish could not agree. The Cornish had also 'done well' in Australia, as they had in all the new world societies to which they had ventured, from the United States of America to South Africa and New Zealand. Cornish hard-rock miners, especially, had been in sustained demand throughout the nineteenth century on the international mining frontier, highly skilled — and well-paid — workers, whose efforts were critical in the swift development

20 Hirst, *Sense and Nonsense*, 13.

21 *Ibid*, 12.

of the international mining economy.[22] Already imbued with a superior sense of self, a manifestation of the 'industrial prowess' that underscored nineteenth-century Cornish society, the emigrant Cornish deployed the myth of 'Cousin Jack' wherever they went. Put simply, this myth insisted that the Cornish were somehow innately qualified above all others as hard-rock miners, that they were especially suited to the rigours of the mining frontiers of the new world, a superiority that placed them in the forefront of the international mining industry and gave them the edge over competing ethnic groups. It was a myth developed in Latin America in the years after 1815, honed on the copper mines of Michigan and South Australia in the 1840s and 1860s, and given expression the world over, culminating in the Cornish dominance of South African mining in the 1880s and 1890s. But the Cornish could also have it both ways, and part of the secret of their success — in Australia as elsewhere — was their ability to temper 'difference' with conformity to the norms and expectations of new world (essentially English-speaking, protestant) societies. In contrast to many other ethnic groups, Cornish conceptions of separate identity were neither subversive nor threatening in the estimation of their host societies.

In Australia, as elsewhere, the myth of Cousin Jack was complemented by an insistence that the Cornish were 'ancient Britons', descendents of the original 'British' inhabitants of Great Britain.[23] Although this sought to distinguish the Cornish from the English — the latter the descendents of Anglo-Saxon interlopers in the British Isles — it nonetheless secured the Cornish in their status as progenitors of Britain's greatness. As the 'original' Britons, the Cornish were somehow more 'British' than the English: they were, after all, direct descendants of Boudicca, the folk-hero so beloved of Victorian history books, who had stood up for Britain against the might of Rome. This image of the martial superiority of the 'ancient Briton' seemed a million miles from English constructions

22 Payton, *Cornish Overseas.*

23 P Payton, 'Cousin Jacks and ancient Britons: Cornish immigration and ethnic identity', *Journal of Australian Studies* 68 (2001) 54–64.

of the 'Celts' — which ranged from hostile imaginings of a feckless, dirty, subhuman race to a more patronisingly affectionate picture of a poetic, dreamy, unworldly people given to drink — but by the end of nineteenth century the terms 'ancient Briton' and 'Celt' had become entwined. Indeed, as early as 1859, the Wesleyan Methodist minister at the Burra copper mine in South Australia had told his Cornish congregation that they, in contradistinction to rival Irish claims, were 'the real descendents of the Celts'.[24]

Here, then, was a hint that the playing field was not always 'level' after all. Irish attempts to promote Gaelic revivalist images of the 'Celt' were met with not only a continuing English disdain for 'Celtic' attributes but also an alternative, competing construction of Celticity offered by the Cornish. For the Cornish, to be Celtic was to be not just British, but ultra-British. The Cornish asserted this 'superiority' — as Cousin Jacks and ancient Britons — in the face of ethnic competitors in the mines of the new world, and in Australia, as elsewhere, this was often in direct opposition to the Irish. A fascinating insight into Cornish-Irish rivalry is provided by the experience at the Kapunda copper mine in South Australia, discovered in 1843–44. As elsewhere in South Australia, the Cornish provided the 'labour aristocracy' at the mine — the captains (managers) and the 'tributers' and 'tutworkmen' (skilled underground miners) — but the workforce also consisted of other ethnic groups, including the Irish. Some of these Irish, indeed, were skilled hard-rock miners, like the Cornish, their presence at Kapunda keenly felt by the Cornish who resisted this ethno-occupational competition in the workplace. The Irish had first arrived at Kapunda in numbers in 1854, in response to the labour shortage occasioned by the departure of many of the Cornish for the goldfields of Victoria, and they were seen immediately by the remaining Cornish as rivals: a rivalry sharpened, of course, by religious prejudice.

In 1862, a number of Kapunda miners claimed that their ores were being unfairly assayed by the mine's staff, so that the value of

24 *South Australian Register* (4 March 1859).

the ore won was being underestimated. This, in turn, it was alleged, led to the miners on 'tribute' contract work being significantly underpaid. Anonymous threatening letters were sent to the mine's chief captain, and a public meeting was held at Kapunda to discuss the issue. The Cornish put their weight firmly behind their captain, implying that the Irish were responsible for the intimidating poison-pen letters, and with the situation becoming a little ugly, several speakers found it politic to express 'their opinion that the writer was neither a Cornishman or an Irishman', in order to diffuse the situation.[25] But the hostility remained. In 1893, there was an outbreak of violence in the elections to the Adelaide parliament, when Patrick McMahon Glynn — the hero of the Irish community at Kapunda — was surprisingly defeated. Glynn blamed his defeat on religious bigotry, and one eyewitness to the violence thought that '[t]he bone of contention was the Irish vote'.[26] In the fighting that followed, two of those most badly beaten both bore Cornish names: W Rowe and James Pengelly. When Michael Davitt, the Irish Land League agitator, visited the district in the 1890s, he felt as though 'Kapunda was somewhere in Connaught instead of being fourteen thousand miles away'.[27]

Like Pekina today, the strength of Irish identity in nineteenth-century Kapunda comes as a surprise. Further research might uncover the extent of the Cornish-Irish rivalry, and shed new light on the way it was expressed over time. Here it might be hypothesised that the conflict at Kapunda mirrored that at Butte, Montana, in the United States of America, where the struggle between the Cornish and the Irish for supremacy in the copper mines and for control of the miners' trade union is well documented. At Butte, as at Kapunda, the Irish were not always the unskilled labourers of popular fancy, but often highly-skilled hard-rock men, much sought after to work the difficult granite of the Butte district. The Irish formed themselves into a distinctive ethno-occupational enclave, and Butte

25 *South Australian Register* (17 May 1862).

26 Anon, *A Circle of Friends: Memories of Kapunda* (Kapunda, 1929) 108.

27 M Davitt, *Life and Progress in Australasia* (London, 1898) 63.

became one of the most 'Irish' towns in America. But there was also a sizeable Cornish ethno-occupational enclave — as there was in every other mining district in the American west — and there was a competing construction of Butte as a 'Cornish' town. The resultant antagonism between the competing claims and ambitions of the Cornish and the Irish had an especially illuminating dimension, for a great many of the skilled Irish miners at Butte had come from the 'Hungry Hill' copper mines of Allihies, in West Cork. There, in an earlier existence, they had already encountered the Cornish, for Cornish miners had been in West Cork as 'labour aristocracy' since the beginning of the nineteenth century. It was not surprising, given their higher wages and superior housing, that the Cornish attracted the resentment of the local Irish at Allihies, a hostility that the Irish took to Butte, and remembered when once again they rubbed shoulders there with the hated Cornish.[28]

Perhaps there were such remembrances at Kapunda. At any rate, it is its Irish identity that Kapunda has often sought to commemorate in recent decades. In the 1970s, the town initiated an 'Irish and Colonial Festival', designed to celebrate Kapunda's early history, but it was not until 1988 (Australia's bicentennial year) that it thought to remind locals and visitors of its Cornish connections — through the erection of a giant statue of a Cornish miner at the town's southern edge. Significantly, perhaps, the committee appointed to manage the project avoided the obvious name for the statue — 'Cousin Jack' — and opted for the more explicitly 'multicultural' 'Map Kernow': son of Cornwall, in the Cornish language. Although Cornish had never been spoken traditionally in South Australia, it was a Celtic language (like Irish), and its use somehow avoided the worst of the superior exclusivity associated with the myth of Cousin Jack. As the leaflet produced by the local council explained, 'Map Kernow stands for all the people who are part of Kapunda's history — the

28 D M Emmons, 'Faction fights: the Irish worlds of Butte, Montana, 1875–1917', 82–98 in P O'Sullivan (ed), *The Irish World Wide: History, Heritage, Identity* Volume 2: The Irish in the New Communities (Leicester, 1992); R A Williams, *The Berehaven Copper Mines* (Sheffield, 1991); Payton, *Making Moonta*, 210–12.

Cornish, Irish, German and other nationalities'.[29]

Be that as it may, the Cornish-Irish antipathy that had characterised nineteenth-century Kapunda was observable elsewhere in Australia, and in the mining industry was often institutionalised into rivalry within the trade union movement, as on the Western Australian goldfields at the turn of the twentieth century. In South Australia, despite the relatively small size of the Irish population, there was concern at the level of Irish influence elsewhere in the continent, particularly after federation, when it was feared that this influence could have major political ramifications across the country. In 1910, John Verran, a Cornish miner and Methodist local preacher from Moonta, became the first Labour premier of South Australia. His government lasted until 1912, his term in office characterised by industrial strife and conflict with the conservative legislative council, the upper house. Defeated at the polls, Verran began to lose the hitherto solid support of the Methodist establishment in South Australia, the *Australian Christian Commonwealth* magazine, published in Adelaide, complaining that he and his cabinet colleagues had been too 'prepared to take their orders from the more violent and revolutionary forces in the party'.[30] Looking anxiously across the state border to Victoria, the magazine detected a sinister Fenian hand in all this, and declared that 'efforts are being made to dominate the Labour Party by the Church of Rome'.[31]

These fears appeared to be confirmed by the conscription controversy during the Great War, when the Methodist church supported attempts to introduce conscription into the armed forces in Australia. The Labor Party, however — in South Australia as elsewhere in the continent — opposed conscription, as did many Roman Catholics and much of Irish-Australian opinion. Most vocal of the Irish-Catholic anti-conscriptionists was Daniel Mannix, newly appointed archbishop in Melbourne. More than just

29 Leaflet produced by the District Council of Kapunda c1989.

30 *Australian Christian Commonwealth* (16 February 1912).

31 *Australian Christian Commonwealth* (1 November 1911).

opposing conscription, which was bad enough for his protestant critics, Mannix seemed cool towards the empire's cause, and would not condemn German aggression until as late as 1917. His was an old-fashioned Irish nationalism, which infuriated empire loyalists and delighted Fenian sympathisers. He was either traitor or hero, depending whose side one was on, but he demanded the respect of Victoria's Catholic population, and by and large he got it. For the next four decades, he would take the salute at the annual Saint Patrick's Day parade in Melbourne. As Blainey has observed, Mannix positioned himself at the top of Bourke Street for the march-past 'as if he was the Pope. To a quarter of Victoria he was'.[32]

In South Australia, the Cornish-Methodist influence in the Labour Party survived the trauma of the conscription issue and the Great War, and managed to outlast the sudden collapse of the Moonta and Wallaroo mines in 1923. Well into the 1930s, argued John Lonie, the Labour Party in 'its composition and ideology reflected the social situation of the 1890s. Of note was the still very strong Methodist flavour which derived in the first place from the mine workers of Burra and Wallaroo who were of Cornish stock'.[33] This was an influence detectable, for example, in the Premiership in 1933 of RS Richards, born at Moonta of Cornish parentage, who continued to represent the constituency of Wallaroo until 1949.[34] In neighbouring Victoria, there was also an enduring Cornish influence in state politics, not so readily observable as in South Australia but detectable nonetheless. Its apogee was the Premiership of Albert Dunstan in the 1930s and 1940s. Dunstan's father was a Cornish miner and Methodist who, like many of his countrymen, had at length abandoned the goldfields to take up farming on what was then Victoria's outback frontier. Albert Dunstan became involved in the Country Party — which in those days had a strong radical

32 Blainey, *History of Victoria*, 157.

33 J Lonie, *Conservatism and class in South Australia during the depression years, 1924–1934* (unpublished MA thesis, University of Adelaide, 1973) 173.

34 Payton, *Making Moonta*, 185–191.

wing, generally supportive of Labor — and in 1926 founded his own breakaway group, the Progressive Country Party. Within weeks it had formed more than 100 branches, mainly in the north-western wheat belt of Victoria, where his father and other former gold-miners had settled a generation before. An astute politician, Dunstan managed to gain — and hold — the balance of power in the Victorian parliament, keeping Labor in power in 1927–28 and 1929–32. He also managed to negotiate the reunification of the Country Party, mainly on his terms, and, after the defeat of the Labor government, joined a coalition administration led by the Liberals. In 1935, now leader of the Country Party, Dunstan shifted his coalition allegiance to the Labor Party, and in doing so became Premier of Victoria, a position he would hold for a decade.[35]

Albert Dunstan's eventual defeat in 1945 heralded the changing nature of post-war politics in Victoria. As Blainey notes, '[t]he nonconformist Protestant lobby in Victoria was powerful [but a]fter 1945 that Protestant lobby suffered defeats. It was vulnerable because its political influence lay essentially in the Liberal and Country parties and not in Labor where Catholics were strong'.[36] Yet the alliance of Catholicism and Labour was not always easy or straightforward, and in 1955 the Labour Party was split asunder when its Catholic right-wing — fearing what it saw as a growing communist influence within the party — broke away to form the Democratic Labor Party (DLP). The Democratic Labor Party was to have an important impact on Victorian and Australian federal politics for a decade and more, its support for the Liberal-Country Party alliance effectively keeping Labor out of government in Canberra until the Whitlam era. Integral to the Catholic identity of the Democratic Labour Party was an enduring Irish influence. Significantly, this Irishness was deployed explicitly in the anti-communist cause, a number of DLP leaders, including Frank McManus and Standish Keon, using their Irish-Australian networks to generate support for Australia's involvement in the Vietnam War. And yet, as Val Noone has shown,

35 Blainey, *History of Victoria*, 196–200.

36 Blainey, *History of Victoria*, 213.

this assertion of 'Irishness' provoked an oppositional reaction, some Irish-Australians remembering their anti-conscription and anti-imperialist credentials, and reacting against DLP support for the war. In this, coincidentally, they were also encouraged by the emergence of the 'Troubles' in Northern Ireland in the late 1960s and 1970s, where the rhetoric of the 'troops out' movement and the focus on the disabilities suffered by the Catholic community also had the effect of radicalising many Irish-Australians. Noone puts the case quite straightforwardly: 'The Irish factor was important in Australian responses to the Vietnam War. Some Australians linked Irishness to support for the anti-communist war in Vietnam while others drew on Irish rebel traditions to oppose it'.[37]

Remarkably, then, the political influence of both Cornish and Irish constructions of Australia could be traced well into the twentieth century. The mining-Methodist 'Cousin Jack' tradition was detectable until at least the Second World War in the activities of men such as RS Richards and Albert Dunstan, the (often competing) Irish-Catholic tradition still visible in the controversies surrounding the Democratic Labor Party and its anti-communist agenda. And yet, as we have seen, by this time the rhetoric of pan-Celticism had already found a voice in Australia, drawing a veil over long-held enmities and antagonisms, and stressing instead the supposed common experience and common cause of the several Celtic peoples. This was, to a degree, a reflection of what was already happening in north-western Europe, where the Celtic Congress and the Celtic League (among other bodies) had pushed a determinedly pan-Celtic agenda, influencing the debates on devolution, regionalisation and self-government as they had re-emerged in the United Kingdom, Ireland and France from the 1960s onwards. It was also part of a redefining 'Britishness' that had become apparent in the United Kingdom by the late 1980s, where a monolithic sense of being 'British' was replaced increasingly by a more conditional identity: one which stressed its English, Welsh,

37 V Noone, 'The impact of Vietnam and Ireland on Australian identity during the 1960s', 137–149 in Wooding and Day (eds), at p 142.

Scots and other components.

But pan-Celticism was also a mirror of what was happening in Australia itself. Pan-Celticism was part of the multicultural unpackaging and repackaging of Australian identities.[38] Here, the notion of a homogeneous 'British'-Australian identity had given way to a more complex reconstruction, one outcome being the hybrid concept of 'Anglo-Celtic', a term which stressed implicitly the numerical strength and cultural significance of the several Celtic peoples in Australian history. This was a strength and significance that, in relative terms, far outweighed the Celtic influence in the United Kingdom itself. But more than that, 'Anglo-Celtic' also intimated the 'level playing field' that many had tried to build in Australia, where English dominance of the UK state had not been transferred uncritically to the established institutions of Australia. Instead, as we have seen, there were attempts at accommodation and convergence, not least in the separation of church and state and the achievement of religious tolerance. The Irish were, as noted above, particular beneficiaries of this. But, paradoxically, the Cornish had been pathfinders in achieving the separation of church and state, especially in South Australia where Cornish Methodists had been a prominent and vocal element of the colony's 'Paradise of Dissent'. To that extent, the 'common experience' and 'common cause' stressed by pan-Celticists was matched by the reality of Australian history. Despite their competing constructions of Celticity, and their mutual antagonisms, both Irish and Cornish had much to give and much to gain as common supporters of the separation of church and state.

This was demonstrated most vividly in the experience of the Returned Servicemen's League (RSL). Although the RSL wisely hoped to avoid issues of religious alignment, it could not ignore them altogether if it wished to encourage a religious dimension to ANZAC Day commemorations. Therefore, it constructed a non-denominational church service to conclude the ANZAC Day parade, hoping to appeal to all shades of religious opinion. But Catholics still felt obliged to fall out on completion of the march,

38 Payton, 'Re-inventing Celtic Australia'.

thus avoiding the service. This was hardly the spirit of solidarity that the RSL sought to encourage, and in 1938 the RSL in Victoria came up with a novel solution to the problem.[39] Dropping the non-denominational religious service, it introduced a new civic service. But there was to be a religious dimension of sorts to this new secular arrangement. Attendees could pray according to their own conscience during the two minutes silence, and the hymn 'Lead, Kindly Light' was sung, an astute choice because it had been written by a Catholic and did not actually mention God (one of the chief concerns of Catholic critics of the earlier RSL services). Archbishop Mannix himself approved the new formula, while those with Cornish-Methodist backgrounds would certainly have welcomed a hymn so popular that it had been for a time almost considered an unofficial 'Cornish national anthem'.[40] It was, as the Cornish — and perhaps the Irish — knew, a hymn so very appropriate for a people so given to emigration (and to mining), as well as for those who had served together in war in distant lands:

> Lead, Kindly Light, amid the encircling gloom,
> Lead Thou me on;
> The night is dark, and I am far from home;
> Lead Thou me on.
> Keep Thou my feet; I do not ask to see
> The distant scene — one step enough for me.[41]

The RSL's simple resolution of an otherwise intractable problem hinted strongly at the civic dimension of Australian nationalism, a nationalism which had been able to accommodate varying traditions,

39 Hirst, *Sense and Nonsense*, 17–19.

40 A K Hamilton Jenkin, *The Cornish Miner* (1927, repr Newton Abbot, 1972) 330; P Payton, *Cornish Carols from Australia* (Redruth, 1984) xi.

41 The almost universal appeal of 'Lead, Kindly Light' is illustrated aptly in W Emilson, 'Gandhi and "Lead, Kindly Light"' 227–237 in C M Cusak and P Oldmeadow (eds), *This Immense Panorama: Studies in Honour of Eric J. Sharpe* (Sydney, 1999). I am grateful to Carole Cusak for drawing my attention to this intriguing piece.

ethnic and religious, but which still allowed space for component identities. It was within this civic dimension that competing Celticities were tempered and moderated, and it was against this background that — notwithstanding the apparently oppositional identities expressed in 'Australia's Little Cornwall' and at Pekina in 2001 — pan-Celticism was able to emerge as a credible force in late twentieth- and early twenty-first-century Australia. As John Hirst has observed, the 'Australian ethos [...] was concerned not to obliterate difference but to overlook it'.[42] It was an ethos expressed by the bush poet Henry Lawson, whose sentiments would no doubt appeal to many present-day pan-Celtic enthusiasts:

> They tramp in mateship side by side
> The Protestant and Roman
> They call no biped Lord or Sir
> And touch their hat to no man.[43]

42 Hirst, *Sense and Nonsense*, 19.

43 H Lawson, 'Shearers', cited in Hirst, *Sense and Nonsense*, 19.